UNDOING BABEL

The Tower of Babel in Anglo-Saxon Literature

Undoing Babel

The Tower of Babel in Anglo-Saxon Literature

TRISTAN MAJOR

UNIVERSITY OF TORONTO PRESS
Toronto Buffalo London

Toronto Buffalo London
www.utorontopress.com

ISBN 978-1-4875-0054-2 (cloth)

Library and Archives Canada Cataloguing in Publication

Major, Tristan, author
Undoing Babel : the Tower of Babel in Anglo-Saxon literature / Tristan Major.

(Toronto Anglo-Saxon series)
Includes bibliographical references and index.
ISBN 978-1-4875-0054-2 (hardcover)

1. English literature – Old English, ca. 450–1100 – History and criticism.
2. Babel, Tower of, in literature. I. Title.

PR173.M35 2018 829'.09372 C2017-904464-8

This book has been published with the help of a grant from the Federation for the Humanities and Social Sciences, through the Awards to Scholarly Publications Program, using funds provided by the Social Sciences and Humanities Research Council of Canada.

University of Toronto Press acknowledges the financial assistance to its publishing program of the Canada Council for the Arts and the Ontario Arts Council, an agency of the Government of Ontario.

Canada Council for the Arts
Conseil des Arts du Canada

Funded by the Government of Canada
Financé par le gouvernement du Canada
Canada

To Zoe

Contents

Acknowledgments

This book is the result of almost a decade of research and writing that first began in Pauline Thompson's graduate class on Ælfric at the University of Toronto, and now concludes at the Library of Qatar University, where I am writing this. Over this decade, I have had the privilege of becoming indebted to numerous people and institutions for providing me with help and insight. At the Centre for Medieval Studies at the University of Toronto, I owe thanks to Michael Elliot, Michael Herren, Toni Healey, David and Ian McDougall, Carol Percy, Pauline Thompson, David Townsend, and Joan Holland, who all supported and encouraged my research. Andy Scheil has also provided invaluable help both as and after agreeing to becoming involved in my research as an external examiner; and Andy Orchard continues to be a profound source of knowledge on so many aspects of Anglo-Saxon literature – I am deeply grateful for his enthusiasm and attentiveness.

I am also grateful to the Social Sciences and Humanities Research Council Canada which generously funded a two-year Postdoctoral Fellowship at the University of British Columbia. During this time, I was granted the space and resources to expand my research in fruitful directions. At UBC I was very fortunate to have been able to work under the mentorship of Gernot Wieland. I am truly grateful for the amount of insight and support he provided me, especially for his careful readings and comments on all aspects of my research.

At Qatar University I have had the benefit of working with extremely talented undergraduate students. I owe thanks to Sarah Maysarah Al-Alami for her help proofreading portions of a draft, and to Mashael Al-Mahmoud for reading the work in its entirety. I am also grateful to Qatar University for providing me with generous financial support for acquiring various resources necessary to bring this work to completion.

Additionally, my thanks extend to the very careful comments of the anonymous reviewers of this book, whose criticism has made it much better, and to Suzanne Rancourt for her attentive work at the University of Toronto Press.

Above all, I owe gratitude to my parents, Wayne and Doris, who have always supported all my endeavours, and to my wife, Zoe Thiessen, who has not only endured my long hours of research with saintly patience, but has also been an unimaginable source of comfort and inspiration. To her this book is dedicated.

Genesis 10–11

Since this book deals with the reception history of the Table of Nations and the narrative of the Tower of Babel (or Babylon), it would be helpful to present the biblical text at the beginning. Starting with Genesis 9:18 the biblical account narrates the story of the repopulation of the world after the Flood up to the introduction of Abraham at Genesis 11:29. Though the majority of these verses are made up of genealogical detail, tracing the lineages of the three sons of Noah, the straightforward genealogical account is interrupted by two dramatic narratives. The first is the cursing of Canaan. Although it is Ham, one of Noah's sons, who sees Noah naked and intoxicated from the wine of his vineyard, Noah utters a curse upon Ham's son, Canaan, that he be "a slave of slaves" to his brothers (Genesis 9:25). The second is the Tower of Babel narrative, which recounts the attempt to build a tower to heaven that is foiled when God divides the languages of the workers. Apart from these two narratives, the overarching account consists of the statement that from the three sons of Noah, "the whole earth was populated" (Genesis 9:19), the so-called Table of Nations (Genesis 10), and Abraham's lineage from Noah's son Shem (Genesis 11:10–28). This book will focus mainly on the Table of Nations and the Tower of Babel narrative, designated as Genesis 10–11, but with the acknowledgement that the Table of Nations is actually introduced in Genesis 9 and that the Babel narrative only comprises the first nine verses of Genesis 11. The biblical text pertinent to this study (Genesis 9:28–9, 10:1–32, 11:1–9) has some important differences in the various versions read throughout history. For simplicity's sake, I use the translation of the Revised Standard Version, which is meant to provide an English rendering of the original Hebrew starting point of the history of the text:

9 18 The sons of Noah who went forth from the ark were Shem, Ham, and
Japheth. Ham was the father of Canaan. 19 These three were the sons of Noah;
and from these the whole earth was peopled....

10 These are the generations of the sons of Noah, Shem, Ham, and Japheth;
sons were born to them after the flood. 2 The sons of Japheth: Gomer, Magog,
Madai, Javan, Tubal, Meshech, and Tiras. 3 The sons of Gomer: Ash′kenaz,
Riphath, and Togar′mah. 4 The sons of Javan: Eli′shah, Tarshish, Kittim, and
Do′danim. 5 From these the coastland peoples spread. These are the sons of
Japheth in their lands, each with his own language, by their families, in their
nations. 6 The sons of Ham: Cush, Egypt, Put, and Canaan. 7 The sons of Cush:
Seba, Hav′ilah, Sabtah, Ra′amah, and Sab′teca. The sons of Ra′amah: Sheba and
Dedan. 8 Cush became the father of Nimrod; he was the first on earth to be a
mighty man. 9 He was a mighty hunter before the Lord; therefore it is said, “Like
Nimrod a mighty hunter before the Lord.” 10 The beginning of his kingdom
was Babel, Erech, and Accad, all of them in the land of Shinar. 11 From that land
he went into Assyria, and built Nin′eveh, Reho′both-Ir, Calah, and 12 Resen
between Nin′eveh and Calah; that is the great city. 13 Egypt became the father
of Ludim, An′amim, Leha′bim, Naph-tu′him, 14 Pathru′sim, Caslu′him (whence
came the Philistines), and Caph′torim. 15 Canaan became the father of Sidon
his first-born, and Heth, 16 and the Jeb′usites, the Amorites, the Gir′gashites,
17 the Hivites, the Arkites, the Sinites, 18 the Ar′vadites, the Zem′arites, and the
Ha′mathites. Afterward the families of the Canaanites spread abroad. 19 And the
territory of the Canaanites extended from Sidon, in the direction of Gerar, as far
as Gaza, and in the direction of Sodom, Gomor′rah, Admah, and Zeboi′im, as
far as Lasha. 20 These are the sons of Ham, by their families, their languages, their
lands, and their nations. 21 To Shem also, the father of all the children of Eber, the
elder brother of Japheth, children were born. 22 The sons of Shem: Elam, Asshur,
Arpach′shad, Lud, and Aram. 23 The sons of Aram: Uz, Hul, Gether, and Mash.
24 Arpach′shad became the father of Shelah; and Shelah became the father of Eber.
25 To Eber were born two sons: the name of the one was Peleg, for in his days the
earth was divided, and his brother’s name was Joktan. 26 Joktan became the father
of Almo′dad, Sheleph, Hazarma′veth, Jerah, 27 Hador′am, Uzal, Diklah, 28 Obal,
Abim′a-el, Sheba, 29 Ophir, Hav′ilah, and Jobab; all these were the sons of Joktan.
30 The territory in which they lived extended from Mesha in the direction of Sep-
har to the hill country of the east. 31 These are the sons of Shem, by their families,
their languages, their lands, and their nations. 32 These are the families of the sons
of Noah, according to their genealogies, in their nations; and from these the nations spread abroad on the earth after the flood.

11 Now the whole earth had one language and few words. 2 And as men
migrated from the east, they found a plain in the land of Shinar and settled

there. [3] And they said to one another, "Come, let us make bricks, and burn them
thoroughly." And they had brick for stone, and bitumen for mortar. [4] Then they
said, "Come, let us build ourselves a city, and a tower with its top in the heavens,
and let us make a name for ourselves, lest we be scattered abroad upon the face of
the whole earth." [5] And the Lord came down to see the city and the tower, which
the sons of men had built. [6] And the Lord said, "Behold, they are one people, and
they have all one language; and this is only the beginning of what they will do;
and nothing that they propose to do will now be impossible for them. [7] Come, let
us go down, and there confuse their language, that they may not understand one
another's speech." [8] So the Lord scattered them abroad from there over the face
of all the earth, and they left off building the city. [9] Therefore its name was called
Babel, because there the Lord confused the language of all the earth; and from
there the Lord scattered them abroad over the face of all the earth.

UNDOING BABEL

The Tower of Babel in Anglo-Saxon Literature

Introduction

In his invective against heathenism and England's marauding Vikings, Wulfstan, Archbishop of York (d. 1023), argues that all paganism can be traced back to the dispersal of humankind after the fall of the Tower of Babel:[1]

> Eala, gefyrn is þæt ðurh deofol fela þinga misfor, 7 þæt mancynn to swyðe Gode mishyrde, 7 þæt hæðenscype ealles to wide swyðe gederede 7 gyt dereð wide. Ne ræde we þeah ahwar on bocum þæt man arærde ænig hæðengyld ahwar on worulde on eallum þam fyrste þe wæs ær Noes flode. Ac syððan þæt gewearð þæt Nembroð 7 ða entas worhton þone wundorlican stypel æfter Noes flode, 7 him ða swa fela gereorda gelamp, þæs þe bec secgað, swa ðæra wyrhtena wæs. Þa syððan toferdon hy wide landes, 7 mancyn þa sona swyðe weox; 7 ða æt nyhstan wurdon hi bepæhte þurh ðone ealdan deofol þe Adam iu ær beswac swa þæt hi worhton wolice 7 gedwollice him hæþene godas, 7 ðone soðan God 7 heora agenne scyppend forsawon, þe hy to mannum gescop 7 geworhte

> O! it is long ago that through the Devil many things went astray, and that humankind so greatly disobeyed God, and that so very widely did paganism greatly injure and continues to injure widely. Yet we do not read anywhere in books that anyone raised up any heathen idol anywhere in the world in any of that time which was before Noah's flood. But afterwards it happened that Nimrod and the giants wrought that astonishing tower after Noah's flood, and then as many languages came upon them as were those workers

1 Wulfstan, *De falsis deis*, 1–15.

> of which the books speak. Then afterwards they dispersed to far off lands, and humankind then immediately grew greatly, and then at last they were deceived by that ancient Devil, who previously before led Adam astray, such that they wrought wickedly and impiously heathen gods for themselves, and forsook the true God and their own creator who created and wrought them as humans.

For modern biblical readers, this may seem a strange interpretation of the Tower of Babel narrative. The Babel narrative in Genesis makes no mention of idolatry, Nimrod, giants, or even "the ancient Devil." But these additions are not at all idiosyncratic to Wulfstan, and comprise some of the commonest elements of the exegetical history of the passage. Wulfstan's homily is, in fact, an abridgement of another Old English homily, by his contemporary Ælfric, whose own homily is a revision of a sixth-century Latin homily by Martin of Braga, who naturally relied on his own sources, and so on.[2] In fact, I cite Wulfstan's rather late example here at the beginning of this book in order to point to the endurance of such a long-standing tradition, parts of which first begin to solidify into an authoritative form in the first centuries BCE, while other parts continue to evolve and transform according to the interests and purposes of later authors.

Through Late Antiquity and the early Middle Ages, the Table of Nations and the Tower of Babel narrative make appearances in a wide variety of genres in a wide variety of forms. Most obviously, works of exegesis and sermons, especially those with pericopes of Genesis 10–11, offer some of the most detailed treatments of the Table of Nations and the Tower of Babel. But explicit references to these texts also appear in histories, chronicles, genealogies, poetical works, travel literature, ethnographies, geographical works, and philosophical tracts, to mention only literary genres. Arno Borst's magisterial work, *Der Turmbau von Babel*, is irreplaceable as an account of the numerous texts across world cultures and times that make mention not only of Genesis 10–11, but also other references to ethnic or linguistic diversity.[3] Since the final volume of *Der Turmbau von Babel* was published in 1963, the extensive scope and quality of Borst's

2 See Szurszewski, "Ælfric's *De Falsis Diis.*"
3 Borst, *Der Turmbau von Babel.*

scholarship continues to be influential.[4] But because of Borst's immense scope, he is rarely able to analyse some of the more complex issues surrounding the ways a specific text or author uses the Table of Nations or the Tower of Babel narrative. Only now, decades after its appearance, have scholarly publications begun to reveal a renewed interest in the subject. Benjamin Braude has published a series of articles on literary traditions involving the sons of Noah in late medieval and early modern texts, to be collected in a forthcoming monograph.[5] David M. Goldenberg has traced the concept of the "Curse of Ham" among ancient sources in a 2003 monograph – a topic that David M. Whitford has since continued for the early modern period, and Stephen R. Haynes for American history.[6] Furthermore, Brian Murdoch has written an influential series of essays on medieval interpretations of Genesis, including a chapter on the Tower of Babel;[7] Daniel Anlezark has addressed the related topic of Anglo-Saxon interpretations of Noah and the myth of the Flood in his 2006 monograph;[8] and Phillip Michael Sherman gives a thorough treatment of ancient Jewish reception of Genesis 11.[9]

Of specific significance for this study is Bruce R. O'Brien's monograph on multilingualism in centuries before and after the Norman conquest. Although he uses the Babel and Pentecost narratives only as a springboard for examining translation theory in early medieval England, O'Brien deals extensively with how multilingualism played out in reality, providing the basis for actual attitudes towards the many non-English languages to be spoken in England.[10] In a sense, my own book aims in part to pick up where O'Brien begins: in the implications of the Tower of Babel for theological, ideological and literary understandings of the origins of multilingualism, particularly among Anglo-Saxon authors. Similarly, Andrew Scheil's recently published study on the Matter of Babylon has many overlaps with

4 As of 10 August 2016, Google Scholar gives a total of 383 citations of *Der Turmbau von Babel.*

5 Braude, "The Sons of Noah and the Construction of Ethnic and Geographical Identities in the Medieval and Early Modern Periods," 103–42; "Cham et Noé," 93–125; and "Michelangelo and the Curse of Ham," 79–92.

6 Goldenberg, *The Curse of Ham*; Whitford, *The Curse of Ham in the Early Modern Era*; and Haynes, *Noah's Curse.*

7 Murdoch, *The Medieval Popular Bible.*

8 Anlezark, *Water and Fire.*

9 Sherman, *Babel's Tower Translated.*

10 O'Brien, *Reversing Babel*, 20–3.

this present book. But because Scheil argues for the prevalence of medieval understandings of Babylon across European and North American culture up to the present, his scope does not allow him to deal with many of the Anglo-Saxon sources examined here. Our general understanding of the evidence, as well as general methodology, does not widely differ, and this book helps serve not only to bolster his argument but also to add new prespective to the evidence.[11]

To complement this scholarship, this book will focus on the reception history of the Babel narrative in Anglo-Saxon England. As O'Brien argues, the Babel narrative provides a literal account of ethnic and linguistic diversity, and must have therefore resonated with those early medieval inhabitants of Britain who were well aware of the island's relatively high degree of multiculturalism and multilingualism. Importantly for Anglo-Saxon Christians, the linguistic implications of Babel become informed by the events at Pentecost, during which the Holy Spirit sanctifies the use of all languages of the world for spreading the Church abroad – or at least that is how the event comes to be interpreted. Together, Babel and Pentecost are primary starting points for understanding the world's (and Anglo-Saxon England's) linguistic and ethnic situation. A significant part of the discussion on the Babel narrative in the primary sources involves Pentecost, and for this reason, my own discussion will pay considerable attention to this New Testament event. But language is not the only element of interpretation and use of the Babel narrative in Anglo-Saxon literature. Anglo-Saxon authors also employed the Babel narrative in many ways that help reveal cultural anxieties and literary concerns. Wulfstan's use of the Babel narrative, for only one example, reveals an anxiety over invading Vikings. Other instances appear across the entire range of Anglo-Latin and Old English literature, from the seventh-century school at Canterbury to the later period of the Benedictine reform in the eleventh century. And in each case, the Babel narrative is developed by and distinguished from earlier texts and traditions. Anglo-Saxon uses of the Babel narrative, therefore, offer an important window into how a biblical text informs and transforms the earliest written literature of England.

11 Scheil, *Babylon under Western Eyes*, which expands upon his earlier article "Babylon and Anglo-Saxon England," 37–58. Because Scheil's monograph has only recently been published, I have not been able to engage with it as closely as I would have liked. I have, however, been able to include reference to any overlapping topic in the footnotes.

Because the literature of Anglo-Saxon England participates within the larger context of European literature, it will be helpful to begin by suggesting some basic categories to facilitate interpretation. Whereas some authors offer relatively idiosyncratic interpretations or adaptations of the Tower of Babel narrative in European literature by deviating more than usual from the discourses of their contemporaries, these discourses typically tend to fall consistently into three broad categories. The first consists of a literal understanding and employment of the Table of Nations and the Tower of Babel narrative as an etiological account for the linguistic and ethnic diversity of the world. The second considers the more dramatic, or at times mythic, features of the biblical text, which not only encourage further development of extra-biblical elements, but also provide the impetus for moral lessons that allow the text to exhibit a cyclical, perpetual, and universal exemplum of evil. The third category, which expands the literalism of the first and the extra-biblical and moral aspects of the second, consists of a fusion of historical details together with transhistorical moral dichotomies in order to inform understandings of present in-group and out-group communities and identities. Though authors almost never treat these three categories distinctly, it is most often the case that when a positive understanding of the linguistic and ethnic diversity of the world is put forth, the negative aspects of the Babel narrative are absent. While some authors will trace the ancestry or origins of a specific figure or people back to a name in the Table of Nations (usually Japheth's supposedly European lineage), these accounts are relatively rare and, for understandable reasons, almost never mention the negative aspects of the biblical narrative.

On the contrary, it is much more frequent that an author will emphasize the negative aspects of the Babel narrative in order to attach these negative aspects to the object of his attack. To take Wulfstan's homily again as an example, the mention of the Tower of Babel is peripheral to the main thrust of the argument. Wulfstan is not concerned with the fact that his presentation of the consequences of the fall of the Tower of Babel does not strictly accord with the actual account given in Genesis 11. By mentioning the Tower of Babel, Wulfstan rhetorically establishes his own identity (and therefore authority) as an orthodox leader of a Christian congregation opposed to the recent wave of pagan Norse invaders. He does not use the Babel narrative to understand the origins of ethnic and cultural differences between the Scandinavians and the English, but rather to attempt to set up a dichotomy between Christian and pagan, English and Viking, Same and Other, that has origins in the struggles between good and evil going back to the beginning of human history. And by evoking a biblical text that aids in explaining the origins of pagan, and therefore Norse, wickedness, Wulfstan signals the need to recognize and conform to the religious values of his congregation, which point to wider Christian identities within Europe. Issues of ethnicity come second to the difference of religious values between the Christian Northumbrians and the heathen Vikings.

As mentioned above, Wulfstan's account is by no means atypical of the wider European literary tradition. Many of the authors who deal with the Table of Nations and the Tower of Babel from the first centuries BCE to later Anglo-Saxon England (and beyond) use the Babel narrative to understand the diversity of the world in a moral framework that either celebrates the diversity of in-group communities, or condemns the diversity of out-group communities. It is important to state, however, that my three categories of the interpretative tradition are only intended to clarify the issue for modern scholarship and do not reflect a conscious and explicit proclamation of the sources. No late antique or medieval author provides any kind of self-reflection on the ways his or her contemporaries adopted and adapted the Table of Nations and the Babel narrative. With that said, it will be helpful to look closer into each of these three categories.

The Literal Babel: Ethnic and Linguistic Diversity

Scholarly examination has proven medieval theories of ethnicity to be extremely divergent and complex. Because this study will partly examine how past perceptions of different communities were influenced by biblical texts, it will not be concerned as much with the immense task of reconstructing the components of actual past communities, as with analysing some of the strategies that lie at the core of communal identification and ascription.[12] At least superficially, the ethnography derived from Genesis 10–11 is best conceptualized and promulgated in easily comprehensible units of distinct communities that are referred to under a number of terms,

---

12 As Susan Reynolds points out, the term community has become almost meaningless; *Kingdoms and Communities in Western Europe 900–1300*, xi. While "almost any geographically delimited section of the population can also be described as a local community" (Reynolds, 2), I might also add that communities are not necessarily delimited by specific geography – and so the term becomes even more vague. This vagueness – tending towards meaninglessness – is, unfortunately, necessary. In general, when I use the term community, I mean something along the lines of "ethnic community" or Reynolds's "community of the realm" (ch. 8).

such as ethnic groups, races, and nations, among others.[13] Because criteria for determining ethnic conformity or difference are completely dependent on individuals interacting with each other in social conditions, not on determined sets of features shared by all the individuals of a supposed ethnic group, it is empirically impossible to determine absolutely what makes up a category such as "ethnic group" or "nation" or "race."[14] All categorization of ethnic groups is dependent upon the ideological positions of those deciding and propagating the very criteria for categorization itself. Along with the concepts of nation and race, ethnicity is extremely fluid not only because of the varianc e of categorizations imposed upon an ethnic group (e.g., language, skin colour, cultural habits), but also because of social conditions necessarily inherent to judgments regarding the identity of self or other (e.g., position of power, notions of normative and deviant behaviour). Research in genetics, a field once used to promote ideas of human subspecies or "races," reveals that biological relationships between individuals of different ethnic groups are too similar and individuals of a single ethnic group too diverse for the term "race" to be at all meaningful.[15] For this reason, Benedict Anderson's well-known term "imagined community" has been an apt starting point for conceptualizing how people in the past (as well as today) came to identify themselves and others collectively.[16] Although Anderson was originally referring to modern nations, his terminology has been applied in a broader sense to include any group of people that is perceived either internally by members who self-identify within the community, or externally by those who claim to recognize and who promulgate categorical differences of a community that they do not self-identify with. This definition provides a framework to examine how

---

13 Scholarship on this late antique and early medieval terminology is vast: see Amory, "The Meaning and Purpose of Ethnic Terminology in the Burgundian Laws," 1–28; Ewig, "Beobachtungen zur politisch-geographischen Terminologie des fränkischen Grossreiches und der Teilreiche des 9. Jahrhunderts," 99–140; Goetz, "*Gens*," 39–63; and Zientara, "Populus – Gens – Natio," 11–20. See also the essays on race in the special edition the *Journal of Medieval and Early Modern Studies* 31.1 (2001).

14 Okamura, "Situational Ethnicity," 452–65.

15 See esp. Isaac, Ziegler, and Eliav-Feldon, "Introduction," in *The Origins of Racism in the West*, 1–31, at 7–8.

16 Anderson, *Imagined Communities*, 5–7. Anderson is, in fact, speaking of the modern "nation" specifically, but his definition can be employed more broadly chronologically and conceptually. For the relevance of Anderson's methodology for medieval studies, see Johnson, "Imagining Communities," 1–19.

ethnic or national communities, though based on arbitrary principles, play a profound and powerful role in the ways people think about and act towards other people. It must also be emphasized that the qualifier "imagined" is not always apparent or accepted by those who participate in general categorizations of different groups. The lack of an objective basis as well as the subjective nature of ethnic categorization is often downplayed, ignored, or rejected, commonly for unscientific or irrational reasons. Of course, this is not to deny the very real existence of different communities, but rather to stress that the common elements that bind communities together are altogether "imagined."

Especially for ethnic and national communities of the past, Anthony D. Smith has argued that the "'core' of ethnicity, as it has been transmitted in the historical record and as it shapes individual experience, resides in this quartet of 'myths, memories, values and symbols' and in the characteristic forms or styles and genres of certain historical configurations of populations."[17] An authoritative text such as the Bible, which remains (it is assumed) unchanging as the Word of God, can produce the myths, memories, values, and symbols that help define and promote an identity. But it is important to bear in mind that while the biblical text for the most part remains the same, the myths, memories, values, and symbols that it produces change and develop according to the needs of the author adapting it. These developments create an interesting dynamic for any type of identity that can refer to the biblical texts to help define itself. In particular, Smith argues that one of the most "crucial features of *ethnie* [i.e., an ethnic group] is the myth of common origin and descent."[18] Such a feature is apparent in late antique and medieval ethnographical accounts that employ the Table of Nations and Tower of Babel.

Because the Table of Nations and the Tower of Babel narrative can be interpreted to offer a biblically sanctioned account of the world's original ethnic and linguistic diversity, it would be natural to assume that these texts played a very influential role in late antique and early medieval Christian thought on the matter. European ethnography in the early modern period certainly contained many theories of original ethnic and linguistic diversity founded on the biblical account. But although it is tempting to base early medieval theories of ethnicity on a homogenous knowledge

17 Smith, *Ethnic Origins of Nations*, 15.

18 Smith, "The Politics of Culture," 706–33, at 710. See also Smith, *Ethnic Origins of Nations*, 24–6.

of the Babel narrative and its etiological implications, such assumptions can be misleading. Not only is there a complete lack of evidence for a homogenous knowledge of the Babel narrative – different authors handle the literal account in a variety of ways – but an interpretation of the account as a biblical (and therefore, it is presumed, universally held) foundation for a theory explaining the existence of the world's ethnic and linguistic diversity is without warrant. The Babel narrative, more typically, is adapted to maintain widely disparate and pre-existing beliefs of specific authors who use the narrative when they find it suitable for their purposes, but ignore it when it confuses or does not support their beliefs, potentially in some cases even undermining them. The absence of the Babel narrative in Bede's *Ecclesiastical History*, despite Bede's lengthy treatment of it in his commentary on Genesis and partial use of it in his chronological works, is telling. Bede evidently did not want to muddy the clear waters of English origin with a confusing and discrepant account, even if from a source as authoritative as Genesis. And when Anglo-Saxon authors do use Genesis 10–11 to explain their own ethnic origins, the results are often strikingly unusual: the fourth son of Noah mentioned in some of the Alfredian texts is a good example. Unlike the putative centrality of a migration myth in Anglo-Saxon culture, as proposed by Nicholas Howe,[19] the Babel narrative, in this case, did not flourish with the same kind of cultural value. Not only does the biblical narrative fail to account for the ethnic origins of the Anglo-Saxons (or any Germanic peoples), but when Bede, for example, does engage with the Table of Nations or the Babel narrative, his dominant focus is on negative moral aspects or the testament of the Church in a diverse world.

This is not to say that the Table of Nations and the Babel narrative lacked any authority for late antique and medieval Christian understandings of ethnic or linguistic diversity. In fact, as one of the commonest focal points for Jewish and Christian identity, the Bible did provide an authoritative basis, both theoretical as well as rhetorical, upon which a particular community could come to know and then propagate its own specific understanding of the world and itself in the world. Because such understanding demands epistemological foundations that deal not only with the existence of one's own social group, but also with the existence of external groups, Genesis 10–11 played an important role in certain treatments

19 Howe, *Migration and Mythmaking in Anglo-Saxon England.*

of ethnic similarities and differences, and of general world geography. Post-biblical Jewish and Christian authors, however, did not limit themselves exclusively to Genesis 10–11 for their understandings of the world, especially since it must have been apparent that the Bible did not reflect the perceived reality of the world's diverse communities well, even if it enjoyed the highest acknowledged form of authority. As a biblical text, Genesis 10–11 could be cited, at least on a superficial level, as an authoritative and true reflection of the world's ethnic diversity. Often, however, it is not the biblical text itself that produces the foundations for understanding the world, but rather previous understandings of the world that produce interpretations of the biblical texts, which then validate those understandings. In the insightful words of Goldenberg, the biblical text is "not so much a framework, conceptual and structural, into which all subsequent thinking must fit (conform), as it is a grid upon which postbiblical thinking asserts itself, and in the process changes the biblical blueprint."[20] The original ethnographical content of the Table of Nations and the Tower of Babel, as understood by modern biblical scholarship, actually has very little significance for most late antique and medieval European ethnography. Instead, Jewish and Christian authors were compelled to use the biblical text alongside other sources of knowledge which contained a higher degree of certainty, though paradoxically a lower degree of acknowledged authority. Or to express it inversely, authors were compelled to conform what the biblical sources stated to their own knowledge and to extra-biblical authorities that helped form and propagate communal or individual values. In the centuries both before and after the common era, one of the most prominent tasks for the exegete (for only one example of a biblical reader) was to interpret the biblical texts in ways that could enhance the knowledge and learning taken from non-biblical sources. It was partly for this reason that the allegorical method of exegesis, often represented by the school at Alexandria, gained such popularity among late antique and medieval biblical scholars in western Europe.[21]

Nevertheless, the centrality of the biblical text in late antique and medieval discourses, as well as a general paucity of contrary evidence, has understandably tempted some modern scholars to evoke a kind of self-intuitive interpretation of the Babel narrative that explains how people of Late

20 Goldenberg, *Curse of Ham*, 8.
21 See Auerbach, "Figura," 11–76, esp. 52–6.

Antiquity and the Middle Ages theoretically thought about ethnic diversity. It follows that unless there is reason to think otherwise, the majority of late antique and medieval readers of the biblical text understood it universally and homogeneously: because the Babel narrative is about linguistic and ethnic diversity, most late antique and medieval readers must have based their views on linguistic and ethnic diversity on the biblical account. But of the many authors writing on ethnicity in Late Antiquity and the Early Middle Ages, most seem not at all concerned with Genesis 10–11; even Isidore gives only passing reference to the narrative.[22] Most other authors dealing with ethnography are surprisingly reticent on the matter, or vague, or even at odds with each other and the biblical account.[23] Bede does not allude to Babel in his *Ecclesiastical History*, nor does Paul the Deacon in his *History of the Lombards*, nor Jordanes in his *Gothic History*. Gregory of Tours refers broadly to the Table of Nations and the Babel narrative in his *Histories of the Franks* to describe the dispersal of humankind ("dissiminatum est genus humanum"), but his focus is more on the origins of idolatry and the consequences of earthly pride.[24] There are certainly other accounts from the period that draw upon the Table of Nations and Babel narrative, such as the world chronicle of Hippolytus or genealogies imitating the Table of Nations, but the majority of the evidence does not suggest a profound level of dependency. In fact, one of the remarkable aspects of Borst's study is how many of the numerous figures exhibiting various outlooks on ethnic or linguistic diversity never actually use or even refer to Genesis 10–11. Even an author like Jerome who devoted much of his life to translation and linguistic problems of the Bible says frustratingly little on the Table of Nations and Babel narrative.[25]

The myths and symbols supported by Genesis 10–11 tend not to reflect much in the way of ethnography, but rather point to only a few of the many complex and multifaceted ways in which authors, usually elites or clerics, promoted ethnic unity or difference for whatever purpose. Because these purposes vary from individual to individual, so does the usage of the text. The authors using Genesis 10–11 in ethnographical, linguistic, or geographical discourses set them up alongside innumerable other myths

22 Isidore, *Etymologiarum sive originum libri XX*, IX.1.1.

23 See Braude, "The Sons of Noah," 109–15.

24 Gregory of Tours, *Libri historiarum X*, I.5, 7; Gregory quotes Genesis 9:19.

25 Borst, *Turmbau von Babel*, gives a detailed section on Late Antiquity and the Middle Ages in vol. 2; for Jerome specifically, see vol. 2, 385–91.

and symbols that conflate with, contradict, or ignore each other. For this reason, any foray into the ways late antique and medieval authors, including the Anglo-Saxons, used the Babel narrative for their understanding of ethnic and linguistic diversity must take into consideration late antique and medieval discourses on that diversity and its significance.

The Extra-Biblical Babel: Interpretative Developments and Innovations

As is the nature of religious literature of divine authority, textual features that are particularly cryptic or confusing in their laconic, apparently contradictory, and often inexplicable nature draw attention to the need for interpretation and, more so, the rules for proper interpretation. Despite the profession of authority bestowed upon the Hebrew and Christian Scriptures, these Scriptures are, practically speaking, subordinate to the higher authority of orthodox interpretation, as determined by the theology of the particular community. Exegetes go to great lengths to ensure that the biblical account was understood according to proper theological and ideological doctrine. Literal interpretation of the anthropomorphism of God in the Hebrew Scriptures, for example, does not easily conform to classical Jewish and Christian theology, which sees God as existing beyond the physical and temporal world. For these Jews and Christians, God could not have "walked" in the Garden of Eden or even planted a garden, at least in any literal sense, despite what Genesis 3:8 states. In this case, various approaches that emphasized the text's figurative, rhetorical, or typological nature aim to restore the integrity of a biblical text that seems to describe God very much like a human and very unlike the classical Jewish and Christian notions of God.[26] But the need to deal with certain confusing or unexplained details in the biblical text tends to allow for a greater number of creative interpretative possibilities that are then accepted or rejected. As religious communities produce, accept, and reject proposed interpretations, interpretative traditions also begin to grow, and the bounds of what is acceptable and authoritative shift. What was unthinkable to past readers

26 For a more thorough presentation, see Turner, "Allegory in Christian Late Antiquity," 71–82.

becomes standard for later readers who must deal with whatever interpretive tradition their community has inherited.[27]

Undoubtedly, Genesis 10–11 produced much speculation from exegetes who were presented with the need to explain confusing narrative details. The discrepancy between the narrative and chronological order, the actual identity of the builders of the tower, their motive for building the tower, the detail concerning the building material, and the eventual fate of the tower, all perturbed later readers who felt the need to add extra-biblical elements to make the biblical text more comprehensible. Especially before the canonization of the Bible, extra-biblical elements began to develop, as later readers accepted, rejected, or modified the earlier literary traditions.[28] Authoritative interpretations tended to be favoured over those deemed heterodox, but this is not always the case, and some atypical features from early obscure texts can suddenly appear centuries later.[29] Though I will discuss these extra-biblical features in more detail throughout this book, there are a few that need further explication from the start.

The association between Nimrod and the Tower of Babel was very common. No individual is mentioned by name in the Babel narrative of Genesis 11:1–9, but because Genesis 10:8–10 states that "Cush became the father of Nimrod ... the beginning of his kingdom was Babel," it is not difficult to imagine how biblical readers could claim that Nimrod was the first tyrant of Babel and the architect of the tower. Other details given in Genesis 10:8–12 provided further grounds and impetus for speculation on the character of Nimrod. Importantly, he was frequently thought to be a giant. As has been well documented,[30] belief in postdiluvian gigantism in ancient Jewish literature derives from two factors. The first is the cryptic

---

27 Braude, "Sons of Noah," 106, insightfully states: "The notion of a fixed, widely available, integral biblical text representing the Word of God speaking directly to mankind ... with little or no gloss, no mediation, and little benefit of tradition, was an invention of Johannes Gutenberg and Martin Luther." See also Hauser and Watson, "Introduction and Overview," in *A History of Biblical Interpretation*, vol. 1, 1–54.

28 Hauser and Watson, "Introduction and Overview," 3: "at these earlier, precanonical stages, interpretation contributes, often in a major way, to the eventual shaping of the written, canonical text itself."

29 For example, Murdoch, *The Medieval Popular Bible*, 137, notes the similarities between the twelfth-century German *Vorauer Bücher Mosis* and the first-century *Liber antiquitatum biblicarum* by pseudo-Philo, which both describe the builders writing their names on the bricks of the tower.

30 See Jeffrey, *A Dictionary of Biblical Tradition in English Literature*, *s.v.* "Giants in the Earth," 303–4; and Speyer, "Gigant," 1247–76, esp. 1259–68.

reference in Genesis 6:4 to the Nephilim, described as "sons of God" and "mighty men" (Hebrew *gibbōrim*),[31] who lived before the Flood "and also afterward." Jewish authors, evidently feeling the need to clarify this verse, expanded the account of the Nephilim, by turning them into fallen angels, the so-called Watchers, who come down to earth, marry the "beautiful daughters" of men (I Enoch 6:1–5), and impregnate them with giants who then turn cannibalistic after eating all the normal food (I Enoch 7:3–6; see also Jubilees 5:1–2). Although the Watchers were supposed to be destroyed in the Flood (Jubilees 7:21), Jewish lore allows a handful of survivors, likely because of biblical references to postdiluvian Nephilim (Genesis 6:4 and Numbers 13:33), as well as the references to postdiluvian *gibbōrim*. Because Nimrod is termed "the first on earth to be a mighty man (*gibbōr*)," he also was soon affiliated with the prediluvian giants.[32] To complicate the matter further, the Septuagint translation renders the word *gibbōr* as *gigans* in Genesis 6 and 10, which in turn is rendered *gigans* in the Vetus Latina. Although the ambiguity had been clarified in Jerome's Vulgate, which uses the words *potens* and *robustus*, the inertia of Jewish tradition, along with the Septuagint and the Vetus Latina, was too great to avert the course of interpretation, and Nimrod was henceforth understood to be the first postdiluvian giant, right into the literature of Anglo-Saxon England.[33] The gigantism (and wickedness) of the Nephilim become, henceforth, associated with Nimrod, and a bridge, so to speak, is formed over the Flood.

It is also due to this new presence of giants in the narrative that a number of other elements are introduced. For example, because of the similarities between the Babel narrative, which can be read as giants striving against God to overtake heaven, and the Greek gigantomachia, which portrays the gigantic Titans striving against the gods, Jewish and Christian authors could use the Babel narrative to promote arguments that diminished the tenets of Greek mythology and validated their own. In fact, the earliest non-biblical text to treat the Babel narrative, the first fragment attributed to the anonymous Samaritan or pseudo-Eupolemus, states that

31 Brown, Driver, and Briggs, eds., *A Hebrew and English Lexicon of the Old Testament*, *s.v.* גִּבּוֹר, 1, 2, 150.

32 Van der Toorn and Van der Horst, "Nimrod before and after the Bible," 1–29, at 16–19.

33 See Mellinkoff, "Cain's Monstrous Progeny in *Beowulf*: Part I, Noachic Tradition," 143–97; "Cain's Monstrous Progeny in *Beowulf*: Part II, Post-Diluvian Survival," 83–97; and Orchard, *Pride and Prodigies*, 58–85. Incidentally, Bede, *In principium Genesis*, II.983–98, distinguishes the Nephilim from the postdiluvian giants, such as Nimrod.

giants survived the Flood, founded Babylon, and built the Tower of Babel before being scattered across the earth; significantly, the names of these founders of Babylon are Belos and Kronos, the Babylonian and Greek divinities.[34] Hence, various sorts of euhemerism, which understand the origins of pagan divinities in heroic figures, are often employed, by way of the Babel narrative, to explain the origins of paganism and idolatry. In Anglo-Saxon England, different authors put the Babel narrative to euhemeristic use in different manners. As will be examined in more detail, Alfred the Great directly equates the gigantomachia with the Tower of Babel, thereby (but unwittingly) participating in a long tradition extending back to Hellenistic Jewish writings of the second century BCE. But Wulfstan, as my opening example reveals, is not as much concerned with the paganism of ancient Greece and Rome as with the paganism of the invading Vikings: his euhemeristic approach transfers the paganism traditionally associated with the Babel account to the mythology of Old Norse.

On the one hand, as mentioned above, when authors used Genesis 10–11 for ethnographical purposes, they tend to treat it positively or neutrally, and suppress any negative aspects of pride, impiety, or gigantism. On the other hand, these negative aspects of the Babel narrative provide suitable moral material that can be used to identify and distinguish proper belief and behaviour from deviant. Much of the appeal and power of the Tower of Babel narrative comes from its presentation as a historical account that depicts not only the very beginnings of ethnic or political diversity, but the wickedness of the later Babylonian Empire. Northrop Frye has aptly articulated this prevalent characteristic of late antique and medieval treatments of the Babel narrative: the Tower of Babel "signifies the aspect of history known as imperialism, the human effort to unite human resources by force that organizes larger and larger social units, and eventually exalts some king into a world ruler"; it is, in other words, a "cyclical symbol" that provides "an example of the rising and falling of great kingdoms that forms a kind of counterpoint to Biblical history."[35] Certainly, like Frye, earlier interpreters were also interested in the story's universal characteristics and emphasized these characteristics accordingly.

Although the Babylonian Empire endured as a strong symbol for Jews and Christians, it was a symbol that owed much of its strength to the fact

---

34 Holladay, ed., *Fragments from Hellenistic Jewish Authors*, vol. 1, F 1.10–15.
35 *Words with Power*, 163.

that the Babylonian Empire no longer existed.[36] For the very reason that the early tower and the later empire had perished, both could be read as potent moral examples, particularly on the dangers of earthly (and therefore temporal) grandeur. Related to this exemplum of the fallen kingdom come other moral themes that help explain the cause of its destruction. In particular, the chief sin of pride becomes one of the dominant lessons of the Babel narrative, especially on account of the interpretative potential of Genesis 11:4: "Come, let us build ourselves a city, and a tower with its top in the heavens, and let us make a name for ourselves." Babel comes to be interpreted as an archetype, and as with most archetypes, it is employed effectively as a moral exemplum that not only reveals how vice leads to destruction, but also shares affinities with a number of other biblical exempla, such as the fall of Lucifer, the city-building Cain, the wickedness of the antediluvian giants, and the arrogance of Nebuchadnezzar, who is connected to Babel's Nimrod as much by shared vices as by shared historical lineage.

Other archetypal characters of the Bible may also display an affinity with Babel through various verbal clues. For example, in the Old English poem *Genesis B* Lucifer is so described: "þohte þurh his anes cræft / hu he him strenglicran stol geworhte, / heahran on heofonum" ("he thought how he might build for himself a stronger throne by means of his own power," 272–4), before repeating this narrative detail in his own words: "ic hæbbe geweald micel / to gyrwanne godlecran stol, / hearran on heofne" (I have much power to make a divine throne higher in heaven; 280–2). And later in the same poem, another devil refers to the fall of demons as forsaking heaven's high building: "monig forleton / on heofonrice heah getimbro" (many left that high building in heaven; 738–9). Because of the extra-biblical nature of the fall of Lucifer and the other demons, there is much room for expanding narrative details. In these instances from *Genesis B*, the theme of building high in heaven naturally recalls the Babel narrative, which also involves workers striving to build high up to heaven. Though chronologically speaking, the Babel narrative comes much later than the fall of the demons, the intertextuality of the two accounts strengthens the archetypal character of Lucifer (and the other demons) by connecting him to the builders of Babel while simultaneously strengthening the archetypal characteristics of the builders of Babel by connecting them to Satan himself. This feat is accomplished through a mere turn of phrase, an added

36 See Scheil, *Babylon under Westen Eyes*, 197–249.

rhetorical detail to the extra-biblical narrative. Other scholars have also found resemblance in the ruined buildings of Old English poetry that recall the archetype of Babel and many of its literary, moral, and ideological implications; for example, the ruined cities of the poems of the Exeter Book laments have been compared with both Babel and Babylon.[37]

The Present Babel: Non-Christian Abnormality and the Conversion of the World

I have briefly dealt with the role Genesis 10–11 plays in explaining European ethnography, and in fostering some of the extra-biblical aspects that help authors interpret the biblical account as a moral, archetypal tale. I will now turn to my third category, which conflates these two. The Table of Nations and the Tower of Babel, or rather the literary traditions that developed out of these texts, aided in the demonization of non-European ethnic groups, as well as non-Christian and heterodox religious groups. The biblical texts provided a useful tool for separating out and discriminating against certain ethnic groups thought to have participated in the wickedness of Babel, but also for identifying with an all-embracing Church that transcends diversity. On the one hand, ethnocentric notions of European, and later Christian, superiority, inherited from classical ethnography, were appropriated into and re-enforced by interpretations of Genesis 10–11. On the other hand, early Christians embraced a theology of ecclesiastical membership that found validity in the notion of a religion that transcended ethnic and linguistic divides. The Church, at least theoretically, had spread or was aiming to spread across the entire world, and the converts its missionaries had won at the very margins of the world legitimized the truth they proclaimed. This paradox of biblically justified ethnocentrism and an all-embracing view of the Church directly relates to the reception history of the Table of Nations and Babel narrative, especially as Christian exegetes increasingly interpreted Genesis 10–11 in light of the account of Pentecost presented in Acts 2.

Before early Jewish and Christian authors found significance in the ethnic division of the descendants of the sons of Noah, they understood the

37 Keenan, "*The Ruin* as Babylon," 109–17; but see Doubleday, "*The Ruin*: Structure and Theme," 369–81; Lee, "*The Ruin*: Bath or Babylon?," 443–55; and Scheil, *Babylon under Western Eyes*, 211–15. See also Liuzza, "The Tower of Babel: *The Wanderer* and the Ruins of History," 1–35.

world according to classical geography and cartography. Early Greek geographers divided the earth's known landmass into three continents: Europe, Asia, and Africa. Though the origins of this tripartite division seem to stem from an early division of land surrounding the Mediterranean,[38] the notion quickly took on larger areas, eventually transforming into a comprehensive, universal geography. With this geographical framework in place, it was no great stretch for early Jewish and Christian authors to see the three continents of the world in accordance with the three sons of Noah: Shem's lineage corresponded with Asia, Ham's with Libya or Africa, and Japheth's with Europe. The growing prominence of Christianity in the Roman Empire likely encouraged the association of the Church with Japheth and Europe; but Roman ethnocentrism also likely encouraged the continued discrimination against the non-European peoples of Africa and Asia. While it must be stated that self-conscious notions of a "European identity" are not articulated during Antiquity or the early Middle Ages,[39] Christian identity, alongside notions of Christendom, especially as it existed in the geographical bounds of Europe, did serve as a base to understand and judge communities outside of Christian Europe. By the fifth century, the relationship between Japheth and Europe, Shem and Asia, and Ham and Africa, as well as theological or moral perceptions associated with each son and group, was well established. Patristic authors of the highest authority, such as Jerome, Augustine, and Orosius, all present a tripartite division of the world made to fit with the Table of Nations.[40]

This matter is of particular importance for the history of racial discrimination, which continued far beyond the Middle Ages. I have already mentioned Goldenberg's book on the theological role of Ham's lineage in the discrimination of certain ancient peoples, followed by Hayne's and Whitford's books on how the "curse of Ham" was evoked to justify slavery.[41] Though examples of specific discrimination derived from theological

38 Hay, *Europe*, 2, referring to the *Hymn of Apollo*. See also Mikkeli, *Europe as an Idea and an Identity*, 5.

39 Mikkeli, *Europe as an Idea and an Identity*, 16.

40 Jerome, *Hebraicae quaestiones in libro Geneseos*, 10.21–10:26–9, 11–14; Augustine, *De ciuitate Dei libri XXII*, XVI.xvii.10–21; Orosius, *Historiarum adversus paganos libri vii*, I.3. See Hay, *Europe*, 9–14.

41 Efforts to analyse past discrimination against other communities have been fruitful. Benjamin, *The Invention of Racism in Classical Antiquity*, has, surprisingly, received some censure for even undertaking such an endeavour; see Isaac, Zieglet, and Eliav-Feldon, "Introduction," 1–31. Benjamin's thesis is that modern racism, defined

readings of the three sons of Noah, such as those given by Goldenberg, Whitford, and Haynes, are elusive in the literature of Anglo-Saxon England, Genesis 10–11 was definitely employed by Anglo-Saxons to discriminate more general categories of people. Bede, for example, makes the typological connection between Ham's lineage and the infidelity of heretics and the wicked. He also claims that the Ethiopians are appropriately listed as descendants of Ham's son Cush since "antiquus hostis semper de obscuro perfidorum populo per exsecutionem doctrinae siue opertationis nequam quasi recens nascitur" (the old enemy is always born as though anew from a black nation of infidels through the wicked execution of teaching or deed) – incidentally, this comment on the "black nation of infidels" contrasts with Bede's positive interpretation of dark skin in the Song of Songs as an allegory of the results of persecution.[42] Alongside Bede, Anglo-Saxon attitudes towards non-Christians living in the allegedly remote and exotic corners of the world are prominent. Non-European continents, and the East, in particular, were of great geographical and ethnographic interest for Anglo-Saxons, who understood Africa and Asia mainly as exotic lands inhabited by deformed humans and monsters. The *Wonders of the East*, the *Letter of Alexander to Aristotle*, and the Latin *Liber monstrorum* are good examples cataloguing the unusual and often dangerous humans and monsters one should expect to find outside of Europe. Though the Tower of Babel does appear in the related accounts after the Anglo-Saxon period – John Mandeville's *Travels* is a classic

somewhat narrowly as irrational discrimination based upon pseudo-scientific discourse, has its origins in classical writings of ancient Greece and Rome.

42 Bede, *In principium Genesis*, III.151–3, 146; Bede, *In Cantica Canticorum*, I.291–2, 197: "sancta ecclesia… persecutionibus adustam esse testatur" (the Holy Church… testifies that it is made dark by persecutions). For early Christian notions of blackness, see Byron, *Symbolic Blackness and Ethnic Difference in Early Christian Literature*; and Snowden, Jr, *Blacks in Antiquity*, esp. ch. 9, 196–215. Elsewhere in Anglo-Saxon literature, the connection between the dark skin of an Ethiopian and the "darkness" of wickedness is prevalent: for example, in a Latin *vita* of St Dunstan, the saint encounters a devil who has taken the form of "homuncii nigelli specie" (a little black man); see Winterbottom and Lapidge, eds., *The Early Lives of St Dunstan*, ch. 31.3 and nt. 272 for other Anglo-Latin examples. In the Latin and Old English *Wonders of the East*, the Ethiopian is described as being black ("ualde nigrum" / "sweartes hiwes") and placed alongside a list of monsters; Orchard, *Pride and Prodigies*, § 32, 180 (Latin), 202 (Old English); see also Estes, "Wonders and Wisdom: Anglo-Saxons and the East," 360–73, at 364.

example[43] – its absent is notable in these earlier texts. The general discourse, however, does participate and likely derives, at least in part, from antique and late antique ethnography of monstrous peoples that becomes connected with the Tower of Babel narrative chiefly as it is presented in the sixteenth book of Augustine's *De ciuitate Dei*.

In his *magnum opus*, Augustine provides a lengthy interpretation of the Table of Nations and the Tower of Babel narrative. He speaks of the world's ethnic and linguistic diversity stemming from the descendants of the sons of Noah; the typological implications of the three sons to the Church; the impiety of the giant Nimrod and his founding of the Babylonian Empire; the ethnic and linguistic lineage of the Hebrew-speaking Jews; and the existence of monstrous peoples. In a discussion on whether monstrous beings are to be considered human or not, Augustine borrows from Pliny to give a catalogue of "monstrosa hominum genera" (monstrous races of humans).[44] He goes on to mention certain humans with a variety of abnormalities, usually of physical deformity, but also of sexual deviance. In this catalogue of monsters, Augustine does not generally give geographical locations for where these peoples can be found; interestingly, his discussion lacks the kinds of geographical stigmatizing found in other authors. He only mentions specific locations alongside specific examples of monstrosity. For example, he states that in Hippo Zaritus (in modern-day Tunisia) there is a man with crescent-shaped feet and hands, lacking all but two toes and fingers on each foot and hand.[45] Other, particularly European, authors, however, do not hesitate to place these monstrous peoples outside of Europe, especially in those parts of the world where the Church was thought to be absent.[46]

Although Greek and Roman ethnography provides the origins for late antique and medieval discourse on monstrous peoples, authors like Augustine were able to employ Genesis 10–11 as scriptural evidence for the continuation of this discourse. Not only does Augustine's list of monstrous peoples fall right in the middle of his examination of the ethnic and

43 *Mandeville's Travels*, ch 6 and 24.

44 Augustine, *De ciuitate Dei*, XVI.viii.3; Pliny, *Natural History*, VII.9–32.

45 Augustine, *De ciuitate Dei*, XVI.viii.42–3.

46 Friedman, *The Monstrous Races in Medieval Art and Thought*, is the standard work among a vast bibliography of the subject. See also Cohen, *Of Giants: Sex, Monsters, and the Middle Ages* ; Williams, *Deformed Discourse*; Bildhauer and Mills, eds., *The Monstrous Middle Ages*; and recently Oswald, *Monsters, Gender and Sexuality in Medieval English Literature*.

linguistic diversity that arises out of the fall of the Tower of Babel, but his interpretation of the three sons of Noah establishes a theological framework that understands Ham's lineage as morally opposed to Shem's and Japheth's lineages, who represent the Church. Ham, whose name, according to Augustine, means "calidus" (hot) signifies the "haereticorum genus calidum" (*hot* type of heretics).[47] To his credit, Augustine is careful not to ascribe any moral fault to the literal peoples who are thought to have descended from Ham. But in this case the figurative sense of the biblical text, which becomes valid chiefly in its liberation from the literal sense, ends up pointing back towards an understanding of the literal sense that favours the descendants of Japheth and Shem as European and Christian and denounces the descendants of Ham as those opposed to Europe and the Church. Similarly, some exegetes felt the need to interpret Shem and his Jewish descendants as in opposition to Japheth and his European, gentile descendants. But unlike interpretations of Ham and his descendants, Genesis 9:26 states that Shem received a divine blessing: "Blessed by the Lord my God be Shem." Numerous interpretative strategies were employed to argue for Christian (and, by implication, European) superiority over Shem's descendants. The result is ambivalence towards the Jewish people, both as a theological construct and a real ethnic group, that ultimately leads to an understanding of a tripartite world with each part opposed to the other two.[48]

With the world partitioned into three general ethnic groups, each representing varying degrees of religious morality, European Christians could interpret Japheth not merely as a symbol for their broad ethnic and geographical community but also, paradoxically, as a symbol of the universality of the Church. Two passages in the New Testament were typologically connected to the Tower of Babel narrative: Luke 10, which describes Jesus sending out the seventy or seventy-two disciples, and Acts 2, which describes the apostolic ability to speak in all the languages of the Jewish

47 Augustine, *De ciuitate Dei*, XVI.ii.13. The word *calidus* is difficult to render in English in this case: according to the *Oxford Latin Dictionary*, *calidus* can mean "having a high temperature" (1a), "having a warm climate" (2a), both of which apply to the supposed geographical area of Ham's descendants, but also "hot-blooded, passionate, lusty" (9a), "excited, angry" (9b), and "hot-headed, rash, hasty" (10a), which apply to Augustine's characterization. To further complicate matters, the word *calidus* has the potential to pun with *callidus*, "crafty, cunning, wily" (*OLD* 3a), which also may align with Augustine's characterization.

48 For attitudes towards Jews in Anglo-Saxon England, see Scheil, *The Footsteps of Israel.*

Diaspora when the Holy Spirit descends at Pentecost. Both of these passages formed the basis for interpreting the early growth and genesis of the Church. Especially after Augustine, Latin Christian authors were able to connect Christ's seventy-two disciples with the seventy-two original nations thought to be presented in the Table of Nations.[49] The mission of these original disciples, though not exactly clear in the biblical account, came to represent the first mission of the Church to convert the entire world: the seventy-two disciples preaching to seventy-two nations. Similarly, the Acts account of Pentecost added a linguistic element to the Church's early mission, as the linguistic diversity created at Babel was overcome by the apostolic ability to speak in whatever language was needed to preach the gospel across ethnic and linguistic boundaries. As will be shown, in Anglo-Saxon England, the conversion of the English is frequently linked to this early ecclesiastical mission.[50] Because depictions of the early Church's mission to convert the world are intricately linked to an ideology that sees diversity beginning with the consequences of wickedness carried out at Babel, this study will really be as much about Anglo-Saxon interpretations of the Pentecostal mission as it is about interpretations of the Babel narrative.

Plan of Book

The main emphasis of this book will be on the Anglo-Saxon period, but earlier periods will be treated in the first two chapters. The treatment of the texts in the first chapters may seem out of place to a reader approaching the book for its information on Anglo-Saxon England. For one, many of the texts that I deal with in the first chapter, besides the biblical text itself and Josephus's *Antiquities of the Jews*, have absolutely no influence on medieval Europe – at least one, the *Genesis Apocryphon*, seems to have been completely unknown after the first century CE until its discovery at Qumran in the early twentieth century. Nevertheless my analysis of the early interpretations of the Table of Nations and the Tower of Babel narrative has three primary goals. The first is to show the degree to which early authors develop the biblical text for their own purposes, revealing a great degree of interpretative variability that will have profound influence on

49 See Major, "Biblical and Hellenistic Beginnings to the Early Middle Ages," 7–45.

50 See Levison, *England and the Continent in the Eighth Century*, ch. 3 and 4, 45–93, for Anglo-Saxon missionary activity on the continent.

later readers. The second goal follows the first in that it aims to fill out interpretative genealogies. The *Genesis Apocryphon*, for example, seems to have influenced Jubilees, which in turn influenced Josephus and the early Christian world chronicles. These chronicles, once having taken Latin forms, became some of the most significant texts for medieval ethnography, geography, and cartography. The third goal aims to sift through the evidence to discover the more prevalent interpretative trajectories that share similarities and differences with Anglo-Saxon understanding and use of Genesis 10–11. Although no direct relationship can be positively established between exegesis of the Babel narrative in Hellenistic Judaism and Anglo-Saxon England, the presentation and study of analogues has value for wider understanding of the literary reception of biblical texts.

At the other end of the spectrum, people continued to read, interpret, and develop the Tower of Babel narrative after 1066. However, the later Anglo-Saxon period provides a fitting watershed that marks the end of the early Middle Ages before new cultural and literary shifts begin to appear in England and in Europe. Unsurprisingly, these shifts bring about new and complex interpretations and uses of the Babel narrative that deserve the patience and careful analysis that present restrictions cannot accommodate. Space also does not allow for a full study of the similarly understudied Irish and Carolingian responses to the Babel narrative.[51] Certainly, Irish, Carolingian, and post-conquest English sources all need to be reassessed, but in separate volumes where adequate space can be devoted to proper examination of the subject. For these reasons, the present book is necessarily limited to the relevant material leading up to and involving Anglo-Saxon England.

When dealing with Anglo-Saxon literature, I follow rough chronological order. After the two initial chapters on the earlier interpretative traditions, the third chapter examines the Anglo-Latin texts connected with Theodore's and Hadrian's Canterbury School, and the revival of learning in late seventh- and early eighth-century England. Because the Canterbury commentaries deal with the book of Genesis, they offer some important information about early Anglo-Saxon interpretations of the Babel narrative. Evidence of Theodore's influence, in particular, reveals an interesting textual engagement with previous Latin and Greek literature that allows for unique readings of the Genesis account. This chapter also examines

51 Borst presents a much more thorough examination of the continental material than he does for Anglo-Latin and Old English literature; *Turmbau von Babel*, vol. 2, 483–541.

how Aldhelm, the most famous student of the Canterbury School, seems to have made use of the Babel narrative, especially in his attitude towards preaching and heretics. The fourth chapter deals with the role Genesis 11 plays in the large corpus of Bede's exegetical and historical material. Bede directly treats the subject on a number of occasions, most thoroughly in his commentary on Genesis, to support a theology that understands the world as ethnically diversified by Babel but united by Pentecost. The later section of this chapter is devoted to Bede's immediate legacy, represented by Alcuin of York, who provides an important bridge to subsequent Carolingian exegesis. In the next chapter, I examine the role of the Babel narrative in the Old English works of King Alfred's translation program. Both the Old English *Boethius* and *Orosius* employ the Tower of Babel as a fitting warning against overly proud governance. Though Daniel Anlezark has published an excellent analysis of the Alfredian Anglo-Saxon genealogies that re-fashion the biblical account to express notions of Anglo-Saxon political unification through the appearance of an extra-biblical son of Noah, in this chapter I briefly take up the issue to clarify some points. This chapter also argues that the Old English poem *Solomon and Saturn II*, which may have been composed in the Age of Alfred, uses the Babel narrative to contrast Christianized Europe (and so Anglo-Saxon England) with a non-Christian East.

Over the next century, the achievements of the Anglo-Latin authors of the Benedictine Reform can be traced back to Alfred's efforts at cultural revival. These authors, whose writings will make up the content of the sixth chapter, share with Alfred underlying ideologies and propagate a perception of the past that stresses the tension between ethnic diversity and religious disorder at Babel, and Christian unity at Pentecost. Furthermore, the most prolific authors of the second generation of the Benedictine Reform, Ælfric of Eynsham and Wulfstan the homilist, make much use of the Babel narrative. Their treatments reveal dependency upon the earlier Anglo-Latin writers of the Reform, but also a marked deviance that comes forth in unique and interesting ways through their use of the vernacular. Ælfric's accounts of the Babel narrative, for example, share enough verbal similarity to resemble formulaic phrasing common not only to Old English poetry but also to Wulfstan. Because of the difficulty of dating Old English poetry, I relegate discussion of the biblical poems of Junius 11 to the final chapter, which takes as its main focus the Old English poems *Genesis A* and *Daniel*. This chapter finds a compromise between two competing scholarly interpretations of *Genesis A* that debate the influence of Augustinian theology on the section on the Tower of Babel. It also argues for reading *Daniel* in a typological framework that employs allusions to Babel as an archetype for Babylon.

Chapter One

Early Jewish and Christian Antiquity

Introduction

The scarcity of dramatic narrative and the ambiguity of detail of Genesis 10–11, as well as its seemingly chronological disorder, did nothing to stifle interest in the narrative. Rather, it allowed for much creative inquiry over the actual nature of the biblical event, which then produced a number of extra-biblical features, both outlandish and conservative, associated with the Table of Nations and Tower of Babel narrative. Some of these extra-biblical features, especially those involving extended narrations of, say, Joktan's strife with the child Abram, would not pass into Christian literary traditions.[1] Other features would become commonplace; Nimrod's gigantism is ubiquitous throughout Late Antiquity and the Middle Ages, and his tyrannical character, which is not an element in the biblical text, can be found even among early Protestant exegetes.[2] Still other features, such as the various motives for building the Tower or the association with the builders and idolatry, would be found among Christian authors seeking to explain the narrative's gaps or simply passing on received interpretation. In these cases, there can be surprising temporal or geographical distances between two or more authors expressing the same feature. For example, the extra-biblical detail of a fourth son born on the ark can be found in such disparate texts as the sixth-century Syriac *Book of the Cave of Treasures*, the eighth-century Greek pseudo-Methodius, and some Latin

1 Pseudo-Philo, *Liber Antiquitatum Biblicarum*, ch. 6.

2 For the biblical text, see Sherman, *Babel's Tower Translated*, 17–42; for the Protestants, see Haynes, *Noah's Curse*, 32–4, 50–2; and Scheil, *Babylon under Western Eyes*, 99–100.

and Old English texts affiliated with King Alfred.[3] Likewise, as already mentioned, Old English euhemeristic associations of the builders of Babel with pagan gods have analogues with the earliest surviving interpretative expression of the Babel narrative, the early Jewish fragments attributed to pseudo-Eupolemus.

These extra-biblical features pose a particular organizational problem for this study. A detailed examination duly tracing the development and reception of each throughout Late Antiquity and the Middle Ages is beyond the present scope; and some helpful studies on the earlier periods have already been published. Sherman in particular covers the early Jewish readings and rewriting of the Babel narrative.[4] In the following chapter, I will focus chiefly on the early development of the reception history of the Table of Nations, which provides the broader patterns of influence regarding ethnic and linguistic diversity, along with a theology aiming to understand diversity incorporated in a single, universal Church.

Ethnography and Geography of Genesis 10–11 and Early Jewish Literature

The first five books of the Hebrew Scriptures seem to have initially been put together as a single unit sometime around 500 BCE by an anonymous author or authors who assembled and revised a number of ancient sources. Whereas the Tower of Babel narrative originally seems to have been taken from the J (Jehovist) source, the Table of Nations is often considered a composition of two sources, J and P (Priestly), sewn together by a redactor.[5] Accordingly, the material of Genesis 10 from the P source, which seems to have been the base text of the Table of Nations, originally presented a straightforward genealogical list that used the formula: "the sons of so-and-so [are] so-and-so." Additions from the older J source were then interwoven with those of P in order to fill out the genealogical account with names of individuals, cities, and tribes, and some narrative detail. Alongside

3 See esp. Gero, "The Legend of the Fourth Son of Noah," 321–30; and below 147–9.

4 Sherman, *Babel's Tower Translated*.

5 The division of the Table of Nations proposed by Wellhausen, *Die Composition des Hexateuchs und der historischen Bücher des alten Testaments*, 6–7, remains the standard. The division for chapter 10 is P: 1a, 2–7, 20, 22–3, 31–2; J: 1b, 8–19, 21, 24–30; for a clear representation of the division of the chapter, see Vawter, *On Genesis*, 142–3, who presents the J additions in italics.

greater textual and narrative complexity, the overall effect is that the descendants of Japheth and Shem, Noah's two "good" sons, are portrayed in a neutral light as groups of people obeying the command to Noah to "be fruitful and multiply and fill the earth" (Genesis 9:1), whereas the descendants of Ham, Noah's "wicked" son, are portrayed as dominant and invasive forces on the earth.[6] It is no coincidence that most of Israel's enemies are classed under Ham's descendants in the Table of Nations. This distinction is important for later interpretations of the text; certain Christian authors of Late Antiquity and the Middle Ages tended to emphasize a tripartite categorization of the world in order to self-identify themselves under Japheth's line literally as Europeans and typologically as Christians who are neither the Jews of Shem's line nor the heathens and heretics of Ham's line.

Although the original P or J sources may not have had the intention of casting Ham's descendants in a negative light, but rather of presenting their dwelling places as historically accurate as possible,[7] the biblical text does present a strong sense of land entitlement and illicit encroachment by some of the descendants of Ham. For instance, in the J source only the descendants of Ham are described as builders of cities, which with the material from P become situated within the part of the world allotted to Shem's descendants. Nimrod, particularly, is singled out as an aggressor who, cryptically, is not only a "mighty hunter before the Lord" (Genesis 10:9), but also a founder of a number of cities (Genesis 10:11–12: Babel, Erech, Accad, Nineveh, Rehoboth-Ir, Calah, and Resen) clearly outside of Ham's (and his) allotted portion of land. On the one hand, it is very probable that the details concerning Nimrod's cities reflect a conflation of Ham's son Kush (the father of Nimrod and the ancient name for Ethiopia) with the Kassites, a Mesopotamian people, who ruled Babylon between 1595 and 1145 BCE in an area the Table of Nations allots to Shem's descendants.[8] But on the other hand, these details, by rupturing an otherwise relatively neat categorization, give grounds to an interpretation that sees

6 Ross, "The Table of Nations in Genesis 10 – Its Content," 22–34, at 30.

7 This is the view of VanderKam, "Putting Them in their Place," 476–99, at 483. See also Alexander, "Geography and the Bible," 977–88, at 980: "thus the Canaanites, despite being for the most part ethnically Semites are said to be descended from Ham, not Shem (v. 6), presumably because the land of Canaan was regarded by the compiler of the P-Table as related politically to Egypt, one of Ham's other sons."

8 Goldenberg, *The Curse of Ham*, 20.

the Table of Nations as reflecting negative attitudes towards the aggression of Israel's enemies. Even if the redactor was merely trying to portray Nimrod's kingdom as he understood it – that is, more historically and ethnically connected to the nations of northeast Africa than to Israel – it is still unlikely that he viewed the presence of Nimrod's kingdom in Shem's allotted land neutrally; elsewhere in the Table, the J account is used to state that the descendants of Ham's specifically cursed son Canaan have increased their borders as far as Gaza (10:18–19). Like Nimrod's Babylon, which later became a dangerous threat to the Israelites and which is treated contemptuously in the following narrative of the Tower of Babel, the depiction of Canaan not only as the cursed grandson of Noah, but also as an illegitimate possessor of Israel's land, gives some warrant to Israel's later aggression towards the Canaanite people (Joshua 10–11; see also Deuteronomy 7:1–2).

Instead of being an isolated Jewish text unaware of other Mediterranean literary cultures, the Table of Nations conforms to other ancient representations of ethnic diversity. According to the evidence that survives, people living around the eastern Mediterranean in the first millennium BCE tended to see the world as a circular-shaped landmass formed around the Mediterranean Sea, and surrounded at its own extremities by another outlining body of water, often termed *okeanos* (ocean) in the Greek sources. The centres of these circular worlds differed according to the perspectives of the authors. The earliest known example is the late eighth- or seventh-century BCE Babylonian World Map (British Museum 92687), which places Babylon roughly in the centre.[9] Later, ancient Greek geography displays a comparable tendency. Alongside the geography of Homer, which seems to have placed the centre of the earth in the Aegean Sea, the so-called Ionian world maps, as described by later authors, placed the island of Delphi at the centre or the *omphalos* (navel) of the world – an orientation commonplace in classical Greek geography and literature.[10]

---

9 Horowitz, *Mesopotamian Cosmic Geography*, 21–5 (text and translation), 26 (date), 402–3, 405–6 (photographs). See also an inscription on the tomb of Darius I at Naqsh-e Rustam that gives a list of nations in a geographical sequence that resembles a circular map of the world with Persia at the centre; Goukowsky, *Essai sur les origines du mythe d'Alexandre (336–270 av. J.-C.)*, vol. 1, 222–3.

10 Romm, *The Edges of the Earth in Ancient Thought*, 63 and 65–7; and Ciholas, *The Omphalos and the Cross*. See also Neiman, "Ethiopia and Kush," 34–42, at 42; and Alexander, "Notes on the 'Imago mundi' of the Book of Jubilees," 197–213, at 198.

Notions of centrality are also apparent in the Table of Nations, although not as explicit as elsewhere in ancient Jewish literature. Naturally, it is rather difficult to determine the specific geographical regions that are mentioned in the Table of Nations, especially since the mental map of the redactor must have looked much different than today's maps. In all probability the redactor of the Table of Nations saw the world in line with the mental maps of his relative contemporaries and the later Jewish authors who added helpful geographical information to the Table of Nations. With the evidence admittedly scant, the Table does seem to portray the ethnicity of the world in tripartite geography. Japheth's descendants occupy the North, Ham's the South, and Shem's the East. In this scheme Palestine falls roughly in the middle, intersecting three general ethnic groups of the world. This notion of centrality also accords with other passages in the Hebrew Bible itself, which provide explicit references to the centrality of Israel and Jerusalem in particular. Ezekiel, notably, describes Jerusalem as being in the middle of the nations (5:5) and at the centre of the earth (38:12; see also I Enoch 26.1) – a description that echoes the Greek term *omphalos* (navel) and is rendered as such in the Septuagint.[11]

The centrality of Israel in the Table of Nations becomes more apparent in the subsequent adaptations of the chapter in Jewish pseudepigraphical literature. One of the earliest texts to employ the Table of Nations is the Dead Sea *Genesis Apocryphon*, an Aramaic adaptation of some of the stories of Genesis, particularly centred around Noah and Abraham. Although there is considerable debate over the date of the *Genesis Apocryphon*, its most recent editor, Daniel A. Machiela, has exhaustively examined the available evidence to make a compelling case for its composition in the late third or early second century BCE.[12] In two damaged columns (16–17), the author condenses some of Genesis 10 and expands other parts, notably by including a number of specific geographical details.[13] As far as can be known from the fragmented evidence, the author first outlines the general portions of land allotted to Noah's three sons according to bodies of water (16:8–28), before reiterating the geographical boundaries allotted to the

11 See Alexander, "Jerusalem as the *Omphalos* of the World," 104–19.

12 Machiela, *The Dead Sea Genesis Apocryphon*, 134–42. Translations of the *Genesis Apocryphon* will be from this edition.

13 Scott, *Geography in Early Judaism and Christianity*, 25, notes that the unspecified boundaries in the Table of Nations "invited geographical speculation and allowed revision in the course of time."

immediate grandsons of Noah, again according to bodies of waters and the occasional reference to a mountain range (17:7–24).

As Ester Eshel has argued, the focus on geography, in contrast to ethnicity, in the *Genesis Apocryphon* is heavily reliant on classical world maps. First, Eshel has detected the geographical perspective of the *Genesis Apocryphon* as one that understands what is likely the Sea of Azov (just north of the Black Sea) as "the sea of the East" (17:10). This perspective must, according to Eshel, reflect an "orientation from Greece, namely with Delphi at the center"; for only "someone using Delphi as a reference point could refer to the Sea of Azov as 'the Sea of the East.'"[14] Second, Eshel claims that specific geographical sequences in the *Genesis Apocryphon* differ from the ordering of the names in the Table of Nations to better mirror classical world maps of Ionia: "underlying the arrangement in the *Genesis Apocryphon* – Japheth, Shem, and Ham – are directional considerations ... [that proceed] from north to south, clockwise, which is from left to right on ancient maps"; likewise, Shem's lineage "proceeds from east to west, counter-clockwise, or from top to bottom on ancient maps."[15] Although there is nothing in columns 16–17 of the *Genesis Apocryphon* that indicates north as left or south as right, two other passages, which describe north as left (21:8, 22:10),[16] may indicate that the author thought to present the world as a map aligned with East at the top, North to the left, and South to the right. As Alexander notes, a related section in Jubilees which describes the South as right "suggests that south was on the right of the map."[17] On the contrary, the words for North and South in Hebrew and other Semitic languages are synonyms of the words left and right, possibly because of an ideological orientation to the East, not because of any standardization in cartography.[18]

Likewise, the book of Jubilees, a second-century BCE pseudepigraphon, which likely (but not positively) post-dates the *Genesis Apocryphon* and either borrows from it or from a common extra-biblical source, expands upon the Table of Nations in similar manners. Although Jubilees

14 Eshel, "The *Imago mundi* of the *Genesis Apocryphon*," 111–31, at 123; Eshel's article seems to have a typographical error – *Mauq* for *Me'at* – which causes confusion for Machiela, *The Dead Sea Genesis Apocryphon*, 67, nt. 17:10.

15 Eshel, "The *Imago mundi* of the *Genesis Apocryphon*," 125–6.

16 See Fitzmyer, ed., *The Genesis Apocryphon*, 220, 244.

17 See Alexander, "The *Imago mundi* of Jubilees," 204.

18 Wilson, "South," 590; and Hartley, "North," 550–1.

reveals a great deal of Hellenization, the author was likely a priest of the Hasidic or Essene branch of Judaism,[19] and in his expansion and rewriting of Genesis and Exodus he firmly and explicitly interprets Judaic centrality into the Table of Nations. A number of scholars have also pointed out the significant role that Greek geography plays on the account of the nations in Jubilees 8–9. The author of Jubilees seems to have been acquainted with the Ionian world maps,[20] as well as the geographical traditions that later influence Strabo and Dionysius Periegetes of Alexandria.[21] But despite the influence of Hellenism, the geography of Jubilees naturally differs over the exact location of the centre of the world. Much like Ezekiel and other texts such as I Enoch, the descendants of Shem are described as inhabiting the "center of the earth" with Mount Zion "in the middle of the navel of the earth" (Jubilees 8:19). Again, the word *omphalos* (navel) parallels Greek notions of centrality, and reveals an element of the literary discourse that the author was writing within and, to some extent, against.[22]

Jubilees also discloses further degrees of Hellenization by emphasizing a tripartite division of the world. Unlike the Table of Nations and the *Genesis Apocryphon*, Jubilees explicitly states that peoples of the earth are divided into three parts (8:10) according to the descendants of Shem, Ham, and Japheth; he reiterates his division by referring to the division of Ham as the "second portion" (8:22), and the division of Japheth as the "third portion" (8:25) – interestingly, the lack of a number for Shem's portion indicates its status as normative and self-identifying. This tripartite division of the world also reflects a similar Greek understanding of geography: Hecataeus of Miletus divided the world into the three parts of Europe, Asia, and Libya (or Africa), and Herodotus reaffirms this division with his own modification that Europe is the size of Asia and Africa put together (4.42). As with the *Genesis Apocryphon*, this tripartite division of the earth is apparent in the so-called Sallust maps of the first century BCE, as well as the later T-O maps that separated the world into the three continents Asia, Africa, and Europe by a graphical division that has the semblance of a T inside of an O.[23] Since the Table of Nations in Genesis had already

19 Wintermute, trans., *Jubilees*, in *The Old Testament Pseudepigrapha*, vol. 2 , 45.
20 Alexander, "Notes on the 'Imago mundi,'" 198–9.
21 Scott, *Geography in Early Judaism and Christianity*, 32.
22 Alexander, "Jerusalem as the *Omphalos* of the World."
23 See Woodward, "Reality, Symbolism, Time, and Space in Medieval World Maps," 510–21, at 511; and "Medieval *Mappaemundi*," 286–370, at 343–4.

provided a nascent framework through its land division according to the three sons of Noah, it would have been no great task for the author of Jubilees to emphasize the tripartite nature of his own mental map and thereby syncretise further with the Greek geography in vogue.

Moreover, the author of Jubilees attributes climate zones to his three parts of the world. He writes that the land of Japheth is "cold, and the land of Ham is hot"; and not surprisingly that "the land of Shem is not hot or cold because it is mixed with cold and heat" (8:30). This division of a hot southern climate, a cold Northern climate, and a moderate central climate can be traced back to the influence of Greek geography. For example, the anonymous fifth-century BCE work *Airs Waters Places*, often attributed to Hippocrates, contains a similar climatic division of a cold North in Europe, a hot South in Libya, and a mixed moderate climate in Asia, which may here be referring to Asia Minor.[24] As is to be expected, the centre displays the normal; the peripheries display the abnormal. Plato, likewise, reveals a significant element to these geographical oppositions by attaching moral import to the three climatic zones. In *The Republic*, he has Socrates state that the northern regions possess high-spiritedness or aggression (*thumos*), whereas the southern regions are consumed by love of money. Of course, the middle regions held by the Greeks are typified by their love of learning or philosophy (IV 435e).[25] Elsewhere in Plato's works, the home of the Greeks, and the city of Athens in particular, is awarded the best place for acquiring virtue on account of its mixed, moderate climate (*Timaeus* 24c–d; *Laws* 747d–e; *Epinomis* (ps.-Plato?) 987d). And after Plato, Aristotle follows the same train of thought, placing Greece in the middle of two climatic and moral extremes.[26] The North has spirit but lacks intelligence; the South has intelligence, but lacks spirit; only the moderate zone of Asia Minor has both spirit and intelligence, and, therefore, the true capacity to be powerful. By means of such an understanding of the world, Aristotle is able to make his famous claim that "Greek stock" would rule the world if only it could unite itself under one state (*Politics* VII.7). Furthermore, the supposed centre of the world shifts according to the perspectives of the writer. Early first-century pagan authors Strabo and Vitruvius both relocate the centre of the world from

---

24 Romm, "Continents, Climates, and Cultures," 215–35, at 221. See also Romm, *Edges of the Earth in Ancient Thought*, 45–81.

25 See Romm, "Continents," 224.

26 Ibid., 224–5.

Greece to Rome and claim that from this temperate position Rome enjoyed a superiority to command the peoples living in the southern and northern regions of the world.[27]

Although the author of Jubilees does not go to the same lengths as Plato and Aristotle (or Strabo and Vitruvius), he does reveal a similar dichotomous sense of normality and abnormality among the peoples of the earth based on climatic zones – Shem's descendants (and therefore the ancestors of the author of Jubilees) enjoy the moderate centre, whereas Japheth's and Ham's descendants are constrained to peripheries lacking climates needed for optimum human living. Although the geographical superiority of Shem's allotted land is absent from the *Genesis Apocryphon*, the author of that text similarly emphasizes Shem's superiority over the Asiatic portion of land alongside tensions hinted at in the Table of Nations, and further developed in Jubilees.[28] James M. Scott even goes so far as to interpret the centralization of Shem's allotted land in Jubilees as containing further significance for the acts of Japheth and Ham's descendants that hint at future "imperialistic world conquerors such as the Greco-Macedonians (Seleucids) and later the Romans."[29]

As already mentioned, the author of Jubilees was likely a Hasidic or Essene priest, writing for a Jewish (albeit Hellenized Jewish) audience. He does not need to alter the Table of Nations much, but rather emphasizes certain elements in order to use the rhetorical strategies of Hellenistic geographic and ethnographic discourse. He identifies himself and all Jewish people with Shem, who is allotted the best portion of the earth for normal human living and, therefore, normal human nature itself. Although neither Jubilees nor the *Genesis Apocryphon* would have much or any influence on later Latin Christians of Late Antiquity and the early Middle Ages,[30] the tendency to interpret the Table of Nations, first according to

27 Scott, *Geography in Early Judaism and Christianity*, 33. For Strabo, see *Géographie*, vol. 3, , VI.4.1; and Clarke, *Between Geography and History: Hellenistic Constructions of the Roman World*, 210–28. For Vitruvius, see *De l'Architecture livre VI*, VI.1.6–7, and Callebat's comments at 80–1.

28 Eshel, "The *Imago mundi* of the *Genesis Apocryphon*," 130–1.

29 Scott, *Geography in Early Judaism and Christianity*, 35; see also Eshel, "The *Imago mundi* of the *Genesis Apocryphon*," 127–9.

30 Jubilees was read sporadically in Late Antiquity (Jerome cites it and it is among the list of books condemned by the Gelasian Decree); in Anglo-Saxon England, only the biblical commentaries of the Canterbury School show some knowledge of it. See Biggs, ed., *Sources of Anglo-Saxon Literary Culture: The Apocrypha*, 7.

contemporary geographical and political knowledge, and second according to centric notions that help the author and his audience identify with people favoured by God and disassociated with the rest of the world, would prevail. Part of this interpretative tradition and tendency is no doubt attributed to the reworking of the Table of Nations by Josephus, whose influence on later Christians cannot be understated.

Despite the priority of the *Genesis Apocryphon* and Jubilees, the account of Flavius Josephus (37–c. 100) would have enormous influence on the intellectual traditions of Late Antiquity and the Middle Ages. Josephus's *Antiquitates Iudaicae*, first composed in Greek in the first century CE, and later translated into Latin at Cassiodorus's school at Vivarium,[31] was widely read – not only do a large number of manuscripts survive, but countless authors reveal familiarity with what Walter Berschin has called one of the "basic historical texts in the Latin Middle Ages."[32] Because of his Jewish ethnicity and yet wide readership among Christian authors, Josephus stands as a kind of lynchpin between early Jewish literature and the Roman gentile world, including the emerging Christians.[33] Importantly for this study, Josephus's *Antiquitates* provides an extended revision of the Table of Nations and explicatory details of the Babel narrative, both of which would profoundly influence subsequent treatments of the biblical texts.

Because the details that Josephus introduces to the Babel narrative have been treated recently by other scholars,[34] I will only touch briefly on them here. One of the main exegetical problems of Genesis 10–11 concerns the narrative relationship between the Table of Nations and the consequences of building the Tower of Babel. The biblical text appears to offer two explanations, back-to-back, for the same event: ethnic and linguistic diversity. While some clues in the biblical text hint at the narrative uniformity of the two accounts, for the most part the task of preserving the integrity of the text was left to later exegetes. Josephus's lengthy account of the Babel narrative is one of the first to tackle this issue in depth, providing later

31 Cassiodorus, *Institutiones*, I.xvii.1. For the first volume of the Latin translation, see Josephus, *The Latin Josephus*.

32 Berschin, *Greek Letters and the Latin Middle Ages*, 78.

33 Bibliography on Josephus and his role as mediator between the two cultures is enormous. For two succinct studies, see Bilde, *Flavius Josephus between Jerusalem and Rome*; and Feldman, "Josephus (CE 37–*c.* 100)," 901–21.

34 Notably, Inowlocki, "Josephus' Rewriting of the Babel Narrative (Gen 11:1–9)," 169–91; and Sherman, *Babel's Tower Translated*, 153–94. See also Franklin, *Genesis and the "Jewish Antiquities" of Flavius Josephus*, 93–116.

readers with a solid foundation to further develop the interpretative history. Most significantly, Josephus reframes the Babel narrative to emphasize God's wish for the people to colonize the earth, a kind of prophylactic that aims to prevent the civil strife inevitable with over-population.[35] But after the Flood, the descendants of Noah prove reluctant to obey the command to "fill the earth" (Genesis 9:1); due to their fear of a second flood, they are even reluctant to come down from the mountains, until Japheth, Ham, and Shem first descend and ensure that the lower plains are safe to inhabit.[36] As Sabrina Inowlocki points out, Josephus's aversion to a unified people is also reflected in his near contemporary, Philo of Alexandria, whose *De confusione linguarum* presents the unity of language at Babel as "the unity of evil and of the corporeal world."[37] Importantly, Josephus is also one of the earliest authors to connect Nimrod explicitly with the building of the Tower of Babel.[38] Josephus has him play the role of a tyrant able to organize the people lest they "be scattered abroad upon the face of the whole earth" (Genesis 11:4). By stoking the fears of another flood, Nimrod is able to convince the people to erect a thick, waterproof tower.[39] Naturally, his efforts fail and the people are scattered across the earth, filling each continent, according to God's original wish.[40] The tower eventually topples from divine winds.[41]

Josephus solves the problem created by the biblical order by simply rearranging the narrative. Unlike Genesis and Jubilees, he records the Table of Nations after recounting the Babel narrative. And unlike Jubilees and the *Genesis Apocryphon*, Josephus does not display much hostility towards non-Semitic people in Asia. As F. Schmidt writes,

> Josephus is representative of a social environment for which Hellenism scarcely constituted a danger; indeed, it was perceived of as a reality with which

35 Josephus, *Libri antiquitatum Iudaicarum*, vol. 1, I.110.

36 Ibid., I.109.

37 Inowlocki, "Josephus' Rewriting," 176.

38 The *Liber antiquitatum biblicarum* of pseudo-Philo, a work thought to be contemporary with Josephus, also implicates Nimrod with building the Tower; see van der Toorn and van der Horst, "Nimrod before and after the Bible," 19–20.

39 Josephus, *Libri antiquitatum Iudaicarum*, vol. 1, I.114; see also I.135.

40 Ibid., I.120.

41 Ibid., I.118, citing the third Sybil. Inowlocki, "Josephus' Rewriting," 182–4, also offers further a fascinating reading of this passage that connects Josephus's account with his condemnation of contemporary politics, particularly involving Jewish Zealots.

> Judaism had to come to terms. Therefore the image of the world suggested by the historian is altogether different: Shem, Ham, and Japhet share Asia among them; the Greek names of both nations and places are substituted for the traditional ones. The cultural universe is not seen as a threat.[42]

Josephus stands in contrast to his predecessors not only because he treats the ethnic and linguistic diversity of the world in a neutral or positive light, but also because he updates the names in the Table of Nations to conform to contemporary nations, cities, or other geographical landmarks.[43] Even Josephus's statements that the Hebrew text best represents the original names of the nations, which the Greeks later hellenized in their contemporary forms, serve merely to preserve the integrity of the Hebrew Scriptures in light of new geographical understanding.[44]

Along with updating the names in the Table of Nations to accord with contemporary terminology, Josephus reveals an approach that would have importance for later ethnographical methods. He allows for changes in the existence of ethnic groups. Unable to find contemporary nomenclature for a name mentioned in Genesis 10, Josephus at times glosses over the discrepancy with a historical event that explains the disappearance of an ethnic community. For example, since he can find no nation that represents the later descendants of the Ludim ("Λουμαίου"), Anamim ("Ἀναμία") and Lehabim ("Λαβίμου") mentioned in Genesis 10:13, Josephus states that the Ethiopian War destroyed their cities, evidently leaving knowledge only of their names.[45] This strategy thereby retains the reliability of both the biblical text and contemporary ethnographical knowledge. Even though Josephus gives consideration to the biblical numeration of the descendants of the sons of Noah, the notion of lost ethnic groups implies that the Table of Nations does not necessarily need to be seen as a static account at odds with Greek and Roman ethnography. All ethnic diversity, in other words, begins with the Tower of Babel, but ethnic communities are destroyed, or over time grow into new ones. Though Josephus is not often given the credit he deserves for this subtle innovation, the disconnect

42 Schmidt, "Jewish Representations of the Inhabited Earth During the Hellenistic and Roman Periods," 133–4, quoted from Eshel, "The *Imago mundi* of the *Genesis Apocryphon*," 130.

43 Josephus, *Libri antiquitatum Iudaicarum*, vol. 1, I.122–47.

44 Ibid., I.120, I.122, and I.129.

45 Ibid., I.137; see also I.139.

between Genesis 10 and contemporary ethnography is a necessary feature of all subsequent Christian ethnography and geography.

Christian Ethnography and Geography

As is apparent with Josephus, during the first centuries before and after Christ, Greek and Roman imperialism gave Jewish and Christian authors access to texts that offered new information about the ethnic diversity of the world that did not agree with that of the Table of Nations. Most significantly, the Table of Nations lists seventy to seventy-three names depending on the version and method of counting.[46] By the time early Christians were composing the texts of the New Testament, it had become the norm to understand that there were either seventy or seventy-two original languages and nations that dispersed after the fall of the Tower of Babel. Luke, for example, has Jesus sending out seventy or seventy-two disciples, depending on the manuscript variants and biblical testimonia – a number that is easily connected to the supposed number of "nations" listed in Genesis 10.[47] But any standardized number for the totality of nations will eventually clash with other accounts and observations. Classical Greek and Roman opinions regarding the number of nations or ethnic groups in the world naturally varied from that of the Table of Nations. Many of the barbarian tribes mentioned by Pliny, Livy, and Tacitus, among others, did not have any direct correspondence with the names in the Table, and by the fourth century, historians such as Ammianus Marcellinus could describe the Scythian peoples as innumerable: "gentesque Scytharum innumerae, quae porriguntur ad usque terras sine cognito fine distentas" ([there are] innumerable tribes of the Scythians which extend even to lands that stretch to unknown boundaries).[48]

Despite this clash between pagan and Jewish accounts, efforts were made among Christians to facilitate the differing cultural notions regarding ethnic diversity. Along with his mention of seventy or seventy-two disciples, Luke elsewhere provides his own version of the Table of Nations in his account of Pentecost, where the Holy Spirit descends and grants

46 See Major, "The Number Seventy-Two," 9–14.

47 For the Lukan variants, see Metzger, "Seventy or Seventy-Two Disciples?," 67–76; and Verheyden, "How Many Were Sent According to Lk 10,1?," 193–238.

48 Ammianus Marcellinus, *Ammianus Marcellinus*, vol. 2, XXII.8.42; see also Geary, *Myth of Nations*, 48.

universal linguistic understanding (Acts 2:1–13). Despite the small number of nations mentioned, Luke not only uses representatives roughly grouped in the three parts of the world (Asia, Europe, and Africa), he also updates his list of ethnic groups to correspond to his own interests and literary purposes, which understandably differ from those of Genesis 10.[49] Notably, the updated list includes lands in Asia Minor (in particular Roman provinces in what is now modern Turkey) that will play an important role in the later parts of Acts, as the Gospel is brought to the Gentiles of Asia Minor and eventually to Rome.

Early Christians continued to develop the geographical implications of Genesis 10, especially in light of Acts 2. For example, Tertullian presents a revised list of nations that expands Luke's account. After posing the rhetorical question, "In quem enim alium uniuersae gentes crediderunt, nisi in Christum, qui iam uenit" (in whom else do all the nations believe except Christ who has already come), Tertullian lists the nations mentioned in Acts 2:9–11, before supplementing it:[50]

> et ceterae gentes, ut iam Getulorum uarietates et Maurorum multi fines <et> Hispaniarum omnes termini et Galliarum diuersae nationes et Britannorum inaccessa Romanis loca, Christo uero subdita, et Sarmatarum et Dacorum et Germanorum et Scytharum et abditarum multarum gentium et prouinciarum et insularum nobis ignotarum [et], quae enumerare minus possumus

> and there are other nations such as the various ones of the Gaetuli, and the many boundaries of the Moors, and all the borders of the Spanish, and the diverse nations of the Gauls and the realms of the British that are inaccessible to the Romans but are subject to Christ, and those places of the Sarmatians and Dacians and Germans and Scythians and many other hidden nations and provinces and islands that are unknown to us, and those which we are not able to recount.

49 Acts 2:9–11: "Par'thians and Medes and E'lamites and residents of Mesopota'mia, Judea and Cappado'cia, Pontus and Asia, Phryg'ia and Pamphyl'ia, Egypt and the parts of Libya belonging to Cyre'ne, and visitors from Rome, both Jews and proselytes, Cretans and Arabians." See Metzger, "Ancient Astrological Geography and Acts 2:9–11," 123–33; and Gilbert, "The List of Nations in Acts 2," 497–529, esp. 503–5.

50 Tertullian, *Aduersus Iudaeos*, VII.4.23–37.

Significantly, this list starts with the Gaetuli in Northern Africa, who are just west of Carthage where Tertullian himself was writing, and proceeds clockwise up along Europe and into the steppes, where the nice systematic order becomes, admittedly, a bit jumbled, but then ends in order with the Scythians, who were often considered a people living on the outer limit of the known world. Incidentally, Tertullian's mental map of the nations who "believe in Christ" also presents a kind of dichotomy between the converted northwesterly nations and the unconverted southeasterly nations, especially India, which was understood as an exotic land inhabited by marvels and monsters.

In addition, the early Christian author Origen, in his book *Against Celsus*, revises the Babel narrative to match a geographical tradition stemming from Polybius.[51] Origen states that all humans originally spoke in a divine language (*τῇ θείᾳ διαλέκτῳ*) and lived in the East (*τῶν ἀνατολῶν*).[52] But once they moved out of that preferred position, their thoughts strayed from those that were fitting for the East, and they built the Tower of Babel. The consequent division that Origen describes places moral and linguistic superiority in the East but conforms to a climatic model of the Greeks:[53]

> παραδιδόσθωσαν ἕκαστος κατὰ τὴν ἀναλογίαν τῆς «ἀπὸ ἀνατολῶν» κινήσεως, ἐπὶ πλεῖον ἢ ἐπ' ἔλαττον αὐτοῖς γεγενημένης, καὶ κατὰ τὴν ἀναλογίαν τῆς κατασκευῆς τῶν πλίνθως εἰς λίθους καὶ τοῦ πηλοῦ εἰς ἄσφαλτον καὶ τῆς ἐκ τούτων οἰκοδομῆς ἀγγέλοις, ἐπὶ πλεῖον ἢ ἐπ' ἔλλαττον χαλεπωτέροις καὶ τοιοῖδε ἢ ποιοῖσδε, ἕως τίσωσι δίκας ἐφ' οἷς τετολμήκασι· καὶ ὑπὸ τῶν ἀγγέλων ἀγέσθωσαν ἕκαστος τῶν ἐμποιησάντων τὴν οἰκείαν ἑαθτοῖς διάλεκτον ἐπὶ τὰ μέρη τῆς γῆς κατὰ τὴν ἑαυτῶν ἀξίαν, οἵδε μὲν ἐπὶ τὴν φέρ' εἰπεῖν καυσώδη χώραν ἄλλοι δ' ἐπὶ τὴν διὰ τὸ κατεψῦχθαι κολάζουσαν τοὺς ἐνοικοῦντας, καὶ οἱ μὲν ἐπὶ τὴν δυσγεωργητοτέραν ἄλλοι δὲ ἐπὶ τὴν ἔλαττον τοιαύτην, καὶ οἱ μὲν ἐπὶ τὴν πεπληρωμένην θηρίων οἱ δὲ ἐπὶ τὴν ἔλαττον ἔχουσαν αὐτά
>
> And each one is handed over to angels who are more or less stern and whose character varies in proportion to the distance that they moved from the east, whether they had travelled far or a little way, and in proportion to the amount of bricks made into stones and of clay into asphalt and to the size of the

51 Polybius, *ΠΟΛΥΒΙΟΥ ΙΣΤΟΡΙΑΙ*, XXXIV.i.14. See Walbank, *A Historical Companion on Polybius*, 571.
52 Origen, *Origène: Contra Celse*, V.30.4–5.
53 Origen, *Contra Celse*, V.30.19–32; trans. Chadwick, *Contra Celsum*, 287.

> building made out of them. Under them they remained until they had paid the penalty for their boldness. And each one is led by angels, who put in them their native language, to the parts of the earth which they deserve. Some are led to parched land, for example; others to country which afflicts the inhabitants by being cold; and some to land that is difficult to cultivate; others to land that is less hard; and some to country full of wild beasts, and others to country that has them to a lesser degree.

Despite the lack of influence this particular text will have on later authors, there are some noteworthy elements in this passage. The first is the notion of centrality in the East, which is perhaps expected for a writer reliant on Jewish sources. The East, notably where the descendants of Shem dwell, retains its moral and linguistic superiority, so much so that people are punished according to how far they stray from it. Second, Origen underlines an intricate connection between land and people. Unlike the Greek sources that attribute supposed ethnographical characteristics to the environment,[54] Origen goes one step further to state that the sins of the people determined the land they are to inherit. The inevitable conclusion is that those living in favourable conditions have ancestors who are less sinful than those living in unfavourable conditions – a notion that goes hand in hand with early Jewish and Christian racist understandings of the Ethiopians. Whereas ancient Roman and Greek authors claim that the Ethiopians are black because they live so close to the sun, certain Jewish and Christian authors invert the claim by typologically associating dark skin with the "blackness" of sin and the Devil.[55] In other words, it is not so much the environment that determines the character of a people, but that the moral makeup of the people determines the reason why they are living in such an environment.

Third, Origen displays a sixfold division of the inhabited world that echoes the six climatic zones of Polybius. Later Greek and Roman geographers had a more sophisticated view of the climatic division of the world than their predecessors, and although they continued to understand the landmass of the earth as divided into the three parts of Europe, Africa, and Asia, these geographers argued for a spherical world with a number of different zones between the Arctic Circle and the equator. Little survives that

---

54 See Balsdon, *Romans and Aliens*, 59–60; Clarke, *Between Geography and History*, 150–1; and Thümmel, "Poseidonios und die Geschichte," 558–61, at 559–60.

55 Goldenberg, *Curse of Ham*, 47–51.

actually gives a clear indication of what these zones were thought to be like, except that it is cold in the North and hot in the South. Origen, likely drawing on this geographical understanding of the world, uses it as a frame to present his account of the dispersal of the nations after the fall of the Tower of Babel. As with the book of Jubilees, he revises the biblical account to conform more closely to Greek geographical discourses – an interesting strategy for Origen, who here retains the literal historicity of the account instead of resorting to allegory.

Developments of Christian Identity in the Early Church

Within the multicultural and multilingual world of Late Antiquity, the early Church began to develop a theology that proclaimed participation in a distinct identity not dependent on ethnicity, but rather on shared beliefs. In light of the Jewish Table of Nations and Greek and Roman accounts of the world's ethnic diversity, along with the expansion of Christianity to the gentile world, early Christians felt the need to refigure their own relationships with non-Christians in quasi-ethnic terms. Hence arose the notion of the Christian *genus* that tried to distance itself from, or claim superiority over, Jewish and pagan religions, philosophies, and even ethnicity. World diversity occurred at Babel, but especially through the unity of diversity at Pentecost, all Christian people, though separated by culture and language, were united by faith.[56] Barbarian tribes, for example, were no longer necessarily seen in a negative light, but rather as people who potentially played an important role in salvation history. The result of such a shift created new uniting factors; those who believed in the orthodox teachings of Christianity were accepted, at least theoretically, in this separate Christian *genus* regardless of ethnic or cultural backgrounds, whereas those who did not – Jews, pagans, or heretics – became associated with the negativity once attributed by classical authors to those inhabiting cultural peripheries. A dichotomy of identities, inherited from ancient ethnographers, remained intact, though new qualifications arose for inclusion or exclusion among the orthodox Christian *genus*.[57]

---

56 This theme will be important among the writings of Bede; see Tugene, *L'idée de nation chez Bède le Vénérable*, 302: "Il était du moins tenu de justifier en droit cette pluralité de fait, de l'intégrer dans sa vision d'un peuple chrétien indivis dans sa fois."

57 See Johnson, *Ethnicity and Argument in Eusebius'* Praeparatio evangelica, 1–2.

Early Christians, finding themselves in opposition to the classical pagan religions, but no longer compatible with the Jewish religion, found a new route to manoeuvre by identifying themselves as a *tertium genus* (a third race).[58] Clement of Alexandria's *Stromata* is the earliest surviving Christian source to claim identification with the "third race," in a quotation from the now-lost *Kerygma Petri*, a New Testament apocryphal work:[59]

> «νέαν ἡμῖν διέθετο· τὰ γὰρ Ἑλλήνων καὶ Ἰουδαίων παλαιά, ἡμεῖς δὲ οἱ καινῶς αὐτὸν τρίτῳ γένει σεβόμενοι Χριστιανοί.» σαφῶς γάρ, οἶμαι, ἐδήλωσεν τὸν ἕνα καὶ μόνον θεὸν ὑπὸ μὲν Ἑλλήνων ἐθνικῶς, ὑπὸ δὲ Ἰουδαίων Ἰουδαϊκῶς, καινῶς δὲ ὑφ' ἡμῶν καὶ πνευματικῶς γινωσκόμενον
>
> "He conferred upon us a new covenant; for those things of the Greeks and of the Jews are old. But in new ways, we Christians, as a third race, revere him." For clearly, I think, he revealed that the one and only God was known by the Greeks in gentile ways, by the Jews in Jewish ways, and by us in new and spiritual ways.

Although an extensive study of the *tertium genus* is beyond the scope of this study, it is telling how early Christians repositioned themselves in terms of the religious and ethnic diversity around them. Significantly, the notion of Christians as members of a third race later develops into self-identification with the descendants of Japheth who, among the biblical text and some Jewish authors, were neither inherently favoured like the descendants of Shem, nor cursed like the descendants of Ham. By adopting a middle way, the *tertium genus* is able to free itself from the restrictions of ethnicity in salvation history. It distances itself from both the theological concepts of the election of a specific ethnic group, such as the Jews, and the unacceptability of the religions of the pagans. The result was a powerful tool for the early Christians – the ability to be united as a community based on shared faith despite any political, ethnic, or linguistic barriers.

For example, Eusebius of Caesarea (c. 260–340) reveals a theology expressing how Christians constituted a new type of group that transcends

---

58 See Harnack, *The Expansion of Christianity in the First Three Centuries*, vol. 1, 313–52; and Mohrmann, "'Tertium genus' les relations judaïsme, antiquité, christianisme reflétées dans la langue des Chrétiens," 195–210, esp. 195–7.

59 Clement of Alexandria, *Stromata: Buch I–VI*, VI.v.41.6–7; and Cambe, ed., *Kerygma Petri*. Most of the *Kerygma Petri* survives only in quotations from Clement and Origen.

nationalistic or ethnic categories. In his *Historia ecclesiastica*, which played an important role among European readers through its Latin translation by Rufinus, Eusebius claims that Christ is honoured "παρὰ πᾶσιν ἀνθρώποις καθ' ὅλου τοῦ κόσμου" (by all humans and throughout the whole world), and that Christians form a "νέον … ἔθνος, οὐ μικρὸν οὐδ' ἀσθενὲς οὐδ' ἐπὶ γωνίας ποι γῆς ἱδρυμένον, ἀλλὰ καὶ πάντων τῶν ἐθνῶν πολυανθρωπότατόν τε καὶ θεοσεβέστατον" (a new race, not small nor weak nor established in a corner somewhere on the earth, but the most populous and devout of all nations).[60] This desire to establish a connection between the newness of the Christian *genus* and a respected wisdom that reaches back to the beginning of human civilization is typical for Eusebius. As many scholars have pointed out, the Eusebian theology of history is most interested in showing the primacy of the Church to all other religions, including Judaism, which, according to Eusebius, began only with the giving of the Mosaic Law and, thereby, excluded the patriarchs.[61] As Robert W. Hanning states, Eusebius's theology of history "gave a literal fullness to the history of the church even beyond what could be claimed as a result of typology. The patriarchs did not prefigure the church of Christ; they were its first concrete manifestation."[62] Eusebius's theology, Hanning continues, shifts the emphasis away from strict ethnicity "to include not only Israel but all nations in a providential relationship with God," that becomes more of a "battle between the devil and Christ" than the election of one race.[63] Furthering this argument, Arthur J. Droge states that Eusebius has "produced a new kind of national history" that claimed Christianity "was not just a religious movement but a 'nation,'" that defies ethnic categorization by focusing on the congruity of its doctrine and practice with the ancient patriarchs.[64]

Though the need for identifying with a "third race" disappears after the incorporation of Christianity into the Roman Empire, the theological framework continues well afterwards and can be found prominently in Augustine's discussions of the people of the city of God and of the city of

60 Eusebius, *Die Kirchengeschichte*, I.3.19 and I.4.2.

61 See Wallace-Hadrill, *Eusebius of Caesarea*, 168–73; Hanning, *The Vision of History in Early Britain From Gildas to Geoffrey of Monmouth*, 24–8; and Scheil, *Footsteps of Israel*, 111–19.

62 Hanning, *The Vision of History in Early Britain*, 24.

63 Ibid., 26.

64 Droge, "The Apologetic Dimensions of the *Ecclesiastical History*," 492–509, at 500–1.

the Devil.[65] While Augustine's theology of two *populi* differs somewhat from the earlier model of a Christian *genus*, its foundations are still recognizable.[66] Its broader scope is perhaps better able to appropriate biblical ethnicities and geographies and re-use them as theological symbols. In particular, Augustine contrasts Jerusalem, the symbolic city of God, with Babylon (or Babel), the symbolic city of Devil. And Augustine's opposition between the city of the Devil and the city of God lies at the heart of his interpretation of the Tower of Babel narrative.

In *De ciuitate Dei*, Augustine underlines the confusion of Babylon by drawing attention to the Tower of Babel narrative: "Ista ciuitas, quae appellata est confusio, ipsa est Babylon, cuius mirabilem constructionem etiam gentium commendat historia. Babylon quippe interpretatur confusio" (this city, which is called "confusion" is Babylon itself, whose wondrous building, even the history of pagans commends. Indeed, Babylon is interpreted as "confusion").[67] To highlight the confusion of Babylon even further, Augustine uses the word *confusio* alongside Babylon four other times in book sixteen,[68] and twice afterwards.[69] What exactly Augustine means by *confusio*, however, is not clear. Linguistic confusion (as well as ethnic division), which is the basis for the biblical etymology (Genesis 11:11), seems to have receded in favour of spiritual confusion that transcends linguistic and ethnic bounds. In the most succinct account of Augustine's theology of the two cities, which is not found in *De ciuitate Dei*, but rather in his commentary on Psalm 61, Augustine outlines the dichotomy between Babylon and Jerusalem, and the city of the Devil and

65 For Augustine's theology of the two cities, see van Oort, *Jerusalem and Babylon*.

66 Augustine, *De ciuitate Dei*, XIX.xxiv.2–3, defines *populus* as "coetus multitudinis rationalis rerum quas diligit concordi communione sociatus" (a rational assembly of a multitude who are joined by a shared association of the things which they love); see also II.xxi.50–2. For discussion, see Adams, *The* Populus *of Augustine and Jerome*, 17–69 and 123–35.

67 Augustine, *De ciuitate Dei*, XVI.iv.21–4. See Thiel, *Grundlagen und Gestalt der Hebräischkenntnisse des frühen Mittelalters*, 255. The etymology, which derives from Genesis 11:9, is "a polemic pun on the Akkadian 'Babel,' which might actually mean 'gate of the god,'" Alter, *The Five Books of Moses*, 59; see also *Oxford English Dictionary*, *s.v.* "Babel."

68 Augustine, *De ciuitate Dei*, XVI.x.5, xi.6–7, xi.72–3 and xvii.26–7.

69 Ibid., XVII.xvi.62 and XVIII.lxi.70; see also the reference to the "ciuitas confusionis" (city of confusion) at XVIII.li.5.

the city of God, in terms that emphasize spiritual unity and confusion over linguistic or ethnic:[70]

> Quid autem illi diuersi errores inimici Christi, omnes tantum dicendi sunt? nonne et unus? Plane audeo et unum dicere; quia una ciuitas et una ciuitas, unus populus et unus populus, rex et rex. Quid est: una ciuitas et una ciuitas? Babylonia una; Ierusalem una. Quibuslibet aliis etiam mysticis nominibus appelletur, una tamen ciuitas et una ciuitas: illa rege diabolo; ista rege Christo
>
> And why should those diverse errors of the enemy of Christ all be described as such? Are they not one? I dare to say openly they are one, because there is one city and one city, one people and one people, a king and a king. What do I mean by one city and one city? Babylon is one, Jerusalem the other. Whatever other spiritual names are used, there is nevertheless one city and one city: the one has the Devil as its king, the other has Christ as its king.

In line with the early Christian notions of a *tertium genus*, Augustine has abolished all remnants of ethnicity in order to focus on the dichotomy in his theology of the two cities.[71] Identification is no longer dependent on ethnic or linguistic characteristics, but on participation as a citizen in one of the two spiritual cities.

Along with this abolition of ethnic and linguistic identity in lieu of new, spiritual identification, comes an irony that is created by describing a unified *ciuitas* (city) based in diversity and confusion. While, for Augustine, the nations were dispersed at the historical Tower of Babel, the spiritual city of the Devil (Babel or Babylon), is not dispersed, but united (*una*). Indeed, though the city of God is described as united in similar terms, the roles, in a sense, have reversed, and it is now the Church, not the proud builders, that is dispersed throughout the world. As Peter Brown has pointed out, similar sentiment is found elsewhere in Augustine's writings where Augustine speaks of a Jewish, heretical, and pagan "unity over against our Unity" of the Catholic Church, which, nevertheless, "had

70 Augustine, *Enarrationes in Psalmos*, vol. 2, LXI.6.7–13; see also Adams, *The* Populus *of Augustine and Jerome*, 26–7; and Scheil, *Babylon under Western Eyes*, 48–52.

71 See Mohrmann, "Linguistic Problems in the Early Christian Church," 171–96, at 172, writing on the *tertium genus*: "the word γένος ... is used in a religious, spiritual sense. It rises above all ethnical ideas, and indicates that the Christians are new as ἐκκλησία, as a religious community, as much with respect to the Jewish religious community as to paganism."

spread throughout the world" – the "principal argument," according to Brown, "used to impress a pagan."[72] This unity of the Catholic Church finds much strength in its ability to transcend the ethnic boundaries created at Babel and spread across the world.

Augustine proved to be one of the most influential Christian writers of Late Antiquity. And his interpretation of a united Church embracing and remedying a world divided at Babel would have a great impact on subsequent theology. After Augustine, the "third race" of Christendom was no longer articulated as such; instead, the earlier quasi-ethnic terminology was abandoned in favour of an ecclesiastical ethnography that encompassed all ethnicities and languages. By the seventh century, Isidore of Seville, for example, implies that only the Church is capable of spreading across the diversity of the entire globe: "Catholica, universalis, ἀπὸ τοῦ καθ' ὅλον, id est secundum totum. Non enim sicut conventicula haereticorum in aliquibus regionum partibus coartatus, sed per totum terrarum orbem dilatata diffunditur" (Catholic means "universal" from the Greek *καθ' ὅλον*, that is, "according to the whole." For it is not restricted to certain parts of regions like the assemblies of heretics, but it is spread out, extended through the entire world).[73] According to Isidore and the Augustinian tradition that preceded him, the dispersing effects of the Tower of Babel have been adopted to show the solidarity of the Church throughout all the lands – something that neither Jews, nor heretics, nor adherents of pagan cults could claim for themselves.

From its beginnings in the biblical text, the narrative recounted in Genesis 10–11 becomes important for the role it plays in the ways early Jews and Christians understood human diversity. The descendants of the three sons of Noah provide a neat general framework that fits well with Greek geography, and like Greek geography, the Table of Nations could easily be used to inform notions of centrality and marginality, which varied according to the perspectives of the author and audience. The biblical text is reinterpreted not only in attempts to better present contemporary historical developments, but also to assert specific Jewish identity in a

---

72 Brown, *Augustine of Hippo*, 231. Brown cites: *Sermo* 62.18; *Epistula* 232 and *Contra Faustum* XIII.7.

73 Isidore, *Etymologiae*, VIII.i.1. The likely source for this line is from Augustine's *Epistulae*, vol. 2, LII.1: "ipsa est enim ecclesia catholica, unde καθολικὴ graece appellatur, quod per totum orbem terrarum diffunditur."

world increasingly dominated by Greek and Roman hegemony. For Christian theologians, however, the need to be identified as neither Jew nor Greek resulted in new uses of the Table of Nations. Specifically, by the time of Augustine, the Church had expanded beyond its humble beginnings in Palestine to become tolerated and then accepted as the state religion of the Roman Empire. With circumstances that necessitated a theology inclusive of potentially all ethnic and linguistic groups, some authors indicate a new approach to interpreting the Table of Nations that shifts emphasis away from its function as a literal description of ethnic diversity to its value as an allegorical and moral account. Specifically, Augustine's interpretation of Genesis 10–11 as indicative of his theology of the cities of God and the Devil employs this exact strategy. Augustine's theological approach, in fact, epitomizes common attempts to interpret the biblical text as both a literal account that informs the ethnic and linguistic diversity in the world, and an allegorical account that informs the struggle of good and evil in the world.

Chapter Two

Latin Christian Antiquity

Christian Historiography

The first council of the Christian Church, which occurred in Jerusalem around 50 CE (Acts 15:1–29), already had to deal with a problem that would continue to have a bearing on future centuries. Fundamentally, the concern was how non-Jewish Christians were to inherit Christianity's adopted Jewish traditions. Although the issues raised in Jerusalem centred exclusively on the gentile reception of Jewish law, the focus later shifted to concerns over the reception and role of Jewish Scripture and history among Christian communities. By the fourth century a canon of Hebrew Scriptures had crystallized and become authoritative and integral for Christian communities,[1] but there were still a number of different means by which a reader could approach and interpret these texts. Along with the canonization and adoption of the Hebrew Scriptures, came the necessity of adopting Hebrew history, which gave rise to a new need to reconfigure the ethnic or national identities of non-Jewish Christian communities with perceived ethnic or national Jewish identity. As is evident from the council of Jerusalem and some of the letters of Paul, this reconfiguration was complex, for it entailed a rejection of contemporary Jewish identity in conjunction with an adoption of past Jewish identity. One of the methods used to justify this simultaneous rejection and adoption of Jewish identity was to reinterpret, in order to appropriate, Jewish texts. Paul, for example, reinterprets Abraham, the man in whom "all nations shall be blessed"

1 The subject is thoroughly discussed in McDonald and Sanders, eds., *The Canon Debate*. See also Metzger, *The Canon of the New Testament*.

(Genesis 18:18) as a prophetic prefiguration of those who "are of faith" (Galatians 3:9); and elsewhere, he uses a metaphor of gentile branches being grafted into the Jewish tree (Romans 11:17–24).

As Christianity expanded and increasingly clashed with other religious and intellectual paradigms in the Roman Empire, Christians no longer felt the need to ratify their adoption of Jewish Scripture and history. Instead the focus turned to justify their own existence by defending Jewish Scripture and history from their new Roman and Greek opponents. Jewish authors had already begun to defend their texts and traditions in the Greek and Roman world before the advent of Christ. Philo of Alexandria reinterpreted Hebrew Scripture to make it accord with Greek philosophy; and Josephus, who lived in Rome as an exile and who wrote to Greek-speaking audiences, tried to justify Jewish culture and tradition based on its conformity to Greek traditions and on its antiquity (the title of his book, *Antiquitates Iudaicae*, is telling here). In the centuries after Christ, apologetic polemics, which attempted to justify the sudden and quick expansion of Christian identity in the Roman Empire, helped develop nascent Christian historiography.[2] By the third century, pagan critics of Christianity had attacked its lack of antiquity,[3] but because of the continuum between Christianity and Judaism already established among early Christians, Christian apologists used chronological connections between Jewish and Greek history to "christianize" great Greek philosophers. Using Roman and Greek historical methods, Christian scholars could claim that Moses and Plato, or alternatively Moses and Homer, lived at the same time. It was even argued that because the Jewish prophet Jeremiah was in Egypt at the same time as Plato, Jeremiah likely taught Plato his philosophy, and all of Platonism is simply a hashed out form of Judaic (and henceforth Christian) teaching.[4] These comparative methods had far-reaching effects, especially on account of the influence enjoyed by Eusebius's *Chronicon*, which outlined biblical and ancient historical events and figures side by side. As late as the sixth century, Jordanes (following Orosius, following Eusebius)

2 Droge, "Apologetic Dimensions," 494: "above all the Christian apologists of the second and third centuries provided the foundation on which Eusebius [and subsequent Christian historians] constructed his interpretation of history and Christianity's place in it." See also Frede, "Celsus' Attack on the Christians," 218–40; and "Origen's Treatise *Against Celsus*," 131–55.

3 See Droge, "Apologetic Dimensions," 493.

4 Droge, *Homer or Moses? Early Christian Interpretations of the History of Culture*.

claims that Abraham and Ninus, the Assyrian founder of Babylon, were born in the same year (incidentally 2015 BCE).[5]

Roman and Greek authors were often content to begin their historical accounts with some monumental event, such as the founding of Rome; and even the so-called universal histories of pagan authors, which were known through Justinus's *Epitome*, begin with Ninus and the rise of the Assyrian Empire.[6] But the desire to claim antiquity compelled Christian writers to extend their own histories as far back as to creation itself. Orosius, for example, complains about these late beginnings in the classical histories, and states that he will begin his own account briefly with the creation and fall of man.[7] And with the Bible as the foundational text of world history, Christian antiquity was able to extend further back in time than any Greek or Roman historical claim. In particular, the Table of Nations and the Babel narrative, when interpreted as an etiological narrative of the world's diversity, could inform the very origin stories of the Greeks and Romans themselves. The tricky part was harmonizing the material presented in the Hebrew Scriptures with the authoritative historical writings of the Greeks and Romans.

The Christian world chronicles are a unique genre formed out of this apologetic milieu. Following Josephus's example, the chronicle attributed to the third-century historian Hippolytus is one of the first Christian texts to provide a list of the descendants of Noah alongside lists of contemporary nations, regions, and languages of the world. In a section of the chronicle that deals with the diversity of the world in light of the three sons of Noah, Hippolytus (I refer to his authorship for convenience only) states that Japheth had fifteen sons, Ham thirty, and Sem twenty-five, to make a total of seventy descendants.[8] But Hippolytus also disconnects the number of the descendants of Noah from the number of nations that have arisen in the world. Essentially, Hippolytus has updated the Table of

5 Iordannes, *Romana*, 1; Orosius, *Historiarum adversum paganos libri vii*, I.5; Eusebius / Jerome, *Chronicon* Prae.14.17–8 and 20a.1–5.

6 Justinus, *Epitoma historiarum Philippicarum Pompei Trogi*, I.1, 3. For Ninus, see Scheil, *Babylon under Western Eyes*, 23–6. For Justinus's *Epitome* in Anglo-Saxon England, see Crick, "An Anglo-Saxon Fragment of Justinus's 'Epitome,'" 181–96.

7 Orosius, *Historiarum adversum paganos libri vii*, I.1. See Scheil, *Babylon under Western Eyes*, 66.

8 Hippolytus, *Die Chronik*, 56–73 (Japheth's descendants), 92–130 (Ham's descendants), and 158–88 (Shem's descendants); see also Major, "The Number Seventy-Two," 25–8; and Borst, *Turmbau von Babel*, vol. 2, 370–1.

Nations with his own knowledge of contemporary ethnicity: Japheth's fifteen sons give rise to forty-seven nations, and Ham's thirty sons to thirty-two nations. Sem's twenty-five sons are actually reduced to sixteen nations. The later Latin version of Hippolytus's chronicle, the *Liber generationis*, continues this trend by adding three more nations to Japheth's lineage and two more to Sem's.[9] In addition, the Jewish centrality apparent in the Table of Nations and Jubilees shifts in favour of a Mediterranean view point – one that includes relatively exotic languages, such as "Indian" or "British," but gives much more attention to the specific languages and dialects that would be familiar to a Greek audience.[10]

After the decline of antique and late antique Roman hegemony, the so-called barbarian tribes that came to occupy Europe made matters of ethnography more complicated not only through their own ethnic diversity, but also through a reorientation of the centrality of the world away from Rome or Jerusalem and into positions more agreeable to the geographical and ethnic spheres of individual authors. The once-marginal barbarians had adopted the educational tools of the Romans to write about themselves and their own historical or political interests, thereby shifting the focus away from Rome. This shift can be found among authors such as Gregory of Tours (538–94), incidentally a Gallo-Roman, who restructures the geographical bounds of his *Historiae* to focus on Gaul;[11] or the Lombard Paul the Deacon (c. 720–c. 799), who reveals an interesting shift to prefer northern climates over the Mediterranean in the opening of his *Historia Langobardorum*: "Septemtrionalis plaga quanto magis ab aestu solis remota est et nivali frigore gelida, tanto salubrior corporibus hominum et propagandis est gentibus coaptata" (the more the northern region was removed from the heat of the sun and icy in the snowy cold, the more healthy it is for the bodies of humans and was more adapted for propagating nations).[12] Some of

9 Mommsen, ed., *Liber generationis*, in *Chronica minora saec. iv. v. vi. vii.*, vol. 1, 197.

10 See the edition of Hippolytus's list of languages in Borst, *Turmbau von Babel*, vol. 2, 932–6.

11 See Goffart, "Foreigners in the *Historiae* of Gregory of Tours," 275–91, at 290–1. See also Goffart's important caveat that Gregory does not limit himself to a *History of the Franks*, as do his Gallic successors and editors, but rather *histories* of a broader nature; "From *Historiae* to *Historia Francorum* and Back Again," 255–74, esp. 270–1.

12 Paul the Deacon, *Historia Langobardorum*, I.1, 47.25–6. But see Goffart, *The Narrators of Barbarian History*, 383–4, who argues that Paul places a preference on the southern realms for ecclesiastical purposes.

the ways in which Anglo-Saxon authors reorganized their own views on centrality will be touched upon in later chapters.

The so-called *origines gentium* myths were one of the strategies employed to account for the growing discrepancies between the biblical texts and the awareness of ethnic diversity. By tracing back the ethnicities of an individual people, these myths were able to make tenuous connections to a name in the Table of Nations with a contemporary (or more well-known) people.[13] Once a contemporary name is connected to a biblical one, possibilities arise for creating biblically supported attitudes towards a specific people. The church father, Ambrose, seems to be the first of many to make a connection between the contemporary Goths and the biblical Magog, in order to associate the heretical Goths with the same negativity that the Bible allots to Magog. But because there was no actual historical connection between the Goths and Magog, Ambrose had to employ folk etymology based solely on the similarities between the words *Gothus* and *Magog* or its equivalent *Gog*. After this false etymological connection had been established, the apocalyptic disposition of Gog and Magog in Ezekiel 38:2 and Revelation 20:8 could be associated with the Goths, now demonic agents helping to usher in the end of the world.[14] Roman Christians, however, had already viewed the Goths in a negative light because of their adoption of the Arian heresy and their antagonism against the Roman Empire.[15] A connection between the Goths and Magog and Gog was, therefore, not difficult. Folk etymology was simply used to corroborate not

13 See Bickerman, "*Origines Gentium*," 65–81; and Reynolds, "Medieval *Origines Gentium* and the Community of the Realm," 475–390.

14 Ambrose, *De fide ad Gratianum Augustum libri quinque*, PL 16, col. 588A, II.16.138: "Gog iste Gothus est, quem jam videmus exisse"; and Isidore, *Etymologiae*, IX.ii.27: "Magog, a quo arbitrantur Scythas et Gothos traxisse originem"; IX.ii.89: "Gothi a Magog"; and XIV.iii.31: "Scythia sicut et Gothia a Magog." See Borst, *Turmbau von Babel*, vol. 2, 384. However, Jerome, *Hebraicae quaestiones in libro Geneseos*, 10.21, 11, questions the association between Magog and the Goths; and Augustine, *De ciuitate Dei*, XX.xi.13, states that Gog and Magog are not to be understood as "aliqui in aliqua parte terrarum barbari" (certain barbarians in a certain part of the earth).

15 Ambrose hints at this antagonism in *Expositio euangelii secundum Lucam*, II.517–22, 47: "Gothis non imperabat Augustus ... fortasse nos uincunt" (Augustus did not rule over the Goths ... perhaps they are now conquering us). See Ladner, "On Roman Attitudes towards Barbarians in Late Antiquity," 1–26, at 21–3. Gog and Magog also appear on the Anglo-Saxon Cotton Map of British Library, Cotton Tiberius, B.v, fol. 56v, but without "pejorative value," according to Westrem, "Against Gog and Magog," 54–75, at 60.

only an opinion already in existence, but also the biblical account interpreted as providing accurate insights into the actions of future nations. Moreover, the effectiveness of associating Gog and Magog with a negatively viewed ethnic group is attested throughout the Middle Ages: Matthew Paris, a thirteenth-century English chronicler, would connect Gog and Magog to the Mongols,[16] and notably, in Anglo-Saxon England, Wulfstan the homilist, or one of his revisers, would define them as an eastern people who represented helpers of the antichrist: "[God] let þene deofol antecrist rabbian . 7 wedan sume hwile . 7 þa ðe him fylstæð . þæt is gog 7 magog . þæt beoð þa mancyn þe alexander beclysde binnan muntclysan" (God ... allows the devil, the Antichrist, to rage and rave for a while along with those who help him, that is, Gog and Magog: these are the people that Alexander enclosed within a mountain prison).[17]

Although these specific connections are relatively rare, broader connections between Noah's sons Ham, Canaan, and Nimrod were employed to demonize heretical groups or wrong-doers in general. The figure of Nimrod, in particular, was considered not only to be the chief architect of Babel, but also a giant, the world's first tyrant, an astronomer / astrologer, and idol-worshiper, and the second city-builder after Cain.[18] Augustine, in his *De ciuitate Dei*, has an early and one of the most thorough expositions on the matter. Since Nimrod, as the builder of Babel / Babylon, is an archetypal figure of the city of the Devil, Augustine obviously interprets him in a negative light. But before Augustine examines Nimrod's symbolism, Ham's cursed line is associated with heretics: "Cham porro, quod interpretatur calidus ... quid significat nisi haereticorum genus calidum" (indeed because Ham is interpreted as "hot," what can he signify except the hot *genus* of heretics).[19] When Augustine comes to speak of Ham's line again, he more specifically describes Cush as the father of the giant

16 Blurton, *Cannibalism in High Medieval English Literature*, 84–5.

17 Wulfstan, *Secundum Marcum*, transcribed from Oxford, Bodleian, Bodley 343, fol. 141v, and printed in the critical apparatus of *Homilies of Wulfstan*, V.64–6. I am grateful to Andy Orchard for this reference.

18 For the history of interpretation of Nimrod, see Livesey and Rouse, "Nimrod the Astronomer," 203–66; van der Toorn and van der Horst, "Nimrod before and after the Bible," 1–29; Jeffrey, ed., *A Dictionary of Biblical Tradition in English Literature*, *s.v.* "Babel," 66–9; Dean, *The World Grown Old in Later Medieval Literature*, 134–9; Cohen, *Of Giants*, 22–4; Murdoch, *The Medieval Popular Bible*, 129–40; and Fyler, *Language and the Declining World in Chaucer, Dante, and Jean de Meun*, 35–44.

19 Augustine, *De ciuitate Dei*, XVI.ii.9–13.

Nimrod, whose beginning was the city of Babylon itself.[20] After establishing this lineage from Ham's general typology as the *haereticorum genus*, through to Cush, the giant-bearer, Augustine presents the single figure Nimrod as a symbolic representative of the city of the Devil:[21]

> Babylon quippe interpretatur confusio. Vnde colligitur, gigantem illum Nebroth fuisse illius conditorem, quod ... ait initium regni eius fuisse Babylonem ... Erigebat ergo cum suis populis turrem contra Deum, qua est impia significata superbia.
>
> Indeed, Babylon means "confusion." For this reason, it is inferred that that giant Nimrod was its builder, because ... it is said that the beginning of his kingdom was Babylon ... Therefore, Nimrod, along with his people, built a tower against God, which signified his impious pride.

In these lines, Augustine gives future readers further precedent to use Nimrod not only as the symbolic head for all pride and wickedness, but also for paganism and heresy. Nimrod's nature as a giant, strengthened by Augustine, becomes part of the dichotomy between orthodoxy and heresy. And after Augustine, the figure of Nimrod begins to solidify as a symbol for the heresy and the paganism of the world, especially since from an early date, Jewish authors associated Nimrod with the worship of fire, and therefore of Zoroastrianism. Nimrod becomes, in the words of P.W. van der Horst, "the founder of paganism *par excellence*, in this case the influential Zoroaster."[22] Orthodox authors easily connected peripheral groups or ideologies, such as paganism and heresy, to Nimrod, the giant, tyrant, city-builder, and idol worshiper, in order to exploit them as not only wicked, but also monstrous and barbaric.[23]

On the contrary, an ethnic group could be traced back to a biblical name for positive propaganda, especially when the specific author associated himself with that ethnic group. For instance, as soon as a connection

---

20 Ibid., XVI.iii.18 ("pater gigantis Nebroth") and 24 ("initium erat illa nobilissima Babylon ciuitas").

21 Ibid., XVI.iv.23–37, 53–5.

22 Van der Toorn and van der Horst, "Nimrod before and after the Bible," 28; see also 19–20 and 26–8, for an excellent summary of the ancient and late antique sources that connect Nimrod to fire, fire-worshipping, and Zoroaster.

23 See Augustine's claim that the "ciuitas confusionis" (city of confusion) is a city of heretics; *De ciuitate Dei*, XVIII.li.5.

between any ethnic group and the Romans was established (usually a positive connection in itself), a further connection to a name in the Table of Nations was not difficult, since according to many Christian authors, the Romans were descendants of Japheth's son, Kittim.[24] More commonly, ethnic groups were given origins that could be traced back to the fall and dispersal of the people of Troy.[25] In these cases, any ethnic group that could be connected to Troy was then associated with the original grandeur of Troy, which might parallel or even surpass that of the Roman Empire. But in order to make these associations, genealogies had to be fabricated.

For example, the ninth-century *History of the British* by pseudo-Nennius[26] connects the origin of the British people to Troy by means of the supposed founder of Britain, Brutus, who is then connected to the Table of Nations through a complex lineage. The author begins with Noah's sons and proceeds to give a genealogy down to Brutus:[27]

> Aliud experimentum didici de isto Brutone ex antiquis libris nostrorum ueterum. Tres filii Noae diuiserunt orbem terrae in tres partes post diluuium – Sem in Asia, Cam in Africa, Iafeth in Europa – et dilatauerunt terminos suos. Primus homo uenit ad Europam, Alanus cum tribus filiis suis quorum nomina Hisicion, Armenon, Neugio … Ab Hisicione autem ortae sunt quattuor gentes – Franci, Latini, Alamanni, et Bryttones.

> I learned another explanation about that Brutus from the ancient books of our elders. Three sons of Noah divided the earth into three parts after the Flood – Sem in Asia, Ham in Africa, Japheth in Europe – and dispersed to its ends. The first man who came to Europe was Alanus with his three sons

24 See Borst, *Turmbau von Babel*, vol. 2, 935; Jerome, *Hebraicae quaestiones in libro Geneseos*, 10.4.8, 12, however, interprets Kittim as "Citii, a quibus hodieque urbs Cypri Citium nominatur" (the Citii from whom even today the city of Cyprus is called Citium).

25 See Reynolds, "Medieval *Origines Gentium*," 376–7; Wood, "Defining the Franks," 46–57; and Innes, "Teutons or Trojans? The Carolingians and the Germanic Past," 227–49. For the debate on the genre of the *origo gentis*, see Goffart, *The Narrators of Barbarian History*, ix–v; Wolfram, *The Roman Empire and Its Germanic Peoples*, 31–4; and Wolfram, "*Origo et religio*," 70–90. Significantly, the Anglo-Saxons did not employ this origin story, despite their connection to Europe; see Tyler, "Trojans in Anglo-Saxon England," 1–20.

26 For the false attribution to Nennius, see Dumville, "'Nennius' and the *Historia Brittonum*," 78–95.

27 Dumville, ed., *The* Historia Brittonum, 17.

whose names were Hisicion, Armenon and Neugio. And from Hisicion arose four nations – the Franks, the Latini, the Alamanni and the Britons.

In this instance, the mention of the three sons of Alanus, which itself is analogous to the three sons of Noah, has most likely been derived from Graeco-Roman tradition. The attribution of the origins of the Germanic people to three sons appears in Tacitus's *Germania*, which in turn seems to have been influenced by Herodotus' account of the origins of the Scythians.[28] After Tacitus, the three sons appear in the so-called Frankish Table of Nations and then in the *History of the British*.[29] There is also an analogue in Old Norse mythology involving the three first Æsir – Odin, Vili, and Vé,[30] and it is clear that the motif of the three sons could be employed by an author without any specific source in mind.

Furthermore, in accordance with its eclectic nature, the *History of Britain* offers two other elaborate genealogies that give full record of the lineage between Alanus and Adam (via Noah):[31]

Alanus, ut aiunt, filius fuit Fethuir, Fethuir filius Ogomuin, Ogomuin filius Thoi; Thoi filius Boib, Boib filius Simion, Semion filius Mair; Mair filius fuit Ecthactus, Ecthactus filius Aurthact, Aurthact filius Ethec, Ethech filius Ooth, Ooth filius Abir, Abir filius Ra, Ra filius Esraa, Esraa filius Hisrau, Hisrau filius Bath, Bath filius Iobath, Iobath filius Iohan, Iohan filius Iafeth, Iafeth filius Noe, Noe filius Lamech, Lamech filius Matusalem, Matusalem filius Enoch, Enoch filius Iared, Iared filius Malalehel, Malalehel filius Cainan,

28 Geary, *Myth of Nations*, 44 and 51–2. For Tacitus, see *De origine et situ Germanorum*, § 2.8–10: "Manno tris filios adsignant, e quorum nominibus proximi Oceano Ingaevones, medii Hermiones, ceteri Istaevones vocentur" (they assign three sons to Mannus, from whose names are termed the Ingaevones who are closest to the ocean, the Hermiones who are in the middle, and the Istaevones who are the rest). For Herodotus, see *Historiae*, IV.5.2–IV.6.1: "γενέσθαι παῖδας τρεῖς, Λιπόξαϊν καὶ Ἀρπόξαϊν καὶ νεώτατον Κολάξαϊν … ἀπὸ μὲν δὴ Λιπόξαϊος γεγονέναι τούτους τῶν Σκυθέων οἳ Αὐχάται γένος καλέονται, ἀπὸ δὲ τοῦ μέσου Ἀρπόξαϊος οἳ Κατίαροί τε καὶ Τράσπιες καλέονται, ἀπὸ δὲ τοῦ νεωτάου αὐτῶν τοὺς βασιλέας, οἳ καλέονται Παραλάται" (he bore three sons: Lipoxais, Arpoxais and the youngest Kolaxais … From Lipoxais were born the Scythians who are referred to as the Auchatae race; from the middle son Aproxais were born those referred to as Katiarians and Traspians, and from the youngest son were born the kingly [Scythians] who are referred to as Paralatians).

29 See Goffart, "The Supposedly 'Frankish' Table of Nations," 133–65, at 148, 153.

30 See Orchard, *Dictionary of Norse Myth and Legend*, *s.v.* "Odin," 123 and "Vili(r)," 175.

31 Dumville, ed., *The* Historia Brittonum, 7; these passages need not be translated. See also Isidore, *Etymologiae*, IX.ii.102, for the association between Brutus and Britain.

Cainan filius Enos, Enos filius Seth, Seth filius Adam, Adam filius et plasmatio Dei uiui.

Bryttones a Bruto dicti; Brutus filius Hisicionis, Hisicion filius Alani, Alanus filius Reae Silueae, Rea Siluea filia Numae Pampilii, Numa filius Ascanii, Ascanius filius Eneae, Aeneas filius Anchisae, Anchises filius Troi, Troius filius Dardani, Dardanus filius Flisae, Flisa filius Iuuani, Iuuan filius Iafeth.

The first of these genealogies contains a series of Hebrew-looking names, *Ooth*, *Ra*, *Esraa*, *Hirau*, *Bath*, and *Iobath*,[32] to connect Alanus nominally to the Israelites and genealogically to the *Dei uiui* (living God). The author almost certainly did not know Hebrew, but evidently could make a somewhat convincing fabrication. By employing these names, Alanus and therefore the British are granted a lineage that carries some of the esteem usually associated with the Israelites of the Old Testament. Both the early Jews and the British are now the chosen people of God. Likewise, the second genealogy, which offers a completely new, but somehow equally valid lineage, emphasizes the Roman heritage of Aeneas and the Trojans. Much like in the first genealogy, the British are granted a lineage that carries the esteem of the Trojans and Romans. These genealogies claim the best of both worlds for the British: the sacred esteem of the Jews and the secular esteem of the Romans.

Linguistic Diversity

After Hippolytus, the notion of seventy-two nations of the world was not as rigidly held as the notion that there are seventy-two languages in the world. In all likelihood the more or less stable linguistic control that Latin and Greek had over the Roman world prevented discussion on the multiplicity of languages.[33] The kind of theological limitation to linguistic diversity that lies behind the Christian notions of the seventy-two languages of the world does not seem to have been a concern to non-Christian

---

32 See Thiel, *Grundlagen und Gestalt der Hebräischkenntnisse*, 149 (oth), 387 (raah), 309 (Ezra-), 244 (Hira / Aras), 260 (bath), 332 (Jobad)

33 See Balsdon, *Romans and Aliens*, 137–45, esp. 137: "we hear surprisingly little of language difficulties in antiquity; only in the Bible does the story of the Tower of Babel point to the segregation of humanity through differences in language." Balsdon, 144, also provides a few anecdotes on regions thought to contain many more languages than seventy-two.

Romans. However, some Romans did assume that there were potentially just as many languages as there were distinct, and unassimilated, ethnic groups. Pliny the Elder, for example, makes mention of "tot gentium sermones, tot linguae, tanta loquendi varietas" (so many languages of the nations, so many tongues, such great variety of speaking);[34] and later provides an anecdote on the linguistic ability of the Persian king Mithridates, who knew all of the twenty-two languages of the twenty-two *gentes* that he ruled over: "Mithridates duarum et viginti gentium rex totidem linguis iura dixit, pro contione singulas sine interprete adfatus" (Mithridates, king of twenty-two nations, uttered laws in the same number of languages, and spoke to each nation before an assembly without an interpreter).[35] But for the most part, later Christians did not have to take into account the existence of more than seventy-two languages in the world.

In order to reconcile the specific number of languages with the non-specific number of nations, late antique Christian authors employed a variety of different strategies. Augustine, for example, explicitly states that there were numerous African nations who all spoke one language: "Auctus est autem numerus gentium multo amplius quam lingarum. Nam et in Africa barbaras gentes in una lingua plurimas nouimus" (the number of nations has increased more than the number of languages. For in Africa we know that many barbarian nations speak in one language).[36] And Augustine's contemporary, Arnobius, shifts the emphasis from the seventy-two nations to the thousand (ambiguously termed) *patriae* or *generationes* that spoke all together only seventy-two languages.[37] A few centuries later, Isidore gives two of the most explicit statements on the matter: "initio autem quot gentes, tot linguae fuerunt, deinde plures gentes quam linguae; quia ex una lingua multae sunt gentes exortae" (originally there were as many nations as languages, but later more nations than languages, because

34 Pliny, *Natural History*, VII.6.i.

35 Ibid., VII.88.xxiv; see Balsdon, *Romans and Aliens*, 144. Butler gives this example of Mithridates as an analogue to the linguistic capacities of the Anglo-Saxon king Oswald, "Textual Community and Linguistic Distance in Early England," 33, nt. 50.

36 Augustine, *De ciuitate Dei*, XVI.vi.48–50.

37 Arnobius the Younger, *Commentarii in Psalmos*, , CIV.60–78. The transformation and lack of uniformity among the terms *gens*, *natio*, *populus* is noted by Geary, "Ethnic Identity as a Situational Construct," 18–19. See also Adams, *The* Populus *of Augustine and Jerome*, 109–12.

from one language many nations arose),[38] and then, "ex linguis gentes, non ex gentibus linguae exortae sunt" (nations have arisen from languages, not languages from nations).[39]

From the Christian perspective, there seems to be general agreement that, unlike ethnic groups, languages revealed little or no change throughout history. Many authors, for example, argued that the Hebrew language, regarded as the language of Adam, remained unchanged after the manifestation of linguistic diversity at the Tower of Babel.[40] Notably, by the later Anglo-Saxon period, Ælfric is able to claim that the animals Adam named in Eden have retained their Hebrew names up to his day: "adam him eallum naman gesceop. 7 swa swa hé hí þa genamode. swa hí sindon gyt gehatene" (Adam created a name for all [of the animals] and whatever he named them, they are still called).[41] Aramaic (or Chaldean or Syriac, as it was called in Late Antiquity), the language spoken by Israelites in the first centuries after Christ, was considered a language separate from Hebrew, even though philologically it is closely related.[42] Alternatively, dialectal and sociolectal differences were recognized in Late Antiquity. Isidore, for example, lists five different dialects of Greek, and four dialects of Latin,[43] and the enigmatic seventh-century grammarian, Virgilius Maro

38 Isidore, *Etymologiae*, IX.i.1. Despite the word *initio* here, this sentence must refer to *gentes* that arise out of the seventy-two original nations, since earlier Isidore states, "una omnium nationum lingua fuit, quae Hebraea vocatur" (there was one language for all the nations).

39 Ibid., IX.i.14.

40 Resnick, "'Lingua Dei, lingua hominis'," 51–74, at 55–6. See also Mohrmann, "The Ever-Recurring Problem of Language in the Church," and "Linguistische Probleme bei den Kirchenvätern," 143–59, at 145; and 175–92, at 176–7.

41 Ælfric, *Ælfric's Catholic Homilies: The First Series*, I.85–6. But see also Bede's remarks to the contrary, *In principium Genesis*, I.1752–66; Jones, "Some Introductory Remarks on Bede's Commentary on Genesis," 115–98, at 120.

42 Jerome, for example, refers to the Aramaic section of Daniel as *chaldaicus*; *Prologus Hieronymi in Danihele propheta*, 3. But see Daniel 2:4, where the Vulgate has nobles talking *syriace* to the *Chaldeus rex*. Alexander Souter, ed., *A Glossary of Later Latin to 600 A.D.*, *s.v.* "Syriace," 411, defines *syriace* as "in the Aramaic language." See also Isidore, *Etymologiae*, IX.i.9, who states, "Syrus et Chaldaeus vicinus Hebraeo est in sermone" (Syriac and Chaldean are close to Hebrew in speech).

43 Isidore, *Etymologiae*, IX.i.4–7. See also the comment by Servius Grammaticus, *In Vergilii carmina commentarii*, vol. 1, III.122: "quinque Graecae sunt linguae, Aeolica, Iaca, Dorica, Attica, communis" (there are five Greek languages: Aeolian, Ionian, Doric, Attic, and koine).

Grammaticus, proposes that there were twelve "Latinities": "Latinitatis autem genera sunt XII" (there are twelve types of Latinity).[44]

Along with dialectal variation dependent on regional differences, late antique and early medieval authors also show an awareness of sociolectal variation dependent on differences of social class. But as with their treatments of the dialects of Latin and Greek, these authors did not think that sociolectal variations constituted enough difference for new language categorization.[45] For example, the ubiquitous, rhetorical topos of the *sermo rusticus* may in some cases indicate an awareness of the sociolectal variation of the Latin language,[46] though it admittedly provides very limited evidence for real sociolinguistic notions of linguistic hegemony in Late Antiquity and the Middle Ages.[47] Incidental anecdotes have the potential to expose more telling evidence. For instance, Bede offers a story of an Anglo-Saxon prisoner who is recognized as a noble by his appearance, clothing, and speech ("ex uultu et habitu et sermonibus").[48] Such a narrative detail indicates that sociolects were, at least, distinguished in Anglo-Saxon England, but not different enough to be considered separate languages. The limitations that the Bible and other ancient texts placed on linguistic diversity provide a conceivable basis for knowledge of the languages of the world among Christians in Late Antiquity and the Middle Ages. While an author such as Augustine, who had experience with the ethnic diversity of North

44 Virgilius Maro Grammaticus, *Epitomae*, I.64. See also Law, *Wisdom, Authority and Grammar in the Seventh Century*, 88–93.

45 For the sociolinguistic complexities of determining what constitutes a language and what constitutes a dialect or sociolect, see Romaine, *Language in Society*, esp. ch. 1, 1–31.

46 For only one example, see Gregory of Tour's admittance of his own lack of eloquence and condemnation of the "linguae latitudo turpis atque obscoena" (shameful and obscene breadth of language); *Libri historiarum X*, IX.6. Auerbach, *Mimesis: The Representations of Reality in Western Literature*, 67–83; and *Literary Language and its Public in Late Antiquity and in the Middle Ages*, 103–12 are the *loci classici* for Gregory's humble Latinity. For other examples, see Curtius, *European Literature and the Latin Middle* Ages, 411–12.

47 One contrary example made be found in Seneca, *Apocolocyntosis*, 5.3, 36, where Hercules thinks that Claudius's "uocem nullius terrestris animalis sed qualis esse marinis beluis solet" (language was typical of no land animal, but of the sort of a sea monster); see also Balsdon, *Romans and Aliens*, 137.

48 Bede, *Ecclesiastical History of the English People*, IV.22. See Hall, "Interlinguistic Communication in Bede's *Historia Ecclesiastica Gentis Anglorum*," 37–80, at 62; and O'Brien, *Reversing Babel*, 29–33.

Africa, could speak of numerous *gentes*, he could not yet speak of the numerous languages of Africa.

Pentecost and the Evangelization of the Nations

For Christians, issues of linguistic diversity found scriptural basis in the Babel narrative and the New Testament, which played an important role in the new reorientation of the world, as it declaimed the exclusiveness of salvation to the Jews, and revealed a Gospel that did not discriminate among nations. Jesus's Great Commission was to preach the Gospel in order to "make disciples of all nations, baptizing them in the name of the Father, and of the Son, and of the Holy Ghost" (Matthew 28:19). The Book of Acts is essentially a narrative that moves the focal point of the Church from Jerusalem, the capital of a Jewish world, to Rome, the capital of the gentile world.[49] Paul, the apostle to the Gentiles who claims that he himself had "become all things to all men" (1Corinthians 9:22), described the image of Christ as that "where there cannot be Greek and Jew, circumcised and uncircumcised, barbarian, Scyth′ian, slave, free man, but Christ is all, and in all" (Colossians 3:11).[50] And the seventy-two disciples of Christ who were sent out to preach to the nations, along with their typological connections to the seventy-two nations of Babel, underlined the potential universality of Christianity.[51]

Along with these examples, the universalism of the Church expressed in the narrative of Pentecost prevented the early Church, for the most part, from discriminating according to linguistic differences. Although linguistic diversity was created at the Tower of Babel, it was sanctified at Pentecost, and Pentecost became intricately connected to Babel as a New Testament typology. But despite the prominence of this typology in Christian intellectual history, biblical scholars have debated whether Luke, the author of Acts, was deliberately making an allusion to the Babel narrative when he composed the Pentecost narrative. Luke may have had the Table of

49 See Scott, *Paul and the Nations*, 163–5; and *Geography in Early Judaism and Christianity*, 57: "Jerusalem remains the center and focal point of Acts from first to last. Only when Paul finally comes to Rome does Jerusalem recede from view."

50 See Goldenberg, *Curse of Ham*, 43–5; and "Scythian-Barbarian," 87–102.

51 See Major, "The Number Seventy-Two," 21–2; Verheyden, "How Many Were Sent According to Lk 10,1?" 230–7; and Scott, *Geography in Early Judaism and Christianity*, 51–5.

Nations in mind when he wrote the tenth chapter of his Gospel, and it is clear that there are at least thematic similarities between the Babel narrative and the Pentecost narrative. The one separates the nations and languages of the world by divine action, while the other brings them together by divine action. Moreover, the contemporary, albeit much abridged, Table of Nations in Acts 2:9–11 emphasizes the inclusiveness of the Church that transcends ethnic and linguistic boundaries. Along with the Table of Nations and the Tower of Babel narrative, which stressed ethnic and linguistic diversity, Luke's account of Pentecost presented to Christians a world view that emphasized ecclesiastical unity in ethnic and linguistic diversity.

Although the Pentecost narrative does not suggest that all the languages of the world were spoken in Jerusalem on that day, such a notion was quickly adopted, which then facilitated stronger typological connections between Babel and Pentecost. Irenaeus, in his *Adversus haereses*, does not explicitly mention the Tower of Babel in connection to Pentecost, but provides undertones that point to the later development of the typology:[52]

> Hunc Spiritum ... descendisse Lucas ait post ascensum Domini super discipulos in Pentecoste, habentem potestatem omnium gentium ad introitum uitae et adapertionem noui Testamenti; unde et omnibus linguis conspirantes hymnum dicebant Deo, Spiritu ad unitatem redigente distantes tribus et primitias omnium gentium offerente Patri.

> Luke writes that the Spirit, after the ascension of the Lord, which had the power of all nations to introduce life and to disclose the new covenant, had descended upon the disciples on the day of Pentecost; hence those present spoke in all languages and sang hymns to God, as the Spirit brought the separated tribes back into unity and offered them, as the first fruits of all nations, to the Father.

Along with the innovation that all languages (*omnibus linguis*) and nations from around the world (*distantes tribus*) are represented at Pentecost, Irenaeus also introduces an important theme that would prevail in later interpretations of the two events. He implies that the ethnic and linguistic diversity of the world is guided by the Holy Spirit to restore *unitas*. Diversity not only comes to reflect unity, but provides an important tool

52 Irenaeus, *Contre les Hérésies Livre III*, 17.2.23–31.

for legitimizing the claims of Christianity. The success of Pentecost is, therefore, dependent upon the failure of Babel.

After Irenaeus, the typology between the Tower of Babel and Pentecost began to develop among other Christian authors. Gregory of Nazianzus (329–89), for example, in a homily on Pentecost, interprets the coming of the Holy Spirit in light of the division of languages at Babel, and thereby gives further support to the typology among other Greek Fathers, such as his successor as Archbishop of Constantinople, John Chrysostom (347–407), and the important Greek theologian Cyril of Alexandria (d. 444).[53] The homilies of Gregory of Nazianzus were also transmitted into the West soon after their composition through the Latin translation by Rufinus, and were read variously in Anglo-Saxon England.[54] In Rufinus's Latin, the text reads:[55]

> Admiranda quidem fuit et illa linguarum antiqua diuisio, cum ad turris superbam et inpiam constructionem male sibi sociata iniquorum unanimitas concordabat. sed discissione uocis atque in ignotum sonum uersae impiae conspirationis reprimuntur conatus. uerum multo admirabilior est ista diuisio. quod enim fuerat tunc ab una in plures sibi inuicem ignotas discrepantesque diuisum, id nunc per plures ad unam concordem et consonam reuocatur

> Indeed it was an admirable thing, that ancient division of languages, when the unanimity of evil men wickedly bound to each other agreed to the proud and impious building of the tower, but the efforts of their impious conspiracy were repressed by the division of language which was turned into an

53 Cyril of Jerusalem, *Catecheses*, PG 33, col. 989, XVII.xvii; see Borst, *Turmbau von Babel*, vol. 1, 243. John Chrysostom, *Homilia II: de sancta Pentecoste*, PG 50, col. 467; and *Homilia XXXV: In epist. I ad Cor.*, PG 61, col. 296; see Borst, *Turmbau von Babel*, vol. 1, 249–50; and Adler, *Das erste christliche Pfingstfest*, 2–4.

54 Notably, PentI 24 refers to Gregory of Nazianzus, although this may only indicate that Theodore was "quoting here from memory"; Bischoff and Lapidge, *Biblical Commentaries*, 153, nt. 85. Bede also quotes one of Gregory's *Orationes* in his *Expositio Actuum Apostolorum*, II.70–84, which he must defend in his *Retractatio in Actus Apostolorum*, II.45–8; and three manuscripts written or existing in England in the eleventh century contain portions of the *Orationes* (Oxford, Trinity College 4; Salisbury, Cathedral Library 9; and Salisbury, Cathedral Library 89); Lapidge, *The Anglo-Saxon Library*, 307.

55 Gregory of Nazianzus / Rufinus, *De Pentecoste et de Spiritu Sancto*, 16.14–21. The Greek is found in Gregory of Nazianzus, *Oratio XLI: In Pentecosten*, PG 36, col. 449, XVI; see Borst, *Turmbau der Babel*, I.246.

> unfamiliar sound. But more admirable is this division; for that first one (i.e., at Babel) then had been divided by one into many who were discordant and unknown to themselves; this one (i.e., at Pentecost) now is recalled through many to one that is in agreement and harmony.

Unlike Irenaeus, who hints at a connection between Pentecost and Babel that is based solely on the apostles' ability to speak all the languages of the world, Gregory connects the two through a contrast of discordance and harmony. In Rufinus's translation this contrast is given a typological turn that is based on a notion of the two *diuisiones* that occurred at both events. In fact, Rufinus's appellation of Pentecost as *diuisio* seems forced and almost nonsensical. The only purpose it must have served was to strengthen the connection between Babel and Pentecost, which Rufinus evidently thought was missing in Gregory's Greek.[56] What is important, however, is that in both the Greek and the Latin the theme of Pentecostal unity is contrasted and compared with the diversity of Babel. Rufinus's translation of Gregory's homily reveals an important text in the continuation of the typology, for the parallels between the respective *diuisiones* continue to link the two events together.

By the fifth century Augustine would draw similar parallels between the Tower of Babel narrative and Pentecost, and establish the customary typological elements that became popular in the following centuries. But Augustine's comparisons between the two are not uniform, and they reveal that Augustine was still working within a tradition that had yet to become standardized. Language is of primary concern for Augustine in his comparisons and he speaks of the dispersal of languages at the Tower of Babel in numerous places, most famously in his extensive treatment of Genesis 10 and 11 in the sixteenth book of *De ciuitate Dei*.[57] But this treatment does not actually make an explicit connection between Babel and Pentecost, and within Augustine's vast corpus there are relatively few parallels drawn between Babel and Pentecost. In his *De doctrina christiana*, for example, Augustine hints at a theological solution for dealing with the variety of languages through biblical translations. Biblical translators act, in a way, as the apostles at Pentecost:[58]

56 The repetition of the word *diuisio* is Rufinus's; Gregory uses the Greek words: *διαίρεσις*, division, and *θαυματουργουμένη*, miraculous working.

57 See Borst, *Turmbau von Babel*, II.394–404.

58 Augustine, *De doctrina christiana libri IV*, II.v.6.1–5.

> scriptura diuina ... ab una lingua profecta, qua opportune potuit per orbem terrarum disseminari, per uarias interpretum linguas longe lateque diffusa innotesceret gentibus ad salute
>
> divine Scripture, which began in one language, was fittingly able to be spread throughout the globe, having been diffused far and wide through the various languages of translators, and became known to the nations for their salvation.

Likewise, in his commentary on John, Augustine comes closer to making an explicit typological connection between the diversity created at the Tower of Babel and the unity of the Holy Spirit in the image of a dove. Select passages include: "Hoc significauit Spiritus sanctus diuisus in linguis, unitus in columba" (this signifies the Holy Spirit divided in language, united in the dove); "In columba unitas, in linguis gentium societas" (in the dove, unity; in languages, community of the nations); "De una lingua factae sunt multae ... De multis linguis fit una; noli mirari, caritas hoc fecit" (from the one language many were made ... from the many languages, one is made; do not be amazed, love did this).[59] Though the image of the dove in this context would not prevail, the theme of unity among diversity remained commonplace.

Two of the clearest connections between Babel and Pentecost in Augustine's works appear in his commentary on the Psalms and in a sermon on Pentecost. In his commentary on Psalm 54:11, "Submerge, Domine, et diuide linguas eorum" (come down, O Lord, and divide their languages), Augustine expounds upon the division of languages at Babel to introduce the typology:[60]

> Per superbos homines diuisae sunt linguae, per humiles apostolos congregatae sunt linguae: spiritus superbiae dispersit linguas, Spiritus sanctus congregauit linguas. Quando enim Spiritus sanctus uenit super discipulos, omnium linguis locuti sunt, ab omnibus intellecti sunt; linguae dispersae, in unum congregatae sunt
>
> Through proud men, languages were divided; through humble apostles, languages were gathered together. A spirit of pride dispersed the languages;

59 Augustine, *In Iohannis euangelium*, VI.10.10–35. These lines would later be used by Arator; see below, 70.

60 Augustine, *Enarrationes in Psalmos*, vol. 2, LIV.11.20–5.

> the Holy Spirit gathered languages together. For when the Holy Spirit came upon the disciples, they spoke in the languages of all, they were understood by all; the dispersed languages were gathered together into one.

And in his sermon on Pentecost, Augustine again connects the descent of the Holy Spirit with the dispersal of languages at Babel:[61]

> linguae illae quibus loquebantur a Spiritu sancto impleti, per omnium gentium linguas futuram Ecclesiam praesignabant. Sicut enim post diluvium superba impietas hominum turrim contra Dominum aedificavit excelsam, quando per linguas diversas dividi meruit genus humanum, ut unaquaeque gens lingua propria loqueretur, ne ab aliis intelligeretur: sic humilis fidelium pietas earum linguarum diversitatem Ecclesiae contulit unitati; ut quod discordia dissipaverat, colligeret charitas, et humani generis tanquam unius corporis membra dispersa ad unum caput Christum compaginata redigerentur, et in sancti corporis unitatem dilectionis igne conflarentur. Ab hoc itaque dono Spiritus sancti prorsus alieni sunt, qui oderunt gratiam pacis, qui societatem non retinent unitatis

> those languages, which the ones who were filled with the Holy Spirit spoke, prefigured that the Church would exist through the tongues of all nations. For just as after the Flood the proud impiety of men built a tower to the heavens against God, when humankind deserved to become divided through diverse languages in order that each nation would speak in its own language but not be able to understand other languages; so the humble piety of the faithful gathered the diversity of their languages into the unity of the Church in order that what discord had dispersed, love would gather and that the dispersed limbs of each race, as if of one body, would be brought back together and rejoined to the one head, Christ, and would be refined by the fire of love into the unity of the holy body. Therefore, those who hate the grace of peace and who do not retain the fellowship of unity, are utterly outside of this gift of the Holy Spirit.

In these two passages a major theme appears in the history of the typology of Babel: the contrast between *superbia* (pride) and *humilitas* (humility). While other authors previous to Augustine speak about the pride involved at Babel – Gregory of Nazianzus's homily provides a fitting example – Augustine is the first (to my knowledge) to bring the contrasting theme of *humilitas* into the typology. There is really nothing in Acts 2

61 Augustine, *Sermo* CCLXXI: *In die Pentecostes, V*, PL 38, col. 1245–6.

that points specifically to the humility of the apostles, and the addition seems to rely solely on the Augustinian tendency to create a theological dichotomy between the city of God and the city of the Devil, represented by Jerusalem and Babel / Babylon.[62] In a sense, this dichotomy strengthens the earlier treatments of Pentecost and Babel that focused, more or less, on ecclesiastical unity despite ethnic diversity. In Augustine's condemnation of those who built the Tower of Babel and thereby created diversity in the world, he allegorizes the event in a way that confirms an ecclesiastical unity that transcends diversity, but at the same time promotes Christian identity by opposing it to the immorality of the wicked. The application of *humilitas*, one of the great virtues of the Church, to Pentecost is an important step for the later typological developments.

With that said, the textual examples of the typology between Babel and Pentecost in the period immediately after Augustine and before Gregory the Great are fairly limited, perhaps on account of the paucity of sources. Relatively few authors of this period explicitly show much interest in the typological connections between Babel and Pentecost, and there seemed to be a reluctance to connect the seventy-two languages of Babel with the number of languages spoken at Pentecost.[63] However, the sixth-century poet Arator, who enjoyed much influence among the Anglo-Saxons, is an exception; for he associates Babel with Pentecost in his versified version of Acts:[64]

> Spiritus aetherea descendens sanctus ab aula 119
> Inradiat fulgore locum, quo stemma beatum
> Ecclesiae nascentis erat, quibus igne magistro
> Inbuit ora calor dictisque fluentibus exit
> Linguarum populosa seges; non littera gessit

62 See van Oort, *Jerusalem and Babylon*, 115–23.

63 See Major, "The Number Seventy-Two," 41–2.

64 Arator, *Historia apostolica*, I.119–38; see Borst, *Turmbau von Babel*, vol. 2, 427. For Arator in Anglo-Saxon England, see Lapidge, "Versifying the Bible in the Middle Ages," 11–40, at 20–30; Wieland, *The Latin Glosses on Arator and Prudentius in Cambridge University Library MS GG.5.35*, esp. 4; Martin, "The Influence of Arator in Anglo-Saxon England," 75–81; and Orchard, *The Poetic Art of Aldhelm*, 166–70. A ninth-century commentary on Arator survives in the Anglo-Saxon manuscript, British Library, Royal 15.A.v, ed. Orbán, "Ein anonymer Aratorkommentar in Hs. London, Royal MS. 15 A. V. *Editio princeps*, Teil I," 317–51; and "Ein anonymer Aratorkommentar in Hs. London, Royal MS. 15 A.V. *Editio princeps*, Teil II," 131–229. See Gneuss and Lapidge, *Anglo-Saxon Manuscripts*, no. 488.

Officium, non ingenii stillauit ab aure
Vena nec egregias signauit cera loquelas.
Sola fuit doctrina fides opulentaque uerbi
Materies, caeleste datum, noua uocis origo,
Quae numerosa uenit totoque ex orbe disertis
Sufficit una loqui. Dudum uetus aequoris arca
Cum superasset aquas, turrim uoluere maligni
In caelum proferre suam, quibus impia corda
Sermonum secuere modos sociisque superbis
Affectus cum uoce perit. Confusio linguae
Consimili tunc gente fuit; nunc pluribus una est,
Ecclesiae quoniam uenientis imagine gaudet
Concordes habitura sonos et pace modestis
Fit facunda redux humilisque recolligit ordo,
Quod tumidi sparsere uiri.

The Holy Spirit descending from the heavenly hall illuminates that blessed place with radiance where the stem of the nascent Church began. With fire as their teacher, heat inspired their mouths, and with flowing words the populous field of languages went forth. Writing did not carry out this act; the vein of genius did not drip from the ear, nor did a wax tablet help express these outstanding speeches: faith alone was their teaching and the opulent matter of their speech: a gift from heaven, a new beginning of language, which pours forth abundantly and allows these eloquent orators from the entire world to speak together. Formerly, after the ancient ark had overcome the waters of the sea, wicked men desired to build their tower into heaven, but their impious hearts divided the ways of speaking, and in their common pride the will to continue perished with their communication. At that time, there was confusion of language within the same nation; now there is a single language for many nations because this language, which will produce single-minded sounds, rejoices in the image of the emerging Church, becomes eloquent, and restores those moderate people to peace. The humble group recovers what the puffed up men scattered.

The connection in these lines between the Tower of Babel and Pentecost is heavily dependent on Augustine's own treatment of the subject.[65] But the

65 Schwind, *Arator-Studien*, 192–3, reveals the source as Augustine's commentary on John. Deproost, *L'Apôtre Pierre dans une Épopée du VIe Siècle*, 83–4, also cites a few analogues, including Augustine.

connection is not made simply to expound upon the Augustinian contrast between the pride of the builders and the humility of the apostles. Instead, Richard Hillier has argued that the parallel is made specifically as a comment on baptism.[66] Arator's references to Noah's ark, which traditionally signified baptism, and the discussion on the Holy Spirit's presence at Christ's baptism in the Jordan, which appear in the next lines of the poem, both confirm Hillier's interpretation.[67] Arator's treatment of Pentecost and Babel shows that Augustinian typology had begun to take some root, and that notions of a Church, which is dispersed throughout the whole world (*totoque ex orbe*), but remains unified, continued to prevail.

With Pope Gregory the Great (c. 540–604), the so-called apostle to the English,[68] the Augustinian typology between Babel and Pentecost takes the standard form that would prevail among many Anglo-Saxon authors. In his *Homilia* 30, Gregory makes a clear theological parallel based on the multiplicity of languages that is present at both Babel and Pentecost:[69]

> Audistis etenim quia Spiritus sanctus super discipulos in igneis linguis apparuit omniumque linguarum scientiam dedit. Quid scilicet hoc miraculo designans, nisi quod sancta ecclesia, eodem Spiritu repleta, omnium gentium erat uoce locutura? Qui uero contra Deum turrim aedificare conati sunt, communionem unius linguae perdiderunt; in his autem quo Deum humiliter metuebant, linguae omnes unitae sunt. Hic ergo humilitas uirtutem meruit, illic superbia confusionem.

> Indeed you have heard that the Holy Spirit appeared over the disciples in tongues of fire and gave knowledge of all languages to them. What, namely, is signified in this miracle unless that the holy Church, filled by that same Spirit, was about to speak with the voice of all nations? And those who attempted to build a tower against God lost the communion of one language; among these

66 Hillier, *Arator on the Acts of the Apostles*, 27–9.

67 Arator, *Historia apostolica*, I.138–47; and Hillier, *Arator on the Acts of the Apostles*, 28. The Christian interpretation of the ark as the baptism of the Church first appears in the New Testament, 1 Peter 3:20–1; see Anlezark, *Water and Fire*, 35–41, for patristic interpretations.

68 See Gretsch, *Ælfric and the Cult of Saints in Late Anglo-Saxon England*, 21–64; and Lendinara, "Forgotten Missionaries," 365–497; and below, ch. 6. Goffart, "The *Historia Ecclesiastica*," 29–45, at 37, suggests that Gregory's apostolic influence in Northumbria may have waned and been replaced by that of Wilfrid.

69 Gregory the Great, *Homiliae in Euangelia*, XXX.4.99–106.

people, however, when they humbly revered God, all languages were united. Therefore, here humility merited virtue, there pride merited confusion.

The languages of all the nations are said to be spoken by the apostles through the Holy Spirit; the linguistic confusion of Babel is contrasted to the linguistic unity at Pentecost, and *superbia* is contrasted with *humilitas*. Like most preceding authors, Gregory confirms the unity of the Church among the diversity created at Babel, an important theme that appears elsewhere in Gregory's works.[70]

Importantly, Gregory's sermon reveals that by the early seventh century an intellectual tradition for interpreting Babel and Pentecost was becoming more or less standardized, as the eagerness of later authors to draw from authoritative sources ensured that this Augustinian typology would enjoy continued prominence. Along with the theme of diversity within unity, Augustine's innovative contrast between *superbia* and *humilitas* becomes particularly popular, and dominates the way the two biblical passages are interpreted after the time of Gregory. Importantly, this allegorical approach allows a clear moral dichotomy that facilitates understandings of the passage beyond the literal account, which becomes less important with a theology that sees the diversity of the world unified in the Church. In Anglo-Saxon England, with some notable exceptions, the typology between Babel and Pentecost will remain thoroughly Augustinian and Gregorian.

Perceptions of Britain

Despite the potential of non-literal interpretations of Genesis 10–11, the literal elements of the account continued to play an important role in understanding and categorizing the world, particularly for Britain, which was thought to stand on the very peripheries of Europe. As others have already outlined, the mental maps of Late Antiquity understood the British and Irish Isles as representatives of the furthest regions of the inhabitable earth.[71] The Roman province of Britannia was, according to Virgil, "penitus toto diuisos orbe" (fully separated from the entire world),[72] and only the

70 See Meyvaert, "Diversity Within Unity," 141–62.

71 O'Reilly, "Islands and Idols at the Ends of the Earth," and Scully, "Bede, Orosius and Gildas on the Early History of Britain," 119–45 and 31–42; Michelet, *Creation, Migration, and Conquest*, 119–26; and Anlezark, "The Anglo-Saxon Worldview," 66–81, at 70–4.

72 Mynors, *Ecloga I*, in *P. Vergili Maronis opera*, 66.

uninhabitable regions of the quasi-mythical *ultima Thule* extended farther into the Ocean than the islands of the Atlantic archipelago.[73] Christian writers easily appropriated and syncretized these notions of extremity, borrowed chiefly from classical sources, to a geography based on the biblical texts. In the Table of Nations, the descendants of Noah's son Japheth come to inhabit "divisae ... insulae gentium in regionibus" (the islands of the nations that are divided into regions; Genesis 10:5). Despite the geographical ambiguity of this phrase, which almost certainly did not refer to the British and Irish Isles, it was, nevertheless, no great stretch for European Christian exegetes to argue that these *insulae* were those of Britannia, especially in light of the well-established connection between Japheth's descendants and Europe.[74] Orosius, after writing that the world's three continents are all surrounded by water, places Britain in the "oceano infinito" (boundless Ocean) along with the Orkneys and Thule.[75] Though Britain does remain in Europe, Orosius's description suggests that Britain's situation in the Ocean puts it apart and beyond the threefold division of the world, in a realm similar yet different from the rest of Europe. Similarly, Jordanes, in his *De origine actibusque Getarum*, describes Britain immediately after discussing the mostly uninhabited Orkneys and Thule; his description is fairly exotic with its "slow" sea, its goods that nourish cattle rather than people, and all its uncivilized people and kings.[76] Even among British authors, Gildas states that Britain lies almost at the extreme boundary of the globe,[77] and that as a frozen island it gets more rays from Christ than the actual sun:[78]

> glaciali frigore rigenti insulae et velut longiore terrarum secessu soli visibili non proximae verus ille non de firmamento solum temporali sed de summa etiam caelorum arce tempora cuncta excedente universo orbi praefulgidum sui coruscum ostendens ... radios suos primum indulget, id est sua praecepta, Christus

73 Scully, "Bede, Orosius and Gildas," 33. For Thule in the classical tradition, see Romm, *Edges of the Earth*, 157–60.

74 Jerome, *Hebraice quaestiones in libro Geneseos*, 10.4.14–15, p. 12, claims that Japheth's descendants inhabited Britain. See Wright, "'Insulae Gentium,'" 9–21, at 14–15.

75 Orosius, *Historiarum adversum paganos libri vii*, I.2.78.

76 Jordanes, *Getica*, II.12, p 56 ("mari tardo"); II.13, 57 ("pecora magis quam homines alant"); II.14, 57 ("inculti aeque omnes populi regesque populorum").

77 Gildas, *The Ruin of Britain and Other Works*, 3, 89: "in extremo ferme orbis limite." For Gildas's literary inheritance concerning the situation of Britain on the edge of the world, see Kerlouegan, *Le De excidio Britanniae de Gildas*, 155–6.

78 Gildas, *Ruin of Britain*, 8, 91. See also Michelet, *Creation, Migration, and Conquest*, 239–42, for Gildas's two descriptions of Britain.

> That true sun, Christ, reveals his brilliance, gleaming upon the entire world, and primarily bestows his rays, that is his commands, to an island frozen by icy chill and not near to the visible sun, as if in a remote place of the earth, far from not only the temporal firmament but also the highest stronghold that surpasses all times.

This manner of viewing the island of Britain from the southern perspective of Rome, and not from the actual geographical location of the author, suggests Gildas's affirmation of the centrality of the Roman Church. And along with this affirmation, Gildas is able to uphold the capacity of Christ to unite all the diverse regions of the world, even the extreme regions of Britain.[79]

Another one of the key figures in the propagation of this theological geography, which had some influence in Anglo-Saxon literature, is Gregory the Great. As both the anonymous Whitby life of the Pope and Bede's own account state, Gregory had an interest in converting the English before he became the Bishop of Rome.[80] In his *Moralia in Iob*, Gregory interprets Job 36:30 in light of the universality of the Church and the conversion of Britannia:[81]

> Omnipotens enim Dominus coruscantibus nubibus cardines maris operuit, quia emicantibus praedicatorum miraculis, ad fidem etiam terminos mundi perduxit. Ecce enim paene cunctarum iam gentium corda penetrauit; ecce in una fide orientis limitem occidentisque coniunxit; ecce lingua Britanniae, quae nihil aliud nouerat, quam barbarum frendere, iam dudum in diuinis laudibus Hebraeum coepit Alleluia resonare. Ecce quondam tumidus, iam substratus sanctorum pedibus seruit Oceanus; eiusque barbaros motus, quos terreni principes edomare ferro nequiuerant, hos pro diuina formidine sacerdotum ora simplicibus uerbis ligant; et qui cateruas pugnantium infidelis nequaquam metuerat, iam nunc fidelis humilium linguas timet.

---

79 See Howe, "An Angle on this Earth," 3–27, esp. 9–11; and "From Bede's World to 'Bede's World,'" 125–48, esp. 135–6.

80 Bede, *Ecclesiastical History*, II.1; and Colgrave, ed., *The Earliest Life of Gregory the Great*, § 9–10, 90–2. See Harris, "Bede and Gregory's Allusive Angles," 271–89, for a comparative study of the two accounts.

81 Gregory the Great, *Moralia in Iob libri XXXV*, vol. 3, XXVII.21, 64–76. Part of this passage is quoted in Bede, *Ecclesiastical History*, II.1.

> For the omnipotent Lord covered the ends of the sea with flashing clouds, in that he led the end of the world to faith with miracles of the preachers bursting forth. For behold, he has now penetrated the hearts of almost all the nations; behold, he has joined the bounds of East and West in one faith; behold, the language of Britain, which knew nothing other than to gnash in barbaric manner, just recently began to sound the Hebrew Alleluia in divine praises. Behold, the Ocean, once puffed up but now spread out before the feet of saints, serves the Lord; and on account of divine fear, the mouths of priests with simple words bind these barbaric movements of the Ocean, which earthly princes could not dominate with the sword; and the man without faith who by no means dreaded the troops of soldiers, now with faith fears the tongues of the humble.

While there has been some discussion, initiated by Nicholas Howe, on the linguistic theology of this passage, especially in light of the mention of the *lingua Britanniae*,[82] Gregory's main emphasis is not linguistic, but rather ecclesiastical: the Lord has caused the hearts of almost all the nations, from east to west, to be joined *in una fide* (in one faith). Britannia, as an extremity situated in the Ocean of *barbaros motus* (barbaric movements), and indeed Ocean itself, as a metonymy for Britain and the other islands on the edge of the world, become persuasive symbols for the universality of the Church. In practice, Gregory also recognized the theological and pastoral need to maintain ecclesiastical unity by embracing certain diverse cultural aspects. The *Libellus responsionum* – a text contained in the first book of Bede's *Ecclesiastical History* – provides important evidence for Gregory's emphasis on the theme of "diversity within unity."[83] Notably, Augustine of Canterbury's second question to Gregory

82 Howe, *Migration and Mythmaking*, 122–3: "Gregory's own statement depicts the Anglo-Saxon conversion as a linguistic movement from barbaric howl to Hebrew alleluia, from meaningless sounds to divine eloquence"; see also Stanton, *The Culture of Translation in Anglo-Saxon England*, 65–6; and "Linguistic Fragmentation and Redemption before King Alfred," 12–26, at 14–16.

83 Bede, *Ecclesiastical History*, I.27. For the Gregorian authorship of the *Libellus*, see Meyvaert, "Le libellus responsionum à Augustin de Cantorbéry," 543–50; "Bede's Text of the *Libellus Responsionum* of Gregory the Great to Augustine of Canterbury," 15–33; and Flechner, "The Making of the Canons of Theodore," 121–43, at 135–8. For the transmission of the *Libellus*, see Elliot, "Boniface, Incest, and the Earliest Extant Version of Pope Gregory I's *Libellus responsionum* (JE 1843)," 62–111.

involves the different uses of the liturgy throughout the Church. Gregory, with somewhat surprising cultural sensitivity, states:[84]

> siue in Romana siue in Galliarum seu in qualibet ecclesia aliquid inuenisti, quod plus omnipotenti Deo possit placere, sollicite eligas, et in Anglorum ecclesia, quae adhuc ad fidem noua est, institutione praecipua, quae de multis ecclesiis colligere potuisti, infundas. Non enim pro locis res, sed pro bonis rebus loca amanda sunt.

> whatever you find that is able to please almighty God to a greater extent, whether it is in the Roman or Gallic or in whatsoever church, you may carefully select and bring, with special instruction, into the English church, which is still new to the Faith, whatever you have been able to collect from a number of churches. For things should not be loved on account of their places, but places should be loved on account of their good things.

In this passage, Gregory's emphasis on the unity of the Church surpasses uniformity of ecclesiastical practice: ecclesiastical unity transcends diversity within the Church. The focus or centre of Christian identity is no longer only Rome, but rather wherever the *bonae res* are found – even as far away as England.

Especially after the conversion, the Christian inhabitants of Britain themselves became an indication that the Romano-centrism of western Christianity had prevailed even among peripheral geographies and peoples by means of *unitas catholica* (catholic unity).[85] As Fabienne L. Michelet states on the matter, "centrality and marginality cannot be thought of separately, for they are of course the two sides of the same coin," and "to represent distant reaches of the world is to know and to appropriate them."[86] The centre is strengthened by the fact that it can be found not only at what was thought to be the geographical middle, but also at its most outlying points. By adopting the mental maps of Antiquity, Christian authors, interpreting Britain as positioned on the edge of the world, could also argue that its conversion to Christianity signifies the

84 Bede, *Ecclesiastical History*, I.27.

85 For the ecclesiastical shift to the centricity of Rome, see O'Reilly, "Islands and Idols at the Ends of the Earth," 123. See also Howe, "Rome as Capital of Anglo-Saxon England," 101–24, esp. 107.

86 Michelet, *Creation, Migration, and Conquest*, 10.

fulfilment of biblical prophecies that foretold the Church's extension from "sea to sea" (Ps 71:8).[87] While other foreign and exotic realms were thought to exist outside of Europe, such as the supposedly monstrous realms of the East, the position of the province of Britannia at the extreme limits of the Roman Empire allowed Christian authors to claim that the Church really had extended into the most remote parts of the world.[88]

Late antique interpretations of the ethnic and linguistic diversity of the world were widespread and influenced by many sources, biblical or otherwise. The cultural and religious tendencies of the age were moulded together in ways that appeared more syncretic and harmonized. As Christians were forced to deal with issues such as ethnic diversity and proto-nationalism, they were able to use the Tower of Babel narrative to understand and support their emerging beliefs. By allowing for salvation to spread beyond Israel into the numerous nations of the world, Christians of Late Antiquity were able to forge a new identity that, as neither pagan nor Jew, could boast of a universality that transcended and used the ethnic or linguistic boundaries created at Babel. By doing so, these Christians shifted the cultural dichotomy between the centre and peripheries partially away from the realm of geography and ethnicity and focused it on differences of doctrine – on orthodoxy and heterodoxy. The Tower of Babel narrative is continually employed as a reminder of how powerfully textual interpretations could be used when needed to strengthen a specific world view. The literature of Anglo-Saxon England will naturally follow course, as individual authors will adapt the interpretative traditions of Late Antiquity to their own specific perspectives and objectives. As will be shown, the Tower of Babel narrative will be prevalent in supporting ideas of ethnic and linguistic diversity, in creating and promulgating morality based on identity, and in interpreting the trajectory of salvation history from the initial confusion of Babel to the all-embracing order of the Church after Pentecost.

---

87 O'Reilly, "Islands and Idols at the Ends of the Earth," 119–21.

88 Ibid., 122, referring to Jerome, *Epistulae, pars I: epistulae I–LXX*, XL.10, LVIII.3, LX.4; *Commentariorum in Esaiam libri I–XI*, IV.xi.11/14, 154–5; *Tractatus siue homiliae in psalmos*, 95:10; and Augustine, *Epistulae*, vol. 4, CXCIX.47.

Chapter Three

The Early Anglo-Saxon School at Canterbury

Texts From The Canterbury School of Theodore and Hadrian

In 667 the archbishop-elect of Canterbury, Wigheard, who was in Rome seeking the *pallium*, died of the plague, leaving the see at Canterbury vacant. Pope Vitalian, who then took on the responsibility of choosing an archbishop for Canterbury, offered the see to Hadrian, who was at the time an abbot of a certain *monasterium Hiridanum*, not far from Naples.[1] Because of his relative youth and inexperience, Hadrian did not feel worthy of the position, and recommended a Greek monk from Tarsus named Theodore, who was living outside of Rome, most likely in the monastery *ad aquas Saluias*.[2] The Pope accepted Hadrian's request and ordained Theodore to the see of Canterbury on 26 March 668, but not without cautioning Theodore's involvement in arguing the orthodox position against monotheletism (the heresy that Christ has only one will) – this politically sensitive issue had recently climaxed with Emperor Constans II charging Pope Martin and Maximus the Confessor with treason.[3]

1 Bede, *Ecclesiastical History*, IV.1.

2 For the lives of Theodore and Hadrian before their arrival into England, see chs. 2 and 3 of Bischoff and Lapidge, *Biblical Commentaries from the Canterbury School of Theodore and Hadrian*, 5–81 (Theodore); 67–9 (*ad aquas Saluias*); 82–132 (Hadrian); 120–3 (*monasterium Hiridanum*); and Lapidge, "The Career of Archbishop Theodore," 93–121.

3 Bede, *Ecclesiastical History*, IV.1. See Chadwick, "Theodore of Tarsus and Monotheletism," 534–44; "Theodore, the English Church and the Monothelete Controversy," 88–95; and Lapidge, "The Career of Archbishop Theodore," 113–18.

Out of these two figures, Theodore and Hadrian, sprang a golden age of learning in Anglo-Saxon England that was to be one of the high points of scholarship in the early Middle Ages. They founded a school at Canterbury where they taught biblical exegesis through Latin, Greek, and possibly Syriac patristic texts, and provided their students with the ability to read Greek to a limited extent, if not perhaps as fluently as Bede attests.[4] On account of their individual learning, Hadrian was probably responsible for ensuring a high quality of Latinity within the school, and Theodore for the introduction of Greek learning and Eastern exegesis. The extent of Theodore's own Latinity has been questioned, most notably by Carmela Vircillo Franklin and Jane Stevenson. Franklin suggests that the *Passio beati Anastasii*, a work that Bede notes is "male de greco translatum" (poorly translated from the Greek), is to be attributed to Theodore;[5] and Stevenson attributes the *Laterculus Malalianus* to Theodore partially on account of Theodore's "superficial" Latinity, and the "un-Classical characteristics" of the *Laterculus*.[6] Moreover, of the four surviving Latin poems that are attributed to Theodore, each reveals a strong dependence on "Greek anacreontic hymns of late antiquity."[7] The most important Latin works that have come out of Hadrian and Theodore's Canterbury School are the biblical commentaries contained in the manuscript Milan, Biblioteca Ambrosiana, M. 79 sup., which although not written by either Hadrian or Theodore, were composed from the notes of some of the students at the

4 Bede, *Ecclesiastical History*, IV.2, writes, "usque hodie supersunt de eorum discipulis, qui Latinam Graecamque linguam aeque ut propriam in qua nati sunt norunt" (even today there are living some of their students who know Latin and Greek as well as the language in which they were born); see also *Ecclesiastical History*, V.8, V.20 and V.23. For a sceptical view of Bede's statements, see Lapidge, "The Study of Greek at the School of Canterbury," 123–39.

5 Franklin, "Theodore and the *Passio S. Anastasii*," 175–203; and *The Latin Dossier of Anastasius the Persian*, 79–80 and 272–97 (text). The quotation is from Bede, *Ecclesiastical History*, V.24, where Bede states that he has made a revised translation of the *passio*.

6 Stevenson, "Theodore and the *Laterculus Malalianus*," 204–21, at 209 and 219; and *The "Laterculus Malalianus" and the School of Archbishop Theodore*, 74–86 and 120–60 (text). For scepticism of Theodore's authorship, see Winterbottom's review of Stevenson's edition, 457–9.

7 Lapidge, "Theodore and Anglo-Latin Octosyllabic Verse," 225–45, at 240, and 240–5 (text).

Canterbury School sometime between the mid-seventh and mid-eighth century.[8] These commentaries are of particular significance for this study because they provide the earliest Anglo-Saxon references to the Tower of Babel.

According to Bernhard Bischoff's and Michael Lapidge's careful study, it is evident that the sources and the methods of the Canterbury commentaries deviate from the mainstream exegetical traditions of Latin Christianity, conforming closer to the so-called Antiochene approach to Scripture.[9] Alongside Latin patristic writing, Theodore and Hadrian seemed to have introduced an extensive collection of Greek texts to England that apparently included works by "Basil, Cosmas Indicopleustes, Epiphanius, John Chrysostom, Procopius, the Greek Ephremic corpus, perhaps a copy of a Greek *catena*" among others.[10] The nature of these sources, especially in their own treatments of the Babel narrative, facilitates an understanding of the unusual comments on the narrative in the Canterbury commentaries. Notably, although Cosmas Indicopleustes's *Topographia christiana* is an obscure sixth-century Greek work of little influence, it must have had some impact on Theodore's lessons at Canterbury. For, as Bischoff first suggested and Lapidge later confirmed, the Canterbury commentaries remarkably contain a close Latin paraphrase of Cosmas's Greek account of the building of Babel (PentI 86):[11]

> *Faciamus ciuitatem nobis et turrem* [Gen 11:4]. Dicit Christianus Historiographus ideo eos fecisse, quia uoluerunt in caelum uindicare, eo quod inde in diluuio puniti sunt pluuia.
>
> *Let us build a city and a tower for ourselves.* The Christian Historian says that they built these things because they wanted to take vengeance against heaven, for the reason that they were there punished in the Flood by rain.

8 Bischoff and Lapidge, *Biblical Commentaries*, 1. The connection between Biblioteca Ambrosiana, M. 79 sup. and the Canterbury School was made by Bischoff, "Wendepunkte in der Geschichte der lateinischen Exegese im Frühmittelalter," 205–73, at 207–8. A new fragment of the second glosses on the gospels has recently been discovered by Steinova, "Munich, Bayerische Staatsbibliothek," 45–55.

9 Bischoff and Lapidge, *Biblical Commentaries*, 190–242 (sources), 243–74 (exegetical nature).

10 Ibid., 241 and 205–33.

11 Bischoff, "Wendepunkt," 208; and Bischoff and Lapidge, *Biblical Commentaries*, 208–11 and 451–2. See also Borst, *Turmbau von Babel*, II.471.

The commentator, following Theodore's Antiochene exegetical methods and sources, is here interested only in explaining the literal details of the narrative, an approach that accords with the other comments on Genesis 10–11 in the Canterbury commentaries. The commentator makes the common mistake of confusing the ambiguous named city Assur in Genesis 10:11 with the traditional eponymous founder of the Assyrians, Assur (PentI 87);[12] he defines the *plateas ciuitatis* of Genesis 10:11, the Vulgate's translation of the etymological elements of the city Rehoboth, as "uias publicas; quae ducunt per ciuitatem" (public ways; those which go through the city, PentI 88); he explains that the "ciuitas magna" (great city) of Genesis 10:12 refers to Nineveh (PentI 89) – a gloss that clarifies ambiguity in the Vulgate's syntax; and he suggests that the plural vocative in Genesis 11:7, *Venite* (come), is addressed to either angels or the members of the Trinity (PentI 92). According to Bischoff's and Lapidge's edition, there also appears to be a cryptic reference to the names of the tower: "Saba et Ophi et Euilath filii Iecthan [Gen 10:28–9]: de eis dicuntur nomina turris" (Saba and Ophir and Hevila, sons of Iecthan: names of the tower are derived from these, PentI 90), although the manuscript's original reading of *terris* (lands), instead of the corrected *turris* (tower), makes better sense. Along with the general tendency to connect the names of Genesis 10 with peoples or lands, the *Book of the Cave of Treasures*, a sixth-century Syriac text that Theodore seems to have been familiar with, mentions Saba, Ophir, and Havilah together as place names.[13] Though not exactly forthcoming with unambiguous evidence, these examples reveal the commentator's tendency to provide literal geographical and onomastic information over allegory in his account of Genesis 10–11.

Furthermore, in the only gloss on Nimrod in the commentaries, Nimrod is called "rex in Persida et Calanne, in ipso loco ubi aedificata est turris" (king in Persia and Calanne, in that exact place where the tower was built, PentI 86). Lapidge shows that the association with Calanne and the place

12 Bischoff and Lapidge, *Biblical Commentaries*, 320. Most modern translators and commentaries take Nimrod to be the subject of the phrase "de terra egressus est Assur" and *Assur* to be a place name, on the basis of Micah 5:6, which puts "terram Assur" in apposition with "terram Nemrod"; see Wenham, *Genesis 1–15*, 223–4. Jerome and Bede take Assur to be the subject: Jerome, *Hebraicae quaestiones in libro Geneseos*, 10.11, 13; and Bede, *In principium Genesis*, III.164–5.

13 Budge, trans., *The Book of the Cave of Treasures*, 136–7. See Bischoff and Lapidge, *Biblical Commentaries*, 236–7.

where the Tower of Babel was built derives from a gloss in the Septuagint,[14] but the appellation *rex in Persida* seems highly anachronistic. It is possible that the commentator intended to update the geography for his audience with a presentation of current historical circumstances; the prepositional phrase *in Persida*, instead of the expected genitive construction *Persidos* or the nominative adjective *Persis*, gives some support to this interpretation: Nimrod was a king in the land that would become Persia. In any case, the connection between Nimrod and Persia is significant. On the basis of historical probability and two glosses that describe customs of the Persians, Lapidge has argued that Theodore might have even had first-hand experience with invading Persians.[15] In addition, Nimrod was closely connected with Zoroaster in the interpretative traditions, who in turn was connected with the religion of the Persians. In the *Recognitiones* of pseudo-Clement that were translated by Rufinus, Nimrod, who is otherwise called Zoroaster, is said to have gone to Persia where he taught fire-worship;[16] in the *Book of the Cave of Treasures*, Nimrod is presented as a fire worshipper of the East and a magician;[17] and in the *Panarion*, Epiphanius states the opinion that Nimrod was the "ἐφευρετὴς … κακῆς διδαχῆς, ἀστρολογίας καὶ μαγείας, ὥς τινές φασι περὶ τούτου τοῦ Ζωροσάστρου" (inventor … of wicked teaching, astrology and magic – some assert such about Zoroaster), but then goes on to correct this opinion: "πολὺ δὲ ἀλλήλων τῷ χρόνῳ διεστήκασιν ἄμφω, ὅ Νεβρὼδ καὶ ὁ Ζωροάστρης" (the two, Nimrod and Zoroaster, are much separated in time from one another).[18] It is probable that the

14 Lapidge, "The Study of Greek," 126; and Bischoff and Lapidge, *Biblical Commentaries*, 451.

15 Bischoff and Lapidge, *Biblical Commentaries*, 8–9.

16 Pseudo-Clement, *Rekognitionen in Rufins Übersetzung*, I.30.7, p. 26: "apud Babyloniam Nebroth primus regnavit, urbemque construxit et inde migravit ad Persas eosque ignem colere docuit" (Nimrod first ruled at Babylon and built the city, and from there travelled to Persia and taught them to worship fire); and IV.26–9, 159–61, where Nimrod is associated (albeit in a convoluted fashion) with the name Zoroaster. Rufinus's translation of the *Recognitiones* provides a source for the Leiden glossary – a text connected with the Canterbury school; see Bischoff and Lapidge, *Biblical Commentaries*, 175. Similar sentiment on Nimrod is also found in pseudo-Clement, *Homilien*, IX(Θ).4–5, 133.

17 *The Book of the Cave Treasures*, 143–4.

18 Epiphanius, *Panarion*, vol. 1, I.3.2–3, 177; interestingly, Procopius of Gaza, *Commentarius in Genesin*, PG 82, col. 312, another of Theodore's sources, borrows this phrase from Epiphanius, but negates it to say "not much separated in time." See van der Toorn and van der Horst, "Nimrod Before and After the Bible," 27. For the *Panarion* and *Commentarius in Genesin* as sources for the Canterbury commentaries, see Bischoff and Lapidge, *Biblical Commentaries*, 212 and 227–9.

Canterbury commentator, who would have been familiar with these three texts, knew of the connection between Nimrod and Zoroaster and of Zoroaster with Persia.

Because Nimrod's gigantism was such a prominent feature of his perceived character in both Latin and Greek sources, the Canterbury commentator may have felt no need to mention it. But what the commentator does state regarding the giants of Genesis 6 may be interpreted as an explanation for the survival of giants after the Flood. Exhibiting knowledge of biblical measurement, the Canterbury commentator states: "*Gigantes*: dicunt decem et octo cubitorum staturam illorum fuisse, et tribus cubitis supereminebat aquis, dum .xv. cubitis excelsior fuit aqua quam montes" (*Giants*: it is said that their height was eighteen cubits, and three cubits above the waters, since the water was fifteen cubits higher than the mountains, PentI 70). This unusual remark, which has no known source, allows enough (literal) breathing room for the giants to survive, thereby providing, intentionally or not, an explanation of their postdiluvian existence.[19] Does the commentator's need to explain how giants survived the Flood anticipate the mention of Nimrod later in the commentary? Of course, there are too many uncertainties to push the point any further. But it can be stated that this unusual gloss does not seem to have been popular; a corresponding gloss in the second Canterbury commentary on Genesis makes sure to give the giants a height that is one cubit less than the waters, presumably for the opposite reason – to indicate that all the antediluvian giants drowned (Gn-Ex-EvIa 12).

Although these references constitute the sole allusions to the Babel narrative in the texts associated with the Canterbury School, notions of ecclesiastical unity in diversity created at Pentecost, typical of late antique Christian theology, also appear in Theodore's putative corpus. In the *Laterculus Malalianus*, which has been hesitantly attributed to Theodore by its recent editor,[20] the magi and their gifts are given a threefold interpretation: "trinitas adoraretur in Christo, crederetur in mundo, praedicaretur in gentibus" (the Trinity is honoured in Christ, believed in the world and preached among the nations).[21] While allusion to a universal Church in a diverse world is not necessarily explicit in this passage, the allegorical interpretation is in stark contrast to the gloss on the magi in the Canterbury

19 See Bischoff and Lapidge, *Biblical Commentaries*, 449–50; and Mellinkoff, "Cain's Monstrous Progeny in *Beowulf*: Part II," 183–97.

20 See above, 79.

21 Stevenson, ed., *The "Laterculus Malalianus,"* § 15, 140.

commentary, which is not at all concerned with the world's diversity, but rather with the meaning of John Chrysostom's name.[22] A more prominent reference to the universality of the Church in the *Laterculus*, however, can be found a few paragraphs later where the twelve apostles are said to have illuminated the whole world with the sun of justice and the precepts of God:[23]

> sic totum mundum, tanquam menses totius annis, sol in se iustitiae continentes, perlustrauerunt et animas fluctis exuli uagas, lucida Dei praecepta tamquam in lina manibus ecclesia medio concluserunt.
>
> just as months of a whole year, they [i.e., the twelve apostles] went throughout / illuminated the entire world, holding fast the sun of justice in themselves, and with the clear precepts of God, just as with hands on a fishing line they confined in the middle of the Church souls wandering on the waves as though an exile.

The *Laterculus*'s language of illuminating or wandering around the world with the sun of justice is reminiscent of Gildas's comments about the island of Britain,[24] although the phrasing between the *Laterculus* and Gildas is too dissimilar to assert any definitive relationship. It is perhaps the case that, besides the frequency of this motif among Christian texts of Late Antiquity,[25] both authors found the image of a sun fitting for an audience residing in the upper parts of the northern hemisphere. It is also notable that in this passage the author of the *Laterculus* creates an image of confinement within the middle of the Church ("ecclesia medio concluserunt") that evokes notions of centrality in contrast to otherness. As was the case for early Christians, there is a noticeable shift from finding identification in ethnic or linguistic similarity to finding identification in religious belief.

---

22 EvII 3: "Magi duobus annis in uia fuerunt, quia duos annos ante natiuitatem Christi apparuit eis stella, ut Iohannes Constantinopolitanus dixit Crisostomus, quem Graeci Crisostomum .i. os auri clamant" (The magi were on the road for two years, because the star appeared to them two years before the birth of Christ, just as John Chrysostom of Constantinople said, whom the Greeks call Chrysostomus, that is mouth of gold).

23 Stevenson, ed., *The "Laterculus Malalianus,"* § 18, 146.

24 See above, 73–4.

25 The image of Jesus as the sun ultimately stems from John 8:12: "ego sum lux mundi" (I [i.e., Jesus] am the light of the world). See also Radner, "The Christian Mystery of Sun and Moon," 89–176; and Kerlouegan, *Le De excidio Britanniae de Gildas*, 178–80.

The Church is identified as containing, even encapsulating, justice and divine precepts in contrast to those who are wandering about ("animas ... uagas"), as it were, without anything concrete to identify with.[26]

Later in the text, in a discussion on the gifts given by the Holy Spirit at Pentecost, the apostolic ability to speak in all languages is paired with the sacraments and ministry of the Church: "quidquid in diuinis spiritus omnium linguarum elucutione, in sacramento uel ministerio sanctae catholicae ecclesiae gesta sunt" (whatever things are done through the speaking of all languages in the holiness of the Spirit, in the mystery or ministry of the holy catholic Church).[27] The reference to all the languages of the world ("omnium linguarum"), especially when coupled with the mystery and ministry of the whole Church ("catholicae ecclesiae"), sheds further light on the earlier reference to the enclosing of souls within the middle of the Church. As with traditional interpretations of Pentecost in Late Antiquity, in which each language is not only affirmed, but also affirms the unity of the Church, this passage has the Church cross ethnic and linguistic boundaries, thereby, confirming a notion of Christian identity that focuses on the faith and work of the Church ("sacramento uel ministerio") rather than ethnic and linguistic diversity. The diversifying effects of Babel are no longer a hindrance, but rather an important tool for creating and propagating essential characteristics of the Church in the world.

Likewise, another text that has recently been attributed to Theodore, the *Passio beati Anastasii*, presents an eagerness to preach the Gospel throughout all the world:[28]

> eius passionum testes beati apostoli peruenerunt quidem cunctum orbem diuino praedicamento, conuenerunt autem ad pietatem uniuersam ciuitatem et regionem et nationem et populum et tribum et linguam

---

26 For a similar description of Nimrod by Byrhtferth of Ramsey, see below, 167–9.

27 Stevenson, ed., *The "Laterculus Malalianus,"* § 22, 152.

28 Franklin, ed., *Vita et passio beati Anastasii monachi*, in *The Latin Dossier*, § 2.15–20, 273. Bede's revised translation reads: "eius passionis testes beati apostoli, universum mundum peragrantes, divina mandata praedicantes, convenerunt autem ex Dei pietate per civitates et regiones, nationes et populos; tribubus et linguis praedicaverunt" (those blessed apostles, witnesses to his passion, pilgrims throughout the whole world, preachers of the divine commandments, who gathered from the piety of God, throughout cities and regions, nations and peoples, preached to the tribes and languages); Franklin, ed., *Acta et passio beati Anastasii martyris ex Persida ciuitate mense Ian. Die XXII*, in *The Latin Dossier*, § 2.17–21, 388.

> as witnesses of his sufferings, the blessed apostles indeed went throughout the entire world, all the while proclaiming the divine message, and gathered each city and region and nation and people and tribe and language into piety.

These lines, based in part on Revelation 7:9,[29] provide a further example of the tendency to create a Christian identity that transcends the ethnic and linguistic diversity of Babel. While it is a tendency that is by no means exclusive to Anglo-Saxon England, a Christian identity that is said to prevail in all parts of the world surely would have had a strong effect on an audience who saw themselves as living on the very edges of the world. Although recognition of Theodore's authorship does not seem to have lasted long after its composition,[30] the possibility that it was written by a Greek-speaking monk from the distant lands of Tarsus underlines even further the notion that Christian identity has the potential to remain united while transcending all borders.

As the earliest reference to the Table of Nations and the Babel narrative in Anglo-Saxon England, the Canterbury commentaries are not exactly typical. The focus on Antiochene exegetical methods and Greek sources will not continue after the deaths of Hadrian and Theodore. In fact, it is not until Bede's biblical commentaries that Genesis 10–11 are treated again in such a direct manner. But other texts associated with Theodore reveal indirect participation in the reception history of Genesis 10–11. Whereas the *Laterculus Malalianus* and the *Passio Beati Anastasii* do not ever refer explicitly to the Babel narrative, they do reveal interest in the ethnic diversity and ecclesiastical unity customary to Latin Christian authors of Late Antiquity.

Aldhelm

The most famous student of Theodore and Hadrian is without a doubt Aldhelm of Malmesbury (c. 639/10–709/10). According to Lapidge's interpretation of William of Malmesbury's life of Aldhelm, Aldhelm was a son of Centwine, king of the West-Saxons (676–85).[31] After most likely

29 "ex omnibus gentibus et tribubus et populis et linguis" (from all nations and tribes and peoples and languages).

30 Bede, *Ecclesiastical History*, V.24, who calls its author unlearned (*inperitus*), evidently did not recognize Theodorean authorship.

31 Lapidge, "The Career of Aldhelm," 15–69, at 17–18. Besides Bede's brief account (*Ecclesiastical History*, V.18), the two medieval *vitae* of Aldhelm are that of Faricius of

studying with an Irish scholar either at Malmesbury or Iona,[32] Aldhelm left for Canterbury around the age of thirty to study under Theodore and Hadrian; he addresses Hadrian in one of his letters (*Ep* 2), and in another letter (*Ep* 5) recommends both Theodore and Hadrian to Heahfrith as superior teachers over the Irish.[33] After Canterbury he was appointed abbot of Malmesbury, and then Bishop of Sherborne, where Bede states that he presided over the see with much energy.[34] Although Aldhelm is still relatively understudied today for a writer of such copious literary production, he is often referred to as the "first English man of letters." His Latin is full of syntactically dense constructions and difficult vocabulary with an extensive array of Latin and Greek nonce words, and his works were widely read in Anglo-Saxon England and formed part of the educational curriculum for tenth-century hermeneutic Latin.[35]

Aldhelm, while never explicitly mentioning the Tower of Babel, shows much interest in issues involving ethnic and linguistic diversity, the universality of the Church, and the propagation of a centrality that reflects the prominence of orthodoxy. Moreover, Aldhelm's conception of the world is in accordance with the traditional division of the world among authors of Late Antiquity, which has its origins in interpretations of Genesis 10. In numerous instances Aldhelm speaks of a tripartite earth

---

Arezzo (d. 1117); Winterbottom, "An Edition of Faricius, *Vita S. Aldhelm*," 93–147; and Book 5 of William of Malmesbury's (c. 1090–1143) *Gesta pontificum Anglorum*, vol. 1, V.498–662. Modern accounts of Aldhelm's life and works can be found in Ehwald, ed., *Aldhelmi opera*, ix–xxiv; Manitius, *Geschichte der lateinischen Literatur des Mittelalters*, vol. 1, 134–41; Lapidge and Herren, *Aldhelm: The Prose Works*, 5–19; and Orchard, *Poetic Art of Aldhelm*, 1–18.

32 William of Malmesbury, *Gesta pontificum Anglorum*, V.189, asserts that Aldhelm was tutored by the Irishman Maíldub. This assertion has been doubted, however, by Winterbottom, "Aldhelm's Prose Style and its Origins," 39–76; and Lapidge and Herren, *Prose Works*, 6–7. Orchard, *Poetic Art of Aldhelm*, 4–5, 54–60, 96–7, maintains that Aldhelm was taught by an Irishman; and Lapidge, "The Career of Aldhelm," 22–7 et passim, argues that Aldhelm was tutored by the Irish abbot Adomnán at Iona.

33 Aldhelm, *Epistula* II and *Epistula* V, in *Opera*, 478 and 492–3.

34 *Ecclesiastical History*, V.18: "altera [parrochia] Aldhelmo, cui annis quattuor strenuissime praefuit; ambo et in rebus ecclesiasticis et in scientia scripturarum sufficienter instructi" (the other diocese was given to Aldhelm, which he oversaw very energetically for four years; he was sufficiently instructed in both ecclesiastical affairs and the knowledge of the Scriptures).

35 Lapidge, "The Hermeneutic Style in Tenth-Century Anglo-Latin Literature," 105–49; and Orchard, *Poetic Art of Aldhelm*, 239–83.

that represents the traditional division into three continents. Adam and Eve are told to increase and multiply in "triquadra mundi latitudo" (the three-cornered expanse of the world);[36] and Constantina is said to govern a "tripertiti mundi monarchiam" (the monarchy of the tripartite world).[37] On the contrary, at the end of the prose *De uirginitate*, Aldhelm states that the Holy Trinity governs the whole world: "alma trinitas, una deitatis substantia et trina personarum subsistentia, totius mundi monarchiam gubernans" (the gracious Trinity – the one substance of the deity and the threefold subsistence of its persons, controlling the monarchy of the entire universe).[38] In this final example, Aldhelm may not have used his usual tripartite division of the world in order to suppress potential confusion regarding the indivisible nature of the Trinity; it is conceivable that one part of a "threefold subsistence" might be misunderstood as ruling one specific part of a threefold earth.

In other instances where Aldhelm uses the image of a tripartite earth, he includes the image of light and illumination, much like Gildas and the author of the *Laterculus Malalianus* before him. In the prose *De uirginitate*, for example, Aldhelm describes the sun as illuminating or wandering around the earth: "luculentus limpidissimi solis splendor triquadram mundi rotam clarius illustrare credatur" (the bright splendour of the clear sun is thought to illuminate / wander around the tripartite orb of the world more clearly).[39] Elsewhere in the same work, Aldhelm employs similar phrasing to foster a metaphor for the New Testament illuminating the Old: "limpida sequentis testamenti liminaria per gratiam evangelicae praedicationis crassae noctis caliginem illustrantia in triquadro terrarum ambitu diffusius spargerentur" (the clear lights of the subsequent testament, illuminating the darkness of dense night through the grace of gospel preaching, were distributed more widely in the three-cornered ambit of lands).[40] And a few paragraphs later, Aldhelm uses the same image to describe the Apostle Thomas illuminating not a threefold earth, but the more specific, threefold India: "Didymus … Eoae tripertitas Indiae provincias sereno evangelicae

36 Aldhelm, *De Virginitate*, XVIII, in *Opera*, 247.15–16; and Lapidge and Herren, *Prose Works*, 74.

37 Aldhelm, *De Virginitate*, XLVIII, 302.10–11; and Lapidge and Herren, *Prose Works*, 115.

38 Aldhelm, *De Virginitate*, LX, 323.1–2; and Lapidge and Herren, *Prose Works*, 132.

39 Aldhelm, *De Virginitate*, IX, 237.6–7; and Lapidge and Herren, *Prose Works*, 65. For the pun on *illustro*, see Andy Orchard, "Old Sources, New Resources: Finding the Right Formula for Boniface," 15–38, at 23.

40 Aldhelm, *De Virginitate*, XXII, 253.2–4; and Lapidge and Herren, *Prose Works*, 79.

praedicationis lumine illustravit" (Didymus [i.e., Thomas] illuminated the tripartite provinces of eastern India with the clear light of evangelical preaching).[41] For a cleric living in Britain, the metaphor of Christ's illumination of the world as the illumination of the sun probably had some effect, especially since it was a common feature in descriptions of Britain to note the darkness of the winter months.[42] For this reason, Aldhelm's use of the image of illumination to describe Theodore and Hadrian's presence in England is cleverly employed:[43]

> ast tamen climatis Britannia occidui in extremo ferme orbis margine posita verbi gratia ceu solis flammigeri et luculento lunae specimine potiatur, id est Theodoro ... et eiusdem sodalitatis cliente Hadriano

> Britain, although situated in almost the outer limit of the western world, possesses, for example, the luculent likeness, as it were, of the flaming sun and moon, that is, Theodore and his colleague of the same sodality, Hadrian.

Although Aldhelm's primary purpose in these lines is to highlight the grandeur of Theodore and Hadrian, the "astriferis micantium vibraminibus siderum" (stellar flashings of twinkling stars), in comparison to the teachers of Ireland,[44] his manner of description borrows from rhetoric that is often used to assert the universality of the Church. First, by mentioning Britain's geographical position, Aldhelm is able to confirm the validity of the catholic Church which participates in such a prominent unity that two of the world's best scholars can easily be found at the edges of the world. Second, the image of the sun and moon, which is usually reserved for the preaching of Christ's gospel, intricately connects Theodore and Hadrian with the apostolic tradition, and therefore affirms the quality of their orthodoxy over the heterodoxy of the Irish. Just as Christ's disciples are sent throughout the world to illuminate the nations with the light of the Gospel, such as Thomas in India, for example, so also do Theodore and Hadrian fulfill this role. In a very real sense for Aldhelm,

41 Aldhelm, *De Virginitate*, XXIII, 255.16–8; and Lapidge and Herren, *Prose Works*, 81.

42 For example, Bede, *Ecclesiastical History*, I.1; see also Howe, "An Angle on this Earth," 10–11. For the similar comments of Gildas, see above, 73–4.

43 Aldhelm *Epistula* V, 492.15–493.1; and Lapidge and Herren, *Prose Works*, 163.

44 Aldhelm, *Epistula* V, 492.14–5; and Lapidge and Herren, *Prose Works*, 163.

they participate in the mission of the seventy (or seventy-two) disciples to preach to the nations.[45]

In addition, Aldhelm refers numerous times to the notion that the whole world has been encompassed by the Church. To mention only a few examples, Aldhelm refers to the Church's embrace of a tripartite division of humankind: "Porro tripertitam humani generis distantiam orthodoxae fidei cultricem catholica recipit ecclesia" (the catholic Church accepts a threefold distinction of the human race, which increases orthodox faith);[46] he states that the birth of Jesus "totius mundi statum ... beavit" (made happy the condition of the entire world);[47] that the renown of Anatolia and Victoria are "per totos mundi cardines longiuscule crebrescunt" (spread far and wide through all the corners of the world) on account of the shared liturgy of the Church;[48] and that Peter's doctrine has been made clear "omnibus hic geminum digessit dogma per orbem" (to all peoples throughout the world).[49] Another revealing example can be found in Aldhelm's letter to Geraint, where Aldhelm describes the involvement of heretics and schismatics in the world:[50]

> Domus vero haec secundum allegoriam ecclesia per totos mundi cardines diffusa intellegitur. Heretici namque et scismatici ab ecclesiae societate extranei per contentionum argumenta in mundo pululantes et veluti horrenda zizaniorum semina in medio fecundae segitis sata dominicam messem maculabant

> This house, according to allegory, is understood to be the Church, spread throughout all ... points of the world. For indeed, heretics and schismatics, foreign to the society of the Church, sprouting up in the world and like, so to speak, the dreadful seed of darnels sown in the midst of a fertile crop, defile the harvest of the Lord by their contentious arguments.

45 See Aldhelm, *Epistula ad Acircium*, in *Opera*, 67–8; and Lapidge and Herren, *Prose Works*, 38–9, where Aldhelm ascribes seventy tongues to the disciples at Pentecost.

46 Aldhelm, *De Virginitate*, XIX, 248.9–10; and Lapidge and Herren, *Prose Works*, 75.

47 Aldhelm, *De Virginitate*, XXXIX, 291.13–14; and Lapidge and Herren, *Prose Works*, 106.

48 Aldhelm, *De Virginitate*, LII, 308.7–9; and Lapidge and Herren, *Prose Works*, 119.

49 Aldhelm, *Carmina ecclesiastica*, IV.i.4, in *Opera*, 19; and Lapidge and Rosier, *Aldhelm: The Poetic Works*, 50.

50 Aldhelm, *Epistula* IV, 482.7–11; and Lapidge and Herren, *Prose Works*, 156.

While Aldhelm appeals to the familiar portrayal of the Church being spread "per totos mundi cardines" (through all points of the world) to claim that ecclesiastical unity can be found in the midst of diversity, his parallel account of heretics, who are distinguished as outsiders to the fellowship of the Church ("ab ecclesiae societate extranei"), clearly demarcates notions of centrality and marginality. The Church, though spread across the world, nevertheless remains at the centre, while heretics, only sprouting up in the world ("in mundo pululantes"), are at the periphery.

Throughout Aldhelm's corpus, much is made of the wickedness of heretics, magicians, and pagans. Just as his accounts of the spreading of Christianity through a tripartite world echo patristic interpretations of the division of the world at Babel, so do Aldhelm's accounts of heretics and magicians echo the Tower of Babel narrative. In one instance, Aldhelm refers to Simon Magus as the "magicae artis inventorem" (founder of the magical art),[51] even though, according to various Christian authors of Late Antiquity, either Zoroaster or Nimrod is the "magicae artis inuentor,"[52] "primus magicae artis auctor" (first practitioner of magical art) or "primus magica" (first magician).[53] While Aldhelm surely would have known that Zoroaster or Nimrod, not Simon Magus, was the traditional founder of the magical arts, it is possible, as Rosier notes, that in an attempt to condemn the unorthodox practices of tonsuring, Aldhelm connects Simon Magus to both the magical arts and unorthodox tonsuring – a connection possible for the heretic Simon Magus but not for the pre-Christian Zoroaster or Nimrod.[54] Elsewhere in Aldhelm's works, Zoroaster and Simon Magus are closely related. In the prose *De uirginitate*, Aldhelm couples the two, along with Cyprian, as infamous sorcerers: "Cyprianus ... post Soroastren et Simonem magorum praestantissimus fuisse memoratur" (Cyprian ... is said to have been the most outstanding of sorcerers after Zoroaster and Simon Magus).[55] And there is further, albeit slight,

51 Aldhelm, *Epistula* IV, 482.27; and Lapidge and Herren, *Prose Works*, 157.

52 For example, see Augustine, *De ciuitate Dei*, XXI.xiv18–20; and Isidore, *Etymologiae*, IX.2.43.

53 Pseudo-Clement, *Recognitiones*, IV.27.2–3, 159, and IV.29.1, 160. Aldhelm twice refers to the "decem libri Clementis" (ten books of Clement), which are the *Recognitiones* (*Epistula*, IV, 483.29; and Lapidge and Herren, *Prose Works*, 157).

54 See Lapidge and Herren, *Prose Works*, 200, nt. 12, for a possible source being "Eusebius's statement that 'Simon was the prime author of every heresy'" (Eusebius, *Historia ecclesiastica*, XIII.1).

55 Aldhelm, *De Virginitate*, XLIII, 295.9–10; and Lapidge and Herren, *Prose Works*, 109.

evidence that Aldhelm viewed the sorcery and heresy of Simon Magus in light of the Tower of Babel, or at least in light of themes present in the Tower of Babel narrative. Aldhelm narrates that Simon Magus "praecelsa rudis scandit fastigia turris" (climbed the lofty summits of a new tower) in order to attempt to fly.[56] While the account is based on the apocryphal *Actus Petri cum Simone*, Rosier states that Aldhelm has added "a number of details," notably the tower.[57] Along with the epithet usually reserved for Zoroaster or Nimrod, "magicae artis inventor," the addition of a tower strengthens an allusion, admittedly inconclusively, to the Tower of Babel.

In a second instance, Aldhelm seems to give other Babylonian undertones to his narrative by means of a tower. In the prose *De uirginitate*, a pagan *magister militum* is described as building a tower in order to confine his daughter, Christina, and to force her to offer sacrifices to pagan gods: "Pater ... turrem eidem minaci proceritate in edito porrectam et forti liturae compage constructam erexit" (her father erected for her a tower that stretched aloft with a menacing height and was constructed with a strong framework of cement).[58] While it has been recognized that the immediate source of this line is Gildas,[59] its ultimate source can be traced back to Orosius's own description of the Tower of Babel: "domus ... minaci proceritate mirabiles" (buildings that were amazing with their menacing height).[60] Even if Aldhelm did not recognize the Orosian source when he read it in Gildas, the phrase "minaci proceritate" at the very least recalls the Tower of Babel's own threat to reach heaven. Furthermore, the addition of the word *litura* is original to Aldhelm. Whereas the *Dictionary of Medieval Latin from British Sources*, references this line and later Old English glosses on this line in order to define *litura* as an "(act of)

56 Aldhelm, *Carmina ecclesiastica*, IV.i.28, p. 20; and Lapidge and Rosier, *Poetic Works*, 50.

57 Lapidge and Rosier, *Poetic Works*, 239, nt. 42. For the *Actus Petri cum Simone*, see Lipsius and Bonnet, eds., *Acta apostolorum Apocrypha*, vol. 1, XXXI–XXXII, 81–3. See also O'Leary, "Apostolic *Passiones* in Early Anglo-Saxon England," 103–19, at 107–9. For the use of the *Actus Petri cum Simone* in Anglo-Saxon England, see Heuchan, "All Things to All Men: Representations of the Apostle Paul in Anglo-Saxon Literature," 112–44.

58 Aldhelm, *De Virginitate*, XLVII, 301.3–5; and Lapidge and Herren, *Prose Works*, 113–14.

59 See Winterbottom, "Aldhelm's Prose Style and its Origins," 48, esp. nt. 8; and Herren, ed., *The Hisperica Famina*, xxi. Gildas's text reads: "culmina minaci proceritate porrecta in edito forti compage pangebantur" (columns erected with menacing height were brought into the sky with a strong structure); Gildas, *Ruin of Britain*, 3.2, 90.

60 Orosius, *Historiarum adversum paganos*, II.6.10, 97; Bede, *In principium Genesis*, III.540, also quotes these words of Orosius for his description of Babel.

smearing, daubing" and "what is daubed, mortar, plaster,"[61] these senses seem unsatisfactory within the context. A tower fortified by "what is daubed" or even "mortar" is not much of a marvel. In fact, Winterbottom, evidently also unsatisfied with the meaning "smearing" or "mortar," admits that he does not understand Aldhelm's use of this word, and offers a suggestion of John Grady which connects *litura* with *λίθος*, stone, or stonework.[62] If Winterbottom is correct with respect to Grady's suggestion, this meaning would not only heighten the putative strength of the tower, but also allow for a fortuitous lexical parallel to the Septuagint's account of the Tower of Babel (Genesis 11:13), in which the builders make bricks for their stonework ("ἐγένετο αὐτοῖς ἡ πλὶνθος εἰς λίθον"). Along with reference already made to a Babylonian *minaci proceritate*, it is not much of stretch to think that Aldhelm included the word *litura* with its semantic implication of stonework in order to strengthen an allusion to the Tower of Babel.

However, *litura* as "mortar" does make sense if Aldhelm had the Tower of Babel in mind when he included the word to his source material. For the word *litura* has Babylonian overtones in the Septuagint version of Micah 7:10–11, which reads, "ἡμέρας ἀλοιφῆς πλίνθου" (on the day of moulding brick), and is literally translated into Latin as "dies liturae lateris."[63] In this case, the words, *ἀλοιφή*, and *litura*, both mean "smearing" or perhaps in the context, "tempering" or "pugging" the clay of the brick.[64] According to Jerome, this line is referring to the Babylonians who will be crushed "in morem lateris" (in the manner of a brick).[65] Since Aldhelm was familiar with Jerome's commentary on the Minor Prophets,[66] he would likely also have read Jerome's Babylonian interpretation of *dies liturae lateris*, and it is, therefore, possible that Aldhelm's description of the pagan tower in the prose *De uirginitate* reflects Micah's and Jerome's Babylonian

61 *Dictionary of Medieval Latin from British Sources*, *s.v.* "litura," fasc. V.I–J–K–L, 1627. For the Old English glosses, see the *Dictionary of Old English*, *s.v.* "clām."

62 Winterbottom, "Aldhelm's Prose Style and its Origins," 48, nt. 8. See also Lewis and Short, *A Latin Dictionary*, *s.v.* "litura," 1072.

63 Although this Latin translation is not found in the Vulgate, it does appear in Jerome's commentary on the Minor Prophets; Jerome, *In Michaeam*, ed. Adriaen, *Commentarii in prophetas*, II.vii.414.

64 See *Oxford English Dictionary*, *s.v.* "pug, *v.*2," III.4.a.

65 Jerome, *In Michaeam*, II.vii.414.

66 Aldhelm quotes the work in *De Virginitate*, XXXI, 269.22–3; and Lapidge and Herren, *Prose Works*, 90. See also Lapidge, *The Anglo-Saxon Library*, 181 and 314.

litura. Winterbottom is rightly confused over Aldhelm's use of *litura*, especially in this context. But considering its possible reference to Babel and Babylon, it is possible that Aldhelm felt free to use it, as a somewhat exotic word, to add flourish to Gildas's line, and latently allude further to the more infamous Tower. Within the context, a tower fortified with a Babylonian material or method not only makes sense, but it heightens the perceived wickedness of the tower by associating it with Babel.

Furthermore, besides its threatening height and this potential allusion to Babylonian building material, Aldhelm's account contains other parallels to the Tower of Babel. It is associated with idolatry, which, as Aldhelm would have known from his sources, began with Nimrod and the fall of the Tower of Babel. And as if to underline the allusion to Babel further, Aldhelm makes reference to the Babylonian tyrant, Nebuchadnezzar, later in the text: "Chaldaici regnatoris machinas" (ovens of the Chaldaean [i.e., Babylonian] tyrant).[67] Although this last reference is borrowed, perhaps from memory, from Sidonius Apollinaris,[68] it functions to vilify the pagan *magister militum* by comparing his deeds with the cruelty of the Babylonian Empire. Moreover, the *magister militum* is said to have instructed his daughter in "liberalibus sofismatum disciplinis" (liberal disciplines of learning);[69] because astrology was part of a liberal education, there may be a slight allusion to Nimrod here, who was thought to be one of the first astrologers and, according to later authors, the founder of the seven liberal arts, but this point should not be stressed.[70]

Just as Aldhelm's account of the death of Simon Magus from a "rudis turrim" has an underlying allusion to the Tower of Babel, so does the account of the tower of the pagan *magister militum*. Although there are no concrete parallels in either account, it is probably no coincidence that Aldhelm's description of each tower has Babylonian features. The negative characteristics of tyranny, idolatry, and soothsaying may have brought the Tower of Babel narrative to Aldhelm's mind, who in turn introduced

67 Aldhelm, *De Virginitate*, XXXI, 301.16; and Lapidge and Herren, *Prose Works*, 114. Aldhelm also refers to the *Chaldaicus regnator* in *De Virginitate*, XXI, 252.12; and Lapidge and Herren, *Prose Works*, 78.

68 Sidonius Apollinaris, *Epistulae et carmina*, XVI.23: "in Chaldaei positos fornace tyranni" (placed in the furnace of the Chaldean tyrant).

69 Aldhelm, *De Virginitate*, XLVII, p. 301.4; and Lapidge and Herren, *Prose Works*, 114.

70 Livesey and Rouse, "Nimrod the Astronomer," 235–6, cite Hugo of St Victor as associating Nimrod with the seven liberal arts.

his own descriptions of towers within his narrative to heighten the nefarious actions of his villains.

The admittedly scant treatments of the Tower of Babel narrative in the Latin works of early Anglo-Saxon England largely conform to the intellectual tradition that these English authors inherited from both Greek and Latin literature of Late Antiquity. But, far from simply parroting the opinions of earlier authors, Anglo-Saxon authors also reveal a certain degree of variation and originality when treating the narrative, at least so far as the limit evidence suggests. Because it provided a basis for understanding the ethnic and linguistic diversity of the world, Genesis 10–11 must have resonated with those who saw themselves living on the very edges of the world. But along with an understanding of the roots of diversity, early Anglo-Saxon authors also saw the great potential of the narrative for other uses. The Church had the power to transcend the diversity created at Babel, and just as the sun illuminates the earth without discrimination of ethnic or linguistic differences, so does the Church find itself in the corners of Britain, one of the most diverse, ethnically and linguistically, areas of Europe.

Along with the notion that the Church transcends Babel's diversity comes the need to re-interpret Babel in order to re-enforce this new identity that was no longer based, in theory, on ethnicity. The negative features of Babel were emphasized and in turn reapplied to the Church's enemies. Aldhelm's unique association of Simon Magus and the pagan *magister militum* with Babylonian elements such as towers or magic and astrology are likely no coincidence. Though allusions to the Babel narrative are relatively scarce in the works coming from the Canterbury School and Aldhelm (there is only one direct allusion), they are given full treatment in the early Anglo-Saxon England's great Northumbrian luminary, the Venerable Bede.

Chapter Four

Bede and Alcuin

Bede

Never a student of the famous Canterbury School, Bede was nevertheless one of the great scholars of early Anglo-Saxon England, and in fact eighth-century Europe. His learning and reading is immense,[1] his Latin style worthy of its praise,[2] and his influence extensive.[3] It should therefore come as no surprise that Bede was well aware of the writings of previous Christian authors on the subject of the Tower of Babel, which he addresses directly in a number of his biblical commentaries. But despite being heavily influenced by authoritative authors of the past, Bede develops nuanced interpretations of the narrative. His exegetical and homiletic treatments of Babel, which are situated in a typical Augustinian framework, provide the most explicit evidence of Bede's adoption and adaption of the narrative. Naturally, the theology that informs Bede's reading and presentation of Genesis 10–11 prevails throughout his corpus, often employing, reflecting, alluding to, and verbally echoing his comments on the Tower of Babel. The result is a corpus of intricate theological expression that keeps the prevalent aspects of the interpretation of Babel at hand, bringing the narrative into the foreground when the discussion explicitly deals with the subject,

1 Meyvaert, "Bede the Scholar," 40–69; Love, "The Library of the Venerable Bede," 606–32; and Lapidge, *The Anglo-Saxon Library*, 191–228.

2 Grocock, "Bede and the Golden Age of Latin Prose in Northumbria," 371–81; Wetherbee, "Some Implications of Bede's Latin Style," 23–31; Sharpe, "The Varieties of Bede's Prose," 339–55; Shanzer, "Bede's Style," 329–52; and Major, "Words, Wit, and Wordplay in the Latin Works of the Venerable Bede," 185–216.

3 Hill, *Bede and the Benedictine Reform*; Cross, "Bede's Influence at Home and Abroad," 17–29; Willmes, "Bedas Bibelauslegung," 281–314, at 306–14; and Whitelock, *After Bede*.

but also hovering just below the surface among broader issues, such as ethnic and linguistic identity. Bede's training and vocation in the Northumbrian monastery of Wearmouth-Jarrow, where ruminating on biblical and patristic texts was a daily phenomenon, partially explain the pervasiveness of Babel across his writings. But they also create a challenge for discerning instances of concrete allusion. Bede has a number of explicit remarks on Babel, but he also offers some instances where the themes of Genesis 10–11 overlap with, and are reflected in, his wider discussions. Whereas Bede's most concrete remarks on the Tower of Babel can be found in his biblical commentaries and homilies, some of his more subtle allusions appear in the context of ethnic and linguistic diversity presented in his well-known historical work, the *Ecclesiastical History of the English People*, which seems to have been informed by the interpretations of the Babel and Pentecost narratives he articulates elsewhere.

The Contrast between Jerusalem and Babel

The most prevalent and frequent use of the Babel narrative in Bede's corpus is the contrast between the wickedness of Babel / Babylon and the righteousness of Jerusalem, figuratively interpreted as the body of the Church. This contrast, which derives chiefly from Augustine, has the advantage of being rooted in the received historical narrative (the ancient enmity of Israel and Babylon) as well as of informing present ideology and morality. Such a straightforward dichotomy as Babel and Jerusalem, which can so easily be distilled into the struggle between good and evil, certainly appealed to Bede's concern with finding meaning in history. In addition, Christians of Late Antiquity, as previously discussed, tended to embrace all ethnic, linguistic, and geographical identities, at least in theory, by placing emphasis on similarities of faith, doctrine, and morality over differences in culture, language, and location. Any dissimilarity of faith, doctrine, or morality was not only rejected and marginalized, but once marginalized, also demonized, ironically in terms reminiscent of demonized cultures, languages, and locations. For Bede, as for late antique Christians, the contrast between the Tower of Babel and the Church provides a suitable focal point for this tension of acceptance and rejection.

In his exposition on Acts (first version 703 × 709; second version 708 × 716),[4] which is one of his earliest, and perhaps first, written commentaries

4 See Brown, *A Companion to Bede*, 14 and 63–4.

on Babel and the Church, Bede already reveals his deviation from standard interpretation by displaying a more nuanced understanding of a historical narrative guided according to God's providence:[5]

> Vnitatem linguarum quam superbia Babylonis disperserat humilitas ecclesiae recolligit, spiritaliter autem uarietas linguarum dona uariarum significat gratiarum. Verum non incongrue spiritus sanctus intellegitur ideo primum linguarum donum dedisse hominibus, quibus humana sapientia forinsecus et discitur et docetur, ut ostenderet quam facile possit sapientes facere per sapientiam dei quae eis interna est.

> The humility of the Church brings together the unity of languages that the pride of Babylon had dispersed; but in spiritual terms, the variety of languages signifies the gifts of various divine acts. And not inconsistently, the Holy Spirit is understood to have given the first gift of languages to humans – through which human wisdom is learned and taught externally – such that the Spirit showed how easily it could make men wise through the wisdom of God which is internal in them.

By contrasting the positive virtues of the Church in Acts 2:4 with the negative characteristics of Babel, Bede calls attention to the paradoxical image of the disparity of languages and the unity of the Church at Pentecost; the *humilitas ecclesiae*, in Augustinian fashion, stands completely opposed to the *superbia Babylonis*.[6] But Bede goes further than Augustine by interpreting linguistic differences as gifts of various *gratiae* given to humans by the Holy Spirit at the Tower of Babel. The implications of this passage, which Lawrence Martin regards as "Bede's theology of language,"[7] are deceptively profound and original. Because the plural form, *linguarum*, in the phrase "primum linguarum donum" can only refer to the division of languages at the Tower of Babel, Bede must mean that the Holy Spirit acted at both Pentecost and Babel. The Holy Spirit's later descent which brings together, and yet still retains, the diversity of languages becomes the

---

5 Bede, *Expositio Actuum Apostolorum*, II.4.55–61.

6 For helpful analyses of Bede's treatment of Pentecost in light of Babel, see Dekker, "Pentecost and Linguistic Self-Consciousness in Anglo-Saxon England," 345–72, at 350–6; Stanton, *Culture of Translation*, 70–2; and "Linguistic Fragmentation and Redemption before Kind Alfred," 19–22.

7 Martin, "Bede as a Linguistic Scholar," 204–17, at 217. See also Tugene, *L'idée de nation*, 315–16.

concluding element of an act initiated during the Spirit's earlier descent where the *donum* of linguistic diversity was first granted. And just as the Holy Spirit was sent down at Pentecost to unite the languages of the world, so too it was sent down at the Tower of Babel to divide them. Despite the comments on Babel's *superbia*, the passage offers a fairly positive reading of history, forcing a retrospective interpretation of the Tower of Babel narrative that removes, at least partly, its usual characterizations of an immoral event. The Holy Spirit, according to Bede, has from the beginning been working in both linguistic diversity and unity by means of that very diversity. In this providential comprehension of history, the division caused by the wickedness of Babel can only be understood properly in hindsight as the initial impetus in bringing forth the unity of the multilingual Church at Pentecost. The linguistic fragmentation of the Tower of Babel, therefore, loses its negative connotations, and is re-appropriated as an essential moment in salvation history.

Similar theological understanding of the Babel narrative is also characteristic of two slightly later texts, Bede's commentaries on Luke and Mark (709 × 716). In a passage repeated verbatim in both commentaries, Bede follows Augustine by using Babel / Babylon and Jerusalem to make moral contrasts. But in this case, just as with the preceding commentary on Acts, Bede expands the contrast to include the redemption of linguistic diversity by the Holy Spirit. Although the negative connotations of Babel remain, the original "confusion" of linguistic diversity is broadened to general moral confusion:[8]

> *multitudinis credentium erat cor et anima una.* Vnde bene in Babilonis constructione linguarum unitas per spiritum superbiae scissa, in Hierosolima est per gratiam sancti spiritus linguarum uarietas adunata. Et illa confusio, haec uisio pacis interpretatur quia uidelicet electos in pluribus linguis et gentibus una fides ac pietas toto orbe pacificando confirmat; reprobos autem plures sectae quam linguae dissociando confundunt.

> *There was one heart and spirit of the believers in the multitude.* Truly, just as at the building of Babel where the unity of languages was torn apart by a spirit of pride, at Jerusalem the diversity of languages is united by the grace

8 Bede, *In Lucae euangelium expositio*, III.8.754–9; and *In Marci euangelium expositio*, II.5.164; I have here altered the punctuation and capitalization of the Latin.

> of the Holy Spirit. That city is interpreted as "confusion," this one as "vision of peace," namely because the one faith and devotion affirm the elect, who are in a multiplicity of languages and nations, by the pacification of the entire world; but there are more sects than languages which confuse the reprobate in their factions.

Much like the commentary on Acts, this passage underlines the standard notion that linguistic diversity was created by *superbia*, and that ecclesiastical unity is brought about solely through the *gratia* of the Holy Spirit (interestingly, the notion of *humilitas* has here been removed). But again, because Pentecost has redeemed Babel by appropriating the linguistic diversity of the world to a unified Church that transcends this diversity, the "confusion" of Babel must be reinterpreted and understood in a new light. Following a cue from Augustine, Bede interprets Babylonian confusion not as linguistic confusion, but as the confusion of heretics (*sectae*).[9] Understandably, the "confusion" of Babel / Babylon must retain a morally negative aspect in Bede's exegesis, but the linguistic "confusion" that is so fundamental to the original story is stripped of its previous connotations, once redeemed by the Holy Spirit. For this reason, the "confusion" is transferred to a non-linguistic feature, and in this case, to those who fall outside of the unity of the Church. Bede is then not only able to preserve a theology that interprets the linguistic diversity of the world as a positive gift brought about by the *gratia* of the Holy Spirit, but he can also argue that heretics, who disrupt the unity of the Church, are really what the Babel narrative is all about. Babel means confusion not because of its linguistic diversity, but because of later ecclesiastical diversity.

Bede also deals with this problem of having to reinterpret the narrative to remove negative connotations of linguistic diversity through a second, though closely related, strategy. Much like his interpretation of Babel's "confusion" as the Church's heretics, Bede elsewhere attempts to generalize the moral implications of the narrative into a universal typology of evil. For instance, in his homily, *In uigilia natiuitatis S. Iohannis baptistae*, Bede contrasts Jerusalem and Babel / Babylon in a manner that emphasizes their figurative and moral elements. Again the negative linguistic "confusion" of Babel is absent, in favour of an emphasis on the historical connection to the Babylon of Nebuchadnezzar, which is then easily

9 Incidentally, Bede, *Ecclesiastical History*, I.8, is also concerned with heresies spreading to Britain.

reapplied to sinners everywhere. Similarly, Jerusalem is removed from its specific historical Jewish context and applied to the Church of Christ:[10]

> intellegere didicerit Hierusalem et templum Dei ecclesiam Christi, Babilonem confusionem peccatorum, Nabuchodonosor diabolum, Iesum sacerdotem, magnum uerum aeternumque pontificem esse Iesum Christum.

> we have learned to understand Jerusalem as the Temple of God, the Church of Christ; and Babylon as the confusion of sinners / sins, Nebuchadnezzar the Devil; and the priest as Jesus, the great, true, eternal pontiff Jesus Christ.

Bede's attempt to universalize Babylon and Jerusalem as typologies removes, by necessity, almost any connection to historical context. As with Augustine, Jerusalem is the Church and Babylon is its antithesis. But in this account, Bede so succinctly epitomizes Augustine's theology of the two cities that all narrative or historical detail becomes irrelevant before their roles as typologies. The confusion of Babel is nothing less than the confusion of "peccatorum," which itself is verbally ambiguous, since the phrase can be understood as the confusion of sinners (*peccatorum*, genitive plural of *peccator*), or more generally, as the confusion of sins (*peccatorum*, genitive plural of *peccatum*). Similarly, the historical character of Nebuchadnezzar is blandly and without further comment assigned to a typology of the Devil, just as the Temple priest is assigned to Jesus Christ. Of course, the laconic nature of this passage is suitable for its homiletic context, which does a good job outlining Bede's fundamental understanding of the Babel narrative. Babel and Jerusalem are simply figurative representatives of good and evil: those who are good are identified within the realm of Christianity, while those who are evil are outside of its boundaries.

Bede's commentary on the first half of Genesis, his most extensive treatment of the Babel narrative, is comparable at its core to his previous comments on the subject, despite its numerous additions and expansions.[11] In this work, Bede begins his exegesis of Genesis 10–11 by following Jerome and Josephus across numerous pages outlining the ethnic identities that are listed in the Table of Nations. Unlike his figurative interpretations of

10 Bede, *Homiliae*, I.14.202–5. Bede's homilies have not been dated with any certainty.

11 For the complexity of dating this text, see Kendall, *Bede*, 45–53, who dates books III–IV, which contain Bede's comments on Babel, to *c.* 722 × 725.

the Tower of Babel in this commentary and elsewhere, Bede's interpretation of the Table of Nations remains surprisingly literal. It updates the biblical names by reassigning them to contemporary nations (or at least those nations contemporary for Josephus and Jerome), and only occasionally condemns wickedness or praises righteousness through a nation's putative allegorical meaning;[12] in general, most of the names in the Table of Nations are left as nations. Otherwise, Bede seems to be content with presenting only a few figurative elements from Genesis 10: Babel signifies worldly pride and confusion, and Nimrod the Devil;[13] the descendants of Joktan dwelling on the mount of Mesha signify divine ascension through striving for saintly humility;[14] Japheth's descendants signify the gentile Church enduring persecutions;[15] Ham's signify the reprobate who cannot transcend worldly care;[16] and the seventy-two nations correspond to the seventy-two disciples of Christ who, by their preaching, will gather the nations together in "a single, undivided confession and faith."[17] Interestingly, Bede does not feel the need to include any new information about the English people, or any of the Germanic tribes that come to inhabit Britain, even though he does ascribe origins to the Spanish and the Italians.[18] In fact, the only hint he makes to an English connection to Japheth is derived from Jerome's suggestion that those of Japheth's lineage living in the "islands of the nations" (insulae gentium, Genesis 10:5) include those living on the islands in the "British Ocean" (oceanum … Britannicum).[19] However, this literal information on the British islands does anticipate Bede's later allegorical exposition of Japheth's islands as the gentile Church enduring the waves of persecution.[20] Despite their separation in the commentary, it is not difficult to see how these two passages might suggest that Britain's literal geographical situation is mysteriously

---

12 For example, Bede interprets the old enemy (*antiquus hostis*) as arising from the dark people (*obscurus populus*) of Ethiopia, *In principium Genesis*, III.151–2.

13 Bede, *In principium Genesis*, III.130–47.

14 Ibid., 302–10.

15 Ibid., 310–18.

16 Ibid., 318–25.

17 Ibid., 349–56 and 374: "una et non dispari confessione ac fide."

18 Ibid., III.21, 23.

19 Ibid., 54; Jerome, *Hebraicae quaestiones in libro Geneseos*, 10.4.15, 12. Bede, *In principium Genesis*, III.312–13, also claims that this line indicates "per orbem ecclesias" (churches throughout the world).

20 Bede, *In principium Genesis*, III.310–18.

connected to its role as a stalwart supporter of the catholic Church in the face of oppression.

After his interpretation of Genesis 10, Bede intersperses his literal understanding of the Babel narrative with allegorical interpretations similar to those he expresses elsewhere. As is to be expected, Bede's emphasis is primarily Augustinian: the literal and figurative actions at Babel signify worldly pride and evil that is contrasted with the humility and righteousness of Jerusalem. Moreover, Bede understands the linguistic diversity created at Babel in light of the linguistic harmony created at Pentecost, an understanding that he articulates no fewer than four times in his commentary on Genesis 11:1–9. Significantly, the first example begins with Pentecost as an example of the kind of peacefulness that existed before Babel:[21]

> Quanta autem hominum esse felicitas posset etiam paradiso deiectorum, si uel tunc creatori suo seruire humiliter uellent, testatur gratia eiusdem Domini conditoris ac redemptoris nostri, qui discipulis sibi fideliter adherentibus misso super Spiritu omnium notitiam tribuit linguarum.

> The degree of happiness that could have existed for humans, even though cast out of paradise, or if only they then desired to serve their creator with humility, is seen in the grace of that same Lord, our maker and redeemer, who gave knowledge of all languages to the disciples faithfully following him, when the Spirit was sent down.

Although this passage comes close to suggesting that the division of languages is, at least practically speaking, responsible for the loss of peace after Babel, Bede does ensure that blame is placed on the lack of obedience and humility of those who decided not to serve God. Furthermore, Bede's decision to use Pentecost as an example of peacefulness before the events at Babel ensures a focus on the future linguistic unity at Pentecost. Babel in effect becomes a necessary part of providential history that will enable the much more important events of Pentecost.

As with this example, in the following sections of his commentary on Genesis 11:1–9, Bede's earlier comment on the "gift of languages" granted by the Spirit at Babel is absent, even though he does remain relatively true to his previous understanding of the event by continuing to place the

21 Bede, *In principium Genesis*, III.365–9 (I occasionally alter the punctuation of this edition).

emphasis on the linguistic harmony of Pentecost. Not only does Bede carefully avoid directly casting the division of language in a negative light, but he always seems to understand the division at Babel as a necessary first counterpart to the linguistic unity at Pentecost. In terms reminiscent of his commentaries on Luke and Mark that use the demonstratives *haec* and *illa* to juxtapose the two cities, Bede provides another comparison of Babel and Jerusalem in his exposition of the chapter:[22]

> Meritoque haec ciuitas, in qua linguae diuisae ac gentes sunt dispersae, Babylon, id est "confusio"; illa dicitur Hierusalem, id est "uisio pacis," in qua, adunatis in Dei laudem loquelis uniuersarum gentium, est facta concordia.

> For good reason, this is the city Babylon, in which languages were divided and nations dispersed, which means "confusion"; that city is called Jerusalem, which means "vision of peace," in which occurred a unity of spirit when the languages of all the nations came together in the praise of God.

A third very similar interpretation of the Babel narrative is then repeated and expanded at the beginning of Bede's commentary on Genesis 11:8–9:[23]

> Merito confusum est labium in dispersionem, quia male coniurauerat in locutionem nefariam; ablata est potestas linguae superbis principibus, ne in contemptum Dei subditos possent quae coeperant mala docere. Sicque iudicium diuinae seueritatis in adiutorium humanae uersum est utilitatis, ut tacendo cessarent ab opere, cui peruerse loquendo congregati insistebant. Ac sic descendente ac uidente Domino ciuitatem elationis, Babylonem, hoc est "confusionem," appellari contigit. Cui contrarium satis ciuitas ueritatis sicut nomen ita habet et statum; dicitur enim Hierusalem, id est "uisio pacis," in qua coetum fidelium atque humilium spiritu Dominus uidens, misit gratiam Spiritus sancti, qui eis scientiam omnium tribueret linguarum, quibus imbuti omnes qui in diuersis erant linguis populos ad constructionem eiusdem sanctae ciuitatis, id est ecclesiae Christi, unanimam conuocarent.

---

22 Bede, *In principium Genesis*, III.375–9. It should be noted that Bede speaks about the literal division of languages without mention of Pentecost in his comments on Genesis 10:25; *In principium Genesis*, III.254–9.

23 Bede, *In principium Genesis*, III.486–501.

For good reason, language was confused in the dispersal of nations because it wickedly conspired in evil speech; the power of language was removed from those proud rulers lest they would be able to teach their subjects the evil things they had begun in contempt of God. And the judgement of divine severity was turned into a help of human benefit such that by becoming silent they ceased from that work which by speaking perversely they had taken up as a group. But with the Lord thus descending and seeing that city of pride, it happened that it was called Babylon, which means "confusion." The city of truth is contrary to this city of pride in both name and condition; for it is called Jerusalem, which means "vision of peace," in which the Lord saw the assembly of the faithful and humble in spirit and sent the grace of the Holy Spirit who granted knowledge of all languages to them. With knowledge of these languages, they called all the people who spoke diverse languages to the spiritually unified construction of that same holy city, which is the Church of Christ.

Last, the fourth and again very similar instance occurs in a sustained, almost homiletic, subsection of the commentary on Genesis 11:8–9, where the two narratives are treated allegorically, with special reference to their etymologies:[24]

Quod bene utriusque illius ciuitatis figura significauit, cum, diuisis in Babylonia linguis, nemo uocem proximi sui posset agnoscere. Porro in Hierusalem sociatis etiam exterorum omnium qui aduenerant uocem intellegerent per gratiam Spiritus sancti, fideles et in una omnes compage caritatis ac fidei eundem Deum ac dominum conlaudarent.

The figurative element of each of these cities signifies this well, since no one could understand the language of his own neighbour after the languages at Babel were divided. Later on, in Jerusalem, through the grace of the Holy Spirit, they understood even the language of the community of all the foreigners who had come there, and all the faithful praised that same God and Lord together in a single pact of love and faith.

---

24 Bede, *In principium Genesis*, III.565–71; Jones entitles this subsection *Interpretatio spiritualis*, treating it as removed from the earlier commentary. But such editorial intervention is of limited usefulness and can be misleading.

In all of these examples, Bede's principal method of understanding the origins of multilingualism at Babel is through the later events in Jerusalem at Pentecost.[25] Language differences, according to Bede, may have originated with an evil act of pride, but they are redeemed with the linguistic universality that initiates the foundation of the Church, and for that reason, linguistic confusion at Babel really cannot be understood properly without its New Testament counterpart. On the contrary, although the differences from his earlier commentaries and homily are not striking, Bede's commentary on Genesis may present a development in his exegesis on the issue of the world's multilingualism. By directly engaging with the text of Genesis, Bede cannot avoid the negative associations that the original text places on linguistic "confusion." But because of the multilingual nature of the Church, including the English Church, Bede's interpretations of Babel downplay any negative connotations that Genesis may present. The world's multilingualism thus remains a positive aspect regardless of its origins in evil. And much like his earlier commentaries, once the focus moves away from the "confusion" of a multiplicity of languages, Bede finds new groups to condemn in an attempt to reinterpret what exactly the etymology of Babel really means.

Most tellingly, in his sustained allegorical interpretation of the Tower of Babel, Bede presents a tour de force of his hermeneutical attempts to contemporize the meaning of Babel by associating it with heretics, pagans, Jews, and the generally wicked.[26] Bede begins this section with a reminder that Babel is "the city of the Devil," before associating it with "the whole reprobate crowd of humans,"[27] who are then described with the rhetorical flair of a *tricolon abundans* that defines the target of Bede's condemnation:[28]

> qui sunt nisi magistri errorum, qui uel contrarium ueritati cultum diuinitatis introducunt uel agnitam fidem ueritatis malis actibus siue uerbis impugnant.

> those who are nothing except teachers of errors, who either introduce worship contrary to the truth of the divine, or fight the acknowledged faith of truth with evil actions or words.

---

25 For further examples of this contrast, see Major, "Words, Wit, and Wordplay," 216–18.

26 See Scheil, *Babylon under Western Eyes*, 84.

27 Bede, *In principium Genesis*, III.542–4: "Babylon est diaboli ciuitas, hoc est reproba hominum multitudo uniuersa."

28 Ibid., III.544–6.

Once his target has been defined, Bede uses a number of features from the Babel narrative to contrast the wickedness of the reprobate to the righteousness of the Church. The many wicked lords of the pagans are contrasted to the one Lord; Babel's muddy, black, baked bricks of carnal desire and heresies to Jerusalem's strong, white, tempered stones of righteousness; and the unanimous rebelling of Jews and heretics to the defeat of falsehood by catholic preaching. In order to make such comparisons, which can then become more applicable to his contemporary audiences, Bede displaces the narrative from its concrete historical setting to such an extent that he claims every instance of wickedness to be a sinner's own individual Tower of Babel: "faciunt sibi ciuitatem omnes reprobi ... Aedificant ciuitatem Babyloniam cum opera confusione digna faciunt" (all the reprobate make a city for themselves ... they build a city of Babel when they do works that are worthy of "confusion").[29] All literal meaning in the Babel narrative is left behind as Bede expounds a figurative interpretation that establishes a framework for understanding Christian identity in the basic terms of good and evil. This framework becomes reliant not so much on the specific makeup of Christian or non-Christian identity, but rather on the contrast between the two. After stating that every reprobate – presumably including those making up his audience – builds his own Tower of Babel whenever he sins, Bede can then define these reprobates broadly as enemies to the faith of God:[30]

> Quod gentiles faciunt multos deos colendo, haeretici fidem unius Dei erroribus polluendo, Iudei filium Dei Christum negando, falsi catholici fidem malis operibus siue schismatibus rectam profanado
>
> The pagans do this by worshipping many gods, the heretics by defiling the faith of the one God with errors, the Jews by denying Christ the son of God, the false catholics by profaning correct faith with evil or schismatic actions.

The contrast continues even to the last sentence of his commentary on Babel, where the lack of unity among the wicked is placed alongside the unity of the Church: "Constat enim quia quanto nequam doctores siue operarii mali ab inuicem dissidente animo secernuntur, tanto magis ecclesiae colligendae spatium tribuunt" (for it is evident that the more that

29 Bede, *In principium Genesis*, III.670–4.
30 Ibid., 678–81.

wicked teachers or workers of evil separate from themselves with dissident minds, the much more they grant space for the Church to come together).[31] As with Bede's earlier condemnation of the confusion of heretics that forms the figurative foundation of the Babel narrative in his commentaries on Luke and Mark, here also it is the Church alone that has unity, whereas those outside of the Church have only disorder and confusion. Babel's confusion extends far beyond mere differences in language; instead, anything or anyone who does not conform to the faith and morality of the unified Church, from pagans to even "false catholics," contributes to the building of that Tower of the city of the Devil.

This sustained allegorical presentation of the Babel narrative is in many ways Bede's most idiosyncratic. Nevertheless, he does not stray far from either a general Augustinian framework or his own comments elsewhere. He continues to appropriate the Babel narrative in order to expound upon a Christian identity that is based on conformity and dissent. Because the literal meaning, strictly speaking, has nothing to do with the Church, the challenge for the Christian exegete is to provide meaning pertinent to immediate or future biblical readers. Bede is concerned with finding meaning in the Babel narrative as a dichotomy between good and evil, between the wicked (widely defined) and the righteous of the Church. The literal implications of ethnic and linguistic diversity that stem from the Tower of Babel deal only with this dichotomy when they are able to highlight ecclesiastical unity. And because ethnic and linguistic diversity across the world is a prominent feature of a Church aiming to spread across the world, Bede tends to look upon the literal division of languages and ethnic groups favourably. Once the literal consequences of Babel are understood as an essential element of later salvation history, the interpretation of the narrative can transcend to distinguish the true faith of the Church from the false beliefs of its enemies.

Ecclesiastical Unity in a Diverse World

As the preceding discussion reveals, ecclesiastical unity is one of Bede's primary concerns. To grossly simplify, he sees the unity of the Church as a sign validating the veracity of the Church, and lack of unity in the Church as an indicator of theological or moral sickness. Unsurprisingly,

31 Bede, *In principium Genesis*, III.706–9.

throughout his corpus, Bede's theology of ecclesiastical unity is a common feature. His explicit comments on the Tower of Babel provide copious evidence of a world view that places chaos, disorder, and confusion outside of the Church and unity and order within. But alongside these explicit remarks, various allusions and verbal echoes reveal how profound was the influence of the Babel narrative on Bede's thought. Intense training in monastic reading seems to have facilitated the formation of vast mental webs of scriptural language and terminology that seem to refer simultaneously to a whole host of biblical and patristic references, practically impossible to sort out with any certainty. For this reason, the interconnectivity of Bede's theological expression makes it a difficult task to exhibit positive evidence for any kind of indirect influence that the Babel narrative had on him. But by closely examining some of Bede's remarks on ecclesiastical unity and on the etymology of the name Japheth, it will become clear that at least in this instance Bede's monastic language employs Genesis 10–11 to address general theological concerns.

In his commentary on Acts, Bede claims that the description of the Holy Spirit's "tongues as fire" (Acts 2:3) indicates "quia sancta ecclesia per mundi terminos dilatata omnium gentium erat uoce locutura" (that the Holy Church spread to the ends of the world was about to speak with one voice of all nations).[32] It is no surprise that Bede's exposition on Pentecost will include a description of the beginnings of the Church spread across the world. Moreover, this phrase, *ecclesia dilatata* and the variant *diffusa* are commonplace in Bede's works, as well as the intellectual tradition that he inherited,[33] to describe the ultimate outcome of the Pentecostal mission. For example, in his commentary on Ezra and Nehemiah, in all probability written closer to the end of his career, Bede uses the participle *dilatata* alongside the synonymous *diffusa* to describe the Church's expansion: "hoc non pauci sed omnis terra facere per quam ecclesia sancta dilatata est ... hoc non paucis auditoribus sed omnibus populis quibus ecclesia constat toto orbe diffusa" (not only a few, but the entire earth makes this through which the Church is spread ... this was heard not by a few listeners but by all the people for whom the Church is spread across

32 Bede, *Expositio Actuum Apostolorum*, II.3.49–51.

33 For only one example, according to searches performed through the Brepolis databases, http://www.brepolis.net (6 January 2017), the search term "ecclesi*+toto+orbe+diffus*" gives 108 hits in the works of Augustine.

the entire world).[34] Likewise, in his *Retractatio in Actus Apostolorum*, Bede writes: "Vbi Latine dicitur *per totam* in Graeco habet καθ' ὅλης, unde notandum quod ex eo catholica cognominatur ecclesia, quod per totum orbem diffusa in una pace uersetur" (where the words *per totam* are used in Latin, in Greek they are *καθ' ὅλης*, from which it should be noted that the catholic Church is named by these words, which is spread across the entire world and moves about in one peace).[35] The addition of the etymology of the word *catholica*, which Bede might have read in Augustine, Isidore, or simply inferred from his own study of Greek,[36] reinforces the view of a diverse but united Church not only conceptually but also by means of verbal similarities provided by etymology: the word *catholica*, literally rendered into Latin as "per totam" (across all) reveals the meaning of a Church "*per totum* orbem diffusa" (spread *across the entire* world, emphasis mine). In his commentary on the Seven Catholic Epistles, which was written closer to the beginning of Bede's career, probably just before or at the same time as his first commentary on Acts,[37] Bede similarly writes: "una ecclesia catholica toto orbe diffusa saepe pluraliter appellantur ecclesiae propter multifaria scilicet fidelium conuenticula uariis tribubus linguis et populis discreta" (although there is one catholic Church spread across the entire world, churches are often referred to in the plural because of the various assemblies – namely of the faithful – that are distinguished by various tribes, languages and peoples).[38] Not only does this line borrow from Revelation 7:9,[39] as does the *Passio beati Anastasii* and Bede's revision of it, but in Gregorian fashion it propagates a theology of localized multiplicity that reinforces, and paradoxically is mutually reinforced by, the Church's universal uniformity. For one final example, Bede's

34 Bede, *In Ezram et Neemiam*, I.673–7. See also Bede, *In Lucae euangelium expositio*, IV.15.2475: "per orbem terrarum ecclesia dilatata atque diffusa" (the Church is spread out and extended throughout all the earth), which is borrowed from Augustine, *Quaestiones euangeliorum*, II.33.103–4. For the date of *In Ezram et Neemiam*, see DeGregorio, "Bede's *In Ezram et Neeiam* and the Reform of the Northumbrian Church," 1–25; and his introduction to *Bede: On Ezra and Nehemiah*, xxxvi–xlii.

35 Bede, *Retractatio in Actus Apostolorum*, IX.31.76–8.

36 For Augustine and Isidore, see above, 48.

37 Bede attached his commentary on 1 John to the copy of his commentary on Acts that he sent to Acca. See Bede, *Expositio Actuum Apostolorum*, pref.76–9.

38 Bede, *In epistulas VII catholicas*, II.5.93–8.

39 Bede's own comments on Revelation 7:9 in *Expositio Apocalypseos*, X.5–8, are not extensive, but do also point towards the spread of the Church to all people. For his revision of Theodore's *Passio beati Anastasii*, see above, 79 and 85–6.

concern with an *ecclesia per orbem dilatata* appears in his homily, *In quadragesima*, where he reveals the significance of the universal Church for various linguistic groups, which presumably would include the Anglo-Saxons:[40]

> Dilatata autem per orbem ecclesia et Graecis ac barbaris in eiusdem fidei unitatem confluentibus curauerunt praesules fidelium ut idem etiam in Graecum Latinumque transferretur eloquium quo modo etiam Marci Lucae et Iohannis euangelia quae deinceps Graeca lingua ediderunt mox in Latinum transfudere sermonem quatenus haec omnes per orbem nationes legere atque intellegere possent

> And since the Church is spread out across the world among both Greeks and barbarians assembling in the unity of the same faith, overseers of the faithful took care that the same eloquence be rendered in both Greek and Latin, in the same manner that the gospels of Mark, Luke and John, which they produced thereafter in Greek, were at once translated into the Latin language so that all these nations throughout the world could read and understand them.

Here the linguistic diversity of the world is made more concrete with an example of the textual history of the translation of the gospels. The repetition of the phrase *per orbem* underlines the necessity of ecclesiastical unity in faith, but not language. Though not explicitly stating such, Bede hints at the ecclesiastical need not only for a Latin or Greek Bible, but also for one that has been translated into the vernacular – a translation that he was supposedly carrying out on his death bed.[41] Bede's theology of a Church within an ethnically and linguistically diverse world does have practical concerns. A Church that is *per orbem diffusa* must deal with overcoming some of the boundaries that make the world diverse, language in particular. For Bede, the *ecclesia dilatata* takes on the role of unifying language, a role that Georges Tugene has observed always accompanies reference to linguistic diversity in the works of Bede.[42]

---

40 Bede, *Homiliae*, I.21.232–9. For discussion on the importance of this homily for issues of language and translation, see Fleming, "'The Most Exalted Language,'" 148.

41 See Cuthbert's *Epistola de obitu Bedae*, in *Ecclesiastical History*, 582. For Bede's attitude towards the vernacular, see Crépin, "Bede and the Vernacular," 170–92, at 183.

42 Tugene, *L'idée de nation*, 299.

The words *diffusa* and *dilatata* are particularly significant for this study because of their involvement of the supposed etymology of Noah's son Japheth. Following patristic tradition, Bede claims that Japheth is not only figuratively the gentile Church which has taken on the blessing of Shem, but also the literal expansion of the Greeks and Romans across the world:[43]

> Diximus in Sem primogenito filio Noe primitiuam ecclesiam, quae ex isahelitico populo collecta est, in Iapheth minimo filio electionem gentium quae secuta est esse designatam
>
> *Dilatiuit quoque Deus Iapheth, ut habitaret in tabernaculis Sem*, ... cum Greci siue Romani, exorti utique de genere Iapheth, regna Asiae, in quibus posteri Sem habitabent, possiderent.
>
> We said that in Shem, the firstborn of Noah, the primitive Church is designated, which was gathered from the people of Israel, and that in Japheth, the last son, the following election of the gentiles is designated.
>
> *God spread abroad Japheth that he should inhabit the tents of Shem* ... when the Greeks or Romans who are born of the lineage of Japheth, took possession of the kingdoms of Asia, which the descendants of Shem held.

Such interpretation is standard enough: Japheth, whose literal descendants are the European Greeks and Romans, historically formed a significant part of the early Church and conquered parts of Asia. By stating that Japheth "should inhabit the tents of Shem," the biblical writer is really expressing future events that will occur in accordance with God's providential plan. But unwittingly or not, the biblical writer also expresses the future of ecclesiastical history in the very name of Japheth himself. Directly between the two passages quoted above, Bede supports his figurative interpretation of Japheth as the gentile Church by examining the meaning of his name:[44]

43 Bede, *In principium Genesis*, II.2347–50 and II.2401–5.
44 Bede, *In principium Genesis*, II.2369–72.

congruit autem profectibus sanctae ecclesiae, quibus orbem impleuit totum, etiam nomen Iapheth, quod latitudo dictitur; unde alludens ad nomen ipsum, dicit Noe, dilatet deus Iapheth id est latitudinem.

The name Japheth, which means "spreading abroad [*lit.* extent or breadth]" is also fitting to the advancements of Holy Church with which it has filled the entire earth; referring to this, Noah plays on Japheth's name when he says, "may God spread abroad Japheth," that is "a spreading abroad."

Japheth is the "spreading abroad" (*latitudo*) that God "spreads abroad" (*dilatet*) in the Church, which also has "spread abroad" (*dilatata*) throughout the entire world.[45] Etymologically and therefore figuratively, Japheth is the *ecclesia dilatata.* Although the supposed wordplay must have originally denoted literal gentile expansion outside of Palestine, Bede fortuitously employs it here to promote his argument that ecclesiastical expansion across the world is mysteriously foreshadowed in the biblical text, right down to the very meanings of names. In other words, the etymology of Japheth makes the best sense when understood in hindsight, after the Church had expanded across the world and after the Greeks and Romans had conquered parts of Asia. Only then can the profound mystery of the biblical text be fully revealed.

Although Bede does not draw attention to the relationship between the etymology of Japheth and the "spreading abroad" of the Church apart from his commentary on Genesis, similar sentiments can be found elsewhere in his works. In his commentary on Revelation, Bede understands the biblical lemma "latitudinem terrae" (Revelation 20:8) as referring to the Church – an understanding that anticipates his later comments on the name Japheth.[46] In his commentaries on the Seven Catholic Epistles, Bede offers a variant on the usual phrase *ecclesia per orbem diffusa*, similar to his later exposition on Japheth's name: "pro omni ecclesia quae per totam mundi latitudinem diffusa est" (on account of the whole Church which is spread through the entire breadth of the world).[47] And in his work *De Templo*,

45 See Thiel, *Grundlagen und Gestalt der Hebräischkenntnisse*, 322.

46 Bede, *Expositio Apocalypseos*, XXXV.106–8: "ecclesia, quam potius nomine latitudinis terrae in omnibus tunc gentibus persequendam" (the Church, which [is referred to] rather with the name "breath of the earth" since it was about to be persecuted then among all the nations).

47 Bede, *In epistulas VII catholicas*, II.2.43–4.

which was written after his commentary on Genesis, Bede interprets the dimensions of the Temple as the Church spread throughout the world: "populi fidelium ex quibus sancta uniuersalis ecclesia consistit quorum dilatationem per orbem latitudo designat" (the peoples of believers from whom the holy universal Church consists, and whose distribution throughout the world is signified by the breadth [of the Temple walls]); and "hoc per totam latitudinem diffusae ecclesiae per orbem" (this [watching and listening of the Lord is] through the whole breadth of the Church, which is spread throughout the earth).[48] While the word *latitudo* in these two instances primarily refers to the physical attributes of the Temple, Bede employs it in such a manner to interpret allegorically the Temple as the Church. Importantly, later in the same commentary, Bede again uses the world *latitudo*, but here in reference to all of humankind, which has descended from the three sons of Noah to fill the breadth of the world: "latitudinem totius orbis impleuit; Sem quippe prosapia Asiam Cham posteri Africam Iafeth suboles Europam et insulas maris obtinuit" ([humankind] has filled the breadth of the whole world; Shem's lineage took Asia, Ham's descendants Africa, and Japheth's offspring Europe and the islands of the sea).[49] The use of the word *latitudo* next to the name Japheth is too closely related to Bede's other comments regarding the Church's dissemination across the world to be without significance.[50] Though it is unlikely that Bede had the Hebrew etymology of the name Japheth in mind every time that he used the word *dilatata* (or its synonym *diffusa*) in reference to the Church, the connection between the etymological meaning of Japheth and the universal Church must have informed Bede's monastic vocabulary. In fact, like much of Bede's exegesis, it is likely that a preconceived notion, in this case, of a Church spread across the world, informs a clever reading of the etymology of Japheth, and not the other way around. For Bede, the diversity of the world in the unity of the Church is a sure fact that the Bible mystically accounts for, from the straightforward narration of Pentecost to the more oblique etymology of Japheth.

48 Bede, *De templo*, I.902–4 and I.1007–8.

49 Ibid., II.658–60.

50 For Bede and wordplay, see Major, "Words, Wit, and Wordplay"; for Anglo-Saxon uses of etymologies, see Howe, "Aldhelm's *Engimata* and Isidorian Etymology," 37–59; and Robinson, "The Significance of Names in Old English Literature," 14–58.

Attitudes towards Language

Despite being cloistered in a Northumbrian monastery for most of his life, Bede was very familiar with the ethnic and linguistic diversity in Britain and in the rest of Europe at the time. Unsurprisingly, Bede himself was a multilingual speaker: he was a native speaker of Old English and wrote his vast corpus in Latin, which he had learned from training in the monastery he was given to as a young boy.[51] His knowledge of Greek also increased throughout his life, and he appears to have been fairly competent by the time he composed the *Retractatio in Actus Apostolorum* in his final years. Bede's knowledge of Hebrew is negligible compared to his knowledge of Latin or Greek, and he certainly could not read the Hebrew Scriptures in their original script and language, but his internalization of Jerome's comments on Hebrew philology is so extensive that before E.F. Sutcliffe proved otherwise, Bede was thought to be one of the most proficient Hebrew scholars of the Middle Ages.[52] Alongside this knowledge of languages, Bede reveals an acute theological understanding of linguistic diversity throughout his works that relies on but also in some cases exceeds that of his patristic predecessors. Bede's understanding of multilingualism is not to deny, of course, that Latin was the desired language of discourse for the monastic *conuersatio* throughout western Europe at the time, but for Bede linguistic uniformity was not practically nor even theologically sound. Rather, linguistic as well as ethnic diversity is both a gift of grace that plays a necessary role in salvation history, and paradoxically a confirmation of the unity of the catholic Church that is most prevalent in diversity itself.

In the opening metrical prologue to his *Vita S. Cuthberti*, Bede presents a rhetorically lavish account of the spread of the Church, depicted metaphorically as light piercing the darkness:[53]

Multa suis dominus fulgescere lumina saeclis
Donavit, tetricas humanae noctis ut umbras

51 For a list of Bede's works, see Plummer, ed., *Historiam ecclesiasticam gentis Anglorum*, vol. 1, cxlv–clix; and Gorman, "The Canon of Bede's Works and the World of Ps. Bede," 399–445, esp. 402–5.

52 For Bede's knowledge of Greek, see Lynch, "The Venerable Bede's Knowledge of Greek," 432–9. For Bede's Hebrew, see Sutcliffe, "The Venerable Bede's Knowledge of Hebrew," 300–6; and Fleming, "'The Most Exalted Language,'" 53–72.

53 Jaager, ed., *Bedas metrische Vita sancti Cuthberti*, lines 1–10. For the date and composition, see Lapidge, "Bede's Metrical *Vita S. Cuthberti*," 339–55. For an excellent rhetorical analysis of these lines, see Steen, *Verse and Virtuosity*, 25–7.

Lustraret divina poli de culmine flamma.
Et licet ipse deo natus de lumine Christus
Lux sit summa, deus sanctos quoque iure lucernae
Ecclesiae rutilare dedit, quibus igne magistro
Sensibus instet amor, sermonibus aestuet ardor;
Multifidos varium lichinos qui sparsit in orbem,
Ut cunctum nova lux fidei face fusa sub axem
Omnia sidereis virtutibus arva repleret.

The Lord gave many lights to shine among his ages / peoples, so that the divine flame might enlighten the dark shades of human night from the height of heaven. And although Christ himself, born to God from light, is the highest light, God also caused his saints to glow red for the Church like a lamp, in whom, with fire as teacher, love might settle in their senses and heat seethe in their words. God scattered the many-sided lamps onto the diverse globe in order that, like a torch spread out, new light of faith might fill all the fields with starry virtues under each region.

Bede then goes on to give specific examples of saints who had preached to unconverted nations throughout the world in order to build up the Church. Peter and Paul are mentioned as missionaries to Rome; John to Asia; Bartholomew to India; Mark to Asia; and so on. At last, Cuthbert is placed among these missionaries as one who taught the English to ascend to the heavens ("Scandere celsa suis docuit jam passibus Anglos," line 29). Bede then appropriately concludes this prologue with an appeal to the Holy Spirit for eloquence similar to the disciples at Pentecost: "Flammivomisque soles dare qui nova famina linguis, / Munera da verbi linguae tua dona canenti" (you, who are accustomed to grant new eloquence with flame-spouting tongues, grant the gifts of the Word to the tongue singing your gifts, lines 37–8).[54] For Bede, Pentecost was the beginning of the Church's mission to convert the world, and in order to do so, linguistic barriers had to be embraced and overcome. Pragmatically as well as theologically, one of Bede's chief symbols of the genesis of the Christian mission was the *linguae* of the Holy Spirit. And Bede's attitudes towards linguistic diversity are positive, stemming from the notion that the

54 Arator, *Historia apostolica*, I.227, provides the ultimate source: "Munera da linguae qui das in munere linguas" (give the gifts of language / tongue, you who give languages / tongues as a gift).

dispersal of languages at Babel is redeemed through the flaming and omnilingual tongues at Pentecost.

This theology of language, formed out of the intertextual relationship between Babel and Pentecost, gives rise to some further implications outside of Bede's exegetical works, especially his well-known historical work, the *Ecclesiastical History of the English People*. A number of scholars have already explored some of these implications of Bede's linguistic theology, especially as it is reflected in the *Ecclesiastical History*.[55] Notably, Tugene has provided an indispensable analysis of the foundation of Pentecost for Bede's views towards linguistic diversity;[56] Kees Dekker reads Bede's narrative of Caedmon as an example of a Pentecostal "miracle of language";[57] and Irina A. Dumitrescu has recently interpreted certain narratives bookending the *Ecclesiastical History* as a program of linguistic freedom that stems in part from Bede's readings of Babel and Pentecost.[58] As is apparent from this scholarship, Bede's use of Babel and Pentecost for language matters has proven to be a fruitful area of study. Most of my own discussion relies on the excellent foundation this scholarship has established, and I will aim only to strengthen and augment it in specific instances.

First of all, Bede, despite his language learning and respect for Latin, Greek, and Hebrew, does not seem to have any entertained any theological notion of linguistic hierarchy,[59] especially that of *sacrae linguae*. Although many of the Church Fathers were themselves multilingual to varying degrees, there seems to be a general lack of preference for certain languages over others. One important exception, however, is the notion of the *tres sacrae linguae* that were written on the *titulus* of the cross of Christ.[60] As Irven M. Resnick has shown, the notion of the *tres sacrae linguae* had

55 Crépin, "Bede and the Vernacular," 183, states that because of Bede's focus on allegorical interpretation, "in Bede's mind the variety of languages in its literal sense does not seem connected with the Tower of Babel" – a statement that I do not think stands up to scrutiny.

56 Tugene, *L'idée de nation*, 294–302. See also Merrills, *History and Geography in Late Antiquity*, 275–6; and Hall, "Interlinguistic Communication," 46.

57 Dekker, "Pentecost and Linguistic Self-Consciousness," 355–6.

58 Dumitrescu, "Bede's Liberation," at 43.

59 For evidence of Bede's sociolinguistic hierarchy of languages, see Hall, "Interlinguistic Communication"; and Crépin, "Bede and the Vernacular," 183–4.

60 John 19:20; the Vulgate and the Greek *textus receptus* also mention the three languages in Luke 23:38. It is also interesting to note that the Vulgate version of Revelation 9:11 includes the Latin word *Exterminans*, which appears alongside the Hebrew *Abaddon* and Greek *Apollyon*, but has no basis in the Greek text.

not been fully developed until it found its strongest expression in Isidore's *Etymologiae*. It is here for the first time that the word *sacrae* appears in connection with *linguae*:[61]

> Tres sunt autem linguae sacrae: Hebraea, Graeca, Latina, quae toto orbe maxime excellunt. His enim tribus linguis super crucem Domini a Pilato fuit causa eius scripta. Vnde et propter obscuritatem sanctarum Scripturarum harum trium linguarum cognitio necessaria est.

> And there are three holy languages: Hebrew, Greek and Latin, which are the most eminent in the whole world. For in these three languages the case of the Lord was written by Pilate upon the cross. Therefore because of the obscurity of Holy Scripture, knowledge of these three languages is necessary.

Previous to Isidore, Hilary of Poitiers mentions *tres linguae* of the cross, and Augustine (Isidore's likely source in this instance) notes that they are "prominent" over other languages: Hebrew, because it is the language of the Law; Greek, because it is the language of the philosophers; and Latin, because it is the language of the Empire.[62] However, Isidore's addition of the word *sacrae* did have some influence over medieval authors, especially Irish scholars,[63] and has become appropriated in modern scholarly terminology for describing the phenomenon of the interest in the three languages on the cross.[64]

Bede was more judicious when it came to such linguistic theology. A number of scholars have already pointed out that Bede does not conform to Isidore's view of sacred languages, and never employs the phrase, *tres sacrae linguae*.[65] If anything, Bede falls more in line with Augustine's approach, which grants some pre-eminence to the languages on the cross,

61 Isidore, *Etymologiarum siue originum libri xx*, IX.1.1, 3.

62 Hilary of Poitiers, *Prologus in librum Psalmorum* 15, PL 9, col. 241B–242A; Augustine, *In Iohannis euangelium tractatus CXXIV*, CXVII.19.4: "hae quippe tres lingaue ibi prae ceteris eminebant"; and Irish-Augustine, *De mirabilibus sacrae scripturae*, PL 35, col. 2161B. See Resnick, "'Lingua Dei, lingua hominis,'" 51–74, at 63–5.

63 McNally, "The 'Tres Linguae Sacrae' in Early Irish Bible Exegesis," 395–403; and Berschin, *Greek Letters and the Latin Middle Ages*.

64 O'Brien, *Reversing Babel*, 23–5.

65 Frank, "Some Uses of Paronomasia in Old English Scriptural Verse," 207–26, at 223; Tugene, *L'idée de nation*, 301; Dekker, "Pentecost and Linguistic Self-Consciousness," 350–2; Stanton, *Culture of Translation*, 65–6; and "Linguistic Fragmentation," 17.

but does not go so far as to consecrate them.[66] A fitting example can be found in Bede's commentary on Luke, where he quotes Philippians 2:11 alongside Augustine's *Tractatus in Iohannem* to undermine a sacred hierarchy of language in favour of an acceptance of all languages:[67]

> hoc nomen Hebraice Graece et Latine scriptum erat hoc est quod idem apostolus subsecutus adnectit: *Et omnis lingua confiteatur quia Iesus Christus in gloria est Dei patris.* Quantum uero ad litteram *hae tres lingua ibi prae ceteris eminebant Hebraea propter Iudaeos in lege gloriantes Graeca propter gentium sapientes Latina propter Romanos multis ac paene omnibus iam tunc gentibus imperantes.* Velint nolint ergo Iudaei omne mundi regnum omnis mundana sapientia omnia diuinae legis sacramenta testantur quia Iesus rex Iudaeorum est, hoc est imperator credentium et confitentium Deum.

> This name had been written in Hebrew, Greek, and Latin, which the same apostle affirms when he adds: *And each tongue should confess that Jesus Christ is in the glory of God the Father.* And according to the literal interpretation, *these three languages are there eminent above the other languages: Hebrew because of the Jews who glorify in the Law, Greek because of the wise men of the nations, Latin because of the Romans who at that time ruled many, almost all, of the nations.* Therefore, whether the Jews wanted it or not, each kingdom of the world, all worldly wisdom and all the mysteries of the divine Law bear witness that Jesus is the king of the Jews, that is, the emperor of those who believe and confess God.

A similar adaptation of the Augustinian passage is also found in Bede's commentary on Ezra and Nehemiah:[68]

> Quem etiam certi nobis mysterii gratia Hebraice Graece et Latine conscripsit quia nimirum omnis diuina lex quam habebant Hebraei omnis sapientia mundana in qua gloriabantur Graeci omne regnum terrestre in quo tunc

66 See Bischoff, "Das griechische Element in der abendlandischen Bildung des Mittelalters," 246–75, at 251. A dislike for Isidore was once suspected in the works of Bede, but see McCready, "Bede and the Isidorian Legacy," 41–73; "Bede, Isidore, and the *Epistola Cuthberti*," 75–94; and Kendall and Wallis, *Bede: On the Nature of Things and On Times*, 13–20.

67 Bede, *In Lucae euangelium*, VI.1649–59.

68 Bede, *In Ezram et Neemiam*, I.316–22. The three languages of the cross are also mentioned in passing in Bede's commentary on 1 Samuel, *In primam partem Samuhelis libri IIII*, IV.765–7.

> maxime praeminebant Romani Christum regem contestatur omnium sanctorum et confitentium Deum.
>
> Pilate also wrote this in Hebrew, Greek, and Latin for the sake of a mystery that is certain to us: that without doubt all the divine Law which the Hebrews had, all the worldly wisdom in which the Greeks gloried, and each earthly kingdom over which the Romans for the most part ruled at that time bear witness that Christ is king of all the saints and of those who confess God.

For Bede, who refrains from any allegorical interpretation of the *titulus*,[69] the languages on the cross merely served the practical purpose of preaching the Gospel in spite of the efforts of the Jews. The linguistic sacrality inherent in Isidore's work is completely absent in Bede's exposition.

The reasons behind Bede's rejection not only of the *tres sacrae linguae* but also of any sacred language at all have been explored more thoroughly by Dekker and Stanton, who independently state that Gregory the Great is partially responsible.[70] The Gregorian text that they both cite appears in the fourth book of the *Dialogues*, which Bede clearly knew and studied.[71] In this book Gregory tells a story about a boy named Armentarius, who had died of the plague but miraculously came back to life. Upon investigation, it is revealed that the boy had learned every language while he was in heaven, and as proof of this miracle he was able to converse both with his Greek-speaking master and a Bulgarian servant in their own languages – languages that the boy previously did not know. The problem with attributing this Gregorian passage to Bede's rejection of the *tres sacrae linguae*, however, is that nothing is explicitly stated regarding the sacrality of any language; it is not a story about the *tres sacrae linguae*. It seems more likely that Bede would not have found much in the way of linguistic theology in this story, but that the story is to be understood *simpliciter*, as a popular narrative that is useful for edifying, in the words of Walter Goffart, the "theologically naive."[72] It is, therefore, questionable whether Bede, or even

69 Although Bede, *In Lucae euangelium*, VI.1649–59, states that he is offering an interpretation *ad litteram* and *In Ezram et Neemiam*, I.316–22, an interpretation *mysterii gratia*, he ends up saying almost the exact same thing.

70 Dekker, "Pentecost and Linguistic Self-Consciousness," 350–2; Stanton, *Culture of Translation*, 65–6; and "Linguistic Fragmentation," 17.

71 See Lapidge, *The Anglo-Saxon Library*, 209. Gregory the Great, *Dialogues*, IV.xxvii.10–12.

72 Goffart, "Bede's *uera lex historiae* Explained," 111–16, at 114.

Gregory, would have interpreted this saint's life as specific proof against the *tres sacrae linguae*. Aside from the story of Armentarius and Bede's commentaries, other circumstantial evidence for a rejection of linguistic sacrality can be found in Bede's *Ecclesiastical History*, which reveals numerous examples of a positive attitude towards linguistic diversity. Narrative details such as the connection between the five languages of Britain and the five books of the Old Testament law, Pope Gregory's famous multilingual puns, scholars and saints as learned in Greek and Latin as their own languages, and Cædmon's divine ability to paraphrase sacred history into vernacular poetry that is better than Bede's own Latinate attempts, are well-known examples that reveal the importance that linguistic diversity has in salvation history. But one feature of Bede's linguistic theology that has not been as thoroughly examined is his subtle condemnation of the neglect of multilingualism in the burgeoning Church in Britain.

One example can be found in Bede's narration of Agilbert, which reveals the negative effects created by a refusal to embrace multilingualism. In this account, which anticipates the multilingualism at Whitby a few chapters later, Bede narrates how Cenwealh, king of the West-Saxons, has Agilbert accept the episcopal see. After a few years, however, the king who, as Bede explains, only knew the Saxon language grew tired of the linguistic differences between himself and Agilbert: "Tandem rex, qui Saxonum tantum linguam nouerat, pertaesus barbarae loquelae, subintroduxit in prouinciam alium linguae episcopum, uocabulo Uini" (at last, the king, who only knew the Saxon language, grew tired of Agilbert's barbarous speaking and introduced another bishop of his own language into his province, who was named Wine, III.7). Because this is done outside of Agilbert's consent, Agilbert leaves the diocese, and after attending the synod of Whitby, goes to Paris where he is installed bishop before he dies, "senex ac plenus dierum" (old and full of days). Meanwhile, Saxon-speaking Wine proves to be a poor choice as bishop and he is expelled from the see shortly afterwards, only to go and commit simony by buying the see of London from the king of Mercia. The West Saxons are left without a bishop and, therefore, without divine protection. As a consequence, Cenwealh suffers "grauissimis regni sui damnis saepissime ab hostibus" (heavy losses in his kingdom at the hands of his enemies), until he realizes his mistake, offers amends, and requests that Agilbert be reinstituted. Because Agilbert cannot now leave his see at Paris, he sends his nephew, Leuthere, who then governs the see appropriately with "sedulo moderamine" (attentive supervision). Although it may be a small point, it is clear that all of Cenwealh's troubles stem from his stubbornness towards and rejection of a speaker of a foreign language. Considering the future role that Agilbert would play at the synod of Whitby, this narration regarding the negative outcomes of monolingualism becomes a foil to the positive role that multilingualism plays at Whitby in the confirmation of catholic doctrine. Through an example of the negative effects of linguistic rejection, linguistic diversity is inversely portrayed in a positive light.

Before turning to Whitby, a second example of the negative effects caused by rejecting multilingualism can be found in the first book of the *Ecclesiastical History*. Augustine of Canterbury and his fellow missionaries have been sent by Pope Gregory to "preach the Word of God to the English nation" (praedicare uerbum Dei genti Anglorum, I.23). Before they reach Britain, however, they decide to turn back, stricken with fear, rather than enter a barbaric, fierce, unbelieving nation, whose language they did not know ("perculsi timore inerti redire domum potius quam barbaram feram incredulamque gentem, cuius ne linguam quidem nossent, adire cogitabant," I.23). Gregory responds by sending a letter, preserved by Bede, that encourages Augustine and his fellow monks "not to let the tongues / languages of evil men deter you" (nec maledicorum hominum linguae deterreant, I.23). Taking this advice to heart, the missionaries return to Britain equipped with Franish interpreters (I.25). Their mission henceforth is a success. Notably, this emphasis on language barriers in evangelization echoes Bede's previous statement on the Christian Britons on the island:[73]

> inter alia inenarrabilium scelerum facta, quae historicus eorum Gildas flebili sermone describit, et hoc addebant, ut numquam genti Saxonum siue Anglorum, secum Brittaniam incolenti, uerbum fidei praedicando committerent.

> among other deeds of indescribable crimes, which their historian Gildas describes in tearful speech, they also added this, that they never sent the Word of faith to the nation of the Saxons or Angles living in Britain with them by preaching.

The same sentiment is repeated at the end of the *Ecclesiastical History* when Bede attributes the errors regarding Easter and the tonsure of the

73 Bede, *Ecclesiastical History*, I.22.

Britons to their lack of preaching to the Anglo-Saxons.[74] But in the earlier instance, the parallels between the lack of preaching by the Britons, and Augustine's initial fears to preach, suggests that the language barrier was a challenge for both groups, especially since Bede highlights the problem of language differences no fewer than three times.

But how do these instances, and others in the *Ecclesiastical History*, relate to Bede's linguistic theology expressed in his discussions of the association between Babel and Pentecost? Despite the, I believe, correct scholarly claim stemming chiefly from Tugene that positive attitudes towards linguistic diversity and multilingualism in the *Ecclesiastical History* must be influenced by Bede's interpretation of Babel and Pentecost, there is a disconcerting lack of direct evidence for this biblical influence on the *Ecclesiastical History* itself. As mentioned earlier, Bede does not trace the ethnic origins of the inhabitants of Britain back to the dispersal of nations at the Tower of Babel, nor does he explicitly connect the conversion of the Anglo-Saxons to the dispersal of the Church at Pentecost. Because, at least in Bede's version, the synod of Whitby is presented as multicultural and multilingual, some scholars have suggested that it reflects a biblical framework concerned with the relationship between Babel and Pentecost and the theological implications of that relationship.[75] To augment this suggestion, further evidence indicates that Bede had his comments on Babel from his earlier commentaries in mind when he composed Wilfrid's speech at the synod of Whitby.

From the outset, Bede emphasizes that the two secular conveners of the council are Anglo-Saxon products of Irish or Roman education. Bede writes that King Oswiu was "a Scottis edoctus ac baptizatus, illorum etiam lingua optime inbutus" (educated and baptized by the Irish, and completely fluent in their language, III.25), but that his son Alhfrith preferred the doctrines of Rome to the Irish because he was educated by Wilfrid, a representative of the Roman side of the debate:[76]

> Preuenit [*sc.* quaestio paschalis] et ad ipsas principum auras, Osuiu uidelicet regis et filii eius Alchfridi, quia nimirum Osuiu a Scottis edoctus ac baptizatus, illorum etiam lingua optime inbutus, nil melius quam quod illi docuissent

---

74 Ibid., V.22. See Charles-Edwards, "Bede, the Irish and the Britons," 42–52.

75 Hall, "Interlinguistic Communication," 46; and Butler, "Textual Community and Linguistic Distance in Early England," 31–5.

76 Bede, *Ecclesiastical History*, III.25.

> autumabat; porro Alchfrid magistrum habens eruditionis Christianae Uilfridum uirum doctissimum (nam et Romam prius propter doctrinam ecclesiasticam adierat, et apud Dalfinum archiepiscopum Galliarum Lugdoni multum temporis egerat, a quo etiam tonsurae ecclesiasticae coronam susceperat), huius doctrinam omnibus Scottorum traditionibus iure praeferendam sciebat.
>
> The Easter controversy also came to the ears of these leaders, namely the king, Oswiu, and his son, Alhfrith. No doubt Oswiu, having been educated and baptized by the Irish, and also completely fluent in their language, affirmed nothing to be better than what they had taught him; and Alhfrith had as a teacher of Christian scholarship the most learned man Wilfrid (for Wilfrid previously had even gone to Rome for ecclesiastical doctrine and spent much time at Lyons with Dalfinus, archbishop of Gaul, from whom he also had received the crown of ecclesiastical tonsure); Alhfrith knew that Wilfrid's doctrine was rightly to be preferred to all the traditions of the Irish.

To further emphasize the multilingualism of the synod, Bede twice mentions the presence of an unbiased interpreter for the synod. This interpreter, however, is not needed, since Agilbert, a non-native speaker of Old English, has Wilfrid speak in his place, instead of an interpreter:[77]

> Respondit Agilberctus: "Loquatur, obserco, uice mea discipulus meus Uilfrid presbyter, quia unum ambo sapimus cum ceteris qui hic adsident ecclesiasticae traditionis cultoribus; et ille melius ac manifestius ipsa lingua Anglorum, quam ego per interpretem, potest explanare quae sentimus."
>
> Agilbert responded: "I beseech, let my disciple Wilfrid the priest speak in my place, because we both feel the same way with other followers of the ecclesiastical tradition who are sitting here; and he can explain better and more clearly in the language of the Anglo-Saxons itself those things, which we declare, than I can through an interpreter."

Despite the fact that Bede purports to be describing a historical event, the emphasis on multilingualism seems to be unique to his account. The version in the *Vita Wilfridi* by Stephen of Ripon, which Bede borrows from, plays down the presence of the multicultural attendees of the

77 Bede, *Ecclesiastical History*, III.25.

council, mentions no interpreter, and does not make it clear that Wilfrid is to speak because of Agilbert's difficulties with the language:[78]

> Imperatum est ab Aegilberchto episcopo transmarino et Agathone presbitero suo, sancto Wilfritho presbitero et abbati suaviloqua eloquentia in sua lingua Romanae ecclesiae et apostolicae sedis dare rationem.
>
> It was commanded by Agilbert the bishop from across the sea and Agatho his priest to saint Wilfrid the priest and abbot that he give the argument of the Roman church and Apostolic see though persuasive eloquence in his own language.

The question then is for what reason does Bede, from the outset, underline the multilingualism of the synod? The most probable explanation is that the multilingualism at Whitby anticipates Wilfrid's argument that linguistic diversity confirms and ratifies Church unity:[79]

> "Pascha quod facimus" inquit "uidimus Romae, ubi beati apostoli Petrus et Paulus uixere, docuere, passi sunt et sepulti, ab omnibus celebrari; hoc in Italia, hoc in Gallia, quas discendi uel orandi studio pertransiuimus, ab omnibus agi conspeximus; hoc Africam, Asiam, Aegyptum, Greciam et omnem orbem, quacumque Christi ecclesia diffusa est, per diuersas nationes et linguas uno ac non diuerso temporis ordine geri conperimus, praeter hos tantum et obstinationis eorum conplices, Pictos dico et Brettones, cum quibus de duabus ultimis Oceani insulis, et his non totis, contra totum orbem stulto labore pugnant."
>
> "The Easter we perform," he said, "we saw celebrated by all in Rome, where the blessed apostles Peter and Paul lived, taught, suffered and were buried; we observed it carried out by all in Italy, in Gaul where we travelled in zeal of learning and praying; we learned that it is performed in Africa, Asia, Egypt, Greece and in all the world, wherever Christ's Church is spread, through diverse nations and languages in one and the same order of time – except for these men only and their accomplices in stubbornness, I mean the Picts and the Britons, with whom from two of the furthest islands in the ocean, and

78 Colgrave, ed., *The Life of Bishop Wilfrid by Eddius Stephanus*, 20. See also Hall, "Interlinguistic Communication," 44–5.

79 Bede, *Ecclesiastical History*, III.25, 300.

not even entirely in these islands, they fight against the whole world with a stupid effort."

In this passage, Wilfrid's speech echoes Bede's comments elsewhere on the dispersal of the Church across the entire world. Notably, Wilfrid's "omnem orbem, quacumque Christi ecclesia diffusa est," and "per diuersas nationes et linguas uno ac non diuerso temporis ordine" are reminiscent of Bede's remarks on the Tower of Babel in his commentary on Genesis, and his *Retractatio in Actus Apostolorum* (similarities underlined):[80]

> sicut hic [*sc.* Babel] linguis ob superbiam diuisis gentes sunt ab inuicem toto orbe disperse, ita illic [*sc.* Ierusalem] ob meritum humilitatis adunata diuersitate linguarum, collecti ex omni natione quae sub caelo est populi, una et non dispari confessione ac fide, laudes et magnalia Dei resonarent.
>
> just as here [at Babel] when the languages were divided on account of pride, the nations were dispersed from each other across the entire world, so there [at Jerusalem] when the diversity of languages was united on account of the merit of humility, the people gathered together from all nations that are under heaven resounded the praises and great things of God in one and the same confession and faith.
>
> electi in multifaria diuisione loquelarum, uno ac non diuiso corde et intentione domino famulantur
>
> the elect, in the many-fold division of languages, serve the Lord with one and the same heart and intention.

It is probably not worth speculating that Bede had, say, his commentary on Genesis in front of him when he wrote his account of Wilfrid's speech, but it is evident that Bede's theology of language, which stems from the division of languages at Babel and the consecration of linguistic diversity in the nature of the Church, permeates his vocabulary even outside of his biblical commentaries. As Jean Leclercq has expressed, the principles of monastic rumination stemming from *lectio diuina* fashion the expressions of the reader "spontaneously in a Biblical vocabulary."[81] Bede lived his

80 Bede, *In principium Genesis*, III.370–5; and *Retractatio in Actus Apostolorum*, 4.124–5.
81 Leclercq, *The Love of Learning and the Desire for God*, 73–6, quote at 75.

entire adult life ruminating over the Scriptures and patristic writings, as he himself makes clear at the end of the *Ecclesiastical History*.[82] He was intimately familiar with their content, rhetoric, and vocabulary. It is, therefore, no surprise that Wilfrid's speech at Whitby echoes Bede's other comments on the diversity of language and the unity of the Church, stemming from the affiliation of Babel with Pentecost. This theology of division and unity is one of the defining characteristics of his writings.

Working within the intellectual traditions of Late Antiquity, Bede saw himself as living on the edges of a Christianized world. As Uppinder Mehan has suggested in a reading of Bede in light of postcolonial theory, "Although such [colonized] writers do not reject the cultural contributions of the colonizer, they regard the colonizer's culture as having also been changed by the culture of the colonized."[83] Whereas Bede's comments on Britain are relatively scarce outside of the *Ecclesiastical History*,[84] this work suggests that Britain does play a theological role in propagating the notion of ethnic and linguistic diversity in ecclesiastical unity. Britain, through its very existence on the margins of Europe (and hence the world), confirms the power of the Church of Rome to reach far beyond its focal point in Italy. Geographically marginal strongholds of Roman faith and doctrine, such as Northumbria, help justify missionary actions from Rome to the extent that Britain and Ireland themselves became centres from which missionary activity spreads out. These British "islands on the edge of the world" develop into a kind of mirror of Rome; by sending missionaries back to the continent, these islands on the margin assume the religious centrality of Europe, while still retaining their conceptually and geographically liminal position. With a mentality formed in part by interpretations of the diversity created at Babel and the unity brought about at Pentecost, Bede considers how, to again borrow from Mehan, the "colonizing" Roman Church is affected and changed by the "colonized" English people, such that these roles come close to being completely reversed. Before Bede composed the *Ecclesiastical History* near

---

82 Bede, *Ecclesiastical History*, V.24: "cunctumque ex eo tempus utiae in eiusdem monasterii habitatione peragens, omnem meditandis scripturis operam dedi" (from the point [I entered the monastery] I have spent all my time in this same monastery, devoting all my work to the meditation of Scripture).

83 Mehan and Townsend, "'Nation' and the Gaze of the Other in Eight-Century Northumbria," 1–26, at 8.

84 Notable exceptions can be found in Bede, *De templo*, II.1044–8; and Bede, *In cantica canticorum*, Pref.508–10.

the end of his life, he revealed a great interest in defining Christian identity as having transcended ethnic and linguistic boundaries. Especially in his many comments on the Tower of Babel and world diversity, Bede advocates for an identity that finds support not only in its connection to the orthodoxy at Rome, but also in its contrast with non-Christian identity.

Alcuin

In or around 735, the year of Bede's death, Alcuin of York (d. 804) was born. Alcuin, who would become one of the most important figures for bridging Anglo-Saxon and Carolingian scholarship, was trained in York by Bede's pupil, Ecgberht (737–58), and Ælberht (767–78).[85] Despite a promising ecclesiastical career in Northumbria, Alcuin left Britain, and in 781 joined the retinue of Charlemagne who was luring scholars across Europe to promote educational reform. An impressive polymath and skilled teacher, Alcuin eventually became the star scholar at Charlemagne's court; Einhard, Charlemagne's biographer, called him "virum undecumque doctissimum" (the most learned man in every respect).[86] After Alcuin's move from York, he returned to Britain only twice, but retained a correspondence with his Anglo-Saxon pupils. With feet in both England and the continent, he did much to continue the exegetical legacy of Bede among Carolingian intellectual culture. His works include an extensive collection of letters, numerous poems, theological tracts, didactic texts, and commentaries.[87]

Most important for this study, Alcuin composed a question-and-answer text dealing with exegesis of Genesis. His *Quaestiones in Genesim* would prove to be one of the most popular commentaries of the Middle Ages: its fifty-two surviving manuscripts more than double the twenty-two of Bede's commentary on Genesis.[88] In this text, Alcuin does not stray far from the established exegetical tradition when he deals with the sons of Noah and the building of the Tower of Babel. Generally following Augustine or Jerome,

85 For Alcuin's Northumbrian years, see Bullough, *Alcuin*, pt. 2, chs. 1–2; modern accounts of Alcuin's life can be found in Manitius, *Geschichte der lateinischen Literatur des Mittelalters*, vol. 1, 273–7; Duckett, *Alcuin, Friend of Charlemagne*; Godman, ed., *Alcuin: The Bishops, Kings, and Saints of York*, xxxv–xxxix; and Garrison, "Alcuin of York," 26–7.

86 Einhard, *Vita Karoli Magni*, § 25, 30.

87 Jullien and Perelman, *Clavis des auteurs Latins du moyen âge, territoire français, 735–987*, vol. 2: *Alcuin*.

88 Fox, "Alcuin the Exegete," 39–60, at 43.

Alcuin states that Shem signifies Asia, Ham Africa, and Japheth Europe (*Quaes.* 141); that their descendants total seventy-two (*Quaes.* 142); that Japheth signifies the the multitude of believers (*Quaes.* 143); that the building of Babel signifies pride (*Quaes.* 145); that its builder was Nimrod, a giant (*Quaes.* 145, 148); that the consequence of linguistic diversity is a practical result of not obeying God (*Quaes.* 145), but that this diversity will be gathered together in the humility of Christ (*Quaes.* 147); that the plural form *descendamus* in Genesis 10:7 signifies the Trinity (*Quaes.* 146); that the original language is Hebrew (*Quaes.* 150); and that the Chaldaeans worship fire, whereas Abraham did not (*Quaes.* 152).[89]

Alcuin also displays a number of unusual features that deserve further examination. For one, he puts forth the question "An unum opus est turris et civitas, vel duo?" (whether the tower and the city are one entity or two? *Quaes.* 149). Alcuin answers that Babylon, meaning "confusion," is the city where the Tower was built and where the languages were divided, but he also explicitly connects the Tower of Babel to the historical city of Babylon, described by what he terms the "history of the pagans," which include further details on the towers of that city. The credibility of the biblical account is, thereby, strengthened through the semblance of unbiased, non-Jewish, or Christian sources, including their specific, though superfluous, details. Moreover, Alcuin's question itself reveals a desire to clarify ambiguity regarding the biblical tower and the historical city and empire. Similar interest in the specific details of the biblical account is found a few questions earlier, when Alcuin clarifies a geographical detail from the Table of Nations (*Quaes.* 144), noting that the phrase "Niniven et Robooth" (Nineveh and Rehoboth,Genesis 10:11) denotes only the city of Nineveh; *Robooth*, he states, means *platea* and therefore denotes the "plateas civitatis" (broad places of the city).[90] It is unclear why Alcuin found the need to include this particular etymological comment, expect perhaps to clarify the verse in the Vulgate, which renders Rehoboth into its etymological elements as "plateas ciuitatis."

89 Alcuin, *Interrogationes et responsiones in Genesin*, PL 100, col. 532C–534B (henceforth *Quaes.*). See O'Keeffe, "The Use of Bede's Writings on Genesis in Alcuin's *Interrogationes*," 463–83; and Houghton, "(Re)Sounding Brass," 149–61.

90 See Thiel, *Grundlagen und Gestalt der Hebräischkenntnisse*, 394; and Laistner, "Notes on Greek from the Lectures of a Ninth Century Monastery Teacher," 421–56, at 449, R7.

A second intriguing feature of Alcuin's commentary on the Babel narrative is the explanation that God, because he rested from work on the seventh day of creation, cannot be said to have made anything new when he divided the languages (*Quaes.* 151). Instead, as Alcuin writes, God "dicendi modos et formas in diversis linguarum generibus divist" (divided the modes and forms of speaking into the diverse kinds of languages, *Quaes.* 151). To support this claim, Alcuin mentions the presence of a Greek and Latin homograph *sidera* (*σιδηρα*) in the respective translations of Psalm 2:9. With an adroit display of Greek (even more impressive considering Alcuin's apparent ignorance of the language),[91] Alcuin can confidently argue that language diversity is not a matter of new creation but rather the jumbling up of language already created. This final feature of his commentary on the Babel narrative displays a fitting conclusion to Alcuin's progression from the ethnic division of the world into three continents (*Quaes.* 141) to linguistic unity, theologically shown in Christ and the Church (*Quaes.* 147), but also technically shown through Greek and Latin philology (*Quaes.* 151), which suggests that the two languages ultimately share a common origin.

Alcuin is also eager to associate the division at Babel with the disciples of Christ. As mentioned above, he claims that the division of languages caused by the pride of Babel's builders is united by the humility of Christ, and that "quos turris dissociaverat, Ecclesia collegit" (what the Tower broke up, the Church brought back together, *Quaes.* 147).[92] Only a few questions earlier, he states likewise that the seventy-two descendants of Noah's sons provide the categorical basis for the mission of the seventy-two disciples of Christ: "ortae sunt gentes septuaginta duae, inter quas misit Dominus discipulos septuaginta duos (seventy-two nations arose, among which the Lord sent seventy-two disciples, *Quaes.* 142). As with Bede, the affiliation between the diversity at Babel and the Church's unification of that diversity through its missions is a significant element of Alcuin's ecclesiastical theology. Aside from these comments in the *Quaestiones*, Alcuin hints at the realistic implications of the apostolic mission to convert an ethnically diverse world in his famous poem on York, *Versus de patribus regibus et sanctis Euboricensis ecclesiae*. In this work,

91 See Laistner, *Thought and Letters in Western Europe, A.D. 500 to 900*, 239–40.

92 This juxtaposition is comparable to Alcuin's statement a few questions later that Hebrew, the original language of Adam when death entered the world, becomes the language of salvation displayed on the *titulus* of the cross of Christ (*Quaes.* 150).

Alcuin relates the mission of Wilfrid to the efforts of the early Church. His verses are particularly reminiscent of Bede's prologue to the metrical *Vita S. Cuthberti* on the missions of the early disciples:[93]

> Tempore nam micuit Uuilfridus episcopus illo,
> virtutum meritis longe lateque per orbem,
> quem Deus omnipotens infudit luce superna,
> errorum tetricas terris ut pelleret umbras:
> per loca perpetuae quapropter multa salutis
> gentibus et populis doctrinae lumina sparsit

> For at that time Bishop Wilfrid shone, with the merits of his virtues, far and wide across the earth, whom omnipotent God filled with heavenly light so that he might drive the gloomy shadows of errors from the lands. For this reason, he strew the lights of the teaching of salvation across many places to nations and peoples.

Just as Christ's seventy-two disciples preached throughout the world to the seventy-two nations, so also, according to Alcuin's verses, do Wilfrid's virtues shine "across the earth," allowing him to participate in the same mission of the first disciples: to teach salvation to "many nations and peoples." Just as the first apostles at Pentecost, Wilfrid becomes a kind of apostle to the Northumbrians, saving them from pagan error by the truth of the gospel.

Alcuin did not stray very far from the exegetical tradition of his predecessors. The very production of an exposition on Genesis itself aligns him with the comparable endeavours of Jerome, Augustine, and Bede, among others. It is therefore no surprise that Alcuin follows his authorities and the interpretative tradition fairly closely. But his innovations to this tradition are certainly significant by revealing close examination and inquiry into the subject. The synonymy of Babel and Babylon was rarely questioned before Alcuin, if at all. And the logical conclusions, based on careful philological examination, that Alcuin draws regarding linguistic separation are impressive. However, Alcuin's comments on Babel, at their heart, do not deviate far from Bede's comments on the Pentecostal mission of the Church in post-Babylonian world. Not only are Christ's disciples

93 Alcuin, *The Bishops, Kings, and Saints of York*, 48–50, lines 577–82.

to preach to all the nations of the world, but conversely, those who preach Christ's gospel to the nations of the world are his disciples.

Both Bede's and Alcuin's works would enjoy much influence among Alcuin's Carolingian peers and pupils, fostering the continuation and development of the reception history of the Babel narrative. Hrabanus Maurus, Claudius of Turin, Angelomus of Luxeuil, and Remigius of Auxerre all employed Bede's and Alcuin's biblical expositions alongside earlier authorities, such as Augustine and Isidore.[94] These Carolingian luminaries contribute much fascinating material to the subject, but close examination of their writings goes beyond my present scope. For that reason, I will pass over Carolingian literature and turn now to the legacy of the early Anglo-Latin authors in Britain, where the Babel narrative would take on a striking new form: for many Anglo-Saxon authors after the ninth century, Old English would replace Latin. And with this linguistic shift came new developments to the reception history of Genesis 10–11.

94 The best account remains Borst, *Turmbau von Babel*, II.483–541.

Chapter Five

Alfred the Great and the Literature of His Reign

Introduction

In order to contextualize the Anglo-Saxon efforts for renewing ecclesiastical learning and culture in the late ninth century, I begin this chapter with Alfred's often cited description of the state of learning from the opening of the Preface to his *Pastoral Care*. After mentioning the happiness and peace that existed throughout Britain, as well as the high degree of teaching and learning that attracted foreigners to the island, Alfred laments:[1]

> Swa clæne hio wæs <oðfeallen nu> on Angelkynne ðætte swiðe feawe wæron behionan Humbre þe hiora ðenunga cuðen understandan on Englisc, oððe furðum an ærendgewrit of Lædene on Englisc areccan; & ic wene ðætte nauht monige begeondan Humbre næren.

> so completely had it [*sc.* wisdom and teaching] fallen among the Anglo-Saxons that there were very few people on this side of the Humber who could understand their official duties in English or even translate one letter from Latin into English; and I suppose that there were not many beyond the Humber.

Although there has been much debate over the veracity of this statement, the evidence seems to suggest that Alfred's dismal view of education in ninth-century Britain was accurate. Nicholas Brooks, in his examinations of the scriptorium at Canterbury, is able to conclude that the level of

1 Sweet, ed., *King Alfred's West-Saxon Version of Gregory's Pastoral Care*, Pref., 2.

Latin learning in Britain (and in particular in one of Britain's great centres of learning) was abysmal. Lapidge comes to similar conclusions through an examination of Anglo-Saxon literary output before Alfred's translation programs; and the studies of Gameson and Gneuss both understand the manuscript evidence (or lack thereof) as an indication of low levels of learning.[2]

Much had happened in Britain between the writings of Bede in the first half of the eighth century and Alfred's translation program at the end of the ninth. The Viking invasions had hindered the earlier great age of learning, and by the time relative stability returned, different cultural interests and emphases had emerged.[3] From the initial raid at Lindisfarne in 793 to around 865, many of the monasteries were destroyed and the many treasures, literary or otherwise, of the monastic libraries were irretrievably lost. It was not until 878 that King Alfred was able to defeat the Viking raiders at Edington, and make the initial steps for military, political, and, most important for this study, literary and cultural reforms. In imitation of Charlemagne, Alfred surrounded himself with a select group of national and international scholars, whose efforts resulted in a large group of Old English translations of Latin texts. This literary reform, which consisted mainly of translating "sumæ bec, ða ðe niedbeðearfosta sien eallum monnum to wiotonne" (certain books that are most necessary for all men to know),[4] sowed the initial seeds for vernacular writing in Anglo-Saxon England and forms a large part of the Old English corpus that survives today. By the late ninth century, the prestige and use of Old English had advanced to such an extent as to rival Latin as the written language of Britain. Even though Old English must have prevailed previously as the main language of oral discourse, the surviving corpus of Old English texts before Alfred's translation program is relatively small when compared to

2 Brooks, "England in the Ninth Century," 1–20, at 12; *The Early History of the Church of Canterbury*, 171; Lapidge, "Latin Learning in Ninth-Century England," 409–54; Gneuss, "Anglo-Saxon Libraries from the Conversion to the Benedictine Reform"; "King Alfred and the History of Anglo-Saxon Libraries"; and Gameson, "Alfred the Great and the Destruction and Production of Christian Books," 180–210. For alternative interpretations of the evidence, see Tunberg, "King Alfred's Letter as a Source on Learning in England," 87–110; and "Dated and Datable Manuscripts copied in England during the Ninth Century," 512–38.

3 Two succinct and valuable overviews of King Alfred are Franzen, *King Alfred*; and Keynes and Lapidge, *Alfred the Great*, esp. 9–63.

4 Alfred, *Pastoral Care*, Pref., p. 7.

the large number of Latin texts.[5] After the ninth century the reverse is true. Stronger "nationalistic" tendencies that had begun to arise with the political unity promoted by Alfred facilitated writing in English instead of Latin,[6] making Old English one of the first widely written vernaculars of the early Middle Ages. As Sarah Foot argues, Alfred "sought to persuade [his West Saxon and Mercian peoples] that he was restoring the English, whereas, albeit following a model provide by Bede, he was inventing them."[7] Unlike Bede, who stressed the ecclesiastical unity of a *gens Anglorum* speaking a plurality of languages, the Alfredian texts seem to stress English unification through the promotion of a single vernacular language.[8] Although Alfred's own involvement and claims to authorship in this translation program have been questioned ever since William of Malmesbury first attempted to define the Alfredian corpus,[9] Alfred, like Charlemagne, was nevertheless the central driving force behind the creation and distribution of one of the most important literary movements of the Anglo-Saxon era.[10]

---

5 See Orchard, "Latin and the Vernacular Languages," 191–219, esp. 213–18. For a survey of Old English texts before 900, see Bately, "Old English Prose Before and During the Reign of Alfred," 93–138.

6 The secondary literature is vast. Select studies include: Davis, "National Writing in the Ninth Century," 611–37; Foot, "The Making of *Angelcynn*," 51–78; Harris, *Race and Ethnicity in Anglo-Saxon Literature*, 83–105; Stodnick, "The Interests of Compounding," 337–67; and Pratt, *The Political Thought of King Alfred the Great*, 130–78.

7 Foot, "The Making of *Angelcynn*," 55–6. For the later historical creation of the English kingdom, see Molyneaux, *The Formation of the English Kingdom in the Tenth Century*.

8 For Bede, see Wormald, "Bede, the *Bretwaldas* and the Origins of the *gens Anglorum*," 106–34. For Britain's multilingualism in the ninth century with a focus on Scandinavian language contact, see O'Brien, *Reversing Babel*, 72–5.

9 Mynors, ed., *Gesta regum Anglorum*, vol. 1, II.123.1–2, 192.

10 See Bately, "The Alfredian Corpus Revisited," 107–20; Pratt, *The Political Thought of Alfred the Great*, part II, 113–337; and Whitelock, "The Prose of Alfred's Reign," 67–103. For scepticism regarding Alfred's authorship, see Godden, "Did King Alfred Write Anything?," 1–23; and Busse, "Die 'karolingische' Reform König Alfreds," 169–84. Alfred is most likely the main author of the translation of Augustine's *Soliloquies*, Boethius' *De consolatione Philosophae*, Gregory the Great's *Cura pastoralis*, and the first fifty psalms. Translations that appear to be connected to his scholarly circle are Bede's *Ecclesiastical History*, Gregory the Great's *Dialogues* by Werferth of Worcester, and Orosius's *Historiae adversos paganos*. Recently, Treschow et al., "King Alfred's Scholarly Writings and the Authorship of the First Fifty Prose Psalms," have cast doubt on Alfred's authorship, for which see the responses by Bately, "Did King Alfred Actually Translate Anything?," 189–215; and "Alfred as Author and Translator," 113–42. For a very useful

In effect, the new cultural and political conditions that dominated English sentiment inevitably manifested in all literary spheres, and the various interpretations and literary employments of the Tower of Babel narrative are no exception. The political uniformity of Anglo-Saxon England after the late ninth century (albeit at times very unstable) was not so much concerned with justifying its position within a multicultural and multilingual Church as it was with preserving that homogenous identity and cultural independence. The inherited elements of late antique and early Anglo-Saxon traditions that interpreted the ethnic and linguistic diversity of the Tower of Babel in light of the unity of the universal Church are often downplayed in Alfredian texts. Other elements of the Babel narrative such as the transience of glory, the wicked builders of the Tower, or the origins of paganism, take the forefront.

With that said, the new political and cultural situations of Britain, present during Alfred's tenure as King of Wessex (871–99), forced reconsiderations of linguistic issues, especially those involving the vernacular. Alfred's translation program is a direct result of the reassessment not only of linguistic diversity, but also of linguistic hierarchy. Although there is no direct evidence that the Tower of Babel narrative, along with its typological counterpart, Pentecost, played a part in forming the ways that ninth-century Anglo-Saxons looked at and justified the use of Old English, the inherited biblical and patristic tradition that understood the world's linguistic diversity to have resulted from the Tower of Babel and to have been legitimized at Pentecost was certainly at work. After outlining various interpretations of Babel and Pentecost among authors familiar to Alfred, Robert Stanton argues: "Alfred made no grand claims for the sacrality of English or the Pentecostal possibilities of his reforms. But following many eminent thinkers before him, he valorized the vernacular through simple usage, which after all was what gave the three sacred languages their authority."[11] Stanton is also careful to emphasize the pragmatic necessity behind Alfred's translation program and the desire to foster learning by disseminating texts that were linguistically accessible.[12]

annotated bibliography on the subject, see Discenza and Szarmach, "Annotated Bibliography on the Authorship Issue," 397–415.

11 Stanton, *Culture of Translation*, 72; see also Stanton, "Linguistic Fragmentation and Redemption," 26.

12 Stanton, "Linguistic Fragmentation and Redemption," 26.

It is, therefore, a pragmatic rather than theological impulse that appears in Alfred's preface to his translation of Gregory's *Pastoral Care*:[13]

> Ða gemunde ic hu sio æ wæs ærest on Ebreisc geðiode funden, & eft, þa þa hie Crecas geleornodon, þa wendon hi hie on hiora ægen geðiode ealle, & eac ealle oðre bec. And eft Lædenware swa same, siððan hi hie geleornodon, hi hie wendon ealle ðurh wise wealhstodas on hiora agen geðeode. & eac ealla oðra Cristena ðioda sumne dæl hiora on hiora agen geðiode wendon.

> Then I reflected on how the law was first found among the Hebrew language, and afterward, when the Greeks learned it, they translated it completely into their own language, and also other books completely. And afterwards the Romans did the same; after they learned it, they translated it completely through wise interpreters into their own language; and so all other Christian nations translated some part of it into their own languages.

Although Alfred recognizes that all the world's different Christian ethnic groups are permitted to render the originally Hebrew "æ" (law), into their own languages, it is significant that Alfred stresses the order in which translation occurs. Both the Greeks and the Romans learned the law before making their own translations. Unlike at Pentecost, where the Gospel was preached simultaneously to every language group present, in this case, the necessity of already knowing the wisdom of a text precedes translation of that text. Of course, practically speaking, every translator must know the language of the text that is to be translated, but Alfred's emphasis on the prior learning of the Greeks and Romans is curious. He provides a justification for translation into the vernacular, but at the same time qualifies the need of competence to translate. Is Alfred, therefore, offering his own credentials with an inference that he himself has learned the text before undertaking his translation? In any case, neither Babel nor Pentecost seems to be at the forefront of Alfred's mind in these lines. Rather there is

13 Alfred, *Pastoral Care*, pref. 4.25–6.6. It should be noted, however, that according to tradition, the Israelites were given the Law on the same day as Pentecost. See, for example, Isidore, *Quaestiones in vetus testamentum*, PL 83, col. 300B–C: "Jam deinde quinquagesima die post actum pascha data est lex Moysi. Ita et quinquagesima die post passionem Domini, quam pascha illud praefigurabat, datus est Spiritus sanctus" (then on the fifteenth day after the event of Passover, the Law of Moses was given. So also the fifteenth day after the passion of the Lord, which prefigures that Passover, the Holy Spirit was given). See also Adler, *Das erste christliche Pfingsfest*, 46–54.

an eagerness for the vernacular to participate in the dissemination of Christian law through the act of translation – an act that Alfred contextualizes as part of the progression of the Mosaic law through to Anglo-Saxon legal codes in his preface to the Old English *Domboc*.[14] At the same time, the underlying justification for vernacular participation is not possible without a theological framework of the consecration of linguistic diversity at Pentecost.

Old English *Boethius*

Elsewhere in the Alfredian corpus, the Tower of Babel narrative plays an important role. In the Old English translation of the *Consolation of Philosophy*, Alfred expands upon Boethius's Latin by including mention of Nimrod and the building of Babel. Whereas the Boethian reference to the gigantomachia, the mythological war between the giants and the gods, is for Alfred "leasunga" (lies) that are told "on ealdum leasum spellum" (in old lying tales), the true story ("soðspell") tells of Nimrod and the builders of the Tower of Babel.[15] Boethius's Latin, "Accepisti ... in fabulis lacessentes caelum Gigantas" (you have heard ... in the fables of the Giants that harass heaven),[16] effectively becomes with Alfred a long discussion syncretizing the gigantomachia and the Tower of Babel narrative that provides extra-biblical material on the site of the Tower, the builders' intentions, and a moral lesson:[17]

> Hwæt ic wat þæt ðu geherdest oft reccan on ealdum leasum spellum þætte Iob Saturnes sunu sceolde beon se hehsta god ofer ealle oðre godas, and he scelde bion þæs heofenes sunu and scolde ricsian on heofenum. And scoldon gigantas bion eorþan suna, and þa sceoldon ricsian ofer eorðan ... Þa sceolde þam gigantum ofþincan þæt he hæfde hire rice, woldon ða tobrecan þone hefon under him ... Ðyllice leasunga hi worhton, and mihton eaðe secgan

14 Liebermann, ed., *Die Gesetze der Angelsachsen*, I.26–47. See Wormald, *The Making of English Law*, 265–85; and Treschow, "The Prologue to Alfred's Law Code," 79–110.

15 Alfred, *The Old English Boethius*, B text, 35.117 and 126–7, vol. 1, 333–4. For Alfred's use of classical material, see Grinda, "The Myth of Circe in King Alfred's *Boethius*," 237–65; Irvine, "Ulysses and Circe in King Alfred's *Boethius*," 387–401; "Wrestling with Hercules," 171–87; Bately, "Those Books that Are Most Necessary for All Men to Know," 45–78; and Otten, *König Alfreds Boethius*, 125–41.

16 Boethius, *Philosophiae consolatio*, III, 12.59–60.

17 Alfred, *The Old English Boethius*, B text, 35.116–40, vol. 1, 333–4.

soðspell gif him þa leasunga næron swetran, and þeah swiðe gelic þisum. Hi mihton secgan hwylc dysig Nefrod se gigant worhte. Nefrod wæs Chuses sunu; Chus wæs Chaames sunu, Chaam Noes. Se Nefrod het wyrcan anne tor on þam felda þe Sennar hatte, and on þære ðiode þe Deira hatte swiðe neah þære byrig þe mon nu hæt Babilonia. Þæt hi dydon for þam ðingum þæt hi woldon witon hu heah hit wære to þam hefone and hu þicke se hefon wære and hu fæst, oððe hwæt þær ofer wære. Ac hit gebyrede, swa hit cynn was, þæt se godcunda anweald hi tostente ær hi hit fullwyrcan moston, and towearp þone torr, and hiora manigne ofslog, and hiora spræce todælde on twa and hundseofontig geþeoda. Swa gebyreð ælcum þara ðe winð þam godcundan anwealde. Ne gewexð him nan weorðscipe on þam, ac wyrð se gewanod þe hi ær hæfdon.

Lo, I know that you often heard tell in old false tales that Jupiter, son of Saturn, was supposedly the highest god over all other gods, and he was supposedly the son of heaven and supposedly ruled in heaven. And the giants were supposedly the sons of the earth and they supposedly ruled over the earth ... Then it supposedly displeased the giants that Jupiter had their kingdom, and they wanted to break heaven under him ... The poets made up such lies and they could have easily told the truth if the lies were not more pleasant; nevertheless, there is one very similar to these lies. They could have told what foolishness the giant Nimrod did. Nimrod was the son of Chus; Chus was the son of Ham, and Ham the son of Noah. Nimrod commanded that a tower be built on that field which is called Shinar, and in that region which is called Deira – very near to the city which people now call Babylon. They did that because they wanted to know how high it was to heaven and how thick heaven was and how secure, or what was beyond it. But it happened, as was fitting, that the divine power dispersed them before they could complete it, and cast down that tower, and slew many of them, and divided their speech into seventy-two languages. Thus does it happen to those who strive against divine power. No honour accumulates for them in that, but that which they previously had becomes diminished.

Much commentary has attempted to explain the presence of and a source for this Alfredian addition. The conflation of the giants and builders of the Tower of Babel may have initially arisen on account of a gloss in Alfred's Latin copy, such as one by the St Gall commentator which states: "loquitur secundum fidem gentilium vel etiam tangit veritatem, quando divisio linguarum facta est" (s/he [i.e., Lady Philosophy; or perhaps Boethius, the author] is speaking according to the faith of the pagans or also touches the truth [concerning the time] when the division of languages happened).[18] As Godden and Irvine suggest, "the O[ld] E[nglish] author may have been prompted by some such gloss, but his retelling of the two stories [i.e., Babel and the gigantomachia] develops a more detailed parallel than this brief comment suggests."[19] In fact, a long tradition connecting Nimrod and the biblical giants to the gigantomachia had already been established by the ninth century. Though ultimately uncertain regarding Alfred's immediate source, John H. Brinegar outlines many biblical or patristic analogues that might have influenced Alfred, the most probable being Avitus's *De deluuio mundi*.[20] Bede also refers to the connection between the giants of Greek fables and Babel in his commentary on Genesis, though it is not certain how familiar Alfred would have been with Bede's work.[21] Before Bede and Avitus, the tradition extends as far back as pseudo-Eupolemus and the Jewish Sibylline oracles,[22] and it is quite possible that Alfred did not use any one direct source when he connected the pagan giants with the builders of Babel.

In Alfred's account, he states that intellectual curiosity is behind the motives of the builders of the Tower. Rather than instigating a rebellion against God, creating shelter for a second flood, or even making a name for themselves, the builders simply want to discover the nature of heaven:

---

18 Otten, *König Alfreds Boethius*, 129; see also Godden and Irvine, *The Old English Boethius*, vol. 2, 409; and Frankis, "The Thematic Significance of *enta geweorc* and Related Imagery in *The Wanderer*," 253–70, at 262. The relationship between Alfred's Old English text and medieval Latin glosses of Boethius's *Consolatio* has proven vexing to scholars. See Schepss, "Zu König Alfreds *Boethius*," 149–60, at 152; and Donaghey, "The Sources of King Alfred's Translation of Boethius's *De consolatione philosophiae*," 23–57, at 36–7 and 52–3.

19 Godden and Irvine, *The Old English Boethius*, vol. 2, 409.

20 Brinegar, "'Books Most Necessary,'" 71–85. For Avitus, see *Liber quartus de diluuio mundi*, 108–22, 239: "Haec sunt priscorum quae de terrore gigantum / Carmine mentito Grai cecinere poetae ... Non prius absistens, subitas discordia linguas / Quam daret et varius confunderet omnia sermo" (these are those which the Greek poets sang about in a lying song on the terror of the first giants ... [that race] did not subsist [in its madness] before discord gave unexpected languages and various speeches confused everything).

21 Bede, *In principium Genesis*, II.983–6: "Gigantes ... etiam post diluuium, id est temporibus Moysi uel Dauid multos fuisse legimus, qui nomen habent Grece ex eo quod illos iuxta fabulas poetarum terra genuerit" (we read that there were many giants after the Flood, that is, in the times of Moses and David; they have their name in Greek because according to the fables of the poets, the earth bore them).

22 Menner, "Nimrod and the Wolf in the Old English *Solomon and Saturn*," 332–54, at 339. See also Speyer, "Gigant," 1271, for other examples.

"Þæt hi dydon for þam ðingum þæt hi woldon witon hu heah hit wære to þam hefone and hu þicke se hefon wære and hu fæst, oððe hwæt þær ofer wære" (they did that because they wanted to know how high it was to heaven and how thick heaven was and how secure, or what was beyond it). While it is likely that Alfred includes this motive in order to ridicule the absurdity of the builders, the motive does seem disconnected with the moral provided at the end of the passage: "Swa gebyreð ælcum þara ðe winð þam godcundan anwealde. Ne gewexð him nan weorðscipe on þam, ac wyrð se gewanod þe hi ær hæfdon" (thus does it happen to those who strive against divine power. No honour accumulates for them in that, but that which they previously had becomes diminished). Apparently, too much inquiry into the things that lie beyond human understanding is equivalent to rebellion against divine power. But it is also possible that the intellectual curiosity of the builders regarding the heavens reflects the association between Nimrod and astrology that appears in some depictions of the giant.[23]

Another interesting Alfredian addition is the distinction between the Tower of Babel and Babylon, along with the specific details of the field of Shinar and the province of Deira. As previously mentioned, throughout Late Antiquity, Babel and Babylon were near synonyms; if a distinction was to be made, it was according to chronology: Babel was the original Babylon. By the time Alfred is translating Boethius's *Consolatio*, however, evidently some confusion had arisen over the two different names. Using an example from the previous chapter, Alcuin's *Quaestiones* clarifies: "aestimatur a pluribus arcem esse civitatis Babyloniae turrem illam" (it is thought by many that the citadel of the city of Babylon is that Tower).[24] Likewise, in *Genesis A* there seems to be a discrepancy between the field of Shinar and the city of Babylon; for after describing how the builders scattered in four directions, leaving the Tower behind them (1697–1701), the poet notes that Abraham was born in Babylon (1706–10). Though this detail may stem from an interpretation of the place "Ur Chaldeorum" in Genesis 11:31,[25] it does seem odd after the description of the scattering of nations from Babel. But unlike Alcuin's clarification,

23 Nimrod is most prominently associated with astrology in the *Liber Nimrod*; see Livesey and Rouse, "Nimrod the Astronomer." See also the account of Byrhtferth below, 167–9.

24 Alcuin, *Interrogationes*, PL 100, col. 533C, 149. See Frankis, "The Thematic Significance," 263.

25 See Doane, ed., *Genesis A*, 353–4.

which unequivocally locates the Tower of Babel within the city of Babylon, the Old English *Boethius* distinctly dislocates Babel and Babylon: the Tower is not in but "swiðe neah þære byrig þe mon nu hæt Babilonia" (very near to the city which people now call Babylon). Perhaps the author is simply attempting to reconcile the idea that the city of Babylon, which has its origins in Babel, still stands, despite later notions that Babylon had been destroyed, or that the site of the city of the Tower of Babel had become uninhabitable.[26]

The mention of the field of Shinar in the province of Deira is also interesting. According to Genesis, Shinar is both the land that held the field where the Tower of Babel was built, "campum in terra Sennaar" (a field in the land of Shinar) (Genesis 11:2), as well as the home of Nimrod (Genesis 10:10). The presence of Shinar in a description of Babel is, therefore, not surprising, even if it is applied to the field instead of the land: "felda þe Sennar hatte" (the field which was called Shinar).[27] The addition of the place name Deira, on the other hand, is unusual. Originally derived from the place name Dura in Daniel 3:1, where Nebuchadnezzar makes a golden idol "in campo Dura provinciae Babylonis" (on the field of Dura in the province of Babylon), the reference to Deira in the Old English Boethius serves a dual purpose. First, even though Alfred abstains from identifying Babel with Babylon, the reference to Deira helps to unite the two by creating a common locale for both. It connects Babel and Babylon not only spatially, since it locates Shinar and Babylon within the same general region (*ðiode*), but also temporally, since the place name Dura is used in the Bible only for the later Babylon of Nebuchadnezzar's empire. With the inclusion of the place Deira, Alfred can insinuate that ancient Babel's lineage extends to modern Babylon, even if they are not exactly synonymous. Second, the resemblance of Alfred's Babylonian Deira to the Anglo-Saxon kingdom of Deira cannot have been missed by an Anglo-Saxon audience, even if the surviving Old English forms of the kingdom are not *Deira* but "*Deiri*" and "*Dere.*"[28] It would be astonishing to think that Alfred's Anglo-Saxon audience should be so naive as to think that the

26 See the Middle English accounts of Babel in *Mandeville's Travels*, 28; and in John Lydgate's *Fall of Princes*, part 1, I.1139–48.

27 The C text of Alfred, *Boethius*, 22.100, p. 487, contains the unusual form "Nensar."

28 Alfred, *The Old English Boethius*, vol. 2, 410. The Latin form, however, is *Deira*, as apparent in Gregory the Great's famous pun in Bede, *Ecclesiastical History*, II.1. Godden and Irvine also note that the variant *Deira* for Babylonian *Dura* is found in Jerome, *Commentariorum in Danielem libri III*, I.iii.473 (see also I.i.25–7). This commentary

site of the building of the Tower of Babel was as close as Anglo-Saxon Deira. But it is not inconceivable that an Anglo-Saxon would recognize the English region Deira as analogous with Alfred's Babylonian Deira, at least on a paronomastic level. In fact, the verbal similarities between the Babylonian region and the Anglo-Saxon kingdom may have been poignantly reinforced by the further connections between Nebuchadnezzar's idolatry in Dura / Deira, and the Vikings' idolatry in Deira, "an area rich in the remains of the past, both Roman and Northumbrian, and in Alfred's day an area of pagan Scandinavian settlement."[29] By this subtle verbal connection, the moral lessons of Babel / Babylon are reinforced to become relevant to Anglo-Saxon England, despite its remove from the place and time of the original tower and city.

The Old English *Orosius*

The Old English translation of Orosius's *Historiae aduersum paganos*, a text that does not seem to have been translated by Alfred himself, but rather by an author or authors connected to his translation program,[30] provides further information on Anglo-Saxon treatments of Genesis 10–11. Although the Old English text remains, in general, faithful to its Latin exemplar, there are points where vast differences between the Latin and Old English versions are evident.[31] One such difference is found at the very beginning of the Old English work. Whereas Orosius's Latin account includes a preface and an outline of the work's methodology, the Old English version, after a table of contents, begins immediately with the division of the world into the three continents, "Asiam 7 Europem 7 Affricam" (Asia and Europe and Africa).[32] From this traditional division of the world, the translator, following Orosius's Latin, sets out to provide a universal geography. But instead of rendering a faithful account of the

---

also appears to have been used by the author of *Solomon and Saturn II*; see O'Neill, "On the Date, Provenance and Relationship of the 'Solomon and Saturn' Dialogues," 130–68, at 150–1.

29 Frankis, "The Thematic Significance," 264; see also Orchard, *Pride and Prodigies*, 82.

30 Bately, ed., *Old English Orosius*, lxxiii–xciii. See also Leneghan, "*Translatio Imperii*," 656–705.

31 See Khalaf, "A Study on the Translator's Omissions and Instances of Adaptation in the *Old English Orosius*," 195–222.

32 *Old English Orosius*, 8.14.

Latin, some of the geographical descriptions in the Old English have been added to or even rewritten in order to update the geography of the world, especially that of continental and northern Europe.[33] As Nicole Guenther Discenza points out, despite the authorial liberty to contemporize European geography, the presentation of Britain is much slimmer than what would be expected for an English author: "Britain's peoples are not listed, unlike those of other parts of Europe. The British Isles, like Thule, appear too distant to be known."[34] But, as Discenza goes on to argue, a "geographical recentering" of Britain occurs in the text during the interviews of Ohthere and Wulfstan with King Alfred: "the interviewers say nothing of England itself, but the shifted viewpoint makes that unnecessary: England becomes the center to which these explorers return after they have gone to *more* marginal lands, and Alfred is their 'lord.'"[35] This recentring in the Old English *Orosius* discloses some of the nuances behind the political hegemony forming under King Alfred. The traditional division of the world into the three continents of Noah's three sons is affirmed, but ethnic or national status is also recalibrated to legitimize the political identity of the Anglo-Saxons. Just as the Church validated and empowered the presence of Christianity on the margins of the world, so also is Anglo-Saxon political power presented in such a way as to confirm its control despite its position at the edge of the world.[36]

Outside of the geographical descriptions, the Old English *Orosius*, following the Latin, specifically treats the Tower of Babel. In both the Latin and Old English, Nimrod is termed a giant; the description and measurements of the city and its fortifications are nearly consistent; and the building materials are, with one exception, brick and bitumen.[37] But despite the

---

33 Bately, "The Relationship between Geographical Information in the Old English Orosius and Latin Texts Other than Orosius," 45–62, at 52–4; and *Old English Orosius*, lxvii–lxxii.

34 Discenza, "A Map of the Universe: Geography and Cosmology in the Program of Alfred the Great," 83–108, at 90. For the Old English, see *Old English Orosius*, 19.11–20.

35 Discenza, "A Map of the Universe," 94, emphasis hers. See also Michelet, *Creation, Migration, and Conquest*, 132–9. For the Old English, see *Old English Orosius*, 13.29–18.2.

36 See Harris's arguments for interpreting a shift of focus from "a Roman Christ to a Germanic Christendom," *Race and Ethnicity in Anglo-Saxon Literature*, 90–105; and "The Alfredian World History and Anglo-Saxon Identity," 482–510.

37 Orosius, *Historiarum adversum paganos libri vii*, II.6.6–13; *Orosius*, 43.19–44.6. See Bately, *Old English Orosius*, 235.

relative consistency between the two works, there are some interesting alterations in the Old English. First, after translating the Latin line, "murus coctili latere atque interfuso bitumine conpactus," as "he is geworht of tigelan 7 of eorðtyrewan" (it is made of brick and bitumen), the Old English author mistakes the homonymous form *latere* of Orosius's later line, "utroque latere" (on both sides) as a second reference to the building material *later* (brick). In this case, he is not consistent with his earlier rendition and translates it with the adjective "stænenum" (stone).[38] Not only is the use of the adjective *stænen* remarkable for its variation from the earlier Old English *tigelan* (brick), but as Bately notes, this unusual feature is strikingly at odds with classical descriptions of the city, which mention stone only in reference to a bridge.[39] However, while the inconsistency of translation remains unusual, reference to Babel's stone material, though not in accordance with classical descriptions of the city, can be found elsewhere in Old English literature. Specifically, in *Genesis A* the adjective *stænen* is used to describe the Tower of Babel. Because the association of stone with Babel or Babylon is absent outside of Anglo-Saxon England, these two instances reveal a minor but unique tendency in Old English literature to ascribe stonework to the building of Babel. Without pushing the evidence too far, it is possible that this tendency is related to Anglo-Saxon interpretations of ruined stone buildings as a characteristic of the ancient past.[40]

A second alteration in the Old English *Orosius* expands material regarding Babylon's founders. Whereas the Latin simply states: "namque Babylonam a Nebrot gigante fundatam, a Nino uel Samiramide reparatam multi prodidere" (for many have asserted that Babylon was founded by Nimrod the giant and repaired by Ninus or Semiramis), the Old English renders: "Membrað se ent angan ærest timbran Babylonia 7 Ninus se cyning æfter him. 7 Sameramis his cwen hie geendade æfter him on middeweardum hiere rice" (Nimrod the giant first began to build Babylon, and Ninus the king after him. And Semiramis his queen finished it after him in the middle

38 Orosius, *Historiarum adversum paganos libri vii*, II.6.9–10; *Old English Orosius*, 43.28, 43.32.

39 Bately, *Old English Orosius*, 235. An exception might be Isidore's description of the Babylonian temple as made of marble; *Chronica*, § 22.

40 Frankis, "The Thematic Significance," 265, suggests that the adjective *stænenum* reflects, "the Anglo-Saxon literary preoccupation with specifically stone structures with reference to the work of giants and the theme of ruin."

of her reign).[41] The reasons behind the difference are subtle; the Latin word, *reparatam* (repaired), indicates that city-building ceased when the workers of the Tower of Babel were scattered, only to begin again in the form of a new city of Babylon under Ninus. The Old English, however, is not concerned with the unfulfilled efforts of Nimrod and the builders of Babel, but rather with establishing continuity from the city's early history and its later rulers: Ninus, the first king of the Assyrians, a blood-drinker and the killer of Zoroaster; and his wife, Semiramis, a cruel queen who tries to kill her son after having incestuous relations with him.[42] Without reference to Orosius's Latin text, the Old English account gives the impression that Babel did not fall, but rather that its infamous rulers succeeded one after another. This continuity in the Old English helps to underline the wickedness of the lineage extending from Nimrod, the giant, to Ninus, the tyrant, to Semiramis, the evil queen. By doing so, it better represents the enduring archetype of Babylon, especially as the symbolic head of the Augustinian city of the Devil.

Once this wicked lineage of Babel / Babylon is established, and the city's magnificent architecture has been described, the author turns his portrayal of the city into a moral lesson that has no basis in the Latin. According to Bately, Orosius's Latin word *confirmat* at the end of the description of Babylon "is apparently taken to indicate speech on the part of the city."[43] Whatever the initial inspiration, the Old English deviates from the Latin to have the city itself lament that its former glory has passed and that it is now nothing but a warning to those thinking they are secure or strong enough to last in the world:[44]

> heo wære to bisene asteald eallum middangearde, 7 eac swelce heo self sprecende sie to eallum moncynne 7 cweþe: "Nu ic þuss gehroren eam 7 aweg gewiten, hwæt, ge magan on me ongietan 7 oncnawan þæt ge nanuht mid eow nabbað fæstes ne stronges þætte þurhwunigean mæge."
>
> The city was set as an example to all the world, as if it itself might be speaking and saying to all humankind: "Now I am thus fallen and passed away; see,

41 Orosius, *Historiarum adversum paganos libri vii*, II.6.7; *Old English Orosius* 43.21–3.

42 *Old English Orosius*, 21.23–22.28 and 36.12–28.

43 Bately, *Old English Orosius*, 235; but see Godden, "The Old English *Orosius* and its Sources," 297–320, esp. 319.

44 *Old English Orosius*, 44.1–6.

you can look on me and know that you have nothing with you that is secure nor strong enough to be able to endure."

Although the city of Babylon is here referring to its later destruction by Cyrus, as Frankis states, it is explicitly connected to the original city of Babel through the chain of its original rulers, Nimrod, Ninus, and Semiramis.[45] The city, in other words, was created with evil intent and ruled until its destruction with evil intent. The desire for glory that its builders sought and, to some extent, achieved through its architectural grandeur becomes a moral lesson for the entire world (*eallum middangearde*) that speaks to all humankind (*eallum moncynne*) – a lesson that is poignantly underlined by the ironic fact that the very city where linguistic diversity was created is now lamenting with one voice to everyone. Babel / Babylon, in a sense, is only able to transcend its linguistic punishment by offering a model of the retribution that accompanies such wrongdoing. In this transcendence of its own linguistic punishment, the city's speech serves a fundamental purpose for the Old English author: it gives relevance to Babel / Babylon by turning it into an archetype for the failure of all proud endeavours against God, in much the same way that the building of the Tower provides an exemplum of divine punishment and the futility of earthly glory in the Old English *Boethius*.

The Ark-Born Son of Noah

As mentioned above, the geography of the Alfredian *Orosius* states that there are three continents of the world; this statement, of course, stems from the geographical symbolism attached to the three sons of Noah. However, in some West-Saxon royal genealogies of the ninth and tenth centuries, a fourth son of Noah is included for propaganda purposes. As Thomas D. Hill has shown, the notion of Noah's fourth son is not original to Anglo-Saxon England, and an intriguing analogue can be found in the *Reuelationes* of pseudo-Methodius, an eighth-century work that might have been known among the scholars of Anglo-Saxon England who composed the royal genealogies.[46] Hill argues that the pseudo-Methodius text, which contains the extra-biblical figure of Jonitus, a son of Noah who

45 Frankis, "The Thematic Significance," 265.
46 Hill, "The Myth of the Ark-Born Son and the West-Saxon Royal Genealogical Tables," 379–83, at 381–3. See also Gero, "The Legend of the Fourth Son of Noah."

resembles the traditional characteristics of his later friend and student Nimrod, gives at least one precedent to justify the inclusion of an ark-born son in Anglo-Saxon genealogies.[47] Conversely, Daniel Anlezark rejects any connection between pseudo-Methodius and the Anglo-Saxon genealogies, but argues in favour of the Syriac *Book of the Cave of Treasures* as a more likely candidate. Anlezark bases his argument on the possibility that Theodore, who seems to have known the text, introduced the notion of an ark-born son into Anglo-Saxon England through his Canterbury School. From Theodore, this son became removed from the context of the *Book of the Cave of Treasures* but continued to offer an authoritative precedent to the Anglo-Saxon genealogists.[48] Anlezark's criticism of Hill rests on the date of pseudo-Methodius and the lack of any evidence that it was known by the ninth century in Anglo-Saxon England.[49] But it is just as likely, if not more, that English monks "either in their travels or by courtesy of loans," as Michael W. Twomey suggests,[50] learned of pseudo-Methodius's ark-born son which, removed from its own immediate context, provided a foundation for the ark-born sons of the royal genealogies.

Whatever its origins, the presence of an extra-biblical ark-born son in the West-Saxon genealogies is curious, and Anlezark gives a thorough treatment of the subject with much bibliographical reference that does not need to be repeated here.[51] In sum, Anlezark argues that the ark-born son is an ideological, not theological, development from the time of King Alfred: "the fusion of the heroic Germanic past with the world of the biblical patriarchs which the invention of Sceaf as the fourth son of Noah suggests is certainly an ideological innovation appropriate to the reign of

---

47 See pseudo-Methodius, *Die Apokalypse des Pseudo-Methodius die ältesten griechischen und lateinischen Übersetzungen*, § [3], 4, 82–3.

48 Anlezark, *Water and Fire*, 254–8. See also Biggs, "Cave of Treasures," 6. Borst, *Turmbau von Babel*, II.543, also suggests the *Book of the Cave of Treasures* as an analogue for the ark-born son.

49 For a recent and very thorough study on the *Reuelationes* of pseudo-Methodius in England, see Twomey, "The *Revelationes* of Pseudo-Methodius and Scriptural Study at Salisbury in the Eleventh Century," 370–86, at 377–8.

50 Twomey, "The *Revelationes* of Pseudo-Methodius and Scriptural Study at Salisbury in the Eleventh Century," 378. The Latin note that cites Methodius in the Old English Hexateuch is drawn from Peter Comestor, not first hand knowledge of pseudo-Methodius; see Twomey, "Pseudo-Methodius Revelations," 19.

51 Anlezark, *Fire and Water*, ch. 5, "Planting Noah's Seed," 241–90; and the earlier version, "Sceaf, Japheth and the Origins of the Anglo-Saxons," 13–46.

Alfred."[52] For the purposes of this study, it will be sufficient to mention that the presence of Sceaf as the ark-born son in the royal genealogies (and also the father of Scyld mentioned in the opening lines of *Beowulf*)[53] is important in that it reveals how fluid the interpretative tradition of the Table of Nations could be. Because the invention of a fourth son of Noah is perhaps the most atypical (and audacious) alteration to the biblical account of the descendants of Noah in Anglo-Saxon England, it provides a striking example of the fusion of Anglo-Saxon concerns with authoritative Christian texts. Some of the authors of Anglo-Saxon England were not so bound to the authoritative traditions of the past or of the continent that they were prevented from offering creative deviations for their own specific purposes. Although the notion of an ark-born son of Noah enjoyed limited popularity and acceptance among later Anglo-Saxons,[54] it provides one of the more extreme examples of the freedom to alter the inherited tradition for, in this case, ideological or political purposes.

Solomon and Saturn II

Last, *Solomon and Saturn II*, one of three Old English dialogues between the pagan god Saturn and the Jewish king Solomon, offers some interesting, though opaque, material on Anglo-Saxon usage of the Tower of Babel narrative. Described as one of "the most unusual" poems of Anglo-Saxon literature,[55] *Solomon and Saturn II* has frustrated much scholarly interpretation. It is preserved incomplete in only one manuscript, Cambridge, Corpus Christi College 422,[56] has no known source, and cannot be dated with any certainty. Though Anlezark, the poem's most recent editor, has argued for a later date of composition during Dunstan's time at the monastery at Glastonbury (c. 920–c. 939), Patrick P. O'Neill has found the connections between the poem and the Alfredian texts compelling enough

52 Anlezark, *Fire and Water*, 272.

53 See Orchard, *A Critical Companion to Beowulf*, 100–3.

54 For authors who state there were only eight people in the ark, see Anlezark, *Fire and Water*, 273–82. There is also biblical precedent to enumerate those on the ark as "octo animae salvae factae sunt per aquam" (1 Peter 3:20).

55 Anlezark, ed., *The Old English Dialogues of Solomon and Saturn*, vii.

56 See Anlezark, ed., *The Old English Dialogues of Solomon and Saturn*, 1–4; and Ker, *Catalogue of Manuscripts Containing Anglo-Saxon*, no. 70.

to ascribe it to the earlier Alfredian period.[57] Neither argument is conclusive, but I will discuss *Solomon and Saturn II* here alongside the Alfredian texts, solely because of the thematic relationship of the texts concerning the Babel narrative.

Solomon and Saturn II provides a unique variation on the medieval genre of Solomon dialogues. As Robert J. Menner points out, in other Solomon dialogues of the Middle Ages, Solomon's opponent is not Saturn, but a certain Marcolfus (who is given brief mention in *Solomon and Saturn II*).[58] It is only in the Old English versions that the character of Marcolfus is replaced by the sagacious Chaldean Saturn. This Chaldean (that is Babylonian) characteristic of Saturn, which may not be obvious to the modern reader, would have likely been more evident to a medieval audience familiar with patristic material. Isidore provides a fitting example that, in all probability, provides the origins of the Old English depiction of a Babylonian Saturn:[59] "Bel idolum Babylonium est, quod interpretatur vetus. Fuit autem hic Belus pater Nini, primus rex Assyriorum, quem quidam Saturnum appellant" (Bel is a Babylonian idol, which is interpreted as "old." And this Belus was the father of Ninus, as well as the first king of the Assyrians, whom some call Saturn).

In accordance with Saturn's association with Babylon, the *Solomon and Saturn II* poet has Saturn learn his lore among various eastern (and European) nations at the beginning of the dialogue (7–23),[60] and in the

57 For composition by Dunstan, see Anlezark, ed., *Old English Dialogues*, 49–57. For composition in Alfred's circle, see O'Neill, "On the Date, Provenance and Relationship of the 'Solomon and Saturn' Dialogues," 139–68, at 152–64. For earlier scholarship, which is also inconclusive, see Menner, ed., *The Poetical Dialogues of Solomon and Saturn*, 12–17.

58 Menner, "Nimrod and the Wolf," 350–1; and Anlezark, ed., *Old English Dialogues*, 13–14. The mention of Marcolfus appears in line 11: "Marculfes eard" (the land of Marcolfus). For the Solomon and Marcolfus dialogues, see Ziolkowski, ed., *Solomon and Marcolf*.

59 Isidore, *Etymologiae*, VIII.xi.23; see O'Keeffe, "The Geographic List of *Solomon and Saturn II*," 123–41, at 137, nt. 66; and Anlezark, ed., *Old English Dialogues*, 31–3. Powell, "The Anglo-Saxon Imaginary of the East," 64–6, offers an interesting discussion on the absence of the term Babylon in the poem. O'Neill, "On the Date, Provenance and Relationship of the 'Solomon and Saturn' Dialogues," 157–8, nt. 83, however, questions the usefulness of Isidore for Saturn's association with the Chaldeans.

60 As O'Neill, "On the Date, Provenance and Relationship of the 'Solomon and Saturn' Dialogues," 143, observes, Saturn in *Solomon and Saturn I* obtains his knowledge from "Greece, Libya and India – a synecdoche for the three continents known to the ancient world, Europe, Africa and Asia."

Solomon and Saturn Poetic Fragment, which precedes *Solomon and Saturn II* at the head of the manuscript, but is thought to be the conclusion of the poem,[61] Saturn is referred to as the "Caldea eorl" (chief of the Chaldeans, 7). Likewise, Solomon, who capitalizes on Saturn's association with the Chaldeans, twice alludes to the building of the Tower of Babel. The first allusion appears after a substantial lacuna (one erased folio) that follows the poem's introduction (26–30):[62]

> Wat ic ðæt wæron Caldeas
> guðe ðæs gielpne   ond ðæs goldwlonce,
> mærða ðæs modige,   ðær to ðam moning gelomp
> suð ymbe Sanere feld.

> I know that Chaldeans were so boastful in war and so arrogant with gold, so brave in glory – a warning was given there, south about the field of Shinar.

Later in the poem, Solomon repeats his jab at Saturn and the Chaldean people with another allusion to the Tower of Babel (149–53):

> Swa bið ðonne ðissum modgum monnum,   ðam ðe her nu mid mane lengest
> lifiað on ðisse lænan gesceafte.   Ieo ðæt ðine leode gecyððon,
> wunnon hie wið Dryhtnes miehtum,   forðon hie ðæt worc ne gedegdon.
> Ne sceall ic ðe hwædre broðor abelgan;   ðu eart swiðe bittres cynnes,
> eorre eormenstrynde.   Ne beyrn ðu in ða inwitgecyndo!

> So it is then these proud people who here live longest now with wickedness in this transitory creation. Long ago your people revealed that; they strove against the might of the Lord; for that reason, they did not complete that work. But I must not make you angry, brother; you are of a very bitter nation, an angry and mighty race. Do not move into that evil nature!

As O'Neill has shown, the final lines of this quote find their source in Habakkuk 1:6–7: "Chaldeos gentem amaram et velocem ... horribilis et terribilis est" (the Chaldeans are a bitter and swift nation ... it is horrible

61 Anlezark, ed., *Old English Dialogues*, 45; but see Estes, "Constructing the Old English *Solomon and Saturn Dialogues*," 483–99.
62 See Anlezark, ed., *Old English Dialogues*, 4.

and terrible) and, most likely, Jerome's commentary on Daniel.[63] Furthermore, both of these passages from *Solomon and Saturn II* have similarities with the Alfredian treatments of Babel.[64] Just as the Old English *Orosius* describes Babylon as an example to all humans (*to bisene*), *Solomon and Saturn II* calls Babel a warning (*to ðam moning*). Likewise, just as the Old English *Boethius* describes the builders of the Tower as striving against divine power ("winð þam godcundan anwealde"), *Solomon and Saturn II* describes the Chaldeans as striving against the might of the Lord ("wunnon hie wið Dryhtnes miehtum").[65] In the Old English *Boethius* and *Orosius*, and in this passage of *Solomon and Saturn II*, the Tower of Babel is presented as a moral lesson rather than an etiological explanation of the world's diversity. Saturn, who is presented as a descendant of the builders of Babel, reminds the poem's audience that the danger of divine punishment meted out at Babel continues to exist. As Kathryn Powell argues, the boastful, arrogant, glory-seeking Chaldeans, who evidently have not learned the lesson taught at Babel, are placed in a contrast to the righteousness of Solomon, the spokesperson for western Christendom. The Tower is used for a didactic purpose that makes Solomon "the corrector of Eastern error" and disguises "the fact that error [is] … endemic to the West as well."[66] This dichotomy between good and evil, and West and East, that finds expression in Solomon's words on the Tower of Babel is present throughout the poem. As Anlezark argues, the structure of *Solomon and Saturn II* revolves around the interchange of two typological figures who represent the Augustinian cities of God and the Devil: "Saturn the Chaldean is associated with the sinful confusion of Babel, Solomon with the peace of Jerusalem."[67]

Outside of the more explicit allusions to the Tower of Babel, the opposition between Solomon's Jerusalem and Saturn's Babel also appears in Saturn's first riddle. Solomon, after offering the warning (*moning*) provided by the Tower of Babel, asks about the land where "nænig fyra ne mæg

63 O'Neill, "On the Date, Provenance and Relationship of the 'Solomon and Saturn' Dialogues," 148–52.

64 Ibid., 156–7; and Powell, "Orientalist Fantasy in the Poetic Dialogues of *Solomon and Saturn*," 117–43, at 132–4.

65 See O'Neill, "On the Date, Provenance and Relationship of the 'Solomon and Saturn' Dialogues," 157, nt. 82.

66 Powell, "Orientalist Fantasy," 119.

67 Anlezark, ed., *Old English Dialogues*, 46. See also Major, "Saturn's First Riddle in *Solomon and Saturn II*," 301–13.

fotum gestæppan" (no man may set with feet, 33). Saturn then provides an answer that is more cryptic than Solomon's question itself. Saturn refers to a mysterious *Wulf* who slays serpents but is slain by death, a land where no man, bird, nor beast may go, and where a gleaming sword stands over graves (34–46):[68]

> Se mæra was haten   <mere>liðende [MS sæliðende]
> weallende Wulf,   werðeodum cuð
> Filistina,   freond Nebrondes.
> He on ðam felda ofslog   xxv.
> dracena on dægred,   ond hine ða deað offeoll,
> forðan ða foldan   ne mæg fira ænig,
> ðone mercstede,   mon gesecan,
> fugol gefleogan   ne ðon ma foldan nita.
> Ðanon atercynn   ærest gewurdon
> wide onwæcned,   ða ðe nu weallende
> ðurh attres oroð   ingang rymað.
> Git his sweord scinað   swiðe gescæned,
> ond ofer ða byrgenna   blicað ða hieltas.

> The great sea-traveller was called surging Wulf, known to the people of the Philistines, a friend of Nimrod. On that field he slew twenty-five dragons at dawn, and then death felled him, because no man can seek that land, no one that border-land, nor bird fly there, more than any of the beasts of the earth. From there first arose poison-kind, spread widely, those which surging now through poisonous breath make spacious the entrance. His sword shines yet, highly polished, and its hilt gleams over graves.

This passage has been called "one of the most curious and puzzling passages in the poem,"[69] and there have been numerous attempts at interpretation, some more successful than others. For one, since Menner's edition, much light has been shed on the meaning of various elements of the passage. Anlezark has provided a close Virgilian analogue for the barren lands

68 Translation by Anlezark, ed., *Old English Dialogues*, 81.
69 Menner, "Nimrod and the Wolf," 333; see also Menner, *The Poetical Dialogues of Solomon and Saturn*, 121.

of this first riddle of *Solomon and Saturn II* that also describes a land of ominous steam or breath that is hostile to birds:[70]

> spelunca alta fuit uastoque immanis hiatu,
> scrupea, tuta lacu nigro nemorumque tenebris,
> quam super haud ullae poterant impune uolantes
> tendere iter pennis: talis sese halitus atris
> faucibus effundens supera ad conuexa ferebat.
>
> The deep cave was enormous with a vast opening; it was also rocky and guarded by a black lake and the darkness of trees, over which no bird could have an unpunished journey with their wings: some great steam poured from black fissures and bore itself to the highest vaults.

These lines can be further complemented by the description of the fall of Babylon in Revelation 18:2, a description that would be fitting for Saturn's affiliation to the Chaldeans: "cecidit cecidit Babylon magna et facta est habitatio daemoniorum et custodia omnis spiritus inmundi et custodia omnis volucris inmundae" (the great Babylon has fallen, fallen, and it has been made a habitation of demons and a guardian of each unclean spirit, and a guardian of each unclean bird).[71] Furthermore, along with these Latin sources, Andy Orchard has noted connections of *Solomon and Saturn II* to the Old English poem *Beowulf*, which include sea-faring and dragon-slaying heroes, desolate marchlands (*mercstede*), and gleaming swords. Such connections strengthen the heroic elements of the *Solomon and Saturn II* passage and place both poems firmly into vernacular "traditions concerning antediluvian giants and, after the Flood, mighty human figures of pride."[72]

Despite these putative sources and analogues, one of the most mysterious figures of this passage of *Solomon and Saturn II* remains the figure *Weallende Wulf*, called a friend of Nimrod ("freond Nebrondes"). On account of the heroic events in the passage and the opening verbal phrase "was haten" (he was called), it has often been assumed that *Weallende Wulf*, or simply *Wulf*, is a legendary figure, whose history (now lost) might

70 Virgil, *Aeneid*, in Mynors, ed., *Opera*, VI.236–41. Anlezark, ed., *Old English Dialogues*, 120; and "Poisoned Places," 103–26, at 110.
71 Anlezark, ed., *Old English Dialogue*, 120.
72 Orchard, *Pride and Prodigies*, 84.

have been familiar to the poem's original audience. For this reason, much scholarly effort has been spent trying to explain the origin of this figure. Montague Rhodes James attempts to connect *Wulf* to the giant Og of Bashan; and Menner to the Babylonian Bel and to Marcolfus (and therefore to Saturn himself), but neither of these suggestions is convincing.[73] Likewise, Anlezark, following previous editions,[74] capitalizes *Wulf*, but takes a more cautious approach: "whatever the full significance of the passage, Wulf is clearly a heroic figure whose great deeds lead to his death, linked to the origin of 'poison-kind.'"[75] In an earlier article, I examine the identity of the *weallende wulf* and argue that the phrase is better understood enigmatically as a riff on the Isidorian etymology for the word "lupus" (wolf).[76] The Old English participle *weallende* (from *weallan*)[77] makes better sense here as "to rage," because, according to Isidore, the wolf "rabie rapacitatis quaequae invenerit trucidet" (slaughters whatever it finds with a rage of rapacity).[78] Moreover, I suggest, tentatively, that the *weallende wulf* is to be identified with the classical figure Perseus on account of the "Avernian" elements Anlezark has detected in the Old English passage,[79] as well as wordplay on the name *Nebrond*, which can be interpreted as a kenning for Medusa on account of the elements *neb* (face) and *rond* (shield).[80] The *wulf* of *Solomon and Saturn II*, therefore, is not to be identified as the proper name of a Germanic hero, but rather as an epithet for a classical hero.

These speculations notwithstanding, it is clear that the poet of *Solomon and Saturn II* employs references to the Babel narrative, as well as a description of an "Oriental" landscape that alludes both to Avernian geography and to the field of Shinar. Babel or the later Babylon presents not only an exotic East opposed to a normative West, as Powell has argued, but also a moral exemplum that accords with other treatments of the Babel

73 James, ed. and trans., *The Lost Apocrypha of the Old Testament*, 41; and Menner, "Nimord and the Wolf," 352–3; and *Poetical Dialogues of Solomon and Saturn*, 122–3.

74 Kemble, *The Dialogue of Salomon and Saturnus*, 156; Menner, *Poetical Dialogues of Solomon and Saturn*, 91.

75 Anlezark, ed., *Old English Dialogues*, 46; he later states that Wulf is "apparently a personal name" (119).

76 Major, "Saturn's First Riddle in *Solomon and Saturn II*," 310–11.

77 See Bosworth and Toller, eds. *An Anglo-Saxon Dictionary*, *s.v.* "weallan," VII, 1174.

78 Isidore, *Etymologiae*, XII.ii.23.

79 Anlezark, "Poisoned Places."

80 Major, "Saturn's First Riddle in *Solomon and Saturn II*," 311.

narrative among the Alfredian texts. Aside from these thematic relationships, *Solomon and Saturn II* does merit further examination, especially in accordance with its treatment of its biblical and classical sources, which, if its treatments of the Babel narrative give any indication, are fairly unique to the period.

After the prolific output of early Anglo-Latin biblical exegesis, initiated by Theodore and Hadrian's Canterbury School and brought to its height with Bede and Alcuin, the Alfredian corpus reveals a sharp turn in focus on the Tower of Babel narrative. The conflation of the narrative with the gigantomachia in the Old English *Boethius*,[81] the depiction of the city speaking a warning to all humankind in the Old English *Orosius*, and the appearance of the fourth son of Noah in the West Saxon royal genealogies are all innovations that seem to best reflect the current cultural concerns. Unlike the early Anglo-Latin texts, and specifically Bede, there is very little in the Alfredian corpus that connects the Tower of Babel to linguistic diversity, and even less that affirms the validity of linguistic diversity in the universality of the Church, despite what must have been a very multilingual court.[82] Instead, the role of Old English, despite Alfred's laments on the state of Latin learning in the ninth century, becomes sufficient enough as a national language to no longer create a need to justify the use or even existence of vernacular languages.[83] Regarding the linguistic dominance of Latin across much of the Roman Empire, Umberto Eco writes, "a civilization with an international language does not need to worry about the multiplicity of tongues."[84] Eco's statement in some ways can also be applied to late ninth-century England, where Old English seems to be the only available language for practical administrative and educational use. For this reason, the linguistic elements of the Babel narrative lose some of their force in the Old English texts of the period, which retain and emphasize other moral elements.

These remarks on Babel in the Alfredian corpus, when compared to Bede's comments on the subject, help highlight the central features of both. In light of the lack of concern for linguistic diversity in the Alfredian

81 See also *The Wanderer*, 85–7, which describes the Creator of men destroying a city made by giants.
82 Discenza, "Writing the Mother Tongue in the Shadow of Babel," 33–55, esp. 36–7 and 53–4.
83 See also Discenza, *The King's English*.
84 Eco, *The Search for the Perfect Language*, 11.

texts, Bede's comments reveal a much stronger anxiety over preserving linguistic and ethnic diversity of the Church. At the ends of the known world, the English Church with its diversity in unity confirms, for Bede, the ecclesiastical centre of Rome. For the Alfredian texts, however, it is Alfred's West Saxon court that is presented at least by most of its literary output as monolingual, despite its actual multilingualism. In contrast to Bede, the use of the Babel narrative in the Alfredian texts reveals anxieties that focus on excessive pride (*Boethius*, *Orosius*), and particularly pride stemming from knowledge (*Boethius*, *Solomon and Saturn II*). It is no stretch to understand these anxieties as deriving from the newly formed and ever precarious hegemony of Alfred and his emphasis on educational reform as part of the foundation for a stable kingdom. After Alfred's death in 899, the administrative and educational foundations that he initiated continue with his descendants, who turn the focus of learning in England towards ecclesiastical reforms, attempting to replicate the success of Benedictine monasticism on the continent. Naturally, these descendants have their own new concerns and anxieties, which become reflected in their own uses of the Tower of Babel narrative.

Chapter Six

The Tenth and Early Eleventh Centuries

Æthelstan and the First Half of the Tenth Century

Despite Alfred's attempts to revive ecclesiastical learning in Britain, the Danish invasions had taken too devastating a toll on Anglo-Saxon monasticism for it to recover to the degree that it enjoyed in the early eighth century. Many of the once wealthy monasteries, now dilapidated, abandoned, or under the governance of a lay abbot, were unable to attract new adherents to their monastic rules. As outlined by Robin Fleming in her analysis of Domesday T.R.E. (1066), "the ninth century was a period in which a great deal of land in the north and the midlands was permanently alienated from the Church."[1] And yet Alfred's endeavours to restore a strong ecclesiastical and literary culture were not in vain. A number of his successors continued his initiatives during the tenth century when Anglo-Saxon defences were better able to deter and withstand Viking attacks. After the death of Alfred in 899, his son Edward the Elder (899–924) succeeded as king of the Anglo-Saxons.[2] Though there is significantly less evidence for cultural and literary advancements during Edward's reign than during his father's, it does nevertheless indicate a continuation of manuscript production and renewed interest in both Old English and Latin learning, particularly at Canterbury, Winchester, and Worcester.[3]

1 Fleming, "Monastic Lands and England's Defence in the Viking Age," 247–65, at 250. But see Dumville, "Ecclesiastical Lands and the Defence of Wessex in the First Viking Age," 29–54.

2 For Edward, see the important collection of essays, *Edward the Elder, 899–924*, ed. Higham and Hill.

3 Lapidge, "Schools, Learning and Literature in Tenth-Century England," 1–48, at 12–16.

Moreover, alongside a number of new episcopal sees, Edward founded the monastery of New Minster, and his mother, Ealhswið, the monastery of Nunnaminster, both projects begun at Winchester during Alfred's reign.[4]

It was not until Æthelstan (king of the Anglo-Saxons 924/5–7, king of the English 927–39) became king that a revival of English education began in earnest. Æthelstan was a well-known collector and granter of books[5] and relics;[6] and like Alfred he introduced foreign scholars to his court, who encouraged the composition of what would develop into the hermeneutic Latin of the tenth century,[7] as well as the standardization of "Phase II" of Anglo-Saxon Square minuscule.[8] Æthelstan was also responsible for founding a number of new monasteries and for refurbishing those already in existence with precious books, for which he is recognized in manuscript illuminations[9] and poetry.[10] Unfortunately, Æthelstan's importance for the literary and cultural history of England has been relatively and unduly understudied. Only very recently has the first biography proper of Æthelstan, by Sarah Foot, come to publication;[11] previously, scholarship on Æthelstan

4 See Rumble, "Edward the Elder and the Churches of Winchester and Wessex," 230–47; and Biddle, "*Felix Urbs Winthonia*," 123–40 (notes 233–7), at 127–32.

5 Keynes, "King Athelstan's Books," 143–201.

6 Loomis, "The Holy Relics of Charlemagne and King Athelstan," 437–56; Rollason, *Saints and Relics in Anglo-Saxon England*, 159–62; and Brett, "A Breton Pilgrim in England in the Reign of King Æthelstan," 43–70, at 46–8.

7 Lapidge, "Schools, Learning and Literature," 17–21; "Some Latin Poems as Evidence for the Reign of Athelstan," 49–86; "Israel the Grammarian in Anglo-Saxon England," 87–104; Robinson, *The Times of Saint Dunstan*, 83–4; Wood, "The Making of King Aethelstan's Empire," 250–72, at 258–62; "'Stand Firm Against the Monsters,'" 192–217; "A Carolingian Scholar in the Court of King Æthelstan," 135–62; and Brett, "A Breton Pilgrim." For the improbability of John the Old Saxon's authorship of a poem on Æthelstan, see Wieland, "A New Look at the Poem 'Archalis clamare triumuir,'" 178–92.

8 Dumville, "English Square Minuscule Script," 147–79, at 173–8; and "English Square Minuscule Script,"133–64, at 136–44.

9 London, British Library, Cotton Otho B.xi, destroyed in the Ashburnham House fire of 1731 but described by Thomas Smith (1696) and Humphrey Wanley (1705), and Cambridge, Corpus Christi College 183, fol. 1v. See Keynes, "King Athelstan's Books," 173–4 and 180; and Karkov, *The Ruler Portraits of Anglo-Saxon England*, 56–63.

10 Notably, the poem "Rex pius Æðelstan"; see Lapidge, "Some Latin Poems as Evidence," 81–5.

11 Foot, *Æthelstan*. See also Hill, *The Age of Athelstan*; and Keynes, "England, 900–1016," 456–84, at 466–71.

and his impact on English literature and culture, though excellent, has been scant considering his importance for the field.

The literary witnesses to the cultural activity of Æthelstan's reign, which points to an increase in Latin learning mainly prompted by closer contacts with the continent, including the introduction of foreign scholars to the royal court, is restricted to a handful of Latin poems, inscriptions, law-codes, and charters. For this reason, the evidence for a study on the influence of Genesis 10–11 in the first half of tenth-century England is negligible. But despite its paucity, Æthelstan and his literary circle do exhibit features worth examining. Most significantly, Æthelstan is often credited with becoming the first king of England, and it was during his reign that the political and national unity of Britain, as theorized by Bede under the term *gens Anglorum* and promoted by Alfred under the term *Angelcynn*, started to become a reality.[12] Once Alfred (Æthelstan's grandfather) extended his kingdom north of the Thames into Mercia and London, he legitimized his hegemony by stylizing himself King of the Anglo-Saxons. Though much of Britain was still outside of Alfred's rule, this stylization consciously approaches an understanding of the people of Britain as a homogenous, unified nation. After the successes of Æthelstan's own military conquests, which effectively placed the entire island of Britain under his control, he evidently found his grandfather's methods of legitimization helpful, and restyled himself in terms used for the first time, such as "King of the English" and "ruler of all of Britain," among others. These new titles for Æthelstan, which provide an ostentatious "opportunity for propaganda," appear in inscriptions, charters, coins, shrines, and poems associated with the king.[13]

---

12 The idea of a hegemonic rule of all of Britain precedes Bede; see John, *Orbis Britanniae and Other Studies*, 6. For the problems involved with stylizing Æthelstan, "the first king of the English," see Molyneaux, *Formation of the English Kingdom*, 199–214.

13 John, *Orbis Britanniae*, 49. See also Foot, *Æthelstan*, 212–26; Leneghan, "*Translatio Imperii*," 671–3; and Molyneaux, *Formation of the English Kingdom*, 208–9. Examples of titles expressing Æthelstan's rule over all Britain include: "ÆDELSTAN Anglorum basyleos et curagulus totius Brytannie" (BL, Cotton Tiberius A.ii, fol. 15v, for which see Keynes, "King Athelstan's Books," 149–50); "Æðelstanus nodante Dei gratia basileus Anglorum et equae totius Bryttanniae orbis curagulus" (S 430, 438, 446; see also S 447–8); "Æðelstanus rex Anglorum per omnipatrantis dexteram totius Bryttaniæ regni solio sublimatus" (S 379 [adapted from an authentic text, for which see Miller, ed., *Charters of the New Minster, Winchester*, 47–8], 403, 412–13, 416–17, 418, 418a, 419, 422, 434; see also S 411, 423, 430–1, 437, 440); "Rex tot[ius] Brit[anniae]" (on coins of Æthelstan's reign, for which see Blunt, "The Coinage of Athelstan, 924–939,"

Notably this stylization occurs in a brief Latin inscription on folio 3v of London, Lambeth Palace 1370, the so-called MacDurnan Gospels, edited here metrically by Keynes:[14]

Mæielbriðus MacDurnani
istum textum per triquadrum
Deo digne dogmatizat
ast
Æthelstanus Anglosæxna
rex et rector Doruernensi
metropoli dat per æuum.

Mael Brigte mac Tornain, worthily to God, teaches this text throughout the whole world, but Æthelstan king and ruler of the Anglo-Saxons gives it to the see of Canterbury forever.

The phrase "Æthelstanus Anglosæxna rex et rector" is revealing here not only for Æthelstan's image as a king over all the Anglo-Saxons, but also for its appearance alongside a description of a tripartite division of the world. A number of scholars have noted that the word, *triquadrus*, which likely owes its presence here to the bombastic vocabulary of Aldhelm and the *Hisperica Famina*, appears elsewhere in texts associated with Æthelstan's reign:[15] specifically, the adjective is used in the phrase "triquadri orbis" in three charters ascribed to Æthelstan's reign (S 399 and 400, both dated 16 April 928 at Exeter; and S 404, a spurious charter dated to 930 but "apparently based in part on genuine charters of the alliterative group issued in the 940s").[16] D.A. Bullough, taking a slightly contrary view of

36–160, at 47–8); "rex Ethelstanus, totius Britanniae multarumque gentium in circuitu positarum imperator" (on a shrine seen by William of Malmesbury, *Gesta pontificum Anglorum*, vol. 1, , V.248.3); "Rex pius Æðelstan, patulo famosus in orbe … quem Deus Angligenis … constituit regem"; and "regit cum ista / perfecta Saxonia: / uiuit rex Æþelstanus" (for these poetic lines, see Lapidge, "Some Latin Poems," 83 and 86).

14 Keynes, "King Athelstan's Books," 156. For Mael Brigte, see Dumville, "Mael Brigte mac Tornáin, Pluralist Coarb (†927)," 97–116, at 113–16 for this inscription.

15 Robinson, *Times of Saint Dunstan*, 55–9; Paul Grosjean, "Confusa Caligo, Remarques sur les Hisperica Famina," 35–85, at 66; John, *Orbis Britanniae*, 49–50; Herren, ed., *Hisperica Famina*, vol. 1, 117–18; Keynes, "King Athelstan's Books," 156; and Wood, "Making of King Aethelstan's Empire," 257.

16 Keynes, "King Athelstan's Books," 157; see also Wood, "Making of King Aethelstan's Empire," 257.

the origin of the word's relative popularity, briefly mentions his predilection for Orosian priority: "The words *per cunctam triquadri orbis latitudinem* in the opening clause of the protocol of a diploma of 928, and again in a later one, have an obvious Aldhelmian flavour: but as been long noticed, they are actually closer to Orosius than to anything in Aldhelm's writings."[17] Although Orosius does seem to have been one of the earliest to apply the adjective *triquadrus* to the threefold division of the earth, analogous to the three sons of Noah, it appears only once in the entirety of his *Historiae aduersum paganos*: "Maiores nostri orbem totius terrae ... triquedrum statuere eiusque tres partes ASIAM EUROPAM ET AFRICAM uocauerunt" (our elders determined the whole earth to be tripartite and called its three parts Asia, Europe, and Africa).[18] In contrast, the adjective appears seven times in the works of Aldhelm: once in his *Carmina ecclesiastica* (IV.x), three times in his *Carmen de uirginitate*, and three times in his prose *De uirginitate*.[19] It also appears once in the *Hisperica famina*,[20] a number of Anglo-Saxon glossaries,[21] and an occasional continental text.[22] But it is the first four lines of Aldhelm's poem on Matthew in the *Carmina ecclesiastica* that contain the strongest parallels with the inscription in the MacDurnan Gospels, providing some evidence of direct borrowing:[23]

17 Bullough, "The Educational Tradition in England from Alfred to Ælfric," 297–334, at 304.

18 Orosius, *Historiarum aduersum paganos libri vii*, I.2.1. Manuscripts designated PRBD by Zangemeister use the spelling *triquadrum*.

19 Aldhelm, *Carmina ecclesiastica*, IV.x.4 (see above, 87–9); *Carmen de uirginitate*, lines 85: "triquadro cardine," 1040: "triquadrum ... mundum," 2350: "triquadrum ... orbem"; *De uirginitate*, 237, line 6: "triquadram mundi rotam," 247, lines 15–16: "triquadra mundi latitudo," 253, line 4: "in triquadro terrarum ambitu."

20 Herren, ed., *The Hisperica Famina*, vol. 1, line 7: "mundano triquadrae telluris artico" (earthly region of the tripartite world, trans. Herren, 65).

21 Keynes, "King Athelstan's Books," 156, citing Épinal Glossary 1039 and Corpus Glossary 2052.

22 Lullus, *Epistola* 140, in *Die Briefe des heiligen Bonifatius und Lullus*, 279, line 17: "triquadri orbis"; Nigellus, *In honorem Hludowicii*, II.347: "Hic per triquadrum regnabat, pro dolor, orbem"; Heiricus of Auxerre, *Vita S. Germani*, , VI.426: "mundi ... structura triquadri"; Hrabanus Maurus, *De uniuerso*, PL 111, col. 488B (XVIII.2): "tres partes orbis, quod de tribus filiis Noe exortum in orbe continetur triquadro" (punctuation altered); *Commentaria in Libros IV Regem*, PL 109, col. 231A: "in orbe triquadro"; and *Liber de oblatione puerorum*, PL 107, col. 432B: "in orbe triquadro."

23 Aldhelm, *Carmina ecclesiastica*, IV.x.4.1–4; Lapidge and Rosier, trans., *Poetic Works*, 56.

Matheus egregium describens dogma salutis
Ebrea per simplum digessit dicta libellum
Plurima sanctificis narrans miracula scedis
Quae modo per mundum divulgant scripta triquadrum

Matthew, in setting down the excellent doctrine of salvation, produced his account in Hebrew in the form of a simple book, narrating many miracles in these holy pages, which scripture now makes known throughout the tripartite world.

The two verbal similarities, "dogma" (Aldhelm) / "dogmatizat" (MacDurnan), and "per ... triquadrum," are the most striking, but the content is also revealing. In Aldhelm's verses, Matthew describes, produces, and narrates his "little book"; in the MacDurnan Gospel's inscription, Mael Brigte, a celebrated ninth-century Irish coarb,[24] similarly "propounds" (Keynes's translation) the codex of the gospels. Likewise, the alliterative feature of the inscription, notably on the letter /d/ in the third line, reflects the pattern of alliteration in the Aldhelmian verses on Matthew, two of which alliterate on /d/ and a third which contains a further word beginning with /d/. These analogous features of the two poems (verbal, contextual, and stylistic) are also linked by the fact that the inscription in the MacDurnan Gospels immediately follows the opening verses of the Gospel of Matthew (1:1–17; fols. 2r–3r), preceding a portrait of the evangelist himself (fol. 4*v) and his gospel (fol. 5r).[25] It may even be possible that the parallel between the name *Mæielbriðus* extends beyond Aldhelm's fortuitously similar *Matheus* to present Mael Brigte as an apostolic successor and even evangelist, spreading the physical gospel book to the very corners of the tripartite world.

Admittedly, the use of the adjective, *triquadrus*, especially as it appears in very rhetorical contexts dependent upon the stylized vocabulary of past writers, can reveal little about interpretations of the Table of Nations or the Tower of Babel, or even a geographical concept of the world derived from the convergence of biblical and classical notions in the first centuries BCE. It does, however, garner some interest as the image by which Æthelstan seemed to wish to portray himself: a "king and ruler of the Anglo-Saxons" sending out his apostle to propound the gospel book "throughout the

24 Foot, *Æthelstan*, 106; and Dumville, "Mael Brigte mac Tornáin."
25 Keynes, "King Athelstan's Books," 153.

threefold world." Not only is Æthelstan's England a unified and distinct nation in a tripartite world, but it is also a Christian nation connected to the wider Christian world through its scholars.

The same kind of regal and religious propaganda appears in the important manuscript, Cambridge, Corpus Christi College 183, dated 934 × 939, which, alongside Bede's two *Lives of St Cuthbert* (2r–58r, 70r–92v) and a Mass and Office of St Cuthbert (92v–96v), contains a list of popes (59r–60r), a list of the seventy-two disciples of Christ (60r–60v), a list of British archbishops and bishops (61r–64v), British regal lists and genealogies (65r–67r), and various notes (67r–70r). Significantly, one of these notes includes a typological connection between the seventy-two books of the Bible, the languages of the world and the number of Christ's disciples (69r): "De nouo et uetere canone libri s<un>t .lxxii. sicq<ue> et linguarum numero aeq<ue> et discipuloru<m> chr<ist>i sine numero .xii. apostolorum" (there are seventy-two books from the Old and New Testaments, and the same for the number of languages, as well as the number of Christ's disciples not counting the twelve apostles).[26] Though this passage is not unique – in particular, it appears in the earlier related manuscript London, British Library, Cotton Vespasian B.vi, fol. 106r–v, assembled sometime in the mid ninth century[27] – it is worth noting the possible significance CCCC 183 had for Æthelstan. The first folio with any content (1v) contains an elaborate portrait of Æthelstan presenting a book to St Cuthbert. Outside of the Cuthbert texts, which bookend the manuscript, all the medial material relates to the secular and ecclesiastical rule of Britain in its entirety.[28] In a context that seems to legitimize Æthelstan's rule over all aspects of Britain, the mention of the seventy-two books, languages, and

26 Dekker, "Anglo-Saxon Encyclopaedic Notes," 279–315, at 284, no. 11, and 293–4 (commentary).

27 Keynes, "Between Bede and the *Chronicle*," vol. 1, 47–67, at 49–50 and 60–1; and Dekker, "Anglo-Saxon Encyclopaedic Notes," 301. For a helpful study of the lists in these manuscripts, see Walbers, "Number and Measurement in Anglo-Saxon Christian Culture," esp. 39, Table II.1.

28 See Keynes, "King Athelstan's Books," 181: "the decision to combine Cuthbert material with a collection of episcopal and royal records may have been taken with some ulterior motive in mind: perhaps the purpose of the exercise was mainly educational, but it is conceivable that the king and his advisers hoped to remind the Northumbrian community of the essential unity of the Anglo-Saxon church, and to impress on them the ancient links which bound the various Anglo-Saxon kingdoms together." See also Karkov, *Ruler Portraits of Anglo-Saxon England*, 66–8.

disciples points towards Britain's place in the comprehensiveness of the world and the Church's rule over it. Æthelstan again is the Christian ruler of all Britain, and as the medial texts of CCCC 183 indicate, he is well established within a Christian program that encompasses all the seventy-two languages (and nations) of the world through the mission of the seventy-two disciples proclaiming the seventy-two books of the Bible.[29] This note on the number seventy-two is admittedly brief, but it does point to the prevalence of a Christian ideology based on linguistic, ethnic, and religious diversity at Babel that is reunited through the preaching of Christ's disciples. Just as the inscription in the MacDurnan Gospels calls attention to Æthelstan's role as a promoter and promulgator of the Christian faith, so also do the lists and notes of CCCC 183.

Unlike the Anglo-Saxons of the eighth century, who adopted and adapted the classical and patristic traditions regarding Britain as positioned at the end of the world, such sentiment (to my knowledge) is absent in the Anglo-Saxon literature of the first half of the tenth century, at least in the small portion that survives. England is no longer the outlying symbol of the universal Church spread throughout a tripartite world, but rather a significant, even central, aspect of it. In this way, Æthelstan has yet again carried on the work of his grandfather, by adapting geographical and genealogical notions originally derived from Genesis 10–11 in order to give Anglo-Saxon England a more central place in the Christian world. And this centralization of Anglo-Saxon England, especially in its relationship to the Church, would continue after Æthelstan's death in the climax of ecclesiastical and in particular monastic learning during the later tenth-century Benedictine reform.

The Benedictine Reform

After Æthelstan, Kings Edmund (939–46) and Eadred (946–55) would not be as significant for English monasticism as their predecessor, or their successor, Edgar. They do, however, get credit for involving Dunstan, one of the most significant figures of tenth-century Anglo-Saxon England, in ecclesiastical affairs: Edmund appointed him to the abbacy of Glastonbury, and Eadred helped enrich the same monastery (he also apparently attempted to persuade Dunstan to take the episcopal see of Crediton, but

29 See Dekker, "Anglo-Saxon Encyclopaedic Notes," 303–4.

in vain).[30] However, as many of the later reformers will remember with nostalgia, it was under the reign of King Edgar, "pacificus," (king of the Mercians and Northumbrians 957–9, king of the English 959–75) that the tenth-century Benedictine reform would begin in earnest with the prominent monastic leadership of Dunstan (abbot of Glastonbury, 940 × 946, bishop of Worcester and London, c. 958, and archbishop of Canterbury, 959–88), Æthelwold (abbot of Abingdon, c. 954–63, and bishop of Winchester, 963–84), and Oswald (bishop of Worcester, 961–92, and archbishop of York, 971–92).[31]

Though monastic reform had certainly begun and was slowly gaining momentum since Alfred's efforts, these three reformers enjoyed high-profile influence in both secular and ecclesiastical spheres, and were responsible for revitalizing monastic education in England to levels that began to approach the learning of seventh- and early eighth-century Northumbria. In particular, Æthelwold, with the backing of Edgar, introduced a strict ecclesiastical program based on adherence to the Benedictine Rule interpreted through the *Regularis concordia*, and inspired by the earlier continental programs of Benedictine reform.[32] Secular clergy were forcibly expelled from ecclesiastical institutions and new monastic centres and episcopal sees were founded. To be sure, as Antonia Gransden has argued, the tenth-century Benedictine reform did not break as abruptly and

30 *Vita S. Dunstani*, in Winterbottom and Lapidge, eds., *The Early Lives of St Dunstan*, 19.2–4. See also "King Eadred's Will" (S 1515), in Harmer, ed., *Select English Historical Documents of the Ninth and Tenth Centuries*, 34–5, lines 24–6.

31 See the essays in Yorke, ed., *Bishop Æthelwold*; Ramsay, Sparks, and Tatton-Brown, eds., *St Dunstan*; and Brooks and Cubitt, eds., *St Oswald of Worcester*, all summarized by Cubitt, "Review Article," 77–94. The less prominent but hugely important role of Oda, Archbishop of Canterbury (941–58) in the early reform movement, should also be noted; Darlington, "Ecclesiastical Reform in the Late Old English Period," 385–428, at 387.

32 Bullough, "The Continental Background of the Tenth-Century English Reform," 272–96; Symons, "Sources of the *Regularis Concordia*," 14–36, 143–70, 264–89; "*Regularis Concordia*," 37–59 (notes 214–17); Symons, ed., introduction to *Regularis Concordia / The Monastic Agreement*, ix–lix; and Kornexl, "The *Regularis Concordia* and its Old English Gloss," 95–130, which summarizes her *Die "Regularis concordia" und ihre altenglische Interlinearversion*. See also Hill, "The Benedictine Reform and Beyond," 151–69, at 153–4; and the useful introduction in Hurt, *Ælfric*, 11–22. For continental influence on the individual reformers, see Wormald, "Æthelwold and his Continental Counterparts," 169–206; Nightingale, "Oswald, Fleury and Continental Reform," 23–45; and Brooks, "The Career of St Dunstan," 1–23, at 16–18.

severely with the secular clergy as some monastic documents attest; particularly in Northumbria, the secular clergy continued to thrive.[33] Nevertheless, the rhetoric of the reformers often proclaimed Benedictine monasticism as the only valid way to restore Christianity to England, just as the paganism of the past was overcome only by the advent of Christianity.[34] Perhaps due to the nature of the literature, very few references to the Tower of Babel exist in the Old English and Latin writings of the Benedictine reform outside of the works of Ælfric and Wulfstan. But a reference to Nimrod in Byrhtferth of Ramsey's *Vita S. Ecgwini*, an allusion to Pentecost in Lantfred's *Translatio et miracula s. Swithuni*, and a handful of hymns from the period dealing with Pentecost do indicate some continued literary use of the narrative.

Besides those of Ælfric and Wulfstan, the most explicit reference to the Babel narrative among the Benedictine reformers happens to come from one of their contemporaries. Byrhtferth of Ramsey (c. 970–c. 1016), another important but understudied author of the late Anglo-Saxon period, alludes to both Nimrod and Arator's account of Pentecost at the beginning of his *Vita S. Ecgwini*. Although Byrhtferth frequently invokes the Holy Spirit by quoting Arator's lines, "Spiritus alme ueni, sine quo non diceris umquam / Munera da linguae, qui das in munere linguas" (Come nourishing Spirit, without whom you are never spoken, give the gifts of language / tongue, you who give languages / tongues as a gift),[35] he uses them to ask the Holy Spirit specifically to help him compose his *Vita S. Ecgwini* according to the wisdom of the Three Youths, John the Evangelist, and Pope Gregory, and not according to the pagan learning and eloquence of Homer and Nimrod. As a foil to the saintly wisdom granted by the Holy Spirit, Nimrod is described as "wandering throughout the regions of

33 Gransden, "Traditionalism and Continuity during the Last Century of Anglo-Saxon Monasticism," 159–207, esp. 170–80.

34 For the importance of a past in need of reform and renewal in medieval religious movements, see Constable, "Renewal and Reform in Religious Life," 37–67; for the tenth-century English Benedictine reform, see Lees, *Tradition and Belief*, 88–101; and Jones, "Ælfric and the Limits of 'Benedictine Reform,'" 67–108, at 69–79.

35 Byrhtferth, *Vita S. Ecgwini*, in Lapidge, ed., *Byrhtferth of Ramsey*, Pref., 208 (see 209, nt. 20); quoting Arator, *Historia apostolica*, I.226–7. See also Baker and Lapidge, eds., *Byrhtferth's Enchiridion*, II.3.265–6; and Bryhtferth's *Historia regum*, in Arnold, ed., *Symeonis Monachi opera omnia*, vol. 2, § 30; for Byrhtferth's authorship of the *Historia regum*, see Lapidge, "Byrhtferth of Ramsey and the Early Sections of the *Historia Regum* attributed to Symeon of Durham," 317–42.

the world, conferred nothing upon the holy Church" ("Nichil contulit cursus Nemroth uagus per mundi climata sancte ecclesie").[36] Although Lapidge suggests that the astrological work, *Liber Nemroth*, might be a source for these lines because of the shared word *cursus* and its presence in an eleventh-century manuscript containing "Abbonian computistical materials,"[37] this suggestion must remain inconclusive until more is known about the *Liber Nemroth* and its influence in eleventh-century England. A stronger argument could perhaps be made for Isidore's *Etymologiae* as a source here. In his tract on astronomy, Isidore claims that the Chaldeans (whom Byrhtferth also mentions at the beginning of this preface) were the first to have taught astrology, after the Egyptians discovered it. Some of Isidore's astrological vocabulary, such as *mundus*, *cursus*, *climata*, is also found in Byrhtferth's line on Nimrod.[38]

But despite the verbal connection between Nimrod as a *uagus* and the astrological *uaga Lucina* mentioned a few lines later in the *Vita S. Ecgwini*, there is actually nothing in Byrhtferth's description of Nimrod that indicates specially that Nimrod is to be understood as representing astrological knowledge. Instead, Byrhtferth's presentation of Nimrod corresponds more closely to the traditional architect of the Tower of Babel, one of whose possible etymologies is "profugus," meaning "fugitive" or in a transferred sense "wanderer."[39] The word *profugus* is also placed in apposition to the word *uagus* in Genesis 4:12, where it is applied to Cain: "vagus et profugus eris super terram" (you will be a wanderer and a fugitive upon the earth).[40] And since according to Genesis all the nations scatter throughout the world after the Tower of Babel, it is no stretch to see Nimrod functioning here in the *Vita S. Ecgwini* as a kind of metonym not only for the pagan nations of the world but also for their wisdom. For this reason, Byrhtferth's allusion to Nimrod, and his worldly wisdom, can be seen as

---

36 Byrhtferth, *Vita S. Ecgwini*, Pref., 206.

37 Lapidge, ed., *Vita S. Ecgwini*, 207, nt. 10. The manuscript is Vatican City, Bibliotheca Apostolica Vaticana, Reg. lat. 309 (prov. Saint-Denis).

38 Isidore, *Etymologiae*, III.xxv.1: "Astrologiam … Chaldaei primi docuerunt"; III.xviii.1: "Definit enim quid sit mundi … quid sphaerae situs et cursus … quae sint climata caeli." For Byrhtferth's knowledge of Isidore, see Lapidge, *The Anglo-Saxon Library*, 271.

39 Theil, *Grundlagen und Gestalt der Hebräischkenntnisse*, 367; this etymology is found in Bede, *In principium Genesis*, III.145–6.

40 There is confusion in the early Middle ages between Cain and Cham, the father of Nimrod; see Orchard, *Pride and Prodigies*, 65.

foreshadowing the subsequent reference to Pentecost, where the Church first begins to convert the nations not through worldly wisdom but spiritual truth.

A second text that connects the Benedictine reform in Britain to the initial conversion of the English and to the original apostolic mission can be found in Lantfred's *Translatio et miracula s. Swithuni*, written a few years after Æthelwold translated the remains of Swithun at Winchester on 15 July 971.[41] Lantfred, likely a monk from Fleury living at Winchester around 970, begins the preface to his work with a statement on the universal nature of the Christian faith: "Notum est, fratres, fidelibus ubique gentium degentibus" (It is known, my brothers, to the faithful of the nations living everywhere).[42] This opening phrase establishes one of the themes of the preface: conversion of the gentiles, and specifically conversion of the Anglo-Saxons. After relating the nature of the Trinity, Christ's incarnation, death, resurrection, and ascension, Lantfred turns to Pentecost where the Holy Spirit "quorum [*sc.* fornifori] corda compleuit sancti tanta infusione carismatis, ut in una etiam apostolorum uaticinatione pariter eadem tempestate dinoscerentur sermones omnium consona uoce populorum" (filled their [*sc.* the disciples] hearts with such an infusion of grace that in a single prophecy of the apostles the languages of all the peoples were understood together at the same time with harmonious speech).[43] After this narration of Pentecost, which gives the basic details of Acts 2 in hermeneutic vocabulary and style, Lantfred conflates the early apostolic missions into a few lines:[44]

> Moxque conuersis ad fidem paucis ex eorum consanguineis (respuentibus sanam ceteris doctrinam), didascali, adimplentes ueriloqui mathites quae infit iussionem, "euntes in omnem dogmatizantes orbem euangelium humanae

41 See Lapidge, *The Cult of Swithun*, 217–24 (Lantfred), 224–50 (textual matters) and 252–333 (text and translation).

42 *Translatio et miracula S. Swithuni*, Praef.1, 254.

43 Ibid., Praef.20–2, 256.

44 Ibid., Praef.25–30, 256 (I have slightly altered the punctuation). The notion that the apostles selected certain "provinces" stems from Rufinus's translation of Eusebius, *Historia ecclesiastica*, *Die Kirchengeschichte*, III.1, 189: "sancti vero apostoli… ceterique discipuli ad praedicandum verbum dei per singulas quasque orbis terrae provincias diriguntur." It is also found in Blickling Homily 11, Morris, ed., *The Blickling Homilies*, 121: "hie þysne middangeard on twelf tánum tohluton, & æghwylc anra heora in þæm dæle þe he mid tán geeode."

omni creaturae" [Mark 16:15], Iudaici relicta erroris perfidia, optione bis senas sortiti prouincias totiusque gentilitatis fines adgressi, pene uniuersum Deo fauente cosmum quaterno climate quadrifidum ad Christianae fidei religionem et ad sancte trinitatis agnitionem – signis uirtutibusque miraculorum credulitatem prebentibus – conuerterunt.

And at once, after a few of their relatives had been converted (others had rejected that healthy doctrine), the disciples fulfilled the command of their true speaking teacher which he spoke, "going through the whole world, proclaiming the gospel to every human being," and with the treachery of the Jewish error abandoned, they selected twelve provinces according to their choice and, going out to the ends of all heathendom, they converted – with God's favour – almost the whole fourfold world with its four parts to the religion of the Christian faith and recognition of the Holy Trinity: signs and miracles supported their credulity.

Naturally, in Lantfred's account, the apostolic mission eventually comes to Britain, "Quorum equiperatores nouissime ad gentes peruenerunt felices in Britannie limitibus commorantes que nuncupantur Anglisaxones" ("their peers finally came to the blessed nations dwelling at the edges of Britain who are called Anglo-Saxons"), and the English are converted: "Gentes nimirum prefate Anglorum cum tante sitibundo ardore deuotionis sperma diuini percepere rematis" (certainly, the just mentioned English nations took up the seed of the divine word with such thirsting ardor of devotion).[45] The people of Britain, in other words, are ensnared in heathendom by the traps of the devil until they are converted by those who can trace their lineage back, in this case, to Pentecost, where the first mission to all the nations of the world begins.[46]

---

45 *Translatio et miracula S. Swithuni*, Praef.31–2, 36–7, 256.

46 The tendency to trace Christian missions back to the apostles is typical of the hagiographical genre, though specific references to Pentecost are more unique. See, for example, Wulfstan of Winchester's *Vita S. Æthelwoldi*, in Lapidge and Winterbottom, eds., *The Life of St Æthelwold*, Praef., 2: "[*sc.* Christus] multa per uniuersum orbem diffudit apostolicorum luminaria doctorum … Ex quorum collegio beatus pater et electus Dei pontifex Ætheluuoldus" ([Christ] spread throughout the whole world the many lights of apostolic teachers… From their company is the blessed father and bishop chosen by God Æthelwold).

Interestingly, a little later in his preface, after a brief discussion on the devil, Lantfred turns back to Britain and describes how Edgar's reign reflects a unity in diversity reminiscent of Pentecost:[47]

> aetate sexta (quae est caducorum nouissima), indictione quartadecima [=971], Eadgaro regnante, basileo insigni atque inuictissimo, prepotente ac clementissimo necnon gloriosissimo sceptrigera ditione et feliciter gentibus imperante compluribus habitu distantibus, uoce atque moribus, diffuse in insula commorantibus quae "Albio" nuncupata legitur ab Anglorum fore ueteribus.

> in the sixth age, which is the final age for those mortals, and in the fourteenth indiction (=971), Edgar reigned, that distinguished and unconquerable king, very powerful, most merciful and glorious in his scepter-bearing authority, who blessedly ruled over a number of peoples distinct in appearance, language and customs, who dwelled all around the island which is said to have been called "Albion" by the ancient English peoples.

The statement that "Albion" consisted of inhabitants who differed in appearance, language, and customs ("habitu distantibus, uoce atque moribus") is curious. Though its origin must be Bede's *Ecclesiastical History*, which lists four of Britain's languages all united by the fifth language of Latin, as well as the different *mores* of the Britons, it is likely that Lantfred is deliberately trying to equivocate his description of the apostolic mission at Pentecost with Edgar's (and the reformers') rule over England. Just as Lantfred's portrayal of the early apostolic mission consists of the performance of miracles ("signis uirtutibusque miraculorum") and the proclamation of healthy doctrine ("sanam doctrinam"), so also does his depiction of St Swithun's translation during Edgar's reign coincide with miracles and healing of sick. Lantfred's detail that England's saints cured the sickness of the whole island ("per uirtutem Domini curantes totius insulae egros diuersis languoribus oppressos") not only connects them to the first apostles, but also foreshadows the healing miracles that occur through Swithun.[48]

Alongside Byrhtferth and Lantfred, there are a series of hymns for Pentecost associated with the Benedictine reform. In the ninth century,

---

47 *Translatio et miracula S. Swithuni*, Praef.51–5, 258. For the date, see Lapidge, *Cult of St Swithun*, 258, nt. 32.

48 *Translatio et miracula S. Swithuni*, Praef.41–2, 256.

efforts to replace the so-called Old Hymnal, which dates back to the fifth century, can be detected in France and southwest Germany.[49] Soon afterwards the so-called New Hymnal superseded its predecessors and was introduced in Britain during the tenth century in two groups, the "Canterbury Group," and the "Winchester-Worcester Group."[50] Though the content of the hymns on Pentecost are of continental origin, they are significant here not only as texts sung by tenth-century Anglo-Saxon monks, but also because traces of interaction with these hymns survive as Old English glosses in what is termed the Durham hymnal. Not surprisingly, in three of the four hymns on Pentecost, narrative details on the language miracle of Pentecost are present. The Canterbury hymn for Nocturns states: "Linguis loquuntur omnium. / Turbę pavent gentilium," glossed "mid gereordum hi spræcon ealra / mænigu forhtiaþ hæþenra" (they spoke in the languages of everyone. The crowds of the heathens trembled). The hymn for Lauds (not glossed) states: "Adest probatum testibus / apostolorum vocibus, / cum sit diversis oribus / variis locuti gentibus" (Here is proof in the witnesses of the apostles, their voices, when they spoke with diverse mouths to the various nations). And the second part of a three-part hymn, (that part which was sung at Sext at Canterbury), gives the longest description (glosses are above the line and marked in parentheses):

(stefna mistlice swegdan)
Voces diverse intonant,
(heo spræcon godes mærða)
fantur dei magnalia.
(of ælcere þeode wæron gegæderode wæs samodafaren [glossed coitur])
Ex omni gente cogniti,
(grecisces lydenwaru hæðen)
Grecis, Latinis, barbaris,
(7 eallum wundriendum)
cunctisque ammirantibus
(mid gereordum hi spræcon ealra)
linguis loquuntur omnium

49 Gneuss, "Latin Hymns in Medieval England," ch. 11, 407–24, at 409.

50 Gneuss, *Hymnar und Hymnen in englischen Mittelalter*, 55–74, esp. 71. The Canterbury Hymnal of the Bosworth Psalter, London, British Library, Add. 37517, has been edited by Wieland, ed., *The Canterbury Hymnal*; and the Durham Hymnal, Durham, Durham Catherdal B.III.32 by Milfull, ed., *The Hymns of the Anglo-Saxon Church*.

> Diverse voices sounded out and spoke of the great things of God. They were understood by every nation, Greeks, Romans, Barbarians, and all were amazed as they spoke in the languages of everyone.[51]

One noteworthy point of these hymns is the emphasis on heathenism, slightly more prominent in the Old English, which glosses *gentilium* as *hæþenra* and *barbaris* as *hæþen*. Though the original account in Acts describes the various languages of Jews living in the diaspora, in these Pentecostal hymns, and especially in their Old English glosses, the apostles are speaking to heathens. Through these glosses, the lack of true religion in the subjects of the apostolic mission becomes slightly more apparent, which alongside the reference to multilingualism might recall that the origins of multilingualism and heathenism began at Babel long before the conversion of the gentiles at and after Pentecost. Significantly, the very existence of these Old English glosses points to circumstances of multilingualism in Britain itself. The two languages of the manuscript, Latin and Old English, produce a visual reminder that the Anglo-Saxons themselves participate in the "diverse voices" speaking of the "great things of God ... in the languages of everyone." Old English, in other words, is not absent from the Pentecostal mission propounded in the hymn; it is instead an important element of the multilingualism of salvation history.

Admittedly, the Pentecostal mission to reverse the heathenism of the nations first initiated at Babel and to win over a gentile Church is not prominent in the Latin or Old English texts of the Benedictine reform. Only Byrhtferth, Lantfred, and the authors of the New Hymnal refer to the speaking of all languages at Pentecost, and Byrhtferth alone mentions Nimrod. But when allusions to Pentecost or Babel are used in these cases, they ultimately continue to reinforce the contrast between good and evil in salvation history, and further reveal the ideological foundation of the historical narratives of the Benedictine reform. The pagan gentiles of Jerusalem before Pentecost are comparable not only to the pagan Anglo-Saxons before Gregory's mission, but also to the degenerate ninth-century inhabitants of Britain before the Benedictine reform. This analogy has the benefit of bolstering the reformers to the level of apostles who will convert the island and restore it to the pristine religion of early Christianity. Even

51 Milfull, ed., *Hymns*, no. 77, lines 9–10; no. 78, lines 13–16; and no. 80, lines 9–12. This final hymn was sung as one with nos. 79 and 80 at Vespers at Winchester; Milfull, ed., *Hymns*, 312.

in texts that do not mention Babel or Pentecost this historical ideology is apparent. For only one example, the Old English account of Edgar's establishment of monasteries, a fundamental document of the reform affiliated with the Old English translation of the Rule of St Benedict and likely written by Æthelwold himself,[52] narrates the conversion of Britain initiated by Pope Gregory the Great:[53]

> se mæra Wyrhta þe rihsigende wylt 7 gemetegaþ eal þæt he geworhte, no be þęm anum lætan wolde, ac eornostlice ofer þone garsecg þone ylecan leoman þæs fullan geleafan aspringan let, 7 fornean þæt ytemeste iglond ealles middangeardes, mid Ongolcynne genihtsumlice gefylled, wundorfullice anlyhte 7 mærsode. Soðlice þæt ylece iglond, on ærum tydum mid [h]æðengilde afylled, þearle swiþe beswicyn, deofolgilde þeowode; þeahhwæþere þurh fultum þære þancweroþan Cristes gyfe 7 þurh sanctum Gregorium, þæs Romanisces setles bisceop, fram þæm þystrum heora geleafleaste wearþ genered.
>
> That great Creator who reigns, rules, and controls all that he made, by no means desired to refrain from that sole thing [*sc.* promulgation of faith], and earnestly had that same beam of the full faith spread over the sea, and He wondrously illuminated and exalted that island abundantly filled with the English, which is almost the furthermost of all the world. Truly, that same island, previously filled with heathenism, and very sorely deceived, practiced devil worship; nevertheless through the help of that commendable grace of Christ and through Saint Gregory, bishop of the Roman see, it was saved from the darkness of their faithlessness.

As with Lantfred, the author of this text (whom I will assume is Æthelwold) continues with the conversion of the English, describing an initial

52 Whitelock, "The Authorship of the Account of King Edgar's Establishment of the Monasteries," ch. 7, 125–36. But since part of the text echoes a passage from William of Jumièges, it was likely somewhat revised after the Conquest; see Gransden, "Late Anglo-Saxon Monasticism," 203, nt. 233, who refers to Robinson, *Times of Saint Dunstan*, 160–8. Gretsch, *The Intellectual Foundations of the English Benedictine Reform*, 240–1, argues that Edgar's establishment of the monasteries was originally a preface to the Rule. See also Pratt, "The Voice of the King in 'King Edgar's Establishment of Monasteries,'" 145–204.

53 *An Account of King Edgar's Establishment of Monasteries*, in Whitelock, Brett, and Brooke, eds., *Councils and Synods with Other Documents Relating to the English Church*, 143–4.

"Golden Age" of faith when monasticism thrived in imitation of the Apostles who are of one heart, one soul, and who have no common possessions ("him eallum wæs an heorte 7 an saul, ne heora nan syndrige æht næfde").[54] This high point of monasticism, however, then diminished until Edgar and Dunstan begin to restore it – the rest of the text is devoted to describing the establishment of monasteries, an interesting discussion on translation, comments on the benefits of a monastic life under the Benedictine Rule, and exhortations for abbots, abbesses, and secular rulers. Even without reference to Babel or Pentecost, the underlying influence of these biblical events can be detected in the document's cyclical view of history. According to its proponents, the Benedictine reform falls squarely within the course of salvation history extending from the dispersal of pagan nations at Babel, to their redemption at first-century Jerusalem, and finally to the renewed wickedness and reforming efforts in tenth-century Britain.

Ælfric

After the first generation of the Benedictine reform, Æthelwold's (and possibly Dunstan's) most prolific student, Ælfric of Eynsham, (c. 955–c. 1010), concerned himself with continuing the general goals of tenth-century Benedictine monasticism, albeit it in his own idiosyncratic ways.[55] Ælfric's life, at least after his adolescence, was fully imbued with monasticism, and, at around the age of fifty, after spending eighteen years at the monastery of Cerne Abbas, he became the abbot of a newly established

54 *An Account of King Edgar's Establishment of Monasteries*, 145. Tenth-century England is described as a "aurea secla" in the *Libellus Æthelwoldi*, a twelfth-century text that derives from a now lost Old English work translated into Latin perhaps by Gregory of Ely; Blake, ed., *Liber Eliensis*, 395–9, at 397; see Lapidge and Winterbottom, ed., *The Life of St Æthelwold*, 81–3.

55 The dates of Ælfric's life are difficult to determine. Because the minimum age for ordination as a priest was thirty, Ælfric must have been at least that old when he was sent to Cerne Abbas as a mass-priest in 987, and his last work seems to have been written between 1006 and 1012; see Clemoes, "Ælfric," 176–209, at 179; and Hurt, *Ælfric*, 27. See also Gneuss, *Ælfric of Eynsham*; and Hill, "Ælfric: His Life and Work," 35–65. The bibliography of Ælfrician scholarship is vast; see Reinsma, *Ælfric: An Annotated Bibliography*; Kleist, "An Annotated Bibliography of Ælfrician Studies," 503–52; and Magennis, "Ælfric Scholarship," 5–34. For an important caveat against overemphasizing Ælfric's activities in the mainstream of the Benedictine reform, see Jones, "Ælfric and the Limits of 'Benedictine Reform,'" 104.

monastery at Eynsham.[56] Not long after his move to Eynsham, however, Ælfric's literary output discontinued, either because he decided to retire from writing and recede quietly into a less literary life or because he did not have much longer to live. Although Ælfric never rose to great heights in the ecclesiastical hierarchies – unlike his contemporary Wulfstan the homilist, archbishop of York – Ælfric's outstanding erudition, which comes forth in his numerous and diverse writings, securely ensures his place as one of the most important authors of Anglo-Saxon England.

Specifically, Ælfric was much concerned with overcoming latent heathenism or general wickedness by means of dissemination of the gospel to England. Through evangelical dissemination, Ælfric affirmed and fulfilled the notion of England as a central participant in the universal Church, despite its heathen past. Like the Benedictine reformers who taught him, Ælfric participated in the promulgation of an image of Britain before the advent of the reform as completely lacking education and learning, to the great detriment of its spiritual and secular well-being.[57] In an oft-quoted passage, Ælfric writes:[58]

> Hwanon sceolan cuman wise lareowas on Godes folce, buton hi on iugoðe leornion? And hu mæg se geleafa beon forðgenge, gif seo lar and ða lareowas ateoriað? Is nu forði Godes þeowum and mynstermannum georne to warnigenne, þæt seo halige lar on urum dagum ne acolige oððe ateorige, swa swa hit wæs gedon on Angelcynne nu for anum feawum gearum, swa þæt nan Englisc preost ne cuðe dihtan oððe asmeagean anne pistol on Leden, oð þæt Dunstan arcebisceop and Aðelwold bisceop eft þa lare on munuclifum arærdon.

56 Hurt, *Ælfric*, 37. For the possibility that Ælfric began his education under the secular clergy, see Jones, "Ælfric and the Limits of 'Benedictine Reform,'" 104–7; and Jones, "*Meatim Sed et Rustica*: Ælfric of Eynsham as a Medieval Latin Author," 1–57, at 53–7.

57 See Jones, "Ælfric and the Limits of 'Benedictine Reform,'" 76, who insightfully points out a perceived lapse in learning between the first generation of reformers that Ælfric's desires to re-reform: "[p]aradoxically, in order to lay claim to their own Æthelwoldian heritage, Ælfric's projects involve a rhetoric that *needs* decline to make them off from the very successes they aspire to recreate" (emphasis his). Jones also gives further examples of Ælfric's statements regarding English decline and renewal (73–5), citing Ælfric's *Life of St Swithun*, in Lapidge, *The Cult of St Swithun*, lines 234–44; and *The Prayer of Moses*, in *Aelfric's Lives of Saints*, I.xiii.147–55.

58 *Old English Preface to Grammar*, in *Ælfric's Prefaces*, 3b.15–23.

> From where shall come wise teachers among the people of God unless they learn in their youth? And how may the faith be promulgated, if that teaching and the teachers diminish? It is therefore now the time for God's servants and priests to warn eagerly lest holy teaching grows cold or diminishes in our age, just as it has happened in England now a few years ago, such that no English priest knew how to compose or explicate a single letter in Latin until Archbishop Dunstan and Bishop Æthelwold reinstituted teaching in monastic living.

One of the primary ways in which Ælfric attempted to remedy this English ignorance and the principal cause of wickedness and heathenism was by translating a number of biblical and patristic texts from Latin into Old English. In fact, the passage just quoted comes from the preface of Ælfric's translation of the *Excerptiones de Prisciano*, the first vernacular Latin grammar, which Ælfric hopes will aid schoolboys in their Latin *and* English studies.[59] While the focus on multilingual learning, both Latin and Old English, is remarkable, it is understandable for Ælfric's cultural context. Latin and Old English learning had provided the foundation of Christian education since the early eighth century; it found its most prominent expression in Alfred and continued into the program of the Benedictine reform, chiefly by Æthelwold and then by Ælfric.[60]

Ælfric's own translation efforts are best understood as being in line with those of his teacher. Æthelwold, in addition to being an accomplished Latin author, is also thought to be the proficient translator of the Old English *Regula S. Benedicti*[61] – a proposition that accords well with Wulfstan

59 See also the *Latin Preface to Grammar*, in *Ælfric's Prefaces*, 3a.1–5: "Ego Ælfricus, ut minus sapiens, hac excerptiones de Prisciano minore vel maiore vobis puerulis tenellis ad vestram linguam transferre studui, quatinus ... potestis utramque linguam, videlicet Latinam et Anglicam, vestre tenerritudini inserere" (I, Ælfric, though of little learning, was eager to translate the lesser and greater *Excerptiones de Prisciano* for you tender little children into your language, so that you may be able to sow both languages, that is Latin and English, in your tenderness); and again the *Old English Preface to Grammar*, 3b.24–5: "heo [*sc.* ðeos boc] byð ... sum angyn to ægðrum gereorde" (it [*sc.* this book] is a beginning for [the study of] both languages).

60 See Bullough, "The Educational Tradition"; Smith, "Alfred and Ælfric," 9–20; and Wieland, "Bilingual Education in Anglo-Saxon England," 35–57.

61 The twelfth-century *Liber Eliensis* is the first to mention Æthelwold's translation; Blake, ed., *Liber Eliensis*, II.37: "ille regulam sancti Benedicti in Anglicum idioma de Latino transferret" (he [*sc.* Æthelwold] translated the rule of St Benedict into English from Latin). See especially the studies of Gretsch, *Die Regula Sancti Benedicti in*

of Winchester's, as well as Ælfric's, statement that for Æthelwold, "Dulce namque erat ... Latinos libros Anglice eis [*sc.* adolescentes et iuuenes] soluere" (it was pleasant to translate books into English for [his students]).[62] Significantly, in the Old English account of King Edgar's establishment of the monasteries, Æthelwold (or perhaps an anonymous author) provides some discussion on translation from Latin to Old English:[63]

> Ic þ[onne] geþeode to micclan gesceade telede. Wel mæg dug[an hit naht] mid hwylcan gereorde mon sy gestryned 7 to þan soþan geleafan gewæmed, butan þæt an sy þæt he Gode gegange. Hæbben forþi þa ungelæreden inlendisce þæs halgan regules cyþþe þurh agenes gereordes anwrigenesse, þæt hy þe geornlicor Gode þeowien and nane tale næbben þæt hy þurh nytennesse misfon þurfen.
>
> I therefore think translation to be a great method. It cannot really matter much with what language a man is begotten and persuaded to the true faith, except for that one thing, that he goes to God. Therefore let the unlearned people have knowledge of this holy rule through an exposition of their own language so that they may serve God more eagerly and not be reproached that they were compelled to sin through ignorance.

Of course, translation of Latin into the vernacular is not new – Bede, for an early example, encourages it in his letter to Ecgbert and he is said to have been working on an English translation of the Gospel of John on his deathbed.[64] But after Alfred's translation program, and especially during the Benedictine reform, translation of Latin documents into Old English was seen as one of the more prominent steps to reclaiming Britain's Golden

England und ihre altenglische Übersetzung; "Æthelwold's Translation of the *Regula Sancti Benedicti* and its Latin Exemplar," 125–51; "The Benedictine Rule in Old English," 131–58; "Der liturgische Wortschatz in Æthelwold's Übersetzung der Benediktinerregal und sprachliche Normierung in spätaltenglischer Zeit," 310–54; and *Intellectual Foundations of the English Benedictine Reform*, 226–60. See also Gneuss, "Die Benediktinerregal in England und ihre altenglische Übersetzung," 263–84.

62 Wulfstan of Winchester, *Vita Sancti Æthelwoldi*, ch. 31, 46–8; see also Ælfric, *Vita S. Æthelwoldi*, in Lapidge and Winterbottom, ed., *The Life of St Æthelwold*, ch. 20, 77.

63 *An Account of King Edgar's Establishment of Monasteries*, 151–2.

64 *Epistola Bede ad Ecgbertum episcopum*, in Plummer, ed., *Venerabilis Baedae historiam ecclesiasticum*, vol. 1, 409; and *Epistola de obitu Bedae*, in Colgrave and Mynors, ed., *Ecclesiastical History*, 582.

Age of Christianity, and an essential aspect, as is evident from Æthelwold's comments, for much of the reform program. This aspect continued up to the early eleventh century, when Wulfstan the homilist would also encourage vernacular translation of fundamental religious texts.[65]

Ælfric, however, differs from his predecessors and contemporaries in the anxiety that he expresses over translation.[66] In his preface to Genesis, he writes, "Nu þincð me, leof, *þæt* þæt weorc is swiðe pleolic me oððe ænigum men to underbeginnenne" (Now it seems to me, sir, that that work [of translation] is very dangerous for me or any other man to undertake) and "ic ne dearr ne ic nelle nane boc æfter ðisre of Ledene on Englisc awendan" (I neither dare nor desire to translate any book after this one from Latin into English).[67] Similar statements of reluctance towards translation appear elsewhere in Ælfric's Latin preface to the *Lives of Saints*, where he asserts, "Nec tamen plura promitto me scripturum hac lingua, q*u*ia nec conuenit huic sermocinationi plura inseri" (yet I promise not to write more in this tongue because it is not fitting that more is sown into this language);[68] and at the end of the second series of *Catholic Homilies*, where he promises, "Ic cweðe nu þæt ic næfre heononforð ne awende godspel. oþþe godspeltrahtas of ledene on englisc" (I say now that I will never henceforth translate the Gospel or tracts on the Gospel from Latin into English).[69] This anxiety seems to stem chiefly from Ælfric's suspicion that the contents of the "ealda æ" (Old Law), especially Old Testament examples dealing with issues of sexuality, but also the religious and social regulations outlined in the Pentateuch, will be misinterpreted by ignorant readers, who will then turn to heretical error (*gedwyld*) and risk their salvation. If the more difficult contents of the Old Testament are widely available, the risk of error and damnation among his Anglo-Saxon copatriots would, therefore, be greater.

65 Wulfstan, Homilies 7 and 7a, in *Homilies of Wulfstan*.

66 See Stanton, *Culture of Translation*, 131–41; Wilcox, "A Reluctant Translator in Late Anglo-Saxon England," 1–18; Marsden, "Ælfric as Translator," 319–58; Anderson, "The Old Testament Homily," 121–42; and Gittos, "The Audience for Old English Texts," 231–66, at 262–5.

67 *Old English Preface to the Translation of Genesis*, in *Ælfric's Prefaces*, 4.6–7, 116 and 4.111–12, 119.

68 *Aelfric's Lives of Saints*, I.praef.9–11. Note the similar use of the verb *insero* here and in the *Latin Preface to Grammar* quoted above at n. 59.

69 *Ælfric's Catholic Homilies: The Second Series*, 345.5–7.

In the end, however, Ælfric rendered into Old English, either as formal translations or as homiletic pieces, large sections of the Bible, including the first half of Genesis, Numbers, Joshua, Judges, Kings, Esther, Job, Judith, Maccabees, and much of the New Testament Gospels.[70] Moreover, in his *Libellus de ueteri testamento et nouo*, Ælfric even points out his own accomplishments in biblical translation.[71] And on account of his extensive efforts at biblical translation, Ælfric was commemorated in the thirteenth century primarily as a biblical translator:[72]

> Ælfric abbod, þe we Alquin hoteþ,
> He was bocare, and þe [fif] bec wende,
> Genesis, Exodus, Vtronomius, Numerus, Leuiticus,
> Þu[rh] þeos weren ilærde ure leoden on Englisc.

> Abbot Ælfric, whom we call Alcuin, was a scholar, and he translated five books: Genesis, Exodus, Deuteronomy, Numbers, Leviticus – through these books our people were educated in English.

Although, as Milton McC. Gatch insightfully observes, "Ælfric limits himself severely to the historical books [of the Bible] … [and] did not attempt apocalyptic prophecy or wisdom,"[73] his translation efforts were, nevertheless, extensive.

Although realistic awareness of the demands of an audience ignorant of the Latin biblical texts certainly lies behind the discrepancy between

70 *The Old English Heptateuch and Ælfric's Libellus de ueteri testamento et nouo*, 8–51 (Genesis 1–24:22), 144–53 (Numbers 13–36), 177–86 (Joshua1–10), 190–200 (Judges); *Aelfric's Lives of Saints*, I.18, 384–413 (Kings), and II.25, 66–124 (Maccabees); *Angelsächsische Homilien und Heiligenleben*, viii (Esther), and ix (Judith). Ælfric's translations of New Testament passages are too widely spread across his corpus to note here, but see, for example, the pericopes of his two series of Catholic Homilies, discussed throughout by Godden, *Ælfric's Catholic Homilies*.

71 *Libellus de ueteri testamento et nouo*, lines 249–51, 407–8, 461–2, 579–82.

72 *The First Worcester Fragment*, Worcester Cathedral F.174, fol. 63, in Dickins and Wilson, eds., *Early Middle English Texts*, 2; see also Brehe, "Reassembling the *First Worcester Fragment*," 521–36.

73 Gatch, "The Office in Late Anglo-Saxon Monasticism," 341–62, at 361; Gatch, 362, also gives some examples of Ælfric avoiding trickier parts of the biblical narrative, "such as David's relationship with Bathsheba or the Absalom episode." Wilcox, ed., *Ælfric's Prefaces*, 44 and 65, suggests that Ælfric comes to terms with his reluctance to translate by moving away from the need to render literally and by employing greater "interpretative freedoms." See also O'Brien, *Reversing Babel*, 189–90.

Ælfric's theories and practice of biblical translation, Ælfric also expresses theological rationale behind this discrepancy. And that rationale is directly related to his interpretations of the Tower of Babel narrative and its consequences in salvation history. Since Ælfric's biblical training placed him squarely not only in the Benedictine reform but also in the Latin Christian traditions of Late Antiquity and the early Middle Ages, it is no surprise that along with many Christians before him, Ælfric understood the Tower of Babel as a biblical, and therefore authoritative, explanation of the origin of diversity in the world. But also in line with patristic (and tenth-century Benedictine) thought, Ælfric understood that the Church had encompassed the diversity of the world formed at Babel, first with the descent of the Holy Spirit at Pentecost, where the apostles speak all the languages of the world, and second with apostolic preaching to all the nations.[74]

In his corpus of multiple homilies, letters, saints' lives, and scientific and didactic works, Ælfric has essentially six extended treatments of the Tower of Babel outside of his translation of Genesis 11 and Alcuin's *Interrogationes in Genesin*. The first occurs in the opening homily of his first series of Catholic Homilies, *De initio creaturae* (*CHomI.1*), written in 989:[75]

> þa wæs þa sume hwile godes ege on mancynne. æfter þam flode. 7 wæs án gereord on him eallum; Ða cwædon hi betwux him þ[æt] hi woldon wircan ane burh 7 ænne stypel binnan þære byrig. swa heahne þ[æt] his hrof astige up to heofonum. 7 begunnon þa to wyrcanne. þa com god þærto þa ða hi swiðust worhton. 7 sealde ælcum men þe ðær wæs synderlice spræce; þa wæron þær swa fela gereord swa ðær men wæron. 7 heora nan nyste hwæt oðer cwæð; 7 hi ða geswicon þære getimbrunge. 7 toferdon geond ealne middaneard; þa syððan wearð mancyn þurh deofel. beswicen. 7 gebiged fram godes geleafan. swa þ[æt] hi worhton him anlicnyssa. sume of golde sume of seolfre sume eac of stane sume of treowe. 7 sceopon him naman: þæra manna naman þe wæron entas 7 yfeldæde. eft þa ða hi deade wæron. þa cwædan þa cucan þ[æt] hi wæron godas. 7 weorðodon hi. 7 him lac ofredon. 7 comon þa deoflu to heora anlicnyssum. 7 þærón wunedon. 7 to mannum spræcon. swilce hi godas wæron. 7 þ[æt] beswicone mennisc feoll on cneowum to þam anlicnyssum and cwædon ge sind ure godas 7 we besettað urne geleafan. 7 urne hiht on eow; Ða asprang þis gedwyld geond ealne middaneard. 7 wæs se soða scyppend se ðe ana is god forsewen 7 geunweorþod;

74 See Busse, "*Sua gað ða lareowas beforan ðæm folce, & ðæt folc æfter*," 58–106, at 65–6; and Major, "Rebuilding the Tower of Babel: Ælfric and Bible Translation," 47–60.

75 *Ælfric's Catholic Homilies: The First Series*, 1.203–21.

> Then for some time after the Flood humankind held the fear of God, and there was a single language among them all. Then they said among themselves that they wanted to build a single city and a single tower within that city, so high that its roof would rise up to heaven. And they began to build it when God came there where they were most busy building, and gave to each person who was there a different language. Then there were as many languages as there were people, and none of them knew what the other said. And they stopped their construction, and dispersed throughout all the world. Afterwards many were deceived by the devil, and turned away from God's faith such that they made for themselves idols, some of gold, some of silver, some of stone, some of wood; and they gave them names, which were the names of people, who were giants and wicked men. After they were dead, those still living said that they were gods, and they worshipped them and offered sacrifices to them; and devils then came into those idols and dwelled therein, and spoke to people as if they were gods. And those deceived people fell on their knees before those idols and said "you are gods and we place our faith and our hope in you." Then this error sprang up throughout all the world, and the true Creator who alone is God was despised and unhonoured.

After this initial account, a second occurs in the homily *In die sancto Pentecosten* (*CHomI*.22), again from the first series of Catholic Homilies; one in his second series of Catholic Homilies, *Natale Mathei apostoli et euangelistæ* (*CHomII.32*), written in 992; one in his homily, *De falsis diis* (*SHII.21*), written between 992 and 1002; one in the *Libellus de ueteri testamento et nouo* (*LUTN*), written between 1005 and 1006; and one in the related tract, *De sex aetatibus* (*DSA*), written in 1006.[76] The homilies of the first series of Catholic Homilies are Ælfric's earliest accounts of the Tower of Babel, and seem to give rise to numerous features, notably similar or exact phrasing, that appear in the later accounts. For the sake of convenience, the six accounts have been arranged to underline their shared phrasing.

This comparison reveals a great degree of similarity among all the accounts. As is to be expected based on their temporal and textual relationships, the accounts in *CHomI*.1 and *CHomI*.22 are the most similar:

76 *CHomI.22* = *Ælfric's Catholic Homilies: The First Series*, 2.109–27; *CHomII.32* = *Ælfric's Catholic Homilies: The Second Series*, 32.91–105; *SHII.21* = *Homilies of Ælfric: A Supplementary Collection*, vol. 2, 21.72–81; *LUTN* = *Libellus de ueteri testamento et nouo*, lines 139–45; *DSA* = *De sex aetatibus*, , lines 41–57. Dates are from Clemoes, "The Chronology of Ælfric's Works," 29–72; and Pope, ed., *Homilies of Ælfric*, vol. 1, 147.

Similarities in phrasing in Ælfric's discussions of the Tower of Babel[77]

Title	Text			
1 CHomI.1	hi	woldon wircan	ane burh 7	ænne stypel swa heahne
1 CHomI.22	entas	woldon aræran	ane burh 7	ænne stypel swa heahne
1 CHomII.32	men	woldon him arǽran		swa heahne stypel
1LUTN	suna	begunnon to wircenne	wundorlican burh	þone heagan stipel
1DSA	sunan	woldon sona wyrcean	ane burh	ænne heahne stypel
1 SHII.21	entas	worhton	wundorlican	stýpel
2 CHomI.1	þæt his hrof astige up to heofonum		7 begunnon þa to wyrcanne	
2 CHomI.22	þæt his hrof astige oð heofon		7 þæt weorc wæs begunnen	ongean godes willan
2 CHomII.32	þæt his hrof astige to heofenum			
2 LUTN	þe sceolde astigan upp to heofenum			
2 DSA	þe astige upp oð þa heofonan		7 begunnon þa to wyrcenne	ongéan Godes willan
2 SHII.21	*Omitted*			
3 CHomI.1	com god þærto ða hi swiðust worhton			sealde ælcum men þe ðær wæs
3 CHomI.22	God eac for þi hi tosstencte			swa þæt he forgeaf ælcum þæra wyrhtena
3 CHomII.32	se ælmihtiga towearp heora anginn			swa þæt hé forgeaf ælcum ðæra wyrhtena

77 Editorial marks and punctuation have been removed. In order to emphasize similarities some phrases have been silently omitted or placed slightly out of order.

Similarities in phrasing in Ælfric's discussions of the Tower of Babel (*Cont.*)

Title	Text		
3 LUTN	God silf com þærto and sceawode heora weorc		and sealde heora ælcum
3 DSA	God cóm þærto 7 sceawode þone stypell	7 forgeaf þam wyrhtum ælcum	
3 SHII.21	hym swa feala gereorda God þar forgeaf swa þæra wyrhtena wæs		
4 CHomI.1	synderlice spræce		7 heora nan nyste hwæt oðer cwæð
4 CHomI.22	seltcuð gereord		7 heora nan cuðe oþres spræce tocnawan
4 CHomII.32	synderlic gereord		and heora nán nyste hwæt oðer gecwæð
4 LUTN	synderlice spræce		þæt heora ælcum wæs uncuð hwæt oþer sæde
4 DSA	his gereord		þæt heora nan nyste naht oðres sprǽce
4 SHII.21	*Omitted*		
5 CHomI.1	hi ða geswicon þære getimbrunge		7 toferdon geond ealne middaneard
5 CHomI.22	Hi ða geswicon þære getimbrunge		7 toferdon geond ealne middaneard
5 CHomII.32	*Omitted*		
5 LUTN	hi swa geswicon sona þære getimbrunge		and hi ða toferdon to fyrlenum lande
5 DSA	hi swa geswicon sona þæs weorces		7 toferdon to fyrlenum landum
5 SHII.21			Ða þa hi toferdon to fyrlenum landum
6 CHomI.1	þa wæron þær swa fela gereord swa ðær men wæron		
6 CHomI.22	wæron syððan swa fela gereord swa ðæra wyrhtena wæs		
6 CHomII.32	And on swa manegum gereordem swa þæra manna wæs		
6 SHII.21	*See 3*		

despite some minor differences, nearly exact phrasing is used in 1, 2, and 5; and with the exception of 3, close phrasing in 4 and 6. In fact, such similar phrasing, along with that of *DSA*, indicates an interesting omission in *CHomI*.1 of "ongean godes willan" (against God's will) to complete the phrase "7 begunnon þa to wyrcanne" (and they began to work). *CHomII*.32, which was written after the two accounts of the first series of Catholic Homilies, offers an abridged version of the account in *CHomI*.1 and *CHomI*.22. While it shares phrasing with *CHomI*.22 against *CHomI*.1 (1: *arǽran*; 3: *swa þæt hé forgeaf ælcum ðæra wyrhtena*), it also shares phrasing with *CHomI*.1 against *CHomI*.22 (4: *synderlic ... nyste hwæt oðer gecwæð*; 6: *swa þæra manna wæs*). The abridged nature of *CHomII*.32 can be explained by the context of the homily: Ælfric has Matthew state how the apostles came to understand all the languages of the world. Most likely due to a desire to keep background material at a minimum, Ælfric truncated the account of Babel to quicken the pace of the homily.

The account in *SHII*.21 is the most idiosyncratic. The homily seems to have been written after the second series of Catholic Homilies but before Ælfric's collection of saints' lives.[78] It omits many of the phrases found in the other accounts (2, 4, 5) and in one instance conflates two phrases (3, 6) into one: "and hym swa feala gereorda / God þar forgeaf swa þæra wyrhtena wæs" (and God gave them just as many languages as there were workers). The lack of similarity between the account in *SHII*.21 and the accounts in the series of Catholic Homilies suggests that Ælfric did not have copies, or at least did not use copies, of these earlier accounts when he composed these lines. More likely, Ælfric composed the account in *SHII*.21 afresh, perhaps relying on memory of what he had previously written or read.[79]

The other two accounts, those of *LUTN* and *DSA*, both of which were written later in Ælfric's career, have very complex relationships between themselves and the other accounts. They share unique phrasing with each

78 Pope, ed., *Homilies of Ælfric*, vol. 1, 147.

79 For Ælfric's memory, particularly of his Latin sources, see Cross, "Bundles for Burning," 335–46; "More Sources for Two of Ælfric's *Catholic Homilies*," 59–78; "Ælfric – Mainly on Memory and Creative Method in Two *Catholic Homilies*," 135–56; "The Literate Anglo-Saxon," 67–100, at 86–93; and Lees, "The Dissemination of Alcuin's *De virtutibus et vitiis liber* in Old English," 174–89, esp. 182–3.

other in four instances (1: *suna / sunan*;[80] 2: *þe*; 3: *sceawode heora weorc / þone stypell*; 5: *swa … sona*); phrasing shared with at least one of the accounts in the Catholic Homilies in three instances (1: *heagan stipel*; 3: *God cóm þærto*; 5: *hi … geswicon … þære getimbrunge / weorces … 7 toferdon*); and phrasing shared with *SHII*.21 in one instance (5: *to fyrlenum landum / lande*). *DSA* shares features with the accounts in the Catholic Homilies that *LUTN* does not share (1: *ane burh*; 2: *begunnon þa to wyrcenne ongéan Godes willan*; 4: *heora nan nyste … oðres sprǽce*); and *LUTN* shares one feature with *CHomI*.1 (3: *sealde*) and one with *SHII*.21 (1: *wundorlican*) that are not shared with *DSA*. The textual complexity of these relationships implies that Ælfric did not have one single text or even two texts in front of him which he could have copied with slight changes, when he composed his later accounts. Instead, he seems to be drawing from a series of his own homiletic stock-in-trade phrases involving the Tower of Babel narrative that he employed within different contexts, such as the sketches of Old Testament history in *CHomI*.1, *LUTN* and *DSA*; the accounts of Pentecost in *CHomI*.22 and *CHomII*.32, or the explanation of the world's idolatry in *SHII*.21. The shared phrasing in all of Ælfric's accounts of the Tower of Babel reveals that the Babel narrative was important enough for Ælfric not only to record it in writing at least six times, but also to employ a kind of memorized phrasing of the narrative. Although the phenomenon of remembered formulaic phrasing is well documented in Old English homilies, it has rarely been attributed to Ælfric, who is more often praised for his "clear, unmannered, and easily comprehensible prose," or "rhythmic style."[81] Ælfric's formulaic accounts of the Tower of Babel narrative, however, suggest that his method of composition is very much in line with the homiletic tradition of other Old English prose writers, such as Wulfstan.[82]

Furthermore, in his translation of Alcuin's *Interrogationes*, Ælfric deviates from the Latin in a way that corresponds closer to the other accounts.

---

80 Their preceding lines are also similar: "Noes sunan ða syðþan gestry[ndon twa] 7 hundseofontig sunana" (*DSA* 41) / "Noes … suna gestrindon twa and hundseofontig suna" (*LUTN* 135–6). For the significance of the temporal proximity between *DSA* and *LUTN*, see Tristram, *Sex aetates mundi*, 97.

81 Gneuss, *Ælfric of Eynsham*, 18–20. For more recent attention on Ælfric's formulaic style, see Magennis, "Ælfric and Heroic Literature," 31–60, at 50–3; Bredehoft, *Authors, Audiences, and Old English Verse*, 159–67; and Irvine, "Hanging by a Thread," 67–94.

82 See Orchard, "Crying Wolf," 239–64; "On Editing Wulfstan," 311–40; and "Re-editing Wulfstan?," 63–91.

Although in the relevant sections of this work Ælfric follows Alcuin closely by beginning with the division of the world into three parts, he then strays from the Latin in order to connect the seventy-two descendants with the seventy-two builders and the seventy-two languages. In the first instance in the *Interrogationes* where the descendants of Noah's three sons are mentioned, Ælfric translates:[83]

> Hu wæs þes middaneard todæled æfter þa*m* flode? Se yldesta noes sunu sém gestrynde mid his sunu*m* seofon 7 twentig suna. 7 hi gebogodan þone eastdæl middaneardes þe is gehate asia. Se oðer noes sunu chám gestrynde mid his sunu*m* þrittig suna. 7 hy gebogodan þone suðdæl þe is gehaten. affrica. Se þridda noes sunu iafeth gestrynde mid his sunu*m* fiftyne suna. 7 þa gebogodan norðdæl. þe is geháten europa. þas ealle togædere syndon twa 7 hund seofontig þeoda.

> How was the earth divided after the flood? Sem, the oldest of Noah's sons, with his sons, bore twenty-seven descendants, and they inhabited the eastern part of the world which is called Asia. Ham, the second of Noah's sons, with his sons, bore thirty descendants, and they inhabited the southern part which is called Africa. Japheth, the third of Noah's sons, with his sons, bore fifteen descendants, and they inhabited the northern part which is called Europe. All these come to a total of seventy-two nations.

Later in his translation, Ælfric significantly includes material not found in the Latin. Whereas Alcuin writes of Nimrod's involvement as the "exstruendae turris et condendae Babyloniae auctor" (builder of the tower soon to be raised and of Babylon soon to be founded),[84] Ælfric broadens the involvement in the building of the tower by stating: "æt þære getimbrunge þære mycelan byrig babilonian ... hi woldan þone stypel úp to heofenu*m* arǽran. on þære wurdon þa gereord on twa. 7 hund seofantig todæled" (at the building of the great city of Babylon ... they wanted to raise up to

83 Ælfric, "Ælfric's Version of Alcuini Interrogationes Sigeuulfi in Genesin" (henceforth *Interrogationes*), 1–59, at 39–40, § 50–1.367–77; Alcuin, *Quaes.*, 141–2, col. 532C: "Quomodo divisus est orbis a filiis et nepotibus Noe? Sem, ut aestimatur, Asiam, Cham Africam, [et] Japhet Europam sortitus est. Quot gentes singuli eorum procearunt? De Japhet nati sunt filii quindecim, de Cham triginta, de Sem viginti septem: simul septuaginta duo, de quibus ortae sunt gentes septuaginta duae, inter quas misit Dominus discipulos septuaginta duos."

84 Alcuin, *Quaes.*,148, col. 533C.

heaven the tower where languages were divided into seventy-two).[85] In particular, the sentence "hi woldan þone stypel úp to heofenu*m* arǽran" corresponds with only slight variance to the other accounts in 1 and 2. Although earlier in the Latin text, Alcuin writes, "Itaque per linguas divisae sunt gentes dispersaeque per terras" (and so through languages were the nations divided and were dispersed throughout the lands),[86] this sentence does not appear in the Old English. Ælfric evidently found it not specific enough for his purposes to include the seventy-two descendants in the building of the Tower of Babel.

It should, furthermore, be mentioned that, as in his translation of the *Interrogationes*, Ælfric in his *LUTN* refers to a tripartite ethnic and geographical division of the world according to the descendants of Noah after the building of the Tower of Babel:[87]

> Of ðam [*sc.* Sem via Abraham] com Crist siððan, þe eall mancyn alysde. Of Cham, Noes suna, com þæt Chanaeisce folc. And of Iaphet þam gin[g]-stan, þe wæs gebletsod þurh Noe, com þæt norðerne mennisc be þære norðsæ, for þan þe ðri dælas sind gedælede þurh hig: Asia on eastrice þam yldstan suna, Affrica on suðdæle þæs Chames cynne, and Europa on norðdæle Iapheþes ofspringe

> Later from him [Sem via Abraham] came Christ, who redeemed all humankind. From Ham, Noah's son, came the Chanaanite people. And from Japheth, the youngest, who was blessed through Noah, came the northern people near the north sea. Therefore these three parts [of the world] were portioned out through them [the sons]: Asia in the eastern kingdom to the oldest son, Africa in the southern part to the family of Ham, and Europe in the northern part to Japheth's offspring.

Contrary to his translation of the *Interrogationes*, Ælfric here expands on the three parts of the world to provide specific detail about Japheth's line. For one, Ælfric, perhaps as a reflection of Japheth's northern allotment or perhaps in order to provide a kind of *origo gentis* for himself and the West Saxons, places Japheth's lineage in an area around a north sea (not to be

85 Ælfric, *Interrogationes*, 40, § 57.379–3.
86 Alcuin, *Quaes.*, 145, col. 533A.
87 Ælfric, *LUTN*, 166–70.

understood as the modern designation North Sea).[88] Although Ælfric is likely aware that many other *gentes* throughout Europe (not just those *be þære norðsæ*) were thought to be derived from Japheth's line, he may be simplifying the matter for his lay audience. It is probably easier for Ælfric to state that those who settled around the oceanic waters of northern Europe stem from Japheth's line – an area that all Anglo-Saxons would probably generally recognize as their original homeland – than to try to provide an unknown place of origin that connects all the nations of Europe. It is interesting, however, that by locating the origin of Japheth's line to a north sea, Ælfric alters the centricity of Europe, which previous Latin authors understandably placed closer to the Mediterranean Sea. Second, in this passage of the *LUTN*, Ælfric singles out the blessing placed on Japheth's line by Noah. Although Christ came through Sem's line, Japheth "wæs gebletsod þurh Noe" (blessed by Noah); Ham, on the other hand, who is traditionally interpreted allegorically as a reprobate, is only singled out as bearing the *Chanaeisce folc* – traditional enemies of Israel.[89]

One further point regarding Ælfric's six accounts of the Tower of Babel that deserves mention is the different nature of the builders. Although throughout Late Antiquity and Anglo-Saxon England, Nimrod and the builders of Babel are depicted as giants, Ælfric does not show consistency on this point. Whereas he refers to the gigantic builders in his translation of Alcuin's *Interrogationes* ("Nembroð se ént"),[90] in *CHomI*.22 (*entas*), and in *SHII*.21 (*entas*), elsewhere Ælfric describes the builders as the descendants of Noah or simply as humans. Evidently, Ælfric was not committed to one single interpretation of the nature of the builders of Babel and could use whatever suited his purpose. But the rationale behind these purposes is apparent enough. In *SHII*.21, when Ælfric wanted to emphasize the wickedness of idolatry, he refers to the builders as *entas* – a convention that Wulfstan would later employ in his own sermon *De falsis deis*. And in *CHomI*.22, when Ælfric contrasts the pride of Babel with the humility of the Church, he refers to the builders as *entas*, later reinforcing

88 See Borst, *Turmbau von Babel*, II.548.

89 The allegorical interpretation of Ham, which goes back to Philo, figures prominently in Ambrose, *Expositio euangelii secundum Lucam*, VI.44.452–5: "Ex duobus illis [*sc.* Cham et Iaphet] diuersarum nationum populi pullularunt, quorum alter maledictus … benedictus alter" (from these two [Ham and Japheth] the peoples of diverse nations sprang forth: from the one, the people were cursed … from the other, the people were blessed). See Borst, *Turmbau von Babel*, II.385.

90 Ælfric, *Interrogationes*, 379, 40.

the reference with the phrase "enta modignyss" (the pride of giants). However, in *CHomII*.32 where Ælfric is concerned with the linguistic diversity of the world, he plays down the gigantism of the builders by simply calling them *men* (humans). Likewise, Ælfric's three accounts of Babel in works that provide outlines of human history (*CHomI*.1, *LUTN* and *DSA*) do not mention that the Tower was built by giants, but rather by the descendants of Noah. This discrepancy of terminology is particularly emphasized in *CHomI*.1 which interestingly enough connects *entas* with idolatry by stating that after humans built Babel and were dispersed across the world they began to worship past, dead giants (*entas*) as gods.[91] In the three accounts that refer to the building of Babel by humans, the wickedness associated with giants would evidently have less rhetorical effect in a history of humankind, and any reference to giants is either omitted or transferred to a more appropriate place in the homily.

Whereas the Tower of Babel narrative fundamentally explained the linguistic and ethnic diversity of the world, Ælfric seems to have been more interested in its causal relationship with idolatry and error (*gedwyld*), and its redemption through Pentecost. In all of Ælfric's accounts of the Tower of Babel narrative, except *CHomI*.22 and *CHomII*.32, he explains that the nations, following the fall of Babel, took up idolatry. In *CHomI*.1, after cataloguing the different kinds of idolatry that arose after the fall of Babel, Ælfric writes: "Ða asprang þis gedwyld geond ealne middaneard" (then error arose throughout the entire world).[92] Similar lines are repeated in *LUTN*: "On þære ylcan ylde man arærde hæðengild wide geond þas woruld" (in that same age, idolatry was raised widely throughout this world);[93] in the *DSA*: "Æfter þissum wearð wolice afunden / swiðe myce(l gedwyld) on þam manncynne ... *þæt* gedwyld þa a[sprang geond] ealne middaneard" (after this, so much error sorrowfully was found among humankind ... that error arose throughout the entire world);[94] and in *SHII*.21: "man arærde hæþengyld / on eallum þam fyrste ǽr Noes flode, / oðþæt þa entas worhtan þone [wundorlican] stýpel / æfter Noés flóde" (idolatry was raised in that first age that began before Noah's Flood until the giants made that marvelous tower after Noah's Flood), and later, "mancynn þa weox, þa wurdon hi bepæhte / þurh þone ealdan deofol þe Adam ǽr

91 *CHomI*.1.214–19, 186.
92 Ælfric, *CHomI.1* 220–1.
93 *LUTN*, 143–4.
94 *DSA* 51–2, 57.

beswác, / swa þæt hi worhton wolice him godas" (humankind then grew when they became deceived by the old devil, who had deceived Adam, such that they sorrowfully created gods for themselves).[95] Although the connection between the Tower of Babel and idolatry is not new to Ælfric – it occurs as early as Jubilees and is found in both Isidore's and Bede's chronicles[96] – Ælfric places a greater emphasis on it than did previous authors. By doing so, he contextualizes the earlier reform narratives of heathenism in a new framework based on biblical history: whenever heathenism "springs up," whether in ancient Babylon, the pre-conversion island of Britain, or its pre-reform kingdoms, it can be traced back to the heathenism at Babel (and further back, to Adam's fall).

If the problem can be found in the biblical narratives, so can the solution. In contrast to his anxiety over the idolatry and error of the nations, Ælfric was aware that the Church, having spread throughout the world at Pentecost, must act according to the first apostles. Ælfric's first Latin and Old English pastoral letters for Wulfstan provide a fitting example. In the Old English version of the letter, Ælfric inserts lines reminiscent of his other accounts of the rise of heathenism after the Tower of Babel:[97]

> Fram Adame menn wunedon on flæsclicum lustum, and sume on hæþenscype únsnoterlice gelyfdon and mid deofles biggencgum hig-sylfe fordydon and þone scyppend forsáwon, þe hig gesceop to mannum þurh þæs deofles lare, þe Ádam forlǽrde.
>
> After Adam people lived according to carnal desires, and some believed foolishly in heathenism, and by worshipping the devil they undid themselves and forsook the Creator who made them humans, through that teaching of the devil which led Adam astray.

After discussing the role of the law under Moses and the incarnation of Jesus, who established "cristendom and clænnysse" (Christianity and

95 *SHII*.21.72–5, 78–80.

96 Jubilees 11:1–7; Isidore, *Chronica*, §24; and Bede, *De temporum ratione*, LXVI.210–11: "His temporibus primum templa constructa et quidem principes gentium tamquam dii sunt adorati" (In these times [i.e., the second age of the world] temples were first built and indeed the leaders of the nations were worshiped as gods).

97 *Die Hirtenbriefe Ælfrics*, II.9. This section does not appear in the Latin original.

chastity), Ælfric mentions that the twelve apostles, as well as the seventy-two disciples, left their property and wives to live in chastity:[98]

> Eac þa twelf apostolas þe þam hælende folgodan, þa-þa he her on worulde wunode mid mannum, and þa twa and hund-seofontig wera, þe wunedon mid him on his lareow-dome, þa synd leorningc-cnihtas, ealle hi forletan heora æhta and wif and wunedon on clænnysse, Criste folgigende.
>
> Also the twelve apostles who followed Jesus, when he lived here in the world among humans, and the seventy-two men, who lived with him in his teaching – those are disciples – they all gave up their property and wives and lived in chastity, following Christ.

Ælfric then gives more examples of chaste Christian saints before providing a description of Pentecost, where all the languages were understood. As with the previous description of the apostles and disciples as chaste, Ælfric connects Pentecost with the founding of monasticism and the evangelization of the diverse corners of the world: "Her wæs asteald þurh þisne haligan héap þæra muneca lif, þe libbað æfter regule under hyra abbode … Þa to-ferdon þa apostolos to fyrlynum landum, geond ealle þas woruld" (Here the life of those monks who live according to the Rule under an abbot was established by this holy company … Then the apostles spread out to distant lands throughout all the world).[99] So begins, for Ælfric, the first idyllic period of Christian living; but in an interesting phrase that only appears in the Old English version, Ælfric reveals the cyclical nature of his idea of history. Immediately after this initial period when "Godes geleafa weox and wanode se hæþenscype" (faith in God grew and heathenism diminished), Ælfric writes, "Hwæt þa æfter fyrste asprang færlice órmæte ehtnys ofer þa cristenan" (Lo, then after this period, great persecution suddenly sprang up over the Christians).[100] As with Christ's incarnation and the apostolic mission after Pentecost, Constantine's reign then

98 *Die Hirtenbriefe Ælfrics*, II.10–7, quotation at II.12 and II.17. The Latin reads: "instituit christianitatem et castitatem" (2.8) and "Et omnes duodecim apostoli et septuaginta duo discipuli Christi et mones qui eum consecuti sunt, in castitate uixerunt, relinquentes caduca et adquirentes ęterna" (2.12).

99 *Die Hirtenbriefe Ælfrics*, II.42–3. The Latin reads: "Hic incepit uita monachorum, qui sub abbatis iure uiuunt … Postea uero exierunt apostoli per totum mundum, prædicantes euangelium Christi in omnibus terris" (2.41–2).

100 *Die Hirtenbriefe Ælfrics*, II.44–5.

restores the faith "ofer eallne middan-eard" (over the whole world), only to be sullied, again in cyclical fashion, by a series of heretics.[101] All of this progress from evil to good and back again can not only be traced back to the first *hæþenscype* after Adam, which accords with Ælfric's other accounts of heathenism and the Tower of Babel, but it also informs Ælfric's understanding of tenth- and early eleventh-century England, where he scolds the monastic clergy for not living in chastity, and therefore deviating from the true faith of Christ and the first apostolic mission.[102] Because the errors of the present are similar to and have their origins in the errors of the past, they can only be corrected by adherence to the ecclesiastical faith administered in the past, namely at Pentecost where, as Ælfric mentions elsewhere, the apostles taught the gospel in all the languages of the world:[103]

> Ða halgan apostolas þurh þone Halgan Gást
> wurdon swa gelǽrede þæt hi witodlice spræcon
> mid eallum geréordum úncuðra þeoda,
> and hí lǽran mihton mancynn on worulde

> Then the holy apostles through the Holy Spirit became so learned that they certainly spoke with all the languages of foreign people and they could teach humankind in the world.

It is for this reason that Ælfric understood it best to engage with the languages of the nations, including Old English; Pentecost allowed for, and in fact instituted the use of, the vernacular for conversion and correction.

More specifically, in the only two homilies of Ælfric that deal explicitly with both the Tower of Babel and the linguistic abilities of the apostles (*CHomI*.22 and *CHomII*.32), the Babel narrative is used to explain the origins of linguistic diversity in order to highlight the universal mission of the apostolic Church. In *CHomI*.22, Ælfric's description of the Tower of Babel directly contrasts with the event of Pentecost in an Augustinian manner that underscores the linguistic connection in the two events but

101 *Die Hirtenbriefe Ælfrics*, II.47–62, 91–6, quotation at II.47, 91–2. The much abridged Latin is found at 2.46–59, 41–2.
102 For example, *Die Hirtenbriefe Ælfrics*, II.83, p. 102; and II.140, 118.
103 Ælfric, *SHI*.*7*.196–9, 348–9. Similar statements also occur in *CHomII*.*3*.143–5, 23; and *CHomII*.*15*.283–4, 158.

emphasizes the pride of one and the humility of the other. After a brief description of the Tower of Babel, Ælfric immediately notes the linguistic similarities of Pentecost, concluding the whole point of the paragraph (and homily) with a single rhetorical line: "On þysre geferrædene geearnode heora eadmodnys þas mihte. 7 þæra enta modignyss geearnode gescyndnysse" (In this company their humility earned this power, and the pride of the giants earned confusion).[104] Likewise, in the later *CHomII*.32, Ælfric has Matthew narrate the origins of linguistic diversity at the Tower of Babel in order to explain the apostolic ability to speak in all languages. Although Ælfric is here more concerned with the implications of a multilingual Church that has spread across the world, the line: "seo dyrstignys asprang æfter Noes flode" (this presumption rose after Noah's Flood),[105] which refers to the building of the Tower of Babel rather than to idolatry, does give a similar impression of foolishness that needs correcting. Though there is no indication that linguistic diversity is specifically connected here with idolatry, Ælfric does emphasize the ability for the universal Church to use all the languages of the world to preach the Gospel of Christ. Even though *CHomI*.1 does not explicitly connect the Tower of Babel with Pentecost, Ælfric does hint at their relation through an intricate parallelism seen in the homily. Ælfric, after a lengthy section on the early biblical history of the world, states "Ða asprang þis gedwyld *geond ealne middaneard*" (Then this error sprang up *throughout the world*) (emphasis mine). He later echoes this statement by claiming that the disciples, "faran *geond ealne middaneard* bodigende fulluht 7 soðne geleafan" (went *throughout the world*, preaching baptism and the true faith) (emphasis mine).[106] The ancient error that spread throughout the world is remedied by the preaching of baptism and true faith throughout the world. As with other Christian authors before him, Ælfric is also interested in the typological connections between the number of descendants and the number of disciples. As mentioned above, in his translation of Alcuin's *Interrogationes*, after allotting the three continents to the descendants of the three sons, Ælfric translates the Latin line, "ortae sunt gentes septuaginta duae, inter quas misit Dominus

104 Ælfric, *CHomI*.22.126–7. See Godden, *Ælfric's Catholic Homilies*, 179; and Dekker, "Pentecost and Linguistic Self-Consciousness," 358–9, for the sources of this passage.

105 Ælfric, *CHomII*.32.93–4, 275. In this instance, Ælfric loosely follows his source: "nata est praesumptio omnium hominum"; see Godden, *Ælfric's Catholic Homilies*, 609.

106 *CHomI*.1.220, and 283. For Ælfric's use of "sentence parallelism" and "patterning," see Clemoes, "Ælfric," 197–200.

discipulos septuaginta duos,"[107] with "7 swa fela leorníngcnihta sende crist to bodigenne þone soðan geleafan geond ealne middaneard" (and just as many disciples did Christ send to preach the true faith to the entire world).[108] Although Ælfric's reference to the seventy-two disciples is here dependent on Alcuin, the notion of the seventy-two disciples preaching the Gospel across the three continents of the world was important for Ælfric,[109] and it is a motif that he employs elsewhere.

For example, in a homily in his second series of Catholic Homilies on Luke 10:1, the sending out of the disciples, Ælfric mentions the seventy-two disciples alongside a concealed reference to the building of the Tower of Babel:[110]

> Þis godspell belimpð to eallum halgum lareowum: þe on godes gelaþunge his folc læran sceolon; Þa twelf apostolas and ða twa and hundseofontig leorningcnihta: synd ða heafodwyrhtan þyssere getimbrunge. and we sceolon him geefenlæcan; Drihten sende his bydelas ætforan him. and he sylf com æfter. for ðam ðe seo bodung forestæpð. and drihten cymð syþþan to þæs mannes mode ðe þa bodunge gehyrþ
>
> This Gospel is befitting to all holy teachers who in God's Church must teach his people. The twelve apostles and the seventy-two disciples are the chief workers of this building and we should imitate them. The Lord sent his preachers ahead of himself and he himself came afterwards; therefore the preaching precedes and the Lord comes afterwards to the heart of a person who hears the preaching.

In this passage, to which Malcolm Godden does not ascribe a source,[111] Ælfric refers to the seventy-two disciples as the chief-builders of "this building" (*heafodwyrhtan þyssere getimbrunge*) of the Church. Though in this instance the imagery of building is not explicitly connected to the

---

107 Alcuin, *Quaes.*, 142, col. 532C.

108 Ælfric, *Interrogationes*, 40, § 51–2.376–8.

109 Sauer, "Die 72 Völker und Sprachen der Welt," 29–48, at 32.

110 Ælfric, *CHomII*.36.22–8. Ælfric also mentions the seventy-two disciples in his translation of the pericope: "Se hælend geceas him toeacan þam twelf apostolum. twa and hundseofontig leorningcnihta" (*CHomII*.36.2–3). See also the various versions of the Old English Gospels in Skeat, ed., *The Gospel according to Saint Luke in Anglo-Saxon and Northumbrian Versions*, 106–7.

111 Godden, *Ælfric's Catholic Homilies*, 639.

building of the Tower of Babel, it is unlikely that it is merely a fortuitous allusion, especially considering Ælfric's tendency elsewhere to connect the builders of Babel with the seventy-two disciples and the apostles at Pentecost. In a similar manner, in *CHomII*.32 Ælfric, writing of the building of the Tower of Babel, asserts a dichotomy between the wicked building of Babel and the godly building needed to ascend to heaven (emphasis mine):[112]

> men woldon him arǽran swa heahne stypel þæt his hrof astige to heofenum. ac se ælmihtiga towearp heora anginn ... Eft siððan þæs ælmihtigan godes sunu ... hé wolde com to middanearde. and tæhte mid hwilcere *getimbrunge we sceolon to heofonum astigan*

> men desired to raise such a high tower for themselves that its roof would ascend to heaven. But the Almighty overthrew their enterprise ... Afterwards the son of the almighty God ... would come to earth and he taught with what kind of *building we must ascend to heaven.*

The latent allusions to the building of Babel and the building of the Church are again present. For Ælfric, as well as a number of other Benedictine reform texts, the history of humankind is circular and self-reflecting: heathenism with its advent in the fields of Shinar is remedied by Pentecost and the apostolic mission, and though the builders of the Tower of Babel aspired to reach heaven, this aspiration was only truly possible through the building of the Church by the followers of Christ.

It is no surprise that Ælfric placed such significance on the Tower of Babel narrative and that he moulded its essential elements for his own purposes. His six accounts of the Babel narrative, along with the translation of Alcuin's *Interrogationes*, all share some degree of similarity in phrasing; nevertheless that phrasing is employed in different manners for different purposes. Whether Ælfric wanted to describe the roots of idolatry and therefore all error, or to underline the universality of the Church in a multilingual world, he could employ the Tower of Babel narrative in whatever manner suited him best. Just as other authors of Anglo-Saxon

112 Ælfric, *CHomII.32*.94–100, 275. Another analogue can be found in Bede, *In principium Genesis*, III.499–501, where the builders of Babel are contrasted to the apostles who gather the people "ad constructionem eiusdem sanctae ciuitatis, id est ecclesia Christi" (for the construction of that same holy city, that is the Church of Christ).

England could take various elements of the narrative and develop them to underline the moral or rhetorical value, so also did Ælfric use the Tower of Babel narrative to steer his audiences, lay or cleric, away from error to the true faith. Ælfric's uses of the Babel and Pentecost narratives support the image of a man deeply concerned with the salvation of the people of England through teaching in the vernacular, just as the original apostles and disciples did. Through his own labours of vernacular preaching and translating, Ælfric begins to participate in the same apostolic tradition that began at Pentecost, and continued to Britain via Gregory the Great and Augustine of Canterbury, and the later Benedictine reformers under Edgar, up to his own time. It is difficult not to see Ælfric finding affinity with his own descriptions of other ecclesiastical scholars, such as Jerome and Augustine of Hippo, who worked tirelessly translating and disseminating the doctrines of the true faith throughout the entire world, from their remote corners in Palestine and Africa:[113]

se halga hieronimus
be ðam feower godspellerum. ðe gode gecorene synd.
awrat on ðære fore-spræce þaða he awende cristes bóc
of ebreiscu*m* gereorde. and sume of greciscum.
to læden-spræce on þære ðe we leorniað.

in his preface Saint Jerome wrote about the four evangelists who were chosen by God, when he translated the Gospel from Hebrew and some from Greek to the Latin in which we learn.

Ac Augustinus se wisa   us onwreah þas deopnysse,
se þe wæs swa wis   on godes wisdome,
þæt he gesette   þurh his sylfes diht
an þusend boca   be ðam soðan geleafan
and be ðam cristendome,   swa swa Crist him onwreah
on his bisceophade   binnan Affrican scire.
And þa bec syððan   sume becomon to us,
and geond ealle þas woruld   hi synd tosawene,
godes þeowum to lare   and to geleafan trymminge.

113 *Aelfric's Lives of Saints*, I.xv.106–10; and Ælfric, "Sendschreiben on Wulget zu Ylmandun," in *Angelsächsische Homilien und Heiligenleben*, lines 103–11.

> But Augustine that wise man, who was so wise in the wisdom of God, revealed to us that profundity that by his own direction he put into a thousand books on the true faith and Christianity, just as Christ revealed it to him, in his bishopric in Africa. And some of those books afterwards came to us and were sown across the whole world by servants of God for the strengthening of learning and faith.

Among these two great men, Ælfric finds his own humble place in Britain, where he translated Latin texts into Old English in an attempt to combat error and return the island to an age of great religious learning and faith.

Wulfstan

Ælfric was not the only important Anglo-Saxon reformer of the later tenth and early eleventh century who wrote in Old English. His contemporary, Wulfstan (d. 23 May 1023), who corresponded with Ælfric on numerous occasions,[114] was also very much concerned with many of the fundamental goals of the Benedictine reform.[115] Although little is known of Wulfstan's early life besides his caesarean birth, the existence of at least one brother and two sisters, and the likelihood that he was an abbot, by 996 Wulfstan had been ordained the Bishop of London, and by 1002 he held the metropolitan see of York in plurality with Worcester (which he gave up in 1016).[116] In his ecclesiastical and political roles during the turn of the millennium, Wulfstan held a significant position not only through the unfortunate later reign of Æthelred the Unready (978–1016) but also in the transition of the kingdom under Cnut (1016–35). As an influential member of both the Church and state, Wulfstan wrote a number of

---

114 See Clemoes, "The Old English Benedictine Office," 265–83; and Godden, "The Relations of Wulfstan and Ælfric," 353–74.

115 Hill, "Monastic Reform and the Secular Church," 103–17; and "Archbishop Wulfstan: Reformer?," 309–24. But see also Jones, "Wulfstan's Liturgical Interests," 325–52, at 346–9.

116 For Wulfstan in general, see Bethurum, "Wulfstan," 210–46; the numerous essays by Whitelock collected in *History, Law and Literature in 10th–11th Century England*, nos. 8–15, esp. "Archbishop Wulfstan, Homilist and Statesman," no. 11, 42–60; Wormald, "Archbishop Wulfstan and the Holiness of Society," 225–51; "Wulfstan (d. 1023)"; Orchard, "Wulfstan, the Homilist," 494–5; the collection of essays in Townend, ed., *Wulfstan, Archbishop of York*; and Lionarons, *The Homiletic Writings of Archbishop Wulfstan*.

sermons, law-codes for both Æthelred and Cnut, the prose sections of the so-called Old English Benedictine Office, and the texts entitled *Institutes of Polity* and *Canons of Edgar*. It is also possible that he wrote the two tracts on estate management, *Rectitudines* and *Gerefa*, as well as sections of the Anglo-Saxon Chronicle. Significantly, Wulfstan has been associated with a number of manuscripts containing handbooks (often but unhelpfully entitled "Commonplace Books") that reveal not only Wulfstan's reading and compilation tendencies, but also his own hand.[117] Though Wulfstan's writings differ considerably from those of Ælfric in vocabulary, style, and content, he did share a number of concerns, especially in the instruction and religious well-being of England in what he thought of as the final age of the world.

Though the dangers of heathenism and the progression of the world to its detrimental end are ever-present in many of Wulfstan's works, he does have two specific homilies, both based on works by Ælfric, that reveal a fuller picture of salvation history. Wulfstan's Homily 6 (in Bethurum's edition) gives a catechetical account of biblical history based on Ælfric's *CHomI*.1 and a tract by Pirmin of Reichenau.[118] After a typical preamble, Wulfstan begins his homily, much like Ælfric does, with an account of Creation that proceeds through early biblical and extra-biblical history until after the Flood when heathenism first appears in the world. Although Wulfstan does not specifically mention the building of the Tower of Babel, he does give a brief description of the descendants of the sons of Noah dispersing across the world: "ða syððan þæt wæs þæt se flod gesette 7 Noe 7 his suna landes geweald ahtan, hy gestryndan fela bearna, 7 of heora ofsprincge com þæt eft wearð folces unlytel" (after the Flood subsided and after Noah and his sons took possession of the land, they begot many children and from their offspring it happened that there was again no small

117 Orchard, "Wulfstan's Library," 694–700; Elliot, "Wulfstan's Commonplace Book Revised," 1–48; Fowler, "'Archbishop Wulfstan's Commonplace-Book' and the *Canons of Edgar*," 1–10; Bethurum, "Archbishop Wulfstan's Commonplace Book," 916–29; and Bateson, "A Worcester Cathedral Book of Ecclesiastical Collections, Made *c.* 1000 AD," 712–31. For Wulfstan's hand, see Ker, "The Handwriting of Archbishop Wulfstan," 9–27; Cross and Brown, "Wulfstan and Abbo of Saint-German-des-Prés," 71–91, at 73–5; and Tunberg, "Scribes, Scribal Habits, Abbreviations, and Word-Separation," 31–49, at 44–9.

118 *Homilies of Wulfstan*, 293, citing Jost, *Wulfstanstudien*, 45–7 and 55–61, who first discovered the sources.

number of people).[119] Again like Ælfric, Wulfstan immediately follows this account of Noah's descendants with an introduction of idolatry as the very next chronological event in salvation history:[120]

> Ða dyde deofol þa gyt, ealswa he a deð, mannum mycle dare; he gedwealde eft mænigne man to þam swyðe þæt hy ofergeaton 7 forgymdon æt nyhstan heora Drihten 7 wurðedon þurh deofles lare mistlice gedwolþing 7 worhton fela gedwimera on anlicnessum 7 ðærto abugan 7 hy ðærto gebædon, 7 wendon þæt heom of ðam come bot 7 willa þæs ðe hy þonne wilniende wæron. Swa hy dwelode deofol 7 adwealde.

> Then the devil, just as he always does, greatly injured the people; he deceived afterwards many people so that they transgressed and finally forgot their Lord, and worshipped through the devil's teaching various idols and made many illusions in the idols and henceforth worshipped and prayed to them. And they supposed that help came from these idols, as well as the desire which they were desiring at that moment. So the devil deceived and seduced them.

Though this passage partially relies on Pirmin's tract, and in general on Ælfric's first homily, the strong emphasis on the devil's involvement in the initial idolatry is Wulfstan's.[121] In fact, his description of the origins of idolatry leads Wulfstan into an exhortative digression on the diabolical dangers and irrationality of idolatry that deviates so greatly from its source that Bethurum suspects it might have been interpolated.[122] Though the textual issues of this passage are beyond the scope of this study, it does provide a worthwhile example not only of Wulfstan's (or perhaps an interpolator's) conception of the chronology of early salvation history and the origins of idolatry, but also his vehement feelings towards the diabolical nature and threat of heathenism.[123] Much like Ælfric before him, Wulfstan locates the origin of idolatry in the dispersal of the nations. Unfortunately,

119 *Homilies of Wulfstan*, 6.67–9.

120 Ibid., 6.70–6.

121 For Wulfstan's slight use of Pirmin in this passage, see Bethurum, *Homilies of Wulfstan*, 295.

122 *Homilies of Wulfstan*, 6. 77–95, and 296.

123 For Wulfstan on heathenism in general, see Meaney, "'And we forbeodað eornostlice ælcne hæðenscipe,'" 461–500. I also note the caution of Godden, "Apocalypse and Invasion in Late Anglo-Saxon England," 130–62, at 152–4, against understanding Wulfstan as associating too readily the Vikings with Antichrist.

he does not provide enough information in this homily to formulate any further speculation on his understanding of the Tower of Babel, or the connection between ethnic and linguistic diversity and heathenism. The rise of heathenism just seems to be the devil doing what he always does.

In the homily *De falsis deis* (sic), a version of Ælfric's *De falsis diis*, Wulfstan expands his association with heathenism and Babel by directly tackling the perceived (at least by Wulfstan) renewal of Norse paganism in Northumbria.[124] Whereas Ælfric's homily had previously confronted paganism from Scandinavia, which as Pope writes, "would hardly have come into being without the sense that the age-old struggle between the true God and the pretenders was being renewed,"[125] Wulfstan's version is much more direct in its demand for an immediate response to the pagan threats. On account of this anxiety towards Norse paganism on display in Wulfstan's homily, it is reasonable to date *De falsis deis* during the renewal of Viking invasions in 1006–7 and 1009–12, but before Cnut ascends to the throne in 1016.[126] This later date also corresponds with Godden's suggestion that Wulfstan had composed the majority of his revisions of Ælfrician work after Ælfric's death around 1010.[127]

Instead of beginning with an exposition on the Trinity as Ælfric does, Wulfstan begins his homily with a lament on the spread of paganism:[128]

> Eala, gefyrn is þæt ðurh deofol fela þinga misfor ... 7 þæt hæðenscype ealles to wide swyðe Gode mishyrde, 7 gyt dereð wide. Ne ræde we þeah ahwar on bocum þæt man arærde ænig hæðengyld ahwar on worulde on eallum þam fyrste þe wæs ær Noes flode.

> O! it is long ago that through the Devil many things went astray ... and that heathenism, altogether so widely, greatly injured and still injures widely. Yet

124 For general analysis on the ways Wulfstan adapted Ælfric's homily, see Szurszewski, "Ælfric's *De falsiis diis*," 115–17. Rudolf, "Style and Composition of Napier XVIII," 107–49, has cast some doubt on Wulfstan's authorship of this homily, but his argument has not been widely accepted; see for example Pons-Sanz, *Norse-Derived Vocabulary in Late Old English Texts*, 91.

125 Pope, *SHII.21*, 668–9.

126 See Keynes, "An Abbot, an Archbishop, and the Viking Raids of 1006–7 and 1009–12," 151–220.

127 Godden, "The Relations of Wulfstan and Ælfric," 367–8.

128 *Homilies of Wulfstan*, 12.3–7.

> we do not read anywhere in books that one raised up any heathen idol anywhere in the world in all that time which was before Noah's flood.

Notably, the line: "hæðenscype ealles to wide swyðe Gode mishyrde, 7 gyt dereð wide," which does not appear in Ælfric's version, has the effect of localizing the pagan threat to Wulfstan's Northumbria and contemporizing it to eleventh-century England. This localizing effect is repeated a few lines later, when Wulfstan alters one of Ælfric's common phrases for the dispersal of the nations, "hi toferdon to fyrlenum landum" (they scattered to distant lands) to "toferdon hy wide landes" (they scattered widely in the land).[129] Although the word *wide* is one of Wulfstan's most frequently used words,[130] its presence in the phrase is not necessary and, strangely enough, breaks Ælfric's alliteration between *toferdon* and *to fyrlenum*. Conversely, it does create the significant result of intensifying the relevance of the homily in an ever-increasing pagan environment. The adverb *wide* indicates space that is much more personal than the adjective *fyrlen*, which merely implies a sense of removal or distance. For Wulfstan, paganism is not spread into distant lands, but rather widely spread in his own land – the wicked paganism of Babel is not restrained to a past, mythological event, but is a continual danger even to the inhabitants of England or, more locally, York.

Likewise, some of Wulfstan's other minor additions to Ælfric's text reveal his homiletic intentions. One of his commonest homiletic phrases, "þurh deofles lare" (through the devil's teaching), is added to the homily no fewer than five times, after the appearance of the related phrase "ðurh deofol" in the very first line.[131] As a stock phrase, it continually helps to remind the audience of the relationship between paganism and the devil, and therefore paganism and evil. Wulfstan also includes six references to heathenism or error that do not appear in Ælfric's version, perhaps in order to underline the growing threat of paganism in Northumbria.[132] And unlike Ælfric, Wulfstan is persistent in describing God as "soð" (true).[133] In both the opening and concluding paragraphs of the homily, Wulfstan

129 *Homilies of Wulfstan*, 12.11.

130 Orchard, "Crying Wolf," 246, fig. 5.

131 *Homilies of Wulfstan*, 12.17, 19–20, 53, 69, 79. See Jost, *Wulfstanstudien*, 129; and Dendle, *Satan Unbound*, 123–4. Note also the presence of this phrase in Homily 6.72–3, quoted above, 200.

132 *Homilies of Wulfstan*, 12.14, 82 (*hæþene*); 49, 53–4, 84 (*hæðenscype*); 56 (*gedwylde*).

133 Jost, *Wulfstanstudien*, 129, also notes Wulfstan's use of *soð*.

expands Ælfric's phrase "þone Scyppend" (the Creator) to "ðone soðan God" (the true God), and elsewhere, consistently replaces Ælfric's description of God as "ana" (one) with a description of Him being true (soð).[134] The adjective *ana* in a discussion on polytheism might not have been forceful enough for Wulfstan. It is possible to conceive of "one" or even "a single" God among many gods; and perhaps for this reason, Wulfstan chose to replace *ana* with the unambiguous adjective *soð*. Last, Wulfstan deviates from Ælfric's version by mentioning Nimrod who, as is to be expected, is included among the giant builders of Babel: "Ac syððan þæt gewearð þæt Nembroð 7 ða entas worhton þone wundorlican stypel æfter Noes flode" (But afterwards it happened that Nimrod and the giants wrought that astonishing tower after Noah's flood).[135] With the possible exception of *Genesis A*, Nimrod is continually judged in a negative light in Anglo-Saxon England,[136] and Wulfstan's reference certainly implies a condemnation of the religious beliefs and practices of contemporary pagans. By including this name, Wulfstan is able to connect the paganism in Northumbria with one of the nefarious giants of the Old Testament.

All of these alterations to Ælfric's homily suggest that the paganism of the Vikings in Northumbria was a more prominent threat for Wulfstan than it was for Ælfric. While Pope can claim that Ælfric "seems to keep the Danish error at an academic distance while he entrenches the Christian stronghold against an attack that has not yet reached dangerous proportions,"[137] the same cannot be said of Wulfstan, who presents a greater sense of urgency in his own version of the homily. In Wulfstan's account, the Tower of Babel narrative is presented as being of greater relevance for his audience; instead of a discussion on the roots of paganism, it reveals the great danger that accompanies the folly of turning from the true God to the false gods, possible even in the present age. Unlike Ælfric, Wulfstan does not reveal the same use of Pentecost as a kind of remedy of the idolatry at Babel. Instead, in this homily he seems to have a more pessimistic view

134 Ælfric, *SHII*.21.81; Wulfstan, *Homilies of Wulfstan*, 12.14–5: "ðone soðan God 7 heora agenne scyppend," and 12.90: "ðone soðan Godd." Ælfric, *SHII*.21.91, 98: "ána God"; Wulfstan, *Homilies of Wulfstan*, 12.26, 33: "soð God." In one instance Ælfric and Wulfstan both have "a(na) soða God" (*SHII*.21.95; *Homilies of Wulfstan*, 12.30).

135 *Homilies of Wulfstan*, 12.7–9.

136 See, for example, Bede, *In principium Genesis*, III.131–6, who equates Nimrod with the devil.

137 Pope, *SHII*.21, 669.

of the progression of history. As outlined in his *Sermo Lupi ad Anglos*, also a product of this later period, Wulfstan famously preaches that the world is continually getting worse: "þeos world is on ofste, 7 hit nealæð þam ende, 7 þy hit is on worlde a swa lengc swa wirse" (this world is hastening on and it is nearing the end, and the longer things go on in the world, the worse it gets).[138] As Patrick Wormald has argued, Wulfstan aimed to legislate a "Holy Society," through the correct living of Anglo-Saxon Christians whose righteousness will prevent any need for a scourge of God – what Lionarons, building on Godden, terms the Old Testament paradigm.[139] A theory of renewal based on the apostolic mission at Pentecost does not present itself as sensibly for such a paradigm. To risk oversimplification, for Ælfric, the threat of heathenism or heretical error was a cyclical feature of history, which could be remedied through the tenets of reformed monasticism that finds its roots in the initial apostolic mission at Pentecost; for Wulfstan, however, there does not seem to be much hope for recovering a golden age – the end is too near for that, and the first appearance of heathenism is merely the workings of the devil who will be a nuisance in the world until Christ comes on Judgment Day.[140] Although a homogenous interpretation of either author cannot accurately reflect the very diverse range of thought expressed throughout the works of Ælfric and Wulfstan, their treatments of Genesis 10–11 nevertheless do provide some support for the two authors' different approaches towards specific historical paradigms, at least as articulated in the works examined above.

One final text with loose associations with Wulfstan reveals a more optimistic view of history aligning closer to the notion of a post-Pentecostal, universal Church. The manuscript Cambridge, Corpus Christi College 201 contains a number of Wulfstan's works.[141] In particular, the sections of the Old English Benedictine Office in CCCC 201, whose prose sections are Wulfstan's, contain the Old English metrical version of the Lord's Prayer (*Lord's Prayer II*).[142] Under the lemma *Sanctificetur nomen tuum*, the

138 *Homilies of Wulfstan*, 20.7–8.

139 Wormald, "Archbishop Wulfstan and the Holiness of Society"; Lionarons, *Homiletic Writings*; and Godden, "Apocalypse and Invasion," 154–6.

140 See Constable, "Renewal and Reform," 41, and Godden, "The Relations of Wulfstan and Ælfric," 374.

141 See Wormald, *Making of English Law*, 206–10.

142 See Ure, *The Benedictine Office*, 9–12.

poem gives the only reference to the seventy-two languages in the world in Old English poetry (lines 18–26):[143]

Swa is gehalgod þin heah nama
swiðe mærlice manegum gereordum,
twa and hundseofontig, þæs þe secgað bec,
þæt þu, engla god, ealle gesettest
ælcere þeode þeaw and wisan.
Þa wurþiað þin weorc wordum and dædum,
þurh gecynd clypiað and Crist heriað
and þin lof lædað, lifigenda god,
swa þu eart geæþelod geond ealle world.

Thus is your high name hallowed very marvelously in many languages (seventy-two, as the books say), in that you, God of Angels, established all customs and manners for each nation. They honour your work in words and deeds, in accordance with nature they call upon and worship Christ and bring forth your praise, living God, just as you are glorified throughout the whole world.

Although the association between this poem and Wulfstan should not be over-emphasized, it does present an interesting comparison with the homilist. For one, the author of *Lord's Prayer II* favourably alludes to the division of the nations at Babel in order to emphasize the magnitude of God's power and mercy throughout the entire world. Unlike the accounts of Wulfstan and Ælfric, the nations do not fall into heathenism and begin to worship creation over the Creator, but rather see the Creator in his creation and give that work honour ("wurþiað þin weorc wordum and dædum"). This shift in focus is, in fact, remarkable. The Old English poet, who likely saw himself and his audience as living on the edges of the world, encourages a postive view of diversity that takes comfort in a God that blesses all of the dispersed nations. In this poetic rendition, the Lord's Prayer is expanded to include a basis for embracing the world's diversity, which despite its origin in the dispersal of the seventy-two languages at Babel, nevertheless points to the marvellous works of God in salvation history.

143 Sauer, "Die 72 Völker," 30.

The Anglo-Saxon literature of the tenth century displays an intense desire for a revival of religious learning comparable to Alfred's efforts at educational reform. In the earlier literature of Æthelstan's reign and in some of the Latin texts of the Benedictine reform, the available evidence indicates the by now obvious notion that the Church has overcome and encompassed the entire tripartite world. But within this broad notion slightly different emphases can be detected. Admittedly the textual evidence from Æthelstan's reign is too minor to be conclusive, but it does hint at the beginnings and developments of understanding not only a single English Kingdom, but one that is also a Christian nation united under a single king and apostolic Church. As the previous chapter argued, Bede's tendency to present a unified and yet multilingual Church is downplayed in the Alfredian texts, which place much greater emphasis on the use of a single vernacular for a single Anglo-Saxon political unity that must eschew the excessive pride or forbidden knowledge associated with Babel. Continuing this trend, the texts under examination in the present chapter are concerned not so much with the multilingualism that interested Bede but with the presentation of Britain as being legitimately aligned with the Church's missionary activity. With the exception of Byrhtferth, whose reference to Nimrod deals with a separate issue, each of the texts discussed (the poetic inscription in the MacDurnan Gospels, the typological note on the number seventy-two in CCCC 183, Lantferd's *Translatio et miracula s. Swithuni*, the New Hymnal, and the Old English account of Edgar's establishment of the monasteries) presents Britain in some fashion as a participant in the Church's efforts to convert all the nations of the world. This conceptualization of Britain is important. First of all, it seems to be new, even if nascent forms are apparent in some of the early Anglo-Latin texts associated with the Canterbury School and, certainly, in Bede's *Historia ecclesiastica*. Second, although the unity of an English kingdom would only be realized after Æthelstan, the presentation of a discrete religious unity in these post-Alfredian texts parallels the desire to "invent" an English political unity, associated so strongly with Alfred. Admittedly, the texts never go so far as to claim "England" as one of the original seventy-two nations of the world that would then praise God in their respective languages; they do however begin to step in that direction. The implication, even if never expressed, is that the ethnic and linguistic origin of the Anglo-Saxons form a discrete religious (and therefore political) unit that undergoes conversion very much analogous to the other religious and political units of world that are convered after Pentecost. This contextualization of the history of Britain's conversion in the Pentecostal mission, as seen in Lantferd's *Translatio et miracula* and the Old English account of the establishment of the monasteries, participates in a wider discourse aiming to categorize Britain as a distinct but unified nation that plays a valid role in both the multilingualism of the Church, as indicated in the typological note of CCCC 183 and the New Hymnal, and the active promotion of the Gospel, as hinted at in the MacDurnan Gospels.

After the earlier literature of the Benedictine reform, which tends to see monastic practice as a remedy for the evils of the past, Ælfric and Wulfstan are less optimistic. The earlier enthusiasm, which must have stemmed in part from a hope that the Pentecostal mission in Britain would return new levels of religious learning and faith to the island, transforms into a realism contingent upon social and historical circumstances. Ælfric still believes in the fundamental objectives of the reform, but seems to fear that it has not yet gone far enough. Evidently, the temptation of idolatry formed from the Tower of Babel continues to draw people towards heretical error, unless checked by the similar apostolic activity sanctified at Pentecost. Biblical translation, for example, is a necessary act created out of the need to communicate across Babel's diversity of languages, as well as one of the primary methods for conveying the Pentecostal remedy to Babel's diversity. But in his communication of the biblical message, Ælfric does show a great degree of sensitivity towards his source. In order to fulfill specific homiletic goals, he will slightly alter his presentation of the narrative. The builders of Babel are wicked giants when the message needs moral condemnation, and then become human when Ælfric speaks of the origins of ethnic diversity encompassed by the Church. This kind of sensitivity further reveals Ælfric's ability to preach the matter of the biblical text for optimal instruction that again aims essentially to prevent heretical error. Concerns for English religious unity must be put by the wayside for practical matters, even if the use of the verncular for biblical translation continues to validate its status as a tool for promoting Christianity to the nations of the world.

On the contrary, Wulfstan is even more pessimistic, finding no indication that the present and future evils will end before Judgment Day. The "golden age" of Christianity has passed, and according to the cyclical nature of salvation history, it can be expected that England has begun its final descent into the days of the Antichrist. The increase of foreign invaders, who bring with them paganism and the temptation of renewed paganism among the Anglo-Saxons, is a sure sign that the world's final days are near. The evils that originated at Babel have been renewed, and there is no indication that the Holy Spirit's work at Pentecost continues to have any bearing on the ecclesiastical unity of the world – a subject that had little interest for Wulfstan. Naturally, this later pessimism may be explained by the social situations facing the homilist, who employs the more dramatic elements of the Babel narrative, such as the gigantism of its builders, in order to condemn idolatry and paganism threatening England.

Ultimately, all of these cases show that the Anglo-Saxons possessed the freedom to use authoritative texts and interpretations in manners that suited objectives formed by their own cultural and historical situations. The treatments of the past had their authoritative worth, but only to the extent that their authority could be helpful for a specific Anglo-Saxon purpose. These shifting Anglo-Saxon uses of the Tower of Babel narrative reveal the enduring quality not only of the biblical account but also of its interpretive traditions, especially as employed in the dominant trends of the literature across the period.

Chapter Seven

The Biblical Poems of Junius 11

So far I have discussed allusions to the Tower of Babel in the Old English poems *Solomon and Saturn II* and *Lord's Prayer II*. Besides the metrical version of *Genesis*, which will be examined below, scholars have found traces of the Babel narrative in a number of Old English poems. References to ancient destroyed cities, often built by giants, that appear in various poems of the Exeter Book, such as *The Ruin* and *The Wanderer*, have clear analogues to the fall of the Tower of Babel as well as the later destruction of Babylon.[1] Even *Beowulf*, with its hall made by "many nations," seems to contain an allusion to the narrative.[2] In addition to *Beowulf* and the poems of the Exeter Book, the Old English poems of the Vercelli Book deal in large part with the early missionary activities of the apostles and disciples of Christ, which have a basis in Pentecostal theology expressed elsewhere in Anglo-Saxon literature. Even though *The Fates of the Apostles, Andreas*, and *Elene* never allude directly to Genesis 10–11 or Acts 2, they nevertheless present a narrative of conversion that portrays the "Pentecostal Church," in the words of Catharine A. Regan, as "moving toward the completion of its earthly mission."[3]

1 See above, 19 n. 37. The phrase, *enta geweorc* ("work of giants"), occurs with slight variance in *Andreas* 1235, 1495; *Beowulf* 1679, 2717, 2774; *Maxims II* 2; *Ruin* 2; and *Wanderer* 87. See Frankis, "The Thematic Significance," 265. The catalogue of peoples in the poem *Widsið* also has parallels with Genesis 10.

2 See the conclusion below, 239–44.

3 Regan, "Evangelicalism as the Informing Principle of Cynewulf's 'Elene,'" 27–52, at 31. See also McBrine, "The Journey Motif in the Poems of the Vercelli Book," 289–317.

However, the most extensive treatment of the Babel narrative in Old English poetry can be found in the biblical renditions of the manuscript Oxford, Bodleian, Junius 11, which contains over 5,000 lines of Old English verse.[4] While the manuscript itself has been dated to the late tenth century, with its rebinding sometime in the thirteenth,[5] the poems were likely composed much earlier. *Exodus* was once thought to be one of the earliest Old English poems, predating even *Beowulf*, and a tentative date of the eighth century seems to be the current scholarly consensus. Likewise, the antiquity of *Genesis A* and *Daniel* has also been reasserted with some evidence that they were composed in the eighth century. *Genesis B*, an Old English rendition of an Old Saxon poem, which survives interpolated between lines 234 and 852 of *Genesis A*, is thought to be dated around 900. The date of *Christ and Satan* can be set, again tentatively, between *c.* 790–*c.* 820, according to criteria established by the poem's most recent editor.[6] But despite this difference in dates, certain relationships do seem to exist between the poems of Junius 11. *Genesis A* shares a number of unique and rare compounds with *Exodus*.[7] Some scholars have argued that the beginning section of *Daniel*, which has no obvious biblical source, follows naturally

---

4 For the manuscript and the unity of its poems, see Raw, "The Construction of Oxford, Bodleian Library, Junius 11," 187–207; Hall, "On the Bibliographic Unity of Bodleian MS Junius 11," 104–7; Hall, "'The Old English Epic of Redemption,'" 53–68, at 64–6; Portnoy, "'Remnant' and 'Ritual,'" 408–21, at 416–17; and Lucas, "On the Incomplete Ending of *Daniel* and the Addition of *Christ and Satan* to MS Junius 11," 46–59.

5 Lockett, "An Integrated Re-examination of the Dating of Oxford, Bodleian Library, Junius 11," 141–73; and Raw, "The Construction of Oxford, Bodleian Library, Junius 11."

6 See Wrenn, *A Study of Old English Literature*, 97–8. For *Genesis A*, *Exodus*, and *Daniel*, see the chronological tables in Fulk, *A History of Old English Meter*, 61, and Cable, "Metrical Style as Evidence for the Date of *Beowulf*," 77–82, at 80, which have been further affirmed and refined by Cronan, "Poetic Words, Conservatism, and the Dating of Old English Poetry," 23–50; Hartman, "The Limits of Conservative Composition in Old English Poetry," 79–96; and Bredehoft, "The Date of Composition of *Beowulf* and the Evidence of Metrical Evolution," 97–111. Remley, "Aldhelm as Old English Poet," 90–108, has also argued that *Exodus* was written by Aldhelm or someone familiar with Aldhelm's Latin and vernacular poetry; in this case, *Exodus* could be dated to the early eighth century. For *Genesis B*, see Doane, ed., *The Saxon Genesis*, 43–54. For *Christ and Satan*, see Finnegan, *Christ and Satan*, 60–3. It must be noted, however, that the sole use of linguistic criteria for dating Old English texts is problematic, as argued by Amos, *Linguistic Means of Determining the Dates of Old English Literary Texts*.

7 Orchard, "Intoxication, Fornication, and Multiplication," 333–54, at 348. According to Orchard's analysis of rare and unique shared compounds of *Genesis A* and other poems over three hundred lines, only *Judith* shares a greater number than *Exodus*.

from the ending of *Exodus*;[8] and at least one critic has argued for a deliberate thematic connection between *Genesis B* and *Christ and Satan*.[9] Moreover, the treatment of New Testament material in *Christ and Satan* may be accounted for in its explicit, "Finit liber II," which implies the existence of a bipartite compositional scheme behind Junius 11 that would separate the Old Testament poems of a first volume from the New Testament poem of *Christ and Satan* in the second volume.[10]

Although it is now well known that the poems of Junius 11 are not those of Bede's poetic cowherd even if they loosely follow Cædmon's putative corpus, efforts have been made to understand the organization of the manuscript according to the liturgy on the one hand, and according to an Anglo-Saxon catechetical *narratio* on the other hand.[11] While Paul G. Remley shows that the liturgy plays an important part for the composition of the individual poems,[12] it does seem less probable, as J.R. Hall argues, that the lectionary for Holy Saturday influenced the overarching organization of the manuscript.[13] In all probability, the availability of the rather limited number of Old English biblical poems is what guided the organizational scheme, and any theory on the intended content and order of the manuscript may assume too much complexity. The most likely scenario is that the compiler arranged the manuscript according to the

8 See Remley, *Old English Biblical Verse*, 255–72. For proposed biblical sources of the opening of *Daniel*, see Jost, "Biblical Source of Old English Daniel 1–78," 257–62. Likewise, Stévanovitch, "Envelope Patterns in *Genesis A* and *B*," 465–78, at 474–5, has argued that envelope patterns in *Genesis A* (1–14) and *Exodus* (554–64) connect the two works.

9 Young, "Two Notes on the *Later Genesis*," 204–11, at 205–7.

10 The explicit "Finit liber I," if it ever existed, would naturally occur after the lost section of *Daniel*.

11 Bright, "The Relationship of the Cædmonian *Exodus* to the Liturgy," 97–103; Portnoy, "'Remnant' and 'Ritual,'" 319–40, at 339; *The Remnant*, 183; and "*Daniel* and the Dew-Laden Wind," 195–226. Farrell, "The Unity of Old English Daniel," 117–35; Allen, "The Interior Journey"; Remley, *Old English Biblical Verse*, 3–4, 78–87; and Bugge, "Virginity and Prophecy in the Old English Daniel," 127–47, have argued in favour of a liturgical source for specific sections of *Daniel*. For the catechetical tradition in Anglo-Saxon England, see Day, "The Influence of the Catechetical *narratio* on Old English and Some Other Medieval Literature," 51–61; and Fox, "Vercelli Homilies XIX–XXI, the Ascension Day Homily in Cambridge, Corpus Christi College 162, and the Catechetical Tradition from Augustine to Wulfstan," 254–79.

12 Remley, *Old English Biblical Verse*, 136–43, 216–30, 296–301, 359–78.

13 Hall, "On the Bibliographic Unity of Bodleian MS Junius 11"; and "'The Old English Epic of Redemption.'"

canonical order of whatever Old English biblical poems were available at the time and place of copying.

For the purposes of this study, Junius 11 is important since three of its poems contain material on the Tower of Babel narrative: *Genesis A* gives a rendition of the story that falls appropriately in its poetic narration of Genesis 10–11; *Exodus* has a brief digression that mentions the lineage of nations from the sons of Noah (369–74); and *Daniel* alludes to the story in its narration of the later Babylonian kingdom of Nebuchadnezzar and Belshazzar. The other poems of Junius 11, *Genesis B* and *Christ and Satan*, do not contain any explicit reference to the Tower of Babel narrative, though their depictions of Satan conform to archetypal characteristics that share some affinity with other presentations of the builders of the Tower of Babel and the Babylonian king Nebuchadnezzar. This study, however, will focus on only *Genesis A* and *Daniel*, both of which make greater use of the Table of Nations and the Babel narrative, particularly by adding some degree of moral ambiguity to biblical characters often simply interpreted as wicked. Although Nimrod and the builders of Babel in *Genesis A* and Nebuchadnezzar in *Daniel* are portrayed as opponents of God whose best efforts to raise themselves up will eventually fail, the poets do not condemn their efforts outright but even occasionally grant them some restrained praise. By doing so, the struggles of the biblical heroes (Abraham in *Genesis A* and the Jewish captives in *Daniel*) are thrown into relief as the reasons behind success or failure in salvation history become dependent upon human endeavours and desires that are much more understandable than those presented by other Anglo-Saxon authors. Traditionally, evil characters of the Babel / Babylon narratives are treated in a much more sympathetic manner in the poems of Junius 11. The result is a more nuanced presentation of the biblical material that discloses not only the rich interpretative potential of the biblical source but also the extent of innovation in Anglo-Saxon literature when it comes to adaptation of the Bible.

Genesis A

Genesis, as it is titled in the Anglo-Saxon Poetic Records, is one of the longest extant Old English poems at a total of 2,936 lines. But as scholarship has disclosed, the text in Junius 11 actually consists of two poems: *Genesis A* and what is commonly referred to as *Genesis B* or the *Later Genesis* (lines 235–851), a rendition of the temptation of Adam and Eve closely based on an Old Saxon text. Besides this significant interpolation,

Genesis A remains relatively unmodified, with some minor exceptions.[14] After its first 111 lines, which narrate the apocryphal fall of angels, *Genesis A* gives an account of Genesis 1–22 (according to the Vulgate) that follows what Remley has described as the "natural features of an Anglo-Saxon versification."[15] Despite the poet's faithfulness to his biblical source, scholars have traced a number of interesting deviations within the poem to common Anglo-Saxon literary techniques, which employ standard treatments to traditional themes.[16]

Not all scholars, however, agree on the best way for interpreting the poet's method of reasonably faithful rendition that also takes into account literary expectations and tendencies of "Anglo-Saxon versification." After decades of scholarly neglect of the poem, Bernard Huppé argued for the need to recognize the important influence that Christian allegory, particularly as expressed by Augustine in his *De doctrina christiana* and *De ciuitate Dei*, had on Old English literature. Huppé's treatment of the episode of Cain and Abel in *Genesis A* can be taken as a typical example: on account of patristic and medieval exegesis of the episode, Huppé interprets Abel as allegorically representing Augustine's city of God, whereas Cain and his descendants represent the earthly city or the city of Babylon.[17] Although a number of critics have taken issue with Huppé's approach,[18] he has had a pervasive influence on the subsequent scholarship of *Genesis A*.[19] The Old English poet was certainly able to read the Latin of Genesis along with some apocryphal, liturgical, and patristic material, and it is most

14 Estes, "Abraham and the Northmen in *Genesis A*," 1–13, at 3–4, suggests that the poem might have gone through some later revision.

15 Remley, *Old English Biblical Verse*, 114. For the biblical source, see Remley, *Old English Biblical Verse*, 94–149; and "The Latin Textual Basis of *Genesis A*," 163–89.

16 For example, Raw, *The Art and Background of Old English Poetry*, 82.

17 Huppé, *Doctrine and Poetry*, 153–61.

18 Shippey, *Old English Verse*, 140–1; Brockman, "'Heroic' and 'Christian' in *Genesis A*," 115–28; and Boyd, "Doctrine and Criticism," 230–8. See also the references in O'Keeffe, "The Book of Genesis in Anglo-Saxon England," 174–5.

19 For example, Lee, *The Guest-Hall of Eden*, 22–41; Greenfield and Calder, *A New Critical History of Old English Literature*, 207–9; and Fulk and Cain, *A History of Old English Literature*, 114. For some notable examples of allegorical readings of individual episodes of the poem, see Gatch, "Noah's Raven in *Genesis A* and the Illustrated Old English Hexateuch," 3–15; Creed, "The Art of the Singer," 73–80; Frank, "Some Uses of Paronomasia in Old English Scriptural Verse," 211–15; and Orchard, "Conspicuous Heroism," 119–36, at 125–31.

likely that he would have been familiar with the Augustinian theology of the two cities.[20]

Recently, Charles D. Wright has given a cogent rebuttal to this methodology; following J.E. Cross, Wright emphasizes that "persuasive extra-literal reading will normally be supported by textual details that resist or are not adequately accounted for by a literal reading – that is, by something cryptic, incongruous, or supererogatory in the verbal or structural fabric of the text that is more satisfactorily captured by recourse to an extra-literal reading."[21] Wright's approach is important: when a poet introduces an extra-literal element, he will be sure to highlight it verbally or structurally. Indeed, Wright's own analysis of the blood of Abel in the poem provides an excellent example – details that are "cryptic, incongruous, or supererogatory in the verbal or structural fabric of the text" point to an extra-literal reading that in this case can be traced to a passage in Aldhelm's *Carmen de uirginitate* and *Maxims I*.[22]

For the narration of the Table of Nations and the Tower of Babel, the poet of *Genesis A* remains in some aspects surprisingly faithful to the biblical source, but in other aspects reveals a great degree of deviation:[23]

gewiton him þa eastan æhta lædan,
feoh and feorme.   folc wæs anmod;
rofe rincas   sohton rumre land
oð þæt hie becomon   corðrum miclum,
folc ferende,   þær hie fæstlice
æðelinga bearn,   eard genamon.
gesetton þa sennar   sidne and widne
leoda ræswan   leofum mannum
heora geardagum.   grene wongas
fægre foldan   him forðwearde
on ðære dægtide   duguðe wæron,
wilna gehwilces,   weaxende sped.
Ða þær mon mænig   be his mægwine,

20 Note the important caveat of Hall, "Biblical and Patristic Learning," 327–44, at 334–5, that not everyone had access to all the patristic commentaries.

21 Wright, "*Genesis A* ad litteram," 121–71, at 128. See also Cross's review of Huppé, *Doctrine and Poetry*, 561–4.

22 Wright, "Blood of Abel and the Branches of Sin," 7–19.

23 Doane, ed., *Genesis A*, lines 1649–1701.

æðeling anmod,   oðerne bæd
þæs hie him to mærðe,   ær seo mengeo eft
geond foldan bearn   tofaran sceolde,
leoda mægðe   on landsocne,
burh geworhte   and to beacne torr
up ærærde   to rodortunglum.
þæs þe hie gesohton   sennera feld
swa þa foremeahtige   folces ræswan,
þa yldestan,   oft and gelome
liðsum gewunedon,   larum sohton
weras to weorce   and to wrohtscipe
oð þæt for wlence   and for wonhygdum
cyðdon cræft heora.   ceastre worhton
and to heofnum up   hlædræ rærdon,
strengum stepton   stæ*n*en*ne* weall
ofer monna gemet,   mærða georne,
hæleð mid honda.   þa com halig god
wera cneorissa   weorc sceawigan,
beorna burhfæsten,   and þæt beacen somed
þe to roderum up   ræran ongunnon
adames eaforan   and þæs unrædes
stiðferhð cyning   steore gefremede.
þa he reðemod   reorde gesette
eorðbuendum   ungelice
þæt his þære spæce   sped ne ahton
þa hie gemitton,   mihtum spedge,
teoche æt torre   getalum myclum
weorces wisan   ne þær wermægða
ænig wiste   hwæt oðer cwæð.
ne meahte hie gewurðan   weall stænenne
up forð timbran   ac hie earmlice
heapum tohlodon,   hleoðrum gedælde.
wæs oðere   æghwilc worden
mægburh fremde   siððan metod tobræd
þurh his mihta sped   monna spræce.
toforan þa   on feower wegas
æðelinga bearn   ungeþeode
on landsocne.   him on laste bu
stiðlic stantorr   and seo steape burh
samod samworht   on sennar stod.

> They then went into the East, leading their belongings, cattle and provisions. The people were resolute; the brave warriors sought out a more extensive land, until they, the travelling people, arrived in great throngs to where they, the children of nobles, securely seized the land. The leaders of the people settled the far and wide land of Shinar; green fields, fair earth, were enduring for the beloved people in their earlier days; there was prosperity at that time – success of each delight increasing. Then many a person there, many a resolute noble in the company of his relative, asked each other that before the company must go off among the sons of the earth, the tribe of the people, in search of land, they build as a glory for themselves a city, and that they raise up as a sign a tower to the heavens. They therefore sought out the field of Shinar, where the very powerful leaders of the people, the elders, very often dwelled in joy; the men skillfully sought it out for both their work and their crime, until according to their pride and their foolishness they showed their power. They made a city and raised ladders up to heaven; with strength they erected a stone wall beyond moderation, warriors with their hands, eager for glory. Then holy God came and saw the work of those generations of men, the fortified city of warriors, as well as that tower which they, the children of Adam, had begun to raise up to heaven. And the strong-hearted king put a stop to this ill-advised deed, when he angrily created dissimilar languages for the earth-dwellers so that they did not have power over their speech. They then met, powerful in might, the band at the tower with a great number, the leaders of the work, but none of that tribe of warriors there knew what the other said, nor could they agree to build up the stone wall henceforth, but wretchedly they – divided in languages – piled up the work in heaps. Each had become a foreign tribe to the other after the Creator disrupted the speech of men through his mighty power. They then went out in four directions, the children of nobles, separated in language in search of land. Behind them remained both the strong stone tower and the high city, and also that unfinished work in Shinar.

Because the poet does not simply translate or paraphrase his biblical source into Old English verse, this episode has invited a number of different interpretative approaches. Most prominently, one of the poem's editors, A.N. Doane, follows Huppé's general approach and interprets the rendition of Genesis 10–11 in *Genesis A* as participating in the patristic tradition of Augustine, Isidore, and Bede:[24]

24 Doane, ed., *Genesis A*, 348. Doane, 350, also expresses a similar reading for the Tower of Babel episode: "Nemrod was naturally seen as a type of the devil, of heretics, of Jews

> Nemrod was the first tyrant, the first who ruled by large-scale organized violence, and the priority of his evil reign was commonplace. ... Cain founded the City of This World but Nemrod institutionalized it ... The poet is doubtless thinking of Babylon in its widest allegorical sense. With Augustine, and any medieval man, the poet probably thought of Nemrod as a giant.

Because Genesis does not mention Nimrod's involvement in the building of the tower, Doane suggests that the Old English poet, wanting to connect Nimrod to Babel, subtly rearranges the source by "the intercalation of [Genesis] 11:1 between 10:10 and 10:20."[25] Accordingly, the poet translates Genesis 11:1, "Erat autem terra labii unius et sermonum eorundem," as "Reord wæs þa gieta / eorðbuendum an gemæne" (there was still one language common to the earth dwellers, 1635–6), out of biblical order so that it may be specifically applied to Nimrod's reign. Thus Nimrod may be more closely linked to the Babel episode when it appears later. And once Nimrod, "babylones bregorices fruma" (ruler of the kingdom of Babylon, 1633), is associated with the Tower of Babel, an allegorical reading of the poem evidently becomes more apparent. Doane's interpretation has been influential and other scholars have continued to interpret Nimrod's involvement with the building of the Tower Babel in *Genesis A* as participating in Augustinian theology of the two cities.[26]

Despite the degree of influence that the interpretative tradition of Augustine, Isidore, and Bede had on Old English literature, it does not follow that this interpretative tradition must influence Old English literature, even Old English literature dealing with biblical topics. For when the earlier Latin interpretative tradition is disregarded, it does become much more difficult to read the explicit elements of Augustinian theology into this passage of *Genesis A*. In accordance with Wright's methodology, the episode does not seem to present any of the traditional "extra-literal" exegetical and literary interpretations of Genesis 10–11. There is no reference to the number seventy-two with respect to the number of Noah's descendants, even though the account previously mentions each of the sons of

---

and persecutors; his city figures the City of This World, of which all earthly cities are a figure, and his tower is his wickedness as expressed in deed, standing in the broad plains of Senaar ..., a figure of incontinence and lack of subordination to God."

25 Doane, ed., *Genesis A*, 348; see also 71.

26 Swanton, *English Poetry Before Chaucer*, 87; Wilson, "The Rhetoric of *Genesis A*," 225–7; and Olsen, "'Him þæs grim lean becom,'" 127–43, at 136–9.

Noah (1551–2), along with the names of their wives (1546–8),[27] and devotes numerous lines to general descriptions of some of the descendants of each son (Japheth: 1604–14; Ham: 1615–39; Sem: 1640–8). There is also no mention of the traditional tripartite division of the world according to Noah's three sons;[28] and the widespread tradition of describing Nimrod as a giant is absent – indeed, as in the biblical account, Nimrod is not present in the Babel narrative proper. Any attempt to interpret gigantism into the Old English lines "he [*sc.* Nimrod] moncynnes mæste hæfde / on þam mældagum mægen and strengo" (he [Nimrod], most of humankind, had power and strength in those days, 1631–2) fails to take into account the Vulgate's description of figure as "potens in terra" (powerful on the earth, Genesis 10:8).[29] Nor does the Old English poet give any indication that Nimrod is a "tyrant" much less the "first tyrant." More significantly, the poet omits any allegorizing of Babel as confusion (a key element for an Augustinian reading), and does not even mention the name of the Tower itself, resulting in the lack of the etymological punch line of Genesis 11:9 itself: "vocatum est nomen eius Babel quia ibi confusum est labium universae terrae" (its name was called Babel because there, the language of the entire earth was confused).[30] Admittedly, Shinar is mentioned (as *Sennar* 1655, 1668, 1701), which is a near synonym for Babylon elsewhere in Junius 11 when the poet of *Daniel* gives negative implications to "Babilone burh ... Sennera feld" (the city of Babylon ... the field of Shinar, 600–1); and the illustration in the manuscript accompanying the Babel episode (p. 81) places the builders with a crenellated fortress which, as Catherine E. Karkov states, "echoes the crenellated walls of hell from which Satan and his demons gaze upwards."[31] But as features external to the poem itself, the treatment of Shinar in *Daniel* and the illustrations accompanying *Genesis A* can provide only limited help for interpretation of the poem.

27 For the names of Noah's wife and of his sons' wives in Anglo-Saxon and Irish texts, see Wright, "Hiberno-Latin and Irish-Influenced Biblical Commentaries, Florilegia, and Homily Collections," 87–123, at 114.

28 Bridges, "Of Myths and Maps," 69–84, at 79, makes this observation.

29 Wilson, "The Rhetoric of *Genesis A*," 226; and Battles, "*Genesis A* and the Anglo-Saxon 'Migration Myth,'" 43–66, at 48–9, nt. 24, make this connection. Battles also notes that Beowulf is likewise described (196–7; 789–90); for which, see Orchard, *Critical Companion to Beowulf*, 167.

30 For the poet's lack of etymologizing, see Wright, "*Genesis A* ad litteram," 142–9.

31 Karkov, *Text and Picture in Anglo-Saxon England*, 96; see plates VIII ("Fall of the rebel angels"), IX ("Satan in hell"), and XLI ("Nimrod").

Instead, much like the biblical account itself, the poet narrates a literal story of unnamed workers building a tower and city at Shinar. In fact, the overall presentation of the Babel episode in *Genesis A* seems to be remarkably positive, even if the moral condemnation of the builders "for wlence and for wonhygdum" (for pride and foolishness, 1672) is taken into account. Reminiscent of other northern migration tales,[32] the Old English poem can be read as simply portraying people searching out a new homeland, after God frustrates their initial building efforts. The poet provides little explicit guidance on whether the section should be interpreted morally, much less figuratively, and no named person or people is blamed for building the Tower. Even the cursed descendants of Ham, Cush, and Canaan, are said to be "ful freolice feorh" (very noble men, 1618). Indeed, as it stands in the manuscript, the most likely candidates for the actual building of the Tower are the descendants not just of Shem but of Heber, the ancestor of the Hebrews. According to the last antecedent rule, the subject of the verb "gewiton" (1649), which begins the Babel narrative, should be the Hebrews ("ebrei") of the previous line.[33] Likewise, immediately after the episode, the poet again discusses Shem's lineage without any transition to indicate a distinction between the builders of the Tower of Babel and the descendants of Shem. In other circumstances, such attribution would be problematic since biblical commentators often point out that the only people not to have participated in the building of Babel are those of Heber's lineage.[34] But here it is possible that Shem's involvement underscores the connection between the first migration of the world and the later Germanic migrations that eventually settle Britain.

32 See Liuzza "The Tower of Babel," 4; Weelendorf, "The Interplay of Pagan and Christian Traditions in Icelandic Settlement Myths," 1–21; and Battles, "*Genesis A* and the Anglo-Saxon 'Migration Myth,'" 51, who summarizes his important article: "the rendering of the Babel episode in *Genesis A* departs significantly from the source, and these alterations are consistent neither with random amplification nor with a programme of Augustinian exegesis. Important changes include the scale of the tribal movement (great throngs settling Shinar 'far and wide'); a motive that does not fit the circumstances described by the source (search for more spacious territory); a surprisingly sympathetic tone in characterizing the tower-builders before the beginning of their project (they are 'famed warriors' and 'sons of nobles'); and the less ignominious dispersal after Babel (the tower-builders once again become settlers in search of more territory, rather than wretched refugees from God's wrath)."

33 Scheil, *The Footsteps of Israel*, 152–4, may be correct in his interpretation that the "proto-Hebrews" are meant to be understood as the builders of Babel.

34 See, for example, Augustine, *De ciuitate Dei*, XVI.xi.

This positive or at least neutral reading of the beginnings of the Tower of Babel narrative has the virtue of drawing its evidence from the text rather than the putative intellectual tradition in which the poem was written. Nevertheless, evidence both within and outside of the passage indicate that the Babel episode of *Genesis A* should be understood in a more negative light. Though Doane's suggestion that the *Genesis A*-poet attempts to associate Nimrod with Babel by an intercalation of Genesis 11:1 and Genesis 10:10 is unconvincing, further verbal parallels in the poem between Nimrod's multilingual reign and the linguistic confusion at Babel do connect the two. The lines "Reord wæs þa gieta / eorðbuendum an gemæne" (there was still one common language for the earth-dwellers, 1635–6) correspond verbally to "he reðemod reorde gesette / eorðbuendum ungelice" ([God] angrily created dissimilar languages for the earth-dwellers, 1684–5).[35] And while the men at Babel become a "mægburh fremde" (foreign tribe, 1695), the lineage of Shem become a "mægburh Semes" (tribe of Shem, 1703) only eight lines later. The echoic repetition of the second element of the word *mægburh* must have created etymological and oral contrasts with the city or "burh" that is built on the field of Shinar (1666: "burh"; 1680: "burhfæsten"; 1700: "steape burh"), as well as a contrast with both the "mægburh fremde" and the "burh" of Babel in a way that distinguishes between two lineages.[36] Likewise, whereas the Tower of Babel was proudly raised up to the heavens (1167: "up ... to rodortunglum"; 1675: "to heofnum up"; 1681: "to roderum up"), Sem's lineage grows and flourishes humbly under the clouds (1702: "under wolcnum"), though it must be stated that this phrase is used formulaically throughout the poem (916, 1058, 1231, 1392, 1950) and elsewhere in Old English poetry.[37] Along with these repetitions and contrasts, which are typical of the poet's style,[38] contrasting parallels are drawn between Nimrod (a descendant of Ham through Cush) and Eber (a descendant of Shem). Nimrod's appellation, "eafora Chuses" ("Cush's son," 1629), is paralleled only a few

35 Such close proximity of the words *reord* and *eorðbuendum* only occur in these two instances within the entire Old English corpus.

36 For echoic repetition, see Steen, *Verse and Virtuosity*, 31; Kintgen, "Echoic Repetition in Old English Poetry, especially *The Dream of the Rood*," 202–23; and Beaty, "The Echo-Word in *Beowulf* with a Note on the Finnsburg Fragment," 365–73.

37 The phrase occurs 25 times outside *Genesis* and only in Old English poetry, according to a *DOE* corpus search.

38 See, for example, Gardner, *The Construction of Christian Poetry in Old English*, 29–32; Hieatt, "Divisions," 243–51; and Orchard, "Conspicuous Heroism," 122–4.

lines later with Eber's appellation, "eofora Semes" (Shem's son, 1646);[39] and Nimrod's initial monolingual reign of "eorðbuendum" (earth-dwellers, 1636), is contrasted with Eber's one linguistic group, which "ealle eorðbuend Ebrei hatað" (all earth-dwellers call Hebrew, 1648).[40] Along with the general condemnation of the pride of the builders, these verbal parallels subtly hint towards broader theological contrasts. If the poet does not directly associate Nimrod with the building of the Tower, he at least begins to hint at a general ethnic division of the world into wicked and righteous tribes that occurred during the age of Nimrod.

Furthermore, a reading of the episode as merely a migration narrative ignores some of the finer elements of condemnation in the poetic account. Certainly, as Paul Battles has argued, there is strong evidence to show that the episode echoes other accounts of migration in *Genesis A*.[41] But similar evidence also indicates that the episode echoes another, equally pertinent theme: failed settlements of land resembling paradise. As Hugh Magennis and Karin Olsen have outlined, descriptions of spacious, green lands in *Genesis A* recall the verdant garden of Eden lost by Adam and Eve:[42]

neorxnawang stod
god and gastlic, gifena gefylled
fremum forðweardum. fægere leohte
þæt liðe land lago yrnende,
wylleburne. nalles wolcnu ða giet
ofer rumne grund regnas bæron,
wann mid winde hwæðre wæstmum stod
folde gefrætwod.

there was Paradise, good and holy, filled with gifts for its enduring benefits. Running water, a well-spring, irrigated that mild land pleasantly. No clouds as of yet bore rain over that spacious land, clouds black with wind; nevertheless, the ground remained adorned with abundance.

39 As Andy Orchard has pointed out to me, there is also likely a pun made on the name *Eber* and the word *eofera*.

40 Doane, ed., *Genesis A*, 349–50, makes a similar observation on the structure.

41 Battles, "*Genesis A* and the Anglo-Saxon 'Migration Myth.'"

42 Doane, ed., *Genesis A*, lines 208–15; Magennis, *Images of Community in Old English Poetry*, 147–53; and Olsen, "The Theme of Infertility."

Outside of Eden, the poet portrays related imagery for four other locations: the green fields of Noah's vineyard (1558–61); the lush green of Canaan where Abraham will settle (1750–2, 1787–90); the green fields along the Jordan river (1920–4); and the field of Shennar where the Tower of Babel will be built (1655–60). Notably, in two of these cases, people strive against God and, just like Adam and Eve, consequently lose the homelands given to them: the fire that destroys Sodom and Gomorrha will take away the greenness of the Jordan (1924–6, and 2551–2); and the building of Babel causes God to divide language and scatter the builders (1684–1701). The two other cases present the biblical heroes in a more favourable light, especially Abraham, who becomes the hero of the second half of the poem, immediately following the Babel episode.

It is particularly with Abraham that the destruction of Sodom and Gomorrha, and the Tower of Babel provide relevant comparisons. Whereas the builders of Babel acted according to "pride and foolishness" ("for wlence and for wonhygdum"; 1672), the inhabitants of Sodom acted according to pride and drunkenness: "hie þæs wlenco onwod and wingedrync" (so pride grew within them, as well as the drinking of wine, 2581). And like Babel, Sodom is also often portrayed as a splendid city of high walls situated on spacious, green fields (2403–6, 2548–57, and 2585), imagery that connects both cities to the first city of the world, one built by Cain (1056–60). In fact, if read in both historical and narrative order, a certain degree of progression can be detected among these three cities: Cain's city is merely "weallfæstenna / ærest ealra" (the first of all walled fortresses, 1058–9); the Tower of Babel is a "burhfæsten" (fortified city, 1680), a "stiðlic stantorr" (stong stone tower) and "steape burh" (high city, 1700); and Sodom, an accumulation of progressive splendor, is a "goldburg" (golden city, 2551), that is "blæd in burgum" (glorious in its fortresses, 2585), and a "weallsteape burg" (high-walled city, 2405).[43] Although Magennis makes a compelling argument against interpreting all the cities in *Genesis A* as "evil," general similarities between these three cities do indicate some connection between them, which point not so much towards their wickedness per se but rather urban progression that ends in inevitable destruction.[44]

43 Notably, Zoar or Segor, one of the five cities of the plain that is not destroyed because it is where Lot seeks shelter, is also described as a "fæsten … steape" (a high fortress, 2523–4).

44 Magennis, *Images of Community*, 154–9.

In contrast, Abraham is promised vast land and a "steape stanbyrig" (high stone city, 2214) for his descendants. The parallel between this promised city and the Tower of Babel is notable, not only in the verbal similarities, but also because it may explain the cryptic reference to stone as the material for Babel, which conflicts starkly with the biblical and traditional building materials of brick and bitumen.[45] Furthermore, at the end of the poem, Abraham settles in the land of Bersabea where he builds his home: "heah steapreced [*or poss.* heahsteap reced],[46] / burh, timbrede" (he built a high, steep hall, a city, 2841–2) – a feat the builders of Babel are unable to accomplish: "ne meahte hie gewurðan weall stænenne / up forð timbran" (they could not agree to build up the stone wall henceforth, 1691–2). Significantly, the brief account of Abraham's hall at Bersabea begins the poem's final scene and climax, in which Abraham is tested by God and commanded to sacrifice his son Isaac. As the biblical account relates, Abraham obeys God but at the last minute a ram is found nearby and sacrificed in Isaac's place. The poem then ends with Abraham giving thanks for all the gifts given to him by the Lord: "sægde leana þanc / and ealra þara þe he him sið and ær, / gifena, drihten forgifen hæfde" (2934–6). Despite the abruptness of the ending, these final lines do offer a thematically satisfying conclusion. Much like the builders of the Tower of Babel and the inhabitants of the cities of the plain, Abraham has been given prosperous land for himself and for his descendants, and he constructs a building that is described in terms similar to the buildings of Babel and Sodom. But unlike those before him, Abraham remains righteous and faithful, even to the point of sacrificing his son. For this reason, he can give thanks for "ealra þara ... gifena" (all those gifts, 2935–6), because he alone has come as close as possible to obtaining the lost paradise of Eden, "gifena gefylled" (full of gifts, 209). Babel and Sodom, however, remain failed attempts at recovering Eden, if even somewhat noble or grand. Specifically, the efforts of the builders of Babel provide a fitting contrast to Abraham's righteousness not because they fail where Abraham succeeds, but because they fail despite the valiance and magnanimity of their endeavours.

Of all the Anglo-Saxon accounts of the Tower of Babel narrative, the one in *Genesis A* is certainly the most ambiguous. It does not have strong Augustinian overtones that present it as a participant of the city of the

45 Doane, ed., *Genesis A*, lines 1676: "stænenne weall"; 1691: "weall stænenne"; 1700: "stantorr." See also *Old English Orosius*, 43.28 and 43.32.

46 For the variant spacing, see Doane, *Genesis A*, 394.

Devil in a neat dichotomy of good and evil. As is typical for much of the poem, the Babel episode gives no indication of a preference for understanding the event typologically. Even a moral reading of the account is not as immediately apparent as it is in other Anglo-Latin or Old English texts. But the Tower of Babel episode in *Genesis A* does exhibit a number of subtle elements that contrast its builders with the blessed lineage of Shem, and connect it to wider themes of city building after the expulsion from Eden. In this case, the Tower of Babel narrative provides a fitting example of the consequences of misusing God's blessings. The green fields of Shinar end up abandoned as the Tower stands alone and desolate; the pride and foolishness of the builders are punished and their land is lost. But the Babel narrative in *Genesis A* functions most effectively not as a moral tale but rather an enhancement of the poetic structure of one of the overall themes of *Genesis A*. It is a foil to the righteousness and blessing of Abraham, the poem's hero, who is able to resolve the problem of the first fall from paradise through obedience to God, a virtue that points towards the fulfilment of all salvation history in the obedient sacrifice of Christ.

Daniel

The Old English *Daniel* has not garnered the same enthusiastic critical reception as *Genesis A*, *B*, and *Exodus*. In general, many of the poem's commentators, since R.T. Farrell first attempted to rescue the poem in the 1960s, have felt the need to preface their studies with remarks on the misunderstood aesthetic virtue of *Daniel*,[47] and for good reason. There is much opaque or misunderstood aesthetic virtue still to be uncovered in the poem. Lines 279–361, occasionally referred to as the Song of Azarias or *Daniel B*, not only awkwardly interrupt the narrative, but can be partly found in an independent, slightly different, version in the Exeter Book, and may be an interpolation; some narrative details are repeated to confusing effect; and the ending is without doubt missing. Furthermore, despite Remley's meticulous study, the version of the Latin biblical text used by

47 Farrell, "The Unity of Old English Daniel"; and "The Structure of the Old English Daniel," 203–28.

the poet is unknown[48] and, as mentioned above, its relationship to the liturgy has been questioned.[49]

Notwithstanding its occasional structural awkwardness, the poem certainly does have its virtues, most notably its treatment of the psychological development of its main character, Nebuchadnezzar, whose fall from grace and subsequent salvation comprise the greater portion of the narrative.[50] The current scholarly focus on Nebuchadnezzar's development is, however, relatively new. Previous scholars, following Huppé's interpretative trajectory, understood the poem as presenting a dichotomy, essentially of good and evil;[51] some even going so far as to argue for the Augustinian dichotomy of the two cities, particularly on account of the presence of Jerusalem and Babylon in the poem.[52] But much like the poet of *Genesis A*, the poet of *Daniel* is more interested in the literal evolution of a narrative that is reinforced thematically by stylistic techniques, parallel structures, and what is probably best described as a subplot involving the Three Youths in the furnace. This focus on the literal narrative is, in fact, remarkable considering the array of figurative material that must have been available to the poet – the later, prophetic, chapters of Daniel, which Jerome considered of utmost importance, were greatly expanded in medieval commentaries and associated with dream manuals.[53] There is also remarkably little figurative expansion on the meanings of Nebuchadnezzar's dreams in the poem: despite Earl R. Anderson's insistence,[54] Nebuchadnezzar's first

48 Remley, *Old English Biblical Verse*, 231–434. See also Getz, "The Old English Daniel, Line 499b," 305–6.

49 Hall, "'The Old English Epic of Redemption.'"

50 See Overing, "Nebuchadenzzar's Conversion in the Old English *Daniel*," 3–14; Fanger, "Miracle as Prophetic Gospel," 123–35; Harbus, "Nebuchadnezzar's Dreams in the Old English *Daniel*," 261–86; Sharma, "Nebuchadnezzar and the Defiance of Measure in the Old English *Daniel*," 103–26; and Fox, "Denial of God, Mental Disorder, and Exile," 425–50.

51 Huppé, *Doctrine and Poetry*, 224, sums up the poem's theme as "the familiar contrast between the ways of the righteous and the ways of the worldlings." See also Isaacs, *Structural Principles in Old English Poetry*, 145 and 150; Farrell, "The Structure of the Old English Daniel"; Caie, "The Old English *Daniel*," 1–8; and Gardner, *Construction of Christian Poetry*, 34–7.

52 Solo, "The Twice-Told Tale," 347–64, at 358–63; Finnegan, "The Old English *Daniel*," 194–211, at 204–11; and Greenfield and Calder, *New Critical History of Old English Literature*, 218.

53 Harbus, "Nebuchadnezzar's Dreams," 261.

54 Anderson, "Style and Theme in the Old English *Daniel*," 229–60, at 246.

dream does not seem to refer to four empires of the world, as explained in Daniel itself (2:31–45) and developed by later commentators. For Nebuchadnezzar's second dream, Harbus insightfully states, "by presenting an already interpreted dream, the poet ensures that the reader understands it before the king, or even Daniel, does, and thereby removes the need for prophetic explanation."[55] Even when presented with such opportunity to expound upon the extra-literal elements of source, the poet of *Daniel* exercises, in the words of Shippey, immense "self-control" for the sake of the literal narrative.[56]

Yet, the focus on the literal characterization of Nebuchadnezzar does consist of a clear dichotomizing of good and evil. The poet's use of specific vocabulary, first examined by Farrell,[57] establishes an explicit distinction between foolish pride that leads to destructive error, and divine wisdom and council that leads to salvation. It is within this interpretative framework that some of the poem's commentators have been reminded of the Tower of Babel narrative in their readings of *Daniel*, at least in an analogous sense. After all, Nebuchadnezzar's Babylon is the cosmopolitan descendant of the Genesis Babel, and according to the Old English *Orosius* it continues to be an exemplum of worldly glory that will fail despite its grandiose and spectacular character, much like *Daniel*'s Nebuchadnezzar.[58]

It is, however, somewhat surprising that those who see the Tower of Babel in *Daniel* tend to find a connection between Babel and the tree of Nebuchadnezzar's dream more significant than the connection between the earlier city and the later. This connection between Babel and the tree seems to have originated with Alvin A. Lee, who writes, "in [Nebuchadnezzar's] dream his kingdom becomes metaphorically, a *wudubeam wlitig* (498,

55 Harbus, "Nebuchadnezzar's Dreams," 275.

56 Shippey, *Old English Verse*, 145. The closest example to an extra-literal instance in the poem appears when the Three Youths anachronistically evoke the Trinity: "fæder ælmihtig, / soð sunu metodes, sawla nergend, / hæleða helpend, and þec, halig gast" (lines 400–2; see also *Azarias* 103: "Crist cyning"). But, as Remley, *Old English Biblical Verse*, 387, points out, this evocation likely stems from the influence that the liturgical *Canticum trium puerorum* had on the poem, which contains a trinitarian doxology "(as it does in *Daniel*) immediately after the conclusion of the main series of invocations." The poet's use of etymological wordplay, which stems from general knowledge of exegetical methods involving biblical names, has also been observed; see Frank, "Some Uses of Paronomasia," 216–17.

57 Farrell, "Structure"; and Farrell, ed., *Daniel and Azarias*, 34–5; quotations are from Farrell's edition.

58 Scheil, "Babylon and Anglo-Saxon England," 50–1.

beautiful forest tree), towering up, like the fortress of Babel in *Genesis*, to the stars of heaven," and that "the proud, presumptuous figures of Nebuchadnezzar and Belshazzar look back to Lucifer, Cain, the builders of the tower of Babel, and the proud, tyrannical Pharaoh."[59] Whereas the similarities between the Tower of Babel and the tree of Nebuchadnezzar's dream are undeniable, little connects the two accounts outside of the general moral lesson that proud desire to excel will result in destruction. In fact, as Claes Shaar has noted, there is more similarity between Nebuchadnezzar's tree and the cross in Constantine's dream in *Elene* (69–90).[60] As an analogy to each other, an interpretation comparing Nebuchadnezzar's dream to the Tower of Babel is certainly valid; however, many other elements of the poem allude to the Tower of Babel narrative that have so far been overlooked.

Primarily, the biblical book of Daniel itself contains a number of allusions to the Babel narrative that are replicated in the Old English poem. Notably, in the opening chapter of the biblical account, Nebuchadnezzar plunders the Jewish Temple and brings some of the vessels into the land of Shinar ("in terram Sennaar") where the temple of his own god was situated (Daniel 1:2). The mention of Shinar in this verse, one of few references to the place outside of Genesis,[61] reminds the book's audience of the origins of Babylon: its founding by Nimrod and the failed efforts to build a tower to heaven as told in Genesis 10:10 and 11:2.[62] At least this is how some later audiences read the reference. For example, in his commentary on Daniel, Jerome understands the mention of Shinar in Daniel as an allusion to Genesis 11:[63]

> Terra Sennaar locus est Babylonis in quo fuit campus Dura et turris quam usque ad caelum hi, qui ab oriente mouerant pedes suos, aedificare conati sunt; unde et a confusione linguarum locus nomen accepit "Babylon," quae in linguam nostram transfertur "confusio."

---

59 Lee, *Guest-Hall of Eden*, 53, 54. See also Caie, "A Warning Against Pride," 7; and Sharma, "Nebuchadnezzar and the Defiance of Measure," 113. Sharma, 109, also notes the parallel between the phrase "ofer monna gemet" in reference to the Tower of Babel in *Genesis A* 1677, and the defiance of one's measure in *Daniel*.

60 *Critical Studies in the Cynewulf Group*, 235–56.

61 It appears in Genesis 10:10, 11:2, 14:1, 9; Joshua 7:21; Isaiah 11:11; Daniel 1:2; and Zechariah 5:11.

62 See Porteous, *Daniel*, 27.

63 Jerome, *Commentarius in Danielem*, I.i.25.

> The land of Shinar is the location of Babylon, in which was the field of Dura, as well as the location of the tower which those who travelled from the East attempted to build. Accordingly, this place took the name Babylon from the confusion of languages, which is translated in our language as "confusion."

Although the place name Shinar is used elsewhere in the Bible to refer more generally to Babylon, in the entire Old English corpus it is used almost exclusively in reference to the place where the Tower of Babel was built. In fact, only in *Daniel* 601 and 726 is it used to refer to the Babylon of Nebuchadnezzar and Belshazzar, and even then with likely allusion to the field of the Tower of Babel.[64]

Another allusion to Babel can be found in the place name *Dira* in the Old English *Daniel* (171). The prophet Daniel mentions "Dura" as the specific location where Nebuchadnezzar builds his golden idol (Daniel 3:1), which is accordingly rendered in the Old English but with the spelling altered. Admittedly, in both the book of Daniel and the Old English poem there is nothing to suggest that Dura (or Dira) is associated with the earlier city of Babel. But other texts, including the Old English *Boethius*, make the connection between Dura, the field of Shinar, and the Tower of Babel more explicit – a connection that probably reflects Jerome's claim that the Tower of Babel was built at Shinar and Dura. As mentioned in a previous chapter, the Old English *Boethius* not only has a variation on the spelling of Dura similar to that of *Daniel*, but also adds details about Nimrod and the city of Babylon: "Se Nefrod het wyrcan anne tor on þam felda þe Sennar hatte, and on þære ðiode þe Deira hatte swiðe neah þære byrig þe mon nu hæt Babilonia" (Nimrod commanded a tower to be built on the field which is called Shinar and in that nation which is called Deira, very near to the city which people now call Babylon).[65] In addition, Remley has indicated that the Irish *Liber hymnorum* prefaces the Old Latin *Canticum trium puerorum* with a statement connecting *Sennar* and *Dira*: "In campo uero Sennar factus est in campo Diram specialiter" (it happened in the field

64 In reference to the Tower of Babel, the place-name *Sennar* appears at *Genesis A* 1655, 1701, *Old English Heptateuch Genesis* 10:10, and *Gensis* 11:2 (MS C), *Old English Boethius*, B Text 35.131; *Sennera feld* at *Genesis A* 1668; *Senere feld* at *Solomon and Saturn II* 32; and *Senaarlande* at *Old English Heptateuch* 11:2 (MS B). In *Daniel* the phrases are *Sennera feld* (601) and *Sennera wite* (726). *Genesis A* 1963 renders the cryptic reference to Shinar in Genesis 14:1 as *Sennar*.

65 Godden and Irvine, eds., *Old English Boethius*, B.35.130–2.

of Shinar, particularly in the field of Dira).[66] Though no firm conclusion can be drawn from these scant sources, it seems likely that most Anglo-Saxon readers, at least those with an ecclesiastical education, would have understood a reference to Dura / Dira and Shinar to reflect the location of the original Babel and the later Babylon.

Although the Old English reference to Shinar can be found in the poet's source material, it is significant that this reference has been removed from the original biblical order and inserted later in the poem. In Daniel 1:2 Nebuchadnezzar orders the Israelite spoils to be taken to his temple in the land of Shinar. But the Old English poem, when treating this section of the narrative, only states that Israelite treasures and captives are taken "on eastwegas / to Babilonia" (eastward to Babylon, 69–70). It is closer to the end of *Daniel* that the poet includes the reference to Shinar in a description of Babylon through the proud eyes of Nebuchadnezzar:[67]

Ongan ða gyddigan   þurh gylp micel
Caldea cyning   þa he ceastre weold;
Babilone burh   on his blæde geseah,
Sennera feld   sidne bewindan,
heah hlifigan;   þæt se heretyma
werede geworhte   þurh wundor micel.
Wearð ða anhydig   ofer ealle men,
swiðmod in sefan   for ðære sundorgife
þe him god sealde,   gumena rice,
world to gewealde   in wera life:
"Ðu eart seo micle   and min seo mære burh
þe ic geworhte   to wurðmyndum,
rume rice.   Ic reste on þe,
eard and eðel   agan wille."

The king of the Chaldeans began to speak with much boasting when he ruled in his fortress; in his glory he saw the city of Babylon – the wide field of Shinar circling around it – towering high; the king built all that for his army with great wonder. Then he became proud over all men, arrogant in his heart on account of that special gift which God gave him, a kingdom of warriors,

66 Bernard and Atkinson, eds., *Irish Liber hymnorum*, I.195; Remley, *Old English Biblical Verse*, 307.

67 *Daniel*, lines 598–611 (the punctuation has been slightly altered).

> a world to rule in the life of men: "You are the great city, my glorious city, which I built in honour of broad kingdom. I remain in you, and will possess land and home."

Whereas Nebuchadnezzar's direct speech (608–11) is a somewhat faithful rendition of Daniel 4:27 ("nonne haec est Babylon magna quam ego aedificavi in domum regni in robore fortitudinis meae et in gloria decoris mei"), lines 598–607 are original to the Old English poet. Not only do they provide a suitable motive for Nebuchadnezzar's thoughts, as expressed in his soliloquy, but they also create an important intertextual relationship with the Tower of Babel narrative. The reference to Shinar in this passage, dislocated from its biblical source, does more than situate Nebuchadnezzar's cherished city; it recalls the past fall of Babel. The adjective *sidne* modifying *Sennera feld* is also used in *Genesis A* in association with Shinar as the location of the Tower of Babel (1655: "sennar sidne and widne"; and 1963: "of sennar side worulde"). Furthermore, the reference to Shinar in *Daniel* is complemented by the description of Babylon as towering up high in the following verse ("heah hlifigan"; 602).[68] In such close proximity to each other, these details certainly enforce the allusion to Babel, including the aspirations of its builders to make a tower that would reach as high as heaven, in order to parallel the earlier narrative with Nebuchadnezzar's Babylon.

By means of this allusion to the earlier city of Babel, which fell under similar conditions of pride, Nebuchadnezzar's hubris becomes particularly poignant. Like Nimrod (or the anonymous builders), Nebuchadnezzar cannot escape the fate of those who strive against God. He may think that he has succeeded where his predecessors have failed, as he glories in the towering fortress of Babylon, but Nebuchadnezzar will do no better and he will fall along with those who attempted such proud acts before him. Andrew Scheil's observation that the portrayal of Babylon in the Old English *Orosius* finds an analogue in *Daniel* is telling in this instance.[69] For in the Old English *Orosius*, Babel is connected to Babylon not only chronologically and geographically, but also thematically. Just as, according to

68 Babylon is described as high on a number of occasions in *Daniel*: 206: *hean byrig*, 665: *hean burh*, 670: *hea rice*, 672: *widan byrig*, 698: *heahbyrig*, 721: *hea seld*. Jerusalem is also described as high: 38, 54: *hean byrig*.

69 Scheil, "Babylon and Anglo-Saxon England," 50–3. See also Scheil, *Babylon under Western Eyes*, 67–81.

the Old English *Orosius*, Nimrod tyrannically ruled Babel, and Ninus and Semiramis tyrannically ruled Assyrian Babylon, so, according to *Daniel*, does Nebuchadnezzar tyrannically rule Chaldean Babylon. Babel and Babylon are the same city of erroneous "confusion," as attested by the etymology of Genesis 11:9.

Along with the recognition that Babylon is the later form of the original city on the fields of Shinar, a number of other connections between Babel and Babylon underline certain themes throughout the poem. For one, the idols of the biblical book of Daniel are emphasized by the poet in a manner that points back to the Tower of Babel. Although the belief that idolatry first arose after the dispersal of the nations after the Tower of Babel developed long after the book of Daniel was first composed, this belief was widespread by the time the Old English *Daniel* was written down. Nevertheless, in the biblical text itself, the *campus* of Dura, where Nebuchadnezzar's idol is erected, is reminiscent of the *campus in terra Sennaar*, where the Tower of Babel is built; and Nebuchadnezzar's desire that all peoples, tribes, and languages worship the idol (*omnes populi et tribus et linguae*, Daniel 3:4, 3:7) certainly recalls the dispersal of nations and languages at the Tower of Babel, the original Babylon.

While the poet of *Daniel* does not expand this allusion to the Tower of Babel in Nebuchadnezzar's desire to reunite all peoples, tribes, and languages, he does develop his source material to ensure that idolatry is connected to Babylon with verbal clues that allude back to the Tower of Babel narrative. In his description of Babylonian worship of an idol and the Three Youths' refusal to participate, he writes:[70]

ac he wyrcan ongan   woh[71] on felda
þam þe deormode   Diran heton,
se wæs on ðære ðeode   ðe swa hatte,
"bresne Babilonige."   Þære burge weard
anne manlican   ofer metodes est,

70 *Daniel*, lines 170–208.

71 Some editors have suggested that the word *woh*, evil, as it appears in the manuscript should be emended to *weoh*, idol on account of the biblical source: "Nabuchodonosor rex fecit statuam auream" (Daniel 3:1). Farrell, on the contrary, sees this verse represented later in line 174, and understands the initial mention of evil as a general introduction to the king's impiety, later specified. See Farrell, ed., *Daniel and Azarias*, 57, nt. 170; and Krapp, *The Junius Manuscript*, 221, nt. 170. To supplement Farrell and Krapp, Brennan, "The Old English *Daniel*," 85, nt. 170, favours *weoh*.

gyld of golde,   gumum arærde,
for þam þe gleaw ne wæs,   gumrices weard,
reðe and rædleas, riht[72]

Þa wearð hæleða hlyst   þa hleoðor cwom
byman stefne   ofer burhware.
Þa hie for þam cumble   on cneowum sæton,
onhnigon to þam herige   hæðne þeode,
wurðedon wihgyld,   ne wiston wræstran ræd,
efndon unrihtdom,   swa hyra aldor dyde,
mane gemenged,   mode gefrecnod.
Fremde folcmægen,   swa hyra frea ærest,
unræd efnde,   (him þæs æfter becwom
yfel endelean),   unriht dyde.
Þær þry wæron   on þæs þeodnes byrig,
eorlas Israela,   þæt hie a noldon
hyra þeodnes dom   þafigan onginnan,
þæt hie to þam beacne   gebedu rærde,
ðeah ðe ðær on herige   byman sungon.
Ða wæron æðelum   Abrahames bearn,
wæron wærfæste;   wiston drihten
ecne uppe,   ælmihtigne
Cnihtas cynegode   cuð gedydon,
þæt hie him þæt gold   to gode noldon
habban ne healdan,   ac þone hean cyning,
gasta hyrde,   ðe him gife sealde.
Oft hie to bote   balde gecwædon
þæt hie þæs wiges   wihte ne rohton,
ne hie to þam gebede   mihte gebædon
hæðen heriges wisa,   þæt hie þider hweorfan wolden,
guman to þam gyldnan gylde,   þe he him to gode geteode.
Þegnas þeodne sægdon   þæt hie þære geþeahte wæron,
hæftas hearan   in þisse hean byrig,
þa þis hegan ne willað,
ne þysne wig wurðigean,   þe ðu þe to wundrum teodest.

72 There is a lacuna in the manuscript, likely of one folio; see Farrell, ed., *Daniel and Azarias*, 57, nt. 177.

> But he began to build an idol / evil on the field which the brave men called Dira, which was in that nation which was so-called mighty Babylon. The ruler of that city raised for men an image, an idol of gold, contrary to the will of the Creator, because the ruler of the earthly kingdom was not wise, but cruel and reckless, right ... Then the men began to listen, when the sound, the voice of the trumpet, passed over the citizens. Then they kneeled before that idol, they bowed to that image; the heathen people worshiped the image, they did not know the better counsel, they carried out wickedness, just as their leader did, joined with sin, made arrogant in mind. The people did as their lord did first; they carried out an unwise deed – afterwards an evil payment came to them for this; they did a wicked thing. There were three noblemen of Israel in the city of this prince, that would not ever begin to confess the commandment of their prince, that they should lift prayers to this beacon, even though trumpets sounded there before the idol. The children of Abraham were then of a noble lineage; they were true to the covenant; they knew the Lord, eternal up above, the Almighty. The good warriors made it known that they would not have or hold that gold as a god, but they would the high king, the guide of spirits, who gave them grace. Often, in addition, they spoke boldly that they did not care a bit about that idol nor that the leader of that pagan people could command them to those prayers that they should turn hence, men to that golden idol which they set up as a god for themselves. Noblemen said to the prince that they, the more high-minded captives in this high city, were of that intention; "they do not wish to do this, or to worship this idol, which you set up as a glory for yourself."

This lengthy passage has a number of significant details. For one, the semantic variety for the word idol, as well as the great number of times idols are mentioned, is remarkable: *manlica* (174), *gyld* (175, 204), *cumbol* (180), *herg* (181; see also 192, 203 for the homonym *here*), *wihgyld* (182), *beacen* (191), *gold* (197; also 216), *wig* (201, 208). Likewise, the phrase "þe he him to gode geteode" (204) is echoed at line 208, "þe ðu þe to wundrum teodest" and at line 216, "þe he him to gode teode." These instances of idolatry are further complemented by general acts of impiety: *woh* (170), *unræd* (183; also *rædleas* 177, and in contrast, *wræstran ræd* 182), *unrihtdom* (183), *unræd* (186), *unriht* (187); and by references to heathenism: *hæðen* (181, 203; also at 218 and *hæðendom* at 221). Clearly, the poet has taken pains to emphasize the presence of idolatry and paganism in Babylon in a way that brings to mind the belief that idolatry began at Babel. Moreover, the rearing up of the idol, "anne manlican ofer metodes est, / gyld of golde, gumum arærde" (174–5), its description as a *beacen*

(191), and the general lack of *ræd* (177, 182, 186) all recall the account of the builders of the Tower of Babel in *Genesis A*, who raise a *beacen* ("to beacne torr / up arærde," 1666–7) through their *unræd* (1682). For these reasons, the identity of the unnamed leader in *Daniel* who initially carried out foolishness and was afterwards repaid with evil ("hyra frea ærest, / unræd efnde, (him þæs æfter becwom / yfel endelean), unriht dyde," 185–7), wavers ambiguously between Babylon's first foolish king, Nimrod, the builder of the Tower of Babel, and Babylon's later ruler, Nebuchadnezzar, builder of idols.[73]

Nevertheless, it is telling that the poet does not explicitly connect Babel to Babylon in this passage on idolatry. Idolatry is simply the practice of the Chaldeans, just as Nebuchadnezzar's pride is simply a characteristic of the king. In a sense, the presence of any explicit reference to Babel would immediately establish an archetypal connection, which in turn could diminish the importance of the current actions occurring at Babylon. It is exactly the opposite of the formal exegetical technique used, for example, by Bede, which turns Babylon and Nebuchadnezzar into universal typologies that then have far-reaching application. In *Daniel*, if later Babylon is merely an inevitable type of earlier Babel (an archetype of proud idolatry and confused error), the dramatic narrative would indeed be less effective, since the outcome of Nebuchadnezzar's moral choices would be understood as determined and inevitable. This point is important; for in *Daniel* Nebuchadnezzar does escape his destruction by turning to God and becoming redeemed. His redemption would certainly not be suitable for a city that is often epitomized as an archetype of the very enemy of God's people. By merely putting forth an emphasized account of Chaldean idolatry, in contrast to the righteous monotheism of Abraham's lineage, the poet imitates the traditional account of the Tower of Babel, but in this case, Babel becomes a warning of the past, not an indicator of how present events will turn out. Even though Nebuchadnezzar commits similar, even the same, sins as Nimrod and the builders of Babel, he is still able to free himself from the vices of his predecessors and break the archetype.

---

73 In *Genesis A* Nimrod is called "babylones bregorices fruma / ærest æðelinga" (the leader of the city of Babylon / the first noble, 1633–4); and the builder of the Tower of Babel is described as "anmod" (single-minded, 1662), much like Nebuchadnezzar is in *Daniel*, 224.

Furthermore, in *Daniel* the Tower of Babel finds more value as a symbolic device than as an etiological account. There is no hint that world diversity began at Babel. The focus is, of course, on later Babylon, but even the biblical account in Daniel is pared down to highlight the essential moral lesson of the poem: proud strife against God will result in failure. Allusions to the original Tower of Babel are only employed to reinforce that theme. Though it is somewhat surprising that the poet does not exploit the connections between original Babel and later Babylon to a greater extent, it is understandable why the poet remains content to present only literal and succinct details of the narrative of Nebuchadnezzar; just as he left the rich prophetic material alone, so also does he show immense "self-control" regarding the rich archetypal connections between Babel and Babylon which he could have exploited.

It may be significant that *Genesis A* and *Daniel* are often dated to the eighth century, before the reforms of Alfred and the Benedictines. On account of their idiosyncratic nature and deviation from the main biblical interpretative traditions, the approaches to Babel in *Genesis A* and *Daniel* are, in fact, closer to those in the Alfredian texts than they are to those of the Anglo-Latin commentaries of Bede and Alcuin or of the Old English homilies of Ælfric and Wulfstan.[74] Similar to the Alfredian texts, *Genesis A* and *Daniel* adapt the Babel narrative for literary purposes unrelated to the Latin exegetical traditions. The allegorizing of biblical texts that has come to be expected is strikingly absent in favour of transformations of the text that aim to enhance literary presentation over unraveling the profound mysteries of the biblical text.

The poems of the Junius manuscript, therefore, provide important caveats for any interpretation that understands Anglo-Saxon texts as necessarily participating in the dominant intellectual traditions stemming from the authorities of late antique Christianity. Certainly, the general discourse of medieval biblical interpretation focuses intensely on attempts to connect biblical events through allegory and typology, but there also exists a significant lack of homogeneity among writers of the period, and *Genesis A* and *Daniel* are good examples of poetic decisions that disregard the usual typologies of the Babel narrative. The absence of ethnological origins, of a

74 See also Scheil, *Babylon under Western Eyes*, 80.

typology with Pentecost, or of justifications for spreading the Church across the world, do not feature in these two poems, both of which emphasize thematic elements over didactic. Even moral elements of the Babel narrative in the two poems are not immediately obvious. While didactic objectives cannot, of course, be ruled out, the literary value of the use of Genesis 10–11 in the two poems is the dominant feature.

Conclusion

A full documentation of the history of Babel's reception in all times, places, and cultures would be an enormous task. Even Borst's *Der Turmbau von Babel* falls short in many aspects, and in Anglo-Saxon England alone, the various uses and interpretations of the Babel narrative and its specific elements are extremely widespread and complex. This study can, therefore, only serve as one further step for future study of the reception history of Genesis 10–11. But documentation of the interpretations and uses of the Table of Nations and the Tower of Babel narrative help understand elements of medieval culture in general. Most important, this book, which is essentially a series of case studies on the specific developments of the Table of Nations and the Tower of Babel narrative among various authors and cultures of Anglo-Saxon England, hints at some of the trends in the history of biblical interpretation of Late Antiquity and the early Middle Ages specifically, and the history of biblical interpretation in general.

Anglo-Saxon interpretation of the Tower of Babel narrative, which in its original context provides a way of understanding the ethnic and linguistic diversity of the world, shifts away from this original meaning. On account of the conflict between pagan and Christian understandings of the world, new uses of the Babel narrative appear that attempt to syncretize these understandings of the world. From an early date, Christians begin to use the Babel narrative alongside the Pentecost narrative with the result that interpretations of the Babel narrative transform to emphasize the wickedness of the Tower's builders and to polemicize them with the righteousness of the Church. While the Anglo-Saxons, on account of the traditional views of the earth that they inherited, saw themselves as living at the edges of the world, understandings of the ethnic and linguistic diversity are more associated with the Church's identity of transcending diversity and yet retaining unity of belief. The builders of Babel are, therefore, universalized to represent heretics and pagans, as opposed to righteous and orthodox Christians, or they become a useful exemplum of the punishment of pride.

The evolution of interpretation of the Babel narrative reveals the process of development for specific elements that are significant for early medieval cultures. The cultural acceptance of a certain authoritative way of understanding the world is not simply created from nothing. Instead, the inherited tradition of any culture helps dictate what sort of values are to be retained or abandoned. The Tower of Babel narrative in Late Antiquity and Anglo-Saxon England provides important examples of how early medieval cultures interacted and were influenced by their intellectual past. But more important, they show that the ways, by which cultural values can be passed down and evolve through tradition, are very complicated and multifaceted. For this reason, Anglo-Saxon usage and development of Genesis 10–11 is able to help us understand fundamental strategies of biblical reception in medieval and western European culture. As I outlined in the introduction to this book, reception of Genesis 10–11 in late antique and Anglo-Saxon literature fits into three broad and often overlapping categories. For Anglo-Saxon authors, the Babel narrative provides a basis for understanding the world's ethnic and linguistic diversity (though not necessarily for understanding the ethnic and linguistic origins of the Anglo-Saxons); an exemplum that reveals the foundations of immorality, especially among non-Christian and non-European peoples, both ancient and present; and a theological impetus to evangelize non-Christian and non-European people, especially in relation to the mission of the early Church after Pentecost.

Because of the widespread knowledge and authority of the Bible, there is always a temptation to assume that the biblical text is at the forefront of medieval Christian theories. And such a view is not exactly incorrect; a number of late antique and medieval authors do use the information provided by the Table of Nations and the Babel narrative to support their understanding of the world's ethnic and linguistic diversity. A look at how these biblical texts are used throughout the relevant sources shows that while they play a major role in shaping how people thought about themselves and other people, for the most part they do little to produce new attitudes regarding different ethnic, linguistic, or religious groups and much to provide authority made to conform to previously established ideologies. Important conditions that shape identity almost always precede the role Genesis 10–11 played (or did not play) in how people in late antique Europe and Anglo-Saxon England understood their own roles in their communities, especially regarding the world's ethnic, linguistic, and religious diversity in the present as well as in the historic or mythic past. For most of the authors and texts examined in this book, the Babel narrative helps support individual or collective perspectives that begin with markers or identity, whether of ethnicity, language, moral standpoint, or religious affiliation. In this sense, the interpretations and uses of Genesis 10–11 are not only illuminated by what is known of the historical and political situations of the time, but also have the value of revealing cultural concerns and anxieties.

This book has also touched on a number of broad topics, some of which are explicitly connected to Genesis 10–11, others that are distant. And yet these distantly connected topics are still valuable for understanding the overall formation of cultural values and world views present in Anglo-Saxon literature. Because Genesis 10–11 enjoys the canonical authority of a widely read and interpreted scriptural book, it is difficult to determine exactly every instance where Anglo-Saxon authors reveal evidence of being influenced by the Babel narrative, as well as past interpretations of that narrative. There is certainly positive evidence for specific instances of interpretation and influence – an ample amount in fact – but the greater (and perhaps more significant) number of instances can sometimes only exhibit vague affiliation with the Table of Nations and Tower of Babel, especially as it is theologically paired with Pentecost and the post-Pentecostal missions. But the tension between direct references and tenuous affinities should not be seen as a limitation. Rather, it should be seen as an invitation to explore the potential for interpretative possibilities. I began this book with a concrete example of Wulfstan's use of the Tower of Babel narrative. Conversely, to illustrate the potential of the Babel narrative in texts that do not directly refer to it, I will end with a much more oblique example: *Beowulf*.

The most famous of all Old English poems, *Beowulf* has also been one of the most challenging to interpret, allowing for rich and abundant critical readings.[1] The profound complexity of the poem, from its numerous philological and textual cruxes to its grander thematic paradoxes, has deservedly secured it a place among the great works of English literature. A large part of the poem's intricacy lies in the manner which the *Beowulf*-poet has woven the beliefs of early medieval Christianity into a story about

1 See Orchard, *Critical Companion to Beowulf*, 3.

Germanic warriors and monsters. At first glance, Genesis 10–11 might not seem to have too much to do with *Beowulf*, and its focus on the mythological feats of its hero. But the poet was familiar with the early chapters of Genesis, along with some of the traditional interpretations of these chapters.[2] Just after the opening hundred lines, there appears the poem's first monster, the giant named Grendel, who is said to have been created "in Caines cynne" (in the race of Cain).[3] There is then an allusion to the murder of Abel and Cain's punishment from God before the poet states that all the world's monsters are descended from Cain:[4]

> Þanon untydras   ealle onwocon,
> eotenas ond ylfe   ond orcneas,
> swylce gi(ga)ntas,   þa wið Gode wunnon
> lange þrage;   he him ðæs lean forgeald.

> From there all evil offspring awoke, giants and elves and monsters; such giants who struggled against God for a long time – he paid them recompense for that.

However, this genealogy of monsters from Cain presents a problem in continuity with the biblical text, which has all land creatures that did not make it onto the ark destroyed in the Flood. Any postdiluvian creature that claims ancestry of Cain, such as Grendel or his mother, reveals a problem with the biblical account (though not necessarily with the interpretative tradition). This contradiction is even underscored by the *Beowulf*-poet himself, who merges the biblical account of the Flood into the poem with his description of the sword hilt that Beowulf finds in Grendel and his mother's underwater lair:[5]

> hylt sceawode,
> ealde lafe.   On ðæm wæs or writen
> fyrngewinnes;   syðþan flod ofsloh,

2 Ibid., 137–49.

3 Fulk, Bjork, and Niles, eds., *Klaeber's Beowulf*, line 107; see also 1261.

4 *Beowulf*, lines 111–14.

5 *Beowulf*, lines 1687–93. The similarity in phrasing between the two passages also strengthens their connection: 114: *he him ðæs lean forgeald*, and 1692–3: *him þæs endelean … sealde*; see Anlezark, *Water and Fire*, 306–7.

gifen geotende   giganta cyn
frecne geferdon; þæt wæs fremde þeod
ecean dryhtne;   him þæs endelean
þurh wæteres wylm   waldend sealed

he looked at the hilt, the old remnant on which was written the origin of past strife, when the Flood, a rushing ocean, slew the kin of giants – they brought about an audacious deed; that was a race hostile to the eternal God; the Ruler gave them retribution for this through a surge of water.

The *Beowulf*-poet may be attempting to solve the problem of a surviving postdiluvian race of giants by describing both Grendel and his mother as monsters that live under water.[6] Nevertheless, various apocryphal and patristic texts provide numerous analogues of giants surviving the Flood, as Ruth Mellinkoff has shown in two extensive studies;[7] and other Anglo-Saxons have provided their own solutions – the Canterbury biblical commentaries, as mentioned above, describe the giants as being three cubits higher than the Flood waters (PentI 70). Moreover, medieval authors occasionally conflate the antediluvian Cain and the postdiluvian Ham (Cam), in some cases on account of minim confusion.[8]

In any case, it is evident that the *Beowulf*-poet was familiar with at least the early chapters of Genesis and was especially interested in the monstrous elements that traditional interpretations of these chapters could provide. It is therefore likely that the poet was also familiar with the Tower of Babel narrative, even though he never mentions it explicitly. This familiarity might explain a concealed reference to the Tower in the early

6 Orchard, *A Critical Companion*, 139. Moreover, both Grendel and his mother are not described as having an ethnicity (beyond *Caines cynn*) or as having language.

7 Mellinkoff, "Cain's Monstrous Progeny in *Beowulf*: Part I"; and "Cain's Monstrous Progeny in *Beowulf*: Part II." See also Orchard, *Pride and Prodigies*, ch. 3, 58–85.

8 For an overview, see Orchard, *Pride and Prodigies*, 69–79; and Neidorf, "Cain, Cam, Jutes, Giants, and the Textual Criticism of *Beowulf*," 599–632. The *Beowulf*-manuscript itself shows minim confusion; in line 107 the scribe corrects the spelling *cames* to *caines*; and in 1261 the name is spelt *camp*.

part of the poem, where Hroðgar's rise to power and the building of his hall, Heorot, echoes Nimrod and the Tower of Babel:[9]

> Þa wæs Hroðgare heresped gyfen,
> wiges weorðmynd, þæt him his winemagas
> georne hyrdon, oðð þæt seo geogoð geweox,
> magodriht micel. Him on mod bearn
> þæt healreced hatan wolde,
> medoærn micel men gewyrcean
> þon[n]e yldo bearn æfre gefrunon,
> ond þær on innan eall gedælan
> geongum ond ealdum swylc him God sealde,
> buton folcscare ond feorum gumena.
> Ða ic wide gefrægn weorc gebannan
> manigre mægþe geond þisne middangeard,
> folcstede frætwan. Him on fyrste gelomp,
> ædre mid yldum, þæt hit wearð eal gearo,
> healærna mæst; scop him Heort naman
> se þe his wordes geweald wide hæfde.

> Then was military success given to Hroðgar, the glory of battle such that his retainers eagerly obeyed him until those young warriors grew into a great retinue. It came to him in mind that he wanted to order men to make a hall, a mead-hall greater than ever heard of in past age, and therein share out all to young and old, just as God gave to him, with the exception of ancestral property[10] and lives of men. Then I heard far and wide that he commanded the work to many nations throughout this world to adorn the people's place. In time it happened for him, swiftly with men, that it became fully prepared, the greatest of halls; he gave it the name Heorot, who widely held the power of his word.

Just as Nimrod in *Genesis A* was a widely-known man ("widmære wer"; 1630), and increased the glory of his land ("eðelðrym onhof, / rymde and rærde"; 1634–5), Hroðgar's military fame attracts large retinues of young men for whom he builds the greatest mead-hall ever heard of. Even more significant is the account of Heorot being built by many nations throughout

9 *Beowulf*, lines 64–79.
10 For the translation of the crux *folcscare*, see Frank, "*F*-Words in *Beowulf*," 1–22, at 8–9.

the world ("manigre mægþe geond þisne middangeard") – a line that recalls the Tower of Babel narrative:[11] almost the same phrasing is used for the dispersal of Noah's three sons in *Genesis A*: "monna mægðe geond middangeard" (1244).[12] Moreover, although Heorot stands completed for the moment, like Babel it will eventually fall:[13]

Sele hlifade
heah ond horngeap; heaðowylma bad,
laðan liges – ne wæs hit lenge þa gen
þæt se ecghete aþumsweoran
æfter wælniðe wæcnan scolde

The hall towered high and wide-gabled; it waited the hostile flame, the hated fire – it was yet then not long that the sword-hate should awaken to the son-in-law and father-in-law on account of hostility.

Although Heorot is not Babel and Hroðgar is not Nimrod, the *Beowulf*-poet seems to have inserted Babylonian allusions into his description of the building of Heorot, perhaps in order to hint towards the future fall of Heorot and Hroðgar, and emphasize the poem's theme of the transitory nature of glory – the same theme that is present in other Old English accounts of the Tower of Babel.[14] An allusion to Babel at the beginning of the poem also helps reinforce another of the poem's themes: its pre-Christian world. After Heorot is built and Grendel begins his attacks, the Danes turn to idolatry (175–8); of course, it can safely be assumed that the Danes practiced idolatry before these attacks, but the similarities between the idolatry that comes after Babel and the idolatry of the Danes mentioned after the building of Heorot may be more than coincidence. In any case, according to Anglo-Saxon interpretations of salvation history, idolatry that first begins at Babel is not corrected until Pentecost or the missionary activities of the Church. The Danes of *Beowulf*, living in a pre-Christian

11 Hume, "The Concept of the Hall in Old English Poetry," 63–74, at 72, toys with the comparison between Heorot and Babel, but does not note its multinational construction.

12 It should also be noted that in *Beowulf* the related line "manigum mægþa geond þysne middangeard" appears at line 1771, outside of the hall building context.

13 *Beowulf*, lines 81–5.

14 For the association of the ruined hall with transience in Old English poetry, see Hume, "The Concept of the Hall in Old English Poetry," 69–71.

world, would not have access to the grace granted to the gentiles at Pentecost: idolatry, as the *Beowulf*-poet states, is the only "hope of the heathens" ("hæþenta hyht").[15] Although my argument for an allusion to the Babel narrative in *Beowulf* will not convince all, the evidence does, nevertheless, reveal a possibility of intertextuality that may open up new interpretations for one of the most read and examined texts of the period.

Outside of *Beowulf*, the Babel narrative is certainly to be found in other unexpected places. Its origins in the biblical text, and its examination by late antique and Anglo-Saxon exegetes, preachers, and poets certainly helped sustain its popularity and influence. The study of biblical reception, no longer confined to the history of exegesis or topoi, can certainly provide important insights into the cultural concerns and anxieties which produce sometimes surprisingly extensive literary transformations of the highest scriptural authority. Of course, close examination of the reception of other biblical books in Anglo-Saxon England will continue to demonstrate that the interpretation of textual authorities, far from presenting an unchanging, original orthodoxy, is in fact very much dependent on the ideologies of its later readers and re-writers. But since Anglo-Saxon interpretation, rewriting, and adaptation of the biblical texts are generally more concerned with the cultural circumstances at hand, these texts are able to provide the sources and stimuli for much intellectual innovation and literary creativity. The Tower of Babel narrative provides Anglo-Saxons not only authoritative material for understanding the world but also the basis for producing some of the most fascinating literary works of Anglo-Saxon England.

15 *Beowulf*, line 179; see also Stanley, "Hæthenra Hyht in *Beowulf*," 136–51.

Bibliography

Primary Sources

(Primary sources are arranged by author's first name or editor's last name)

Ælfric. *Angelsächsische Homilien und Heiligenleben*. Edited by Bruno Assmann. Rpt. with a supplementary introduction by Peter Clemoes. Darmstadt: Wissenschaftliche Buchgesellschaft, 1964.

– *Ælfric's Catholic Homilies: The First Series*. Edited by Peter Clemoes. EETS s.s. 17. Oxford: Oxford University Press, 1997.

– *Ælfric's Catholic Homilies: The Second Series*. Edited by Malcolm Godden. EETS s.s. 5. London: Oxford University Press, 1979.

– *Aelfric's Lives of Saints*. 4 vols. Edited by Walter W. Skeat. EETS 76, 82, 94, and 114. London: Trübner & Co., 1881, 1900; rpt. 1966.

– "Ælfric's Version of Alcuini Interrogationes Sigeuulfi in Genesin." Edited by George Edwin Maclean. *Anglia* 7 (1884): 1–59.

– *Ælfric's Prefaces*. Edited by Jonathan Wilcox. Durham: Durham Medieval Texts, 1994; corr. rpt. 1996.

– *De sex aetatibus*. Edited by Hildegard L.C. Tristram. *Sex aetates mundi: Die Weltseitalter bei den Angelsachsen und den Iren*. Heidelberg: Winter, 1985.

– *Die Hirtenbriefe Ælfrics in altenglischer und lateinischer Fassung*. Edited by Bernhard Fehr. Rpt. with a supplementary introduction by Peter Clemoes. Darmstadt: Wissenschaftliche Buchgesellschaft, 1966.

– *Homilies of Ælfric: A Supplementary Collection*. 2 vols. Edited by John C. Pope. EETS 259 and 260. London: Oxford University Press, 1967–8.

– *The Old English Heptateuch and Ælfric's Libellus de ueteri testamento et nouo*. Vol. 1. Edited by Richard Marsden. EETS 330. Oxford: Oxford University Press, 2008.

Ælfric / Alcuin. "A Critical Edition of Ælfric's Translation of Alcuin's *Interrogationes Sigwulfi presbiteri* and of the Related Texts *De creatore et creatura* and *De sex etatibus huius seculi.*" Edited by William Proctor Stoneman. PhD diss. University of Toronto, 1982.

Alcuin. *Epistolae*. Ed. Ernst Dümmler. *Epistolae Karolini aevi.* Vol 2. MGH Epp. 4. Berlin: Weidmann, 1895.

– *Interrogationes et responsiones in Genesin*. PL 100. 515–58.

– *The Bishops, Kings, and Saints of York*. Edited by Peter Godman. Oxford: Clarendon Press, 1982.

Aldhelm. *Aldhelm: The Poetic Works*. Translated by Michael Lapidge and James L. Rosier. Cambridge: D.S. Brewer, 1985.

– *Aldhelm: The Prose Works*. Translated by Michael Lapidge and Michael Herren. Cambridge: D.S. Brewer, 1979.

– *Opera*. Edited by Rudolf Ehwald. MGH Auct. antiq. 15. Berlin: Weidmann, 1909.

Alfred. *The Old English Boethius: An Edition of the Old English Versions of Boethius's De Consolatione Philosophiae*. 2 vols. Edited by Malcolm Godden and Susan Irvine. Oxford: Oxford University Press, 2009.

– *West-Saxon Version of Gregory's Pastoral Care*. Part 1. Edited by Henry Sweet. EETS 45 London: Oxford University Press, 1871.

Alter, Robert, trans. *The Five Books of Moses*. New York: Norton & Co., 2004.

Ambrose. *De fide ad Gratianum Augustum libri quinque*. PL 16. 527–698.

– *Expositio euangelii secundum Lucam*. Edited by M. Adriaen. CCSL 14. Turnhout: Brepols, 1957.

Ammianus Marcellinus. *Ammianus Marcellinus*. 3 Vols. Edited by John C. Rolfe. Loeb. Cambridge, MA: Harvard University Press, 1937.

Anlezark, Daniel, ed. *The Old English Dialogues of Solomon and Saturn*. Cambridge: D.S. Brewer, 2009.

Apollinaris Sidonius. *Epistulae et carmina*. Edited by Christian Luetjohann. MGH Auct. antiq. 8. Berlin: Weidmann, 1887.

Arator. *Historia apostolica*. Edited by A.P. Orbán. CCSL 130. Turnhout: Brepols, 2006.

Arnobius the Younger. *Commentarii in Psalmos*. Edited by Klaus-D. Daur. CCSL 25. Turnhout: Brepols, 1990.

Arnold, Thomas, ed. *Symeonis Monachi opera omnia*. 2 vols. RS. London: Longmans and Co., 1882–5.

Augustine. *De ciuitate Dei*. 2 Vol. Edited by Bernard Dombart and Alphonse Kalb. CCSL 47–8. Turnhout: Brepols, 1955.

– *De doctrina christiana libri IV*. Edited by Joseph Martin. CCSL 32. Turnhout: Brepols, 1962.

– *Enarrationes in Psalmos*. Vol. 2. Edited by Eligius Dekkers and Johannes Fraipont. CCSL 39. Turnhout: Brepols, 1956.
– *Epistulae*. Vol. 2. Edited by Al. Goldbacher. CSEL 34.2. Vienna: Tempsky, 1898.
– *Epistulae*. Vol. 4. Edited by Al. Goldbacher. CSEL 57. Vienna: Tempsky, 1911.
– *In Iohannis euangelium tractatus CXXIV*. Edited by Radbod Willems. CCSL 36. Turnhout: Brepols, 1954.
– *Quaestiones euangeliorum*. Edited by Almut Mutzenbecher. CCSL 44B. Turnhout: Brepols, 1980.
– *Quaestionum in Heptateuchum libri septem*. PL 34. 547–824.
– *Sermo* CCLXXI: *In die Pentecostes, V*. PL 38. 1245–6.
Avitus. *Opera*. Edited by Rudolf Peiper. MGH Auct. antiq. 6.2. Berlin: Weidmann, 1883.
Bately, Janet, ed. *The Old English Orosius*. EETS s.s. 6. London: Oxford University Press, 1980.
Bede. *Bedas metrische Vita sancti Cuthberti*. Edited by Werner Jaager. Leipzig: Mayer & Müller, 1935.
– *Bede: On Ezra and Nehemiah*. Translated by Scott DeGregorio. Liverpool: University of Liverpool Press, 2006.
– *Bede: On Genesis*. Translated by Calvin B. Kendall. Liverpool: Liverpool University Press, 2008.
– *Bede: On the Nature of Things and On Times*. Translated by Calvin B. Kendall and Faith Wallis. Liverpool: Liverpool University Press, 2010.
– *De templo*. Edited by David Hurst. CCSL119A. Turnhout: Brepols, 1969.
– *De temporum ratione*. Edited by Ch.W. Jones. CCSL 123B. Turnhout: Brepols, 1977.
– *Ecclesiastical History of the English People*. Edited by Bertram Colgrave and R.A.B. Mynors. Oxford: Clarendon Press, 1969.
– *Expositio Actuum Apostolorum*. Edited by M.L.W. Laistner. *Expositio Actuum Apostolorum et retractatio*. Cambridge, MA: The Medieval Academy of America, 1939. Rpt. without introduction in CCSL 121, Turnhout: Brepols, 1983.
– *Expositio Apocalypseos*. Edited by Roger Gryson. CCSL 121A. Turnhout: Brepols, 2001.
– *Historiam ecclesiasticam gentis Anglorum*. Edited by Charles Plummer. Oxford: Clarendon Press, 1896; rpt. 1975.
– *Homiliae*. Edited by David Hurst. CCSL 122. Turnhout: Brepols, 1955.
– *In Cantica Canticorum*. Edited by D. Hurst, CCSL 119B. Turnhout: Brepols, 1983.
– *In epistulas VII catholicas*. Edited by David Hurst. CCSL 121. Turnhout: Brepols, 1983.

– *In Ezram et Neemiam*. Edited by David Hurst. CCSL 119A. Turnhout: Brepols, 1969.
– *In primam partem Samuhelis libri IIII*, Edited by D. Hurst, CCSL 119. Turnhout: Brepols, 1962.
– *In Lucae euangelium expositio*. Edited by David Hurst. CCSL 120. Turnhout: Brepols, 1960.
– *In Marci euangelium expositio*. Edited by David Hurst. CCSL 120. Turnhout: Brepols, 1960.
– *In principium Genesis usque ad nativitatem Isaac et eiectionem Ismahelis*. Edited by Ch. W. Jones. CCSL 118A. Turnhout: Brepols, 1967.
– *Retractatio in Actus Apostolorum*. Edited by M.L.W. Laistner. *Expositio Actuum Apostolorum et retractatio*. Cambridge, MA: The Medieval Academy of America, 1939. Rpt. without introduction in CCSL 121, Turnhout: Brepols, 1983.
Bernard, J.H., and R. Atkinson, eds. *Irish Liber hymnorum*. 2 vols. London: Henry Bradshaw Soceity, 1898.
Blake, E.O., ed. *Liber Eliensis*. Camden 3rd ser. 92. London: Royal Historical Society, 1962.
Bischoff, Bernhard, and Michael Lapidge, eds. *Biblical Commentaries from the Canterbury School of Theodore and Hadrian*. CSASE 10. Cambridge: Cambridge University Press, 1994.
Boethius. *Philosophiae consolatio*. Edited by Ludwig Bieler. CCSL 94. Turnhout: Brepols, 1957.
Budge, E.A. Wallis, trans. *The Book of the Cave of Treasures*. London: Religious Tract Society, 1927.
Byrhtferth of Ramsey. *Byrhtferth of Ramsey: The Lives of St Oswald and St Ecgwine*. Edited by Michael Lapidge. Oxford: Clarendon Press, 2009.
– *Byrhtferth's Enchiridion*. Edited by Peter S. Baker and Michael Lapidge. EETS s.s. 15. Oxford: Oxford University Press, 1995.
Caie, Graham D., ed. *The Old English Poem* Judgement Day II*: A Critical Edition*. Cambridge: D.S. Brewer, 2000.
Cambe, Michael, ed. *Kerygma Petri*. CCSA 15. Turnhout: Brepols, 2003.
Cassiodorus. *Institutiones*. Edited by R.A.B. Mynors. Oxford: Clarendon Press, 1937; rpt. 1963.
Clement of Alexandria. *Stromata: Buch I–VI*. Edited by Otto Stählin. *Clemens Alexandrinus* 2. GCS 15. Leipzig: Hinrichs, 1906.
Colgrave, Bertram, ed. *The Life of Bishop Wilfrid by Eddius Stephanus*. Cambridge: Cambridge University Press, 1927.
– ed. *The Earliest Life of Gregory the Great*. Lawrence, KS: University of Kansas Press, 1968.
Cyril of Jerusalem. *Catecheses*. PG 33. 370–1128.

Dickins, Bruce, and R.M. Wilson, eds. *Early Middle English Texts.* London: Bowes and Bowes, 1951.

Doane, A.N., ed. *Genesis A: A New Edition, Revised.* Tempe, AZ: ACMRS, 2013.

– ed. *The Saxon Genesis: An Edition of the West Saxon* Genesis B *and the Old Saxon Vatican* Genesis. Madison, WI: University of Wisconsin Press, 1991.

Dumville, David N., ed. *The* Historia Brittonum*: The "Vatican" Recension.* Cambridge: D.S. Brewer, 1985.

Einhard. *Vita Karoli Magni.* 6th ed. Edited by G.H. Pertz, G. Waitz, and O. Holder-Egger. MGH SRG 25. Hannover: Hahn, 1911.

Epiphanius. *Panarion.* Edited by Karl Holl. *Epiphanius: Ancoratus und Panarion.* Vol. 1. GCS 25. Leipzig: Hinrichs, 1915.

Ermoldus Nigellus. *In honorem Hludowicii.* Edited by Ernest Dümmler. MGH PLAC 2. Berlin: Weidmann, 1884.

Eusebius / Rufinus. *Die Kirchengeschichte.* Edited by Eduard Schwartz and Theodor. *Eusebius Werke* 2. GCS 9. Leipzig: Hinrichs, 1903.

Faricius. "An Edition of Faricius, *Vita S. Aldhelm.*" Edited by Michael Winterbottom. *Journal of Medieval Latin* 15 (2005): 93–147.

Farrell, Robert T., ed. *Daniel and Azarias.* London: Methuen, 1974.

Finnegan, Robert Emmett, ed. *Christ and Satan: A Critical Edition.* Waterloo, ON: Wilfrid Laurier Press, 1977.

Fischer, Bonifatius, ed. *Vetus Latina: Die Reste der altlateinischen Bibel.* Vol. 2: *Genesis.* Freiburg: Herder, 1951.

Franklin, Carmela Vircillo, ed. *The Latin Dossier of Anastasius the Persian: Hagiographic Translations and Transformations.* Toronto: PIMS, 2004.

Fulk, R.D., Robert E. Bjork and John D. Niles, eds. *Klaeber's Beowulf.* 4th ed. Toronto: University of Toronto Press, 2008.

Gildas. *The Ruin of Britain and Other Works.* Edited by Michael Winterbottom. Chichester: Phillimore, 1978; rpt. 2002.

Gregory of Nazianzus. *Oration XLI: In Pentecosten.* PG 36. 427–52.

Gregory Naziansus / Rufinus. *De Pentecoste et de Spiritu Sancto.* Edited by August Engelbrecht. *Tyranni Rufini orationem Gregorii Nazianzeni nouem interpretatio.* CSEL 46. Vienna: Tempsky, 1910.

Gregory of Tours. *Libri Historiarum X.* Edited by Bruno Krusch and Wilhelm Levison. MGH Script. rer. mer. 1.1. Hannover: Hahn, 1951.

Gregory the Great. *Dialogues.* Edited by Adalbert de Vogüé. 3 vols. SC 251, 260 and 265. Paris: Les Éditions du Cerf, 1978–80.

Gregory the Great. *Homiliae in Euangelia.* Edited by Raymond Étaix. CCSL 141. Turnhout: Brepols, 1999.

– *Moralia in Iob libri XXXV.* Vol. 3. Edited by Marcus Adriaen. CCSL 143B. Turnhout: Brepols, 1979.

Harmer, Florence E. *Select English Historical Documents of the Ninth and Tenth Centuries*. Cambridge: Cambridge University Press, 1914.

Heiricus of Auxerre. *Vita S. Germani*. Edited by Ludwig Traube. MGH PLAC 3. Berlin: Weidmann, 1896.

Herodotus. *Historiae*. 3rd ed. Edited by Karl Hude. Oxford: Clarendon Press, 1927; rpt. 1986.

Herren, Michael W., ed. *Hisperica Famina: The A-Text*. Toronto: PIMS, 1974.

Hilary of Poitiers. *Prologus in librum Psalmorum*. PL 9.

Hippolytus. *Die Chronik*. Edited by Adolf Bauer and Rudolf Helm. *Hippolytus Werke* 4. GCS 46. Berlin: Akademie, 1955.

Holladay, Carl R., ed. *Fragments from Hellenistic Jewish Authors*. Vol. 1: *Historians*. Chico, CA: Scholars Press, 1983.

Homer. *Iliad*. Edited by David B. Monro and Thomas W. Allen. *Homeri Opera*. 3rd ed. Oxford: Clarendon Press, 1920; rpt. 1989.

Hrabanus Maurus. *Commentaria in Libros IV Regem*, PL 109.

– *De institutione clericorum*. PL 107. 293–420.

– *De universo libri viginti duo*. PL 111. 9–612.

– *Liber de oblatione puerorum*. PL 107.

Irenaeus. *Contre les Hérésies Livre III: Édition critique*. Edited by Adelin Rousseau and Louis Doutreleau. SC 211. Paris: Les Éditions du Cerf, 1974.

Irish-Augustine. *De mirabilibus sacrae scripturae libri tres*. PL 35. 2149–200.

Isidore. *Chronica*. Edited by Jose Carlos Martin. CCSL 112. Turnhout: Brepols, 2003.

– *Etymologiarum sive originum libri XX*. 2 vols. Edited by W.M. Lindsay. Oxford: Clarendon Press, 1911.

– *Quaestiones in vetus testamentum*. PL 83. 207–424.

James, Montague Rhodes, ed. and trans. *The Lost Apocrypha of the Old Testament*. London: Society for Promoting Christian Knowledge, 1920.

Jerome. *Commentarii in prophetas*. Edited by M. Adriaen. CCSL 76. Turnhout: Brepols, 1969.

– *Commentariorum in Danielem libri III*. Edited by François Glorie. CCSL 75A. Turnhout: Brepols, 1964.

– *Commentariorum in Esaiam libri I–XI*. Edited by M. Adriaen. CCSL 73. Tunrhout: Brepols, 1963.

– *Epistulae, pars I: epistulae I–LXX*. Edited by Isidore Hilberg. CSEL 54. Vienna: Österreichischen Akademie der Wissenschaften, 1996.

– *Hebraicae quaestiones in libro Geneseos*. Edited by Paul de Lagarde. CCSL 72. Turnhout: Brepols, 1959.

– *Liber interpretationis hebraicorum nominum*. Edited by Paul de Lagarde. CCSL 72. Turnhout: Brepols, 1959.

– *Prologus Hieronymi in Danihele propheta*. Edited by Robert Weber. *Biblia Sacra iuxta vulgatam versionem*. 4th ed. Stuttgart: Deutsche Bibelgesellschaft, 1994. 1341–2.

– *Tractatus siue homiliae in psalmos*. Edited by G. Morin. CCSL 78. Tunrhout: Brepols, 1958.

John Chrysostom. *Homilia II: de sancta Pentecoste*. PG 50. 463–70.

– *Homilia XXXV: In epist. I ad Cor.* PG 61. 295–306.

John Lydgate. *Fall of Princes*. Part 1. Edited by Henry Bergen. Washington, DC: Carnegie Institution of Washington, 1923.

Jordannes. *Romana et Getica*. Edited by Theodore Mommsen. MGH Auct. antiq. 5. Berlin: Weidmann, 1882.

Josephus. *Libri antiquitatum Iudaicarum*. 4 vols. Edited by Benedict Niese. *Flavii Iosephi opera* 1–4. Berlin: Weidmann, 1887–90.

– *The Latin Josephus*. Vol. 1. Edited by Franz Blatt. Aarsskrift for Aarhus Universitet 30.1. Copenhagen: Universitetsforlaget i Aarhus, 1958.

Justinus. *Epitoma historiarum Philippicarum Pompei Trogi*. Edited by Otto Seel. Stuttgart: B.G. Teubner, 1985.

Kemble, John M., ed. *The Dialogue of Salomon and Saturnus*. London: Ælfric Society, 1848.

Krapp, George Philip, ed. *The Junius Manuscript*. ASPR 1. New York: Columbia University Press, 1931.

Lapidge, Michael and Michael Winterbottom, eds. *The Life of St Æthelwold*. Oxford: Clarendon Press, 1991; rpt. 1996.

Liebermann, F. ed. *Die Gesetze der Angelsachsen*. 3 vols. Halle: Max Niemeyer, 1903–16.

Lipsius, Richard Adelbert and Maximilian Bonnet, eds. *Acta apostolorum Apocrypha*. Vol. 1. Leipzig: Mendelsohn, 1891; rpt. 1959.

Lullus. *Epistolae*. Edited by Michael Tangl. *Die Briefe des heiligen Bonifatius und Lullus*. MGH Epistolae selectae 1. Berlin: Weidmann, 1916.

Machiela, Daniel A., ed. *The Dead Sea Genesis Apocryphon: A New Text and Translation with Introduction and Special Treatment of Columns 13–17*. Leiden: Brill, 2009.

Menner, Robert J., ed. *The Poetical Dialogues of Solomon and Saturn*. London: Oxford University Press, 1941; rpt. 1973.

Milfull, Inge B., ed. *The Hymns of the Anglo-Saxon Church: A Study and Edition of the Durham Hymnal*. CSASE 17. Cambridge: Cambridge University Press, 1996.

Miller, Sean, ed. *Charters of the New Minster, Winchester*. Oxford: Oxford University Press, 2001.

Mommsen, Theodore, ed. *Liber generationis*. *Chronica minora saec. iv. v. vi. vii.* Vol. 1. MGH Auct. Antiq. 9. Berlin: Weidmann, 1892.

Morris, R., ed. *The Blickling Homilies*. EETS 58, 63 and 73. London: Oxford University Press, 1874–80; rpt. 1967.

Orbán, A.P., ed. "Ein anonymer Aratorkommentar in Hs. London, Royal MS. 15 A. V. *Editio princeps*, Teil I." *Sacris Erudiri* 38 (1998): 317–51.

– ed. "Ein anonymer Aratorkommentar in Hs. London, Royal MS. 15 A. V. *Editio princeps*, Teil II." *Sacris Erudiri* 40 (2001): 131–229.

Origen. *Contra Celse*. Vol. 3. Edited by Marcel Borret. SC 147. Paris: Les Éditions du Cerf, 1969.

– *Contra Celsum*. Translated by Henry Chadwick. Cambridge: Cambridge University Press, 1953.

Origen / Rufinus. *Homilien zum Hexateuch in Rufins Übersetzung*. Edited by W.A. Baehrens. *Origenes Werke* 7. GCS 30. Leipzig: Hinrich, 1921.

Orosius. *Historiarum adversum paganos libri VII*. Edited by Karl Zangemeister. CSEL 5. Vienna: Gerold's son, 1882.

Paul the Deacon. *Historia Langobardorum*. Edited by Ludwig Bethmann and Georg Waitz. MGH Script. rer. Lang. Hannover: Hahn, 1878.

Pliny. *Natural History*. Vol. 2. Edited by H. Rackham. Loeb. Cambridge, MA: Harvard University Press, 1947.

Polybius. *ΠΟΛΥΒΙΟΥ ΙΣΤΟΡΙΑΙ: Polybii historiae*. Vol. 4. Edited by Theodor Büttner-Wobst. Leipzig: Teubner, 1904.

Procopius of Gaza. *Commentarius in Genesin*. PG 82.

Pseudo-Clement. *Homilien*. 2nd ed. Edited by Bernhard Rehm. *Die Pseudoklementinen*. Vol. 1. GCS 42. Berlin: Akademie, 1969.

– *Rekognitionen in Rufins Übersetzung*. Edited by Bernhard Rehm. *Die Pseudoklementinen*. Vol. 2. GCS 51. Berlin: Akademie, 1965.

Pseudo-Methodius. *Die Apokalypse des Pseudo-Methodius die ältesten griechischen und lateinischen Übersetzungen*. Edited by W.J. Aerts and G.A.A. Kortekaas. CSCOS 97. Louvain: Peeters, 1998.

Rahlfs, Alfred, ed. *Septuaginta: Id est Vetus Testamentum graece iuxta LXX interpretes*. 2 vols. Stuttgart: Württembergische Bibelanstalt, 1935; rpt. 1971.

Seneca. *Apocolocyntosis*. Edited by P.T. Eden. Cambridge: Cambridge University Press, 1984.

Servius Grammaticus. *In Vergilii carmina commentarii*. Vol. 1. Edited by Georg Thilo and Hermann Hagen. Leipzig: Teubner, 1881.

Seymour, M.C., ed. *Mandeville's Travels*. Oxford: Clarendon Press, 1967.

Skeat, Walter W., ed. *The Gospel according to Saint Luke in Anglo-Saxon and Northumbrian Versions*. Cambridge: Cambridge University Press, 1874.

Stevenson, Jane, ed. *The "Laterculus Malalianus" and the School of Archbishop Theodore*. CSASE 14. Cambridge: Cambridge University Press, 1995.

Strabo. *Géographie*. Vols. 2 and 3. Edited by François Lasserre. Paris: Les Belles Lettres, 1966–7.

Symons, Thomas, ed. *Regularis Concordia / The Monastic Agreement*. London: Thomas Nelson and Sons, 1953.

Tacitus. *De origine et situ Germanorum*. Edited by M. Winterbottom. *Cornelii Taciti opera minora*. Edited by M. Winterbottom and R.M. Ogilvie. Oxford: Clarendon Press, 1975.

Tertullian. *Aduersus Iudaeos*. Edited by Aem. Kroymann. *Quinti Septimi Florentis Tertulliani opera*. Vol. 2. CCSL 2. Turnhout: Brepols, 1954.

Ure, James M., ed. *The Benedictine Office: An Old English Text*. Edinburgh: Edinburgh University Press, 1957.

Virgil. *Opera*. Edited by R.A.B. Mynors Oxford: Clarendon Press, 1969.

Virgilius Maro Grammaticus. *Epitomae*. Edited by Bengt Löfstedt. *Virgilius Maro Grammaticus: Opera omnia*. Leizpig: Sauer, 2003.

Vitruvius. *De l'Architecture livre VI*. Edited by Louis Callebat. Paris: Les Belles Lettres, 2004.

Weber, Robert, ed. *Biblia Sacra iuxta vulgatam versionem*. 4th ed. Stuttgart: Deutsche Bibelgesellschaft, 1994.

Whitelock, D., M. Brett and C.N.L. Brooke, eds. *Councils and Synods with Other Documents Relating to the English Church*. Vol. 1: *A.D. 871–1204*. Part I: *871–1066*. Oxford: Clarendon Press, 1981.

Wieland, Gernot R., ed. *The Canterbury Hymnal*. Toronto: PIMS, 1982.

William of Malmesbury. *Gesta pontificum Anglorum*. Vol. 1. Edited by M. Winterbottom. Oxford: Oxford University Press, 2007.

– *Gesta regum Anglorum*. Vol. 1. Edited by R.A.B. Mynors, R.M. Thompson, and M. Winterbottom. Oxford: Clarendon Press, 1998.

Winterbottom, Michael, and Michael Lapidge, eds., *The Early Lives of St Dunstan*. Oxford: Oxford University Press, 2011.

Wintermute, O.S., trans. *Jubilees*. *The Old Testament Pseudepigrapha*. Vol. 2. Edited by James H. Charlesworth. Garden City, NY: Doubleday & Co., 1985.

Wulfstan. *The Homilies of Wulfstan*. Edited by Dorothy Bethurum. Oxford: Clarendon Press, 1957.

Ziolkowski, Jan M., ed. *Solomon and Marcolf*. Cambridge, MA: Harvard University Press, 2008.

Secondary Sources

Adams, Jeremy duQuesnay. *The* Populus *of Augustine and Jerome: A Study in the Patristic Sense of Community*. New Haven, CT: Yale University Press, 1971.

Adler, Nikolaus. *Das erste christliche Pfingstfest: Sinn und Bedeutung des Pfingstberichtes Apg 2,1–13*. Neutestamentliche Abhandlungen 18.1. Münster: Aschendorff, 1938.

Alexander, Phillip S. "Jerusalem as the *Omphalos* of the World: On the History of a Geographical Concept." In *Jerusalem: Its Sanctity and Centrality to Judaism, Christianity, and Islam*, edited by L.I. Levine. New York: Continuum, 1999. 104–19.
– "Geography and the Bible: Early Jewish Geography." *The Anchor Bible Dictionary*, edited by David Noel Freedman et al. Vol. 2: D–G. New York: Doubleday, 1992. 977–88.
– "Notes on the 'Imago mundi' of the Book of Jubilees." *Journal of Jewish Studies* 33 (1982): 197–213.
Allen, Marjorie Sue. "The Interior Journey: Monastic Spirituality as Theme and Structure in the Junius MS." PhD diss. Princeton University, 1976.
Amory, Patrick. "The Meaning and Purpose of Ethnic Terminology in the Burgundian Laws." *Early Medieval Europe* 2 (1993): 1–28.
Amos, Ashley Crandell. *Linguistic Means of Determining the Dates of Old English Literary Texts*. Cambridge, MA: Medieval Academy of America, 1980.
Anderson, Benedict. *Imagined Communities*. London: Verso, 1983.
Anderson, Earl R. "Style and Theme in the Old English *Daniel*." In *The Poems of MS Junius 11*, edited by R.M. Liuzza. New York: Routledge, 2002. 229–60.
– "Style and Theme in the Old English Daniel." *English Studies* 68 (1987): 1–23.
Anderson, Rachel. "The Old Testament Homily: Ælfric as Biblical Translator." In *The Old English Homily: Precedent, Practice, and Appropriation*, edited by Aaron J. Kleist. Turnhout: Brepols, 2007. 121–42.
Anlezark, Daniel. "The Anglo-Saxon Worldview." In *The Cambridge Companion to Old English Literature*. 2nd ed., edited by Malcolm Godden and Michael Lapidge. Cambridge: Cambridge University Press, 2013. 66–81.
– "Poisoned Places: The Avernian Tradition in Old English Poetry." *ASE* 36 (2007): 103–26.
– *Water and Fire: The Myth of the Flood in Anglo-Saxon England*. Manchester: Manchester University Press, 2006.
– "Sceaf, Japheth and the Origins of the Anglo-Saxons." *ASE* 31 (2002): 13–46.
Auerbach, Erich. "Figura." In *Scenes from the Drama of European Literature*. Minneapolis, MN: University of Minnesota Press, 1984. 11–76.
– *Literary Language and Its Public in Late Antiquity and in the Middle Ages*. Translated by Ralph Manheim. London: Routledge & Kegan Paul, 1965.
– *Mimesis: The Representations of Reality in Western Literature*. Translated by Willard Trask. Princeton, NJ: Princeton University Press, 1953.
Balsdon, J.P.V.D. *Romans and Aliens*. Chapel Hill, NC: University of North Carolina Press, 1979.
Bately, Janet. "Alfred as Author and Translator." In *A Companion to Alfred the Great*, edited by Nicole Guenther Discenza and Paul E. Szarmach. Leiden: Brill, 2014. 113–42.

Bately, Janet. "Did King Alfred Actually Translate Anything? The Integrity of the Alfredian Canon Revisited." *Medium Ævum* 78 (2009): 189–215.
– "The Alfredian Corpus Revisited: One Hundred Years On." In *Alfred the Great: Papers from the Eleventh-Century Conferences*, edited by Timothy Reuter. Aldershot: Ashgate, 2003. 107–20.
– "Those Books that Are Most Necessary for All Men to Know: The Classics and Late Ninth-Century England, A Reappraisal." In *The Classics in the Middle Ages: Papers of the Twentieth Annual Conference of the Centre for Medieval and Early Renaissance Studies*, edited by Aldo S. Bernardo and Saul Levin. Binghamton, NY: Center for Medieval and Early Renaissance Studies, 1990. 45–78.
– "Old English Prose Before and During the Reign of Alfred." *ASE* 17 (1988): 93–138.
– "The Relationship between Geographical Information in the Old English Orosius and Latin Texts Other than Orosius." *ASE* 1 (1972): 45–62.
Bateson, Mary. "A Worcester Cathedral Book of Ecclesiastical Collections, Made *c.* 1000 AD." *English Historical Review* 10 (1895): 712–31.
Battles, Paul. "*Genesis A* and the Anglo-Saxon 'Migration Myth.'" *ASE* 29 (2000): 43–66.
Beaty, John O. "The Echo-Word in *Beowulf* with a Note on the Finnsburg Fragment." *PMLA* 49 (1934): 365–73.
Benjamin, Isaac. *The Invention of Racism in Classical Antiquity*. Princeton: University of Princeton Press, 2004.
Berschin, Walter. *Greek Letters and the Latin Middle Ages: From Jerome to Nicholas of Cusa*, revised and translated by Jerold C. Frakes. Washington, DC: The Catholic University of America Press, 1988.
Bethurum, Dorothy. "Archbishop Wulfstan's Commonplace Book." *PMLA* 57 (1942): 916–29.
– "Wulfstan." In *Continuations and Beginnings: Studies in Old English Literature*, edited by Eric Gerald Stanley. London: Nelson, 1966. 210–46.
Bickerman, Elias J. "*Origines Gentium*." *Classical Philology* 47 (1952): 65–81.
Biddle, Martin. "*Felix Urbs Winthonia*: Winchester in the Age of Monastic Reform." In *Tenth-Century Studies: Essays in Commemoration of the Millennium of the Council of Winchester and* Regularis Concordia, edited by David Parsons. London: Phillimore, 1974. 123–40 and 233–7.
Biggs, Frederick M. "Cave of Treasures." In *Sources of Anglo-Saxon Literary Culture: The Apocrypha*, edited by Frederick M. Biggs. Instrumenta Anglistica Mediaevalia 1. Kalamazoo, MI: Medieval Institute Publications, 2007. 6.
Bilde, Per. *Flavius Josephus between Jerusalem and Rome: His Life, his Works, and their Importance*. Journal for the Study of the Pseudepigrapha s.s 2. Sheffield: JSOT Press, 1988.

Bildhauer, Bettina, and Robert Mills, eds., *The Monstrous Middle Ages*. Cardiff: University of Wales Press, 2003.

Bischoff, Bernhard. "Das griechische Element in der abendlandischen Bildung des Mittelalters." In *Mittelalterliche Studien: Ausgewählte Aufsätze zur Schriftkunde und Literaturgeschichte*. Vol. 2. Stuttgart: Anton Hiersemann, 1967. 246–75.

– "Wendepunkte in der Geschichte der lateinischen Exegese im Frühmittelalter." In *Mittelalterliche Studien: Ausgewählte Aufsätze zur Schriftkunde und Literaturgeschichte*. Vol. 1. Stuttgart: Hiersemann, 1966. 205–73.

Blunt, C.E. "The Coinage of Athelstan, 924–939: A Survey." *British Numismatic Journal* 44 (1974): 36–160.

Blurton, Heather. *Cannibalism in High Medieval English Literature*. New York: Palgrave, 2007.

Borst, Arno. *Der Turmbau von Babel: Geschichte der Meinungen über Ursprung und Vielfalt der Sprachen und Völker*. 4 vols. Stuttgart: Hiersemann, 1957–63.

Bosworth, Joseph, and T. Northcote Toller, eds. *An Anglo-Saxon Dictionary* with a *Supplement* by T. Northcote Toller, with *Addenda and Corrigenda* by Alistair Campbell. Oxford: Clarendon Press, 1972.

Boyd, Nina. "Doctrine and Criticism: A Revaluation of 'Genesis A.'" *Neuphilologische Mitteilungen* 83 (1982): 230–8.

Braude, Benjamin. "Michelangelo and the Curse of Ham: From a Typology of Jew-Hatred to a Genealogy of Racism." In *Writing Race Across the Atlantic World: Medieval to Modern*, edited by Phillip Beidler and Gary Taylor. Gordonsville, VA: Palgrave Macmillan, 2005. 79–92.

– "Cham et Noé: Race, esclavage et exégèse entre islam, judaïsme et christianisme." Translated by Marie-Pierre Gaviano. *Annales: Histoire, Science Sociales* 57 (2002): 93–125.

– "The Sons of Noah and the Construction of Ethnic and Geographical Identities in the Medieval and Early Modern Periods." *The William and Mary Quarterly* 3rd ser., 54 (1997): 103–42.

Bredehoft, Thomas A. "The Date of Composition of *Beowulf* and the Evidence of Metrical Evolution." In *The Dating of Beowulf: A Reassessment*, edited by Leornard Neidorf. Cambridge: D.S. Brewer, 2014. 97–111.

– *Authors, Audiences, and Old English Verse*. Toronto: University of Toronto Press, 2009.

Brehe, S.K. "Reassembling the *First Worcester Fragment*." *Speculum* 65 (1990): 521–36.

Brennan, Francis Costello. "The Old English *Daniel*: Edited with Introduction, Notes, and Glossary." PhD diss. University of North Carolina at Chapel Hill, 1966.

Brett, Caroline. "A Breton Pilgrim in England in the Reign of King Æthelstan." In *France and the British Isles in the Middle Ages and Renaissance: Essays in Memory of Ruth Morgan*, edited by Gillian Jondorf and D.N. Dumville. Woodbridge: Boydell Press, 1991. 43–70.

Bridges, Margaret. "Of Myths and Maps: The Anglo-Saxon Cosmographer's Europe." In *Writing & Culture*, edited by Balz Engler. Tübingen: Gunter Narr, 1992. 69–84.

Bright, James W. "The Relationship of the Cædmonian *Exodus* to the Liturgy." *Modern Language Notes* 27 (1912): 97–103.

Brinegar, John H. "'Books Most Necessary': The Literary and Cultural Contexts of Alfred's *Boethius*.' PhD diss. University of North Carolina at Chapel Hill, 2000.

Brockman, Bennett A. "'Heroic' and 'Christian' in *Genesis A*: The Evidence of the Cain and Abel Episode." *Modern Language Quarterly* 35 (1974): 115–28.

Broderick, H.R. "Observations on the Method of Illustration in MS Junius 11 and the Relationship of the Drawings to the Text." *Scriptorium* 37 (1983): 161–77.

Brooks, N.P. "The Career of St Dunstan." In *St Dunstan: His Life, Times and Cult*, edited by Nigel Ramsay, Margaret Sparks, and Tim Tatton-Brown. Woodbridge: Boydell Press, 1992. 1–23.

– *The Early History of the Church of Canterbury: Christ Church from 597 to 1066*. Leicester: Leicester University Press, 1984.

– "England in the Ninth Century: The Crucible of Defeat," *Transactions of the Royal Historical Society* 29 (1979): 1–20.

Brooks, N.P., and Catherine Cubitt, eds. *St Oswald of Worcester: Life and Influence*. London: Leicester University Press, 1996.

Brown, Francis, S.R. Driver, and Charles A. Briggs, eds. *A Hebrew and English Lexicon of the Old Testament*. Oxford: Clarendon Press, 1907; rpt. 1955.

Brown, George Hardin. *A Companion to Bede*. Woodbridge: Boydell Press, 2009.

Brown, Peter. *Augustine of Hippo: A Biography*. London: Faber & Faber, 1967.

Bugge, John. "Virginity and Prophecy in the Old English Daniel." *English Studies* 87 (2006): 127–47.

Bullough, Donald A. *Alcuin: Achievement and Reputation*. Leiden: Brill, 2004.

– "The Continental Background of the Tenth-Century English Reform." In *Carolingian Renewal: Sources and Heritage: Sources and Heritage*. Manchester: Manchester University Press, 1991. 272–96.

– "The Educational Tradition in England from Alfred to Ælfric: Teaching *utriusque linguae*." In *Carolingian Renewal: Sources and Heritage*. Manchester: Manchester University Press, 1991. 297–334.

Busse, Wilhelm G. "Die 'karolingische' Reform König Alfreds." In *Karl der Große und das Erbe der Kulturen*, edited by Franz-Reiner Erkens. Berlin: Akademie, 2001. 169–84.

– "*Sua gað ða lareowas beforan ðæm folce, & ðæt folc æfter*: The Self-Understanding of the Reformers as Teachers in Late Tenth-Century England." In *Schriftlichkeit im frühen Mittelalter*, edited by Ursula Schaefer. Tübingen: Gunter Narr, 1993. 58–106.

Butler, Emily Elisabeth. "Textual Community and Linguistic Distance in Early England." PhD diss. University of Toronto, 2010.

Byron, Gay L. *Symbolic Blackness and Ethnic Difference in Early Christian Literature*. London: Routledge, 2002.

Cable, Thomas. "Metrical Style as Evidence for the Date of *Beowulf*." In *The Dating of Beowulf*, edited by Collin Chase. Toronto: University of Toronto Press, 1997. 77–82.

Caie, Graham D. "Codicological Clues: Reading Old English Christian Poetry in its Manuscript Context." In *The Christian Tradition in Anglo-Saxon England: Approaches to Current Scholarship and Teaching*, edited by Paul Cavill. Cambridge: D.S. Brewer, 2004. 3–14.

– "Text and Context in Editing Old English: The Case of the Poetry in Cambridge, Corpus Christi College 201." In *The Editing of Old English: Papers from the 1990 Manchester Conference*, edited by D.G. Scragg and Paul E. Szarmach. Cambridge: D.S. Brewer, 1994. 155–62.

– "The Old English *Daniel*: A Warning Against Pride." *English Studies* 59 (1978): 1–8.

Cameron, Angus, Ashley Crandell Amos, Antonette diPaolo Healey, et al., eds. *Dictionary of Old English: A to G online*. Toronto: Dictionary of Old English Project, 2007.

Chadwick, H. "Theodore, the English Church and the Monothelete Controversy." In *Archbishop Theodore: Commemorative Studies on his Life and Influence*, edited by Michael Lapidge. CSASE 11. Cambridge: Cambridge University Press, 1995. 88–95.

– "Theodore of Tarsus and Monotheletism." In *Logos: Festschrift für Luise Abramowski zum 8 Juli 1993*, edited by Hanns Christof Brennecke, Ernst Ludwig Grasmück, and Christoph Markschies. Berlin: de Gruyter, 1993. 534–44.

Charles-Edwards, T.M. "Bede, the Irish and the Britons." *Celtica* 15 (1983): 42–52.

Ciholas, Paul. *The Omphalos and the Cross: Pagans and Christians in Search of a Divine Center*. Macon, GA: Mercer University Press, 2003.

Clarke, Katherine. *Between Geography and History: Hellenistic Constructions of the Roman World*. Oxford: Clarendon Press, 1999.

Clemoes, Peter. "Ælfric." In *Continuations and Beginnings: Studies in Old English Literature*, edited by Eric Gerald Stanley. London: Nelson, 1966. 176–209.
– "The Old English Benedictine Office, Corpus Christi College, Cambridge, MS 190, and the Relations between Ælfric and Wulfstan: A Reconsideration." *Anglia* 78 (1960): 265–83.
– "The Chronology of Ælfric's Works." In *Old English Prose: Basic Readings*, edited by Paul E. Szarmach. New York: Garland Publishing, 2000. 29–72.
Cohen, Jeffrey Jerome. *Of Giants: Sex, Monsters, and the Middle Ages.* Minneapolis, MN: University of Minnesota Press, 1999.
Constable, Giles. "Renewal and Reform in Religious Life: Concepts and Realities." In *Renaissance and Renewal in the Twelfth Century*, edited by Robert L. Benson and Giles Constable. Oxford: Clarendon Press, 1982; rpt. 1985. 37–67.
Creed, Robert P. "The Art of the Singer: Three Old English Tellings of the Offering of Isaac." In *Old English Poetry: Fifteen Essays*, edited by R.P. Creed. Providence: Brown University Press, 1967. 73–80.
Crépin, André. "Bede and the Vernacular." In *Famulus Christi: Essays in Commemoration of the Thirteenth Centenary of the Birth of the Venerable Bede*, edited by Gerald Bonner. London: SPCK, 1976. 170–92.
Crick, Julia. "An Anglo-Saxon Fragment of Justinus's 'Epitome.'" *ASE* 16 (1987): 181–96.
Cronan, Denis. "Poetic Words, Conservatism, and the Dating of Old English Poetry." *ASE* 33 (2004): 23–50.
Cross, J.E. "Bede's Influence at Home and Abroad: An Introduction." In *Beda Venerabilis: Historian, Monk & Northumbrian*, edited by L.A.J.R. Houwen and A.A. MacDonald. Groningen: Egbert Forsten, 1996. 17–29.
– "The Literate Anglo-Saxon – On Sources and Disseminations." *Proceedings of the British Academy* 58 (1972): 67–100.
– "Ælfric – Mainly on Memory and Creative Method in Two *Catholic Homilies*." *Studia Neophilologica* 41 (1969): 135–56.
– "More Sources for Two of Ælfric's *Catholic Homilies*." *Anglia* 86 (1968): 59–78.
– "Bundles for Burning—A Theme in Two of Ælfric's *Catholic Homilies*—with Other Sources." *Anglia* 81 (1963): 335–46.
– Review of Huppé, *Doctrine and Poetry*. *JEGP* 59 (1960): 561–4.
Cross, J.E., and Alan Brown. "Wulfstan and Abbo of Saint-German-des-Prés." *Mediaevalia* 15 (1993): 71–91.
Cubitt, Catherine. "Review Article: The Tenth-Century Benedictine Reform in England." *Early Medieval Europe* 6 (1997): 77–94.
Curtius, Ernst Robert. *European Literature and the Latin Middle Ages.* Translated by Willard R. Trask. New York: Pantheon Books, 1953; rpt. 1963.

Darlington, R.R. "Ecclesiastical Reform in the Late Old English Period." *English Historical Review* 203 (1936): 385–428.

Davis, Kathleen. "National Writing in the Ninth Century: A Reminder for Postcolonial Thinking about the Nation." *Journal of Medieval and Early Modern Studies* 28 (1998): 611–37.

Day, Virginia. "The Influence of the Catechetical *narratio* on Old English and Some Other Medieval Literature." *ASE* 3 (1974): 51–61.

Dean, James M. *The World Grown Old in Later Medieval Literature*. Cambridge, MA: Medieval Academy of America, 1997.

– "Bede's *In Ezram et Neeiam* and the Reform of the Northumbrian Church." *Speculum* 79 (2004): 1–25.

Dekker, Kees. "Anglo-Saxon Encyclopaedic Notes: Tradition and Function." In *Foundations of Learning: The Transfer of Encyclopaedic Knowledge in the Early Middle Ages*, edited by Rolf H. Bremmer Jr and Kees Dekker. Paris: Peeters, 2007. 279–315.

– "Pentecost and Linguistic Self-Consciousness in Anglo-Saxon England: Bede and Ælfric." *JEGP* 104 (2005): 345–72.

Dendle, Peter J. *Satan Unbound: The Devil in Old English Narrative Literature*. Toronto: University of Toronto Press, 2001.

Deproost, Paul-Augustin. *L'Apôtre Pierre dans une Épopée du VI*[e] *Siècle: L'Historia apostolica d'Arator*. Paris: Institut d'Études Augustiniennes, 1990.

Discenza, Nicole Guenther. "Writing the Mother Tongue in the Shadow of Babel." In *Conceptualizing Multilingualism in Medieval England, c. 800–c. 1250*, edited by Elizabeth M. Tyler. Turnhout: Brepols, 2011. 33–55.

– "A Map of the Universe: Geography and Cosmology in the Program of Alfred the Great." In *Conversion and Colonization in Anglo-Saxon England*, edited by Catherine E. Karkov and Nicholas Howe. MRTS 318. Tempe, AZ: ACMRS, 2006. 83–108.

– *The King's English: Strategies of Translation in the Old English* Boethius. Albany, NY: State University of New York Press, 2005.

Discenza, Nicole Guenther, and Paul E. Szarmach. "Annotated Bibliography on the Authorship Issue." In *A Companion to Alfred the Great*, edited by Nicole Guenther Discenza and Paul E. Szarmach. Leiden: Brill, 2014. 397–415.

Donaghey, Brian S. "The Sources of King Alfred's Translation of Boethius's *De consolatione philosophiae*." *Anglia* 82 (1964): 23–57.

Doubleday, James F. "*The Ruin*: Structure and Theme." *JEGP* 71 (1972): 369–81.

Droge, Arthur J. "The Apologetic Dimensions of the *Ecclesiastical History*." In *Eusebius, Christianity, and Judaism*, edited by Harold W. Attridge and Gohei Hata. Leiden: Brill, 1992. 492–509.

– *Homer or Moses? Early Christian Interpretations of the History of Culture*. Tübingen: Mohr-Siebeck, 1989.

Duckett, Eleanor Shipley. *Alcuin, Friend of Charlemagne: His World and His Work*. Hamden, CT: Archon Books, 1951; rpt. 1965.

Dumitrescu, Irina A. "Bede's Liberation Philology: Releasing the English Tongue." *PMLA* 128 (2013): 40–56.

Dumville, David N. "Mael Brigte mac Tornáin, Pluralist Coarb (†927)." *Journal of Celtic Studies* 4 (2004): 97–116.

– "English Square Minuscule Script: The Mid-Century Phases." *ASE* 23 (1994): 133–64.

– "Ecclesiastical Lands and the Defence of Wessex in the First Viking Age." In *Wessex and England from Alfred to Edgar*. Woodbridge: Boydell Press, 1992. 29–54.

– "English Square Minuscule Script: The Background and Earliest Phases." *ASE* 16 (1987): 147–79.

– "'Nennius' and the *Historia Brittonum*." *Studia Celtica* 10–11 (1975–6): 78–95.

Eco, Umberto. *The Search for the Perfect Language*. Translated by James Fentress. Malden, MA: Blackwell, 1995; rpt. 1997.

Elliot, Michael D. "Boniface, Incest, and the Earliest Extant Version of Pope Gregory I's *Libellus responsionum* (JE 1843)." *Zeitschrift der Savigny-Stiftung für Rechtsgeschichte: Kanonistische Abteilung* 100 (2014): 62–111.

– "Wulfstan's Commonplace Book Revised: The Structure and Development of 'Block 7,' on Pastoral Privilege and Responsibility." *Journal of Medieval Latin* 22 (2012): 1–48.

Eshel, Ester. "The *Imago mundi* of the *Genesis Apocryphon*." In *Heavenly Tablets: Interpretation, Identity and Tradition in Ancient Judaism*, edited by Lynn LiDonnici and Andrea Lieber. Leiden: Brill, 2007. 111–31.

Estes, Heide. "Constructing the Old English Solomon and Saturn Dialogues." *English Studies* 95 (2014): 483–99.

– "Wonders and Wisdom: Anglo-Saxons and the East." *English Studies* 91 (2010): 360–73.

– "Abraham and the Northmen in *Genesis A*: Alfredian Translations and Ninth-Century Politics." *Medievalia et Humanistica* n.s. 33 (2007): 1–13.

Ewig, Eugen. "Beobachtungen zur politisch-geographischen Terminologie des fränkischen Grossreiches und der Teilreiche des 9. Jahrhunderts." In *Spiegel der Geschichte: Festgabe für Max Braubach*, edited by Konrad Repgen and Stephan Skalweit. Münster: Aschendorff, 1964. 99–140.

Fanger, Claire. "Miracle as Prophetic Gospel: Knowledge, Power and the Design of the Narrative in *Daniel*." *English Studies* 72 (1991): 123–35.

Farrell, R.T. "The Structure of the Old English Daniel." In *The Poems of MS Junius 11*, edited by R.M. Liuzza. New York: Routledge, 2002. 203–28.

– "The Unity of Old English Daniel." *Review of English Studies* 17 (1967): 117–35.

Feldman, L. "Josephus (CE 37–*c.* 100)." In *The Cambridge History of Judaism. Vol. 3: The Early Roman Period*, edited by William Horbury, W.D. Davies and John Sturdy. Cambridge: Cambridge University Press, 1999. 901–21.
Finnegan, Robert Emmett. "The Old English *Daniel*: The King and His City." *Neuphilologische Mitteilungen* 85 (1984): 194–211.
Flechner, Roy. "The Making of the Canons of Theodore." *Peritia* 17–8 (2003–4): 121–43.
Fleming, Damian Joseph. "'The Most Exalted Language': Anglo-Saxon Perceptions of Hebrew." PhD diss. University of Toronto, 2006.
Fleming, Robin. "Monastic Lands and England's Defence in the Viking Age." *English Historical Review* 395 (1985): 247–65.
Foot, Sarah. *Æthelstan: The First King of England*. New Haven, CT: Yale University Press, 2011.
– "The Making of *Angelcynn*: English Identity before the Norman Conquest." In *Old English Literature: Critical Essays*, edited by R.M. Liuzza. New Haven, CT: Yale University Press, 2002. 51–78.
Fowler, R.G. "'Archbishop Wulfstan's Commonplace-Book' and the *Canons of Edgar*." *Medium Ævum* 32 (1963): 1–10.
Fox, Hilary E. "Denial of God, Mental Disorder, and Exile: The *Rex iniquus* in *Daniel* and *Juliana*." *JEGP* 111 (2012): 425–50.
Fox, Michael. "Vercelli Homilies XIX–XXI, the Ascension Day Homily in Cambridge, Corpus Christi College 162, and the Catechetical Tradition from Augustine to Wulfstan." In *New Readings in the Vercelli Book*, edited by Samantha Zacher and Andy Orchard. Toronto: University of Toronto Press, 2009. 254–79.
– "Alcuin the Exegete: The Evidence of the *Quaestiones in Genesim*." In *The Study of the Bible in the Carolingian Era*, edited by Celia Chazelle and Burton Van Name Edwards. Turnhout: Brepols, 2003. 39–60.
Frank, Roberta. "*F*-Words in *Beowulf*." In *Making Sense: Constructing Meaning in Early English*, edited by Antonette diPaolo Healey and Kevin Kiernan. Toronto: PIMS, 2007. 1–22.
– "Some Uses of Paronomasia in Old English Scriptural Verse." *Speculum* 47 (1972): 207–26.
Frankis, P.J. "The Thematic Significance of *enta geweorc* and Related Imagery in *The Wanderer*." *ASE* 2 (1973): 253–70.
Franklin, Carmela Vircillo. "Theodore and the *Passio S. Anastasii*." In *Archbishop Theodore: Commemorative Studies on his Life and Influence*, edited by Michael Lapidge. CSASE 11. Cambridge: Cambridge University Press, 1995. 175–203.
Franklin, Thomas W. *Genesis and the "Jewish Antiquities" of Flavius Josephus*. Biblica et Orientalia 35. Rome: Biblical Institute Press, 1979.

Franzen, Allen J. *King Alfred*. Boston: G.K Hall, 1986.

Frede, Michael. "Origen's Treatise *Against Celsus*." In *Apologetics in the Roman Empire: Pagans, Jews, and Christians*, edited by Mark Edwards, Martin Goodman and Simon Price. Oxford: Oxford University Press, 1999. 131–55.

– "Celsus" Attack on the Christians.' In *Philosophia Togata II: Plato and Aristotle at Rome*, edited by Jonathan Barnes and Miriam Griffin. Oxford: Clarendon Press, 1997. 218–40.

Friedman, John Block. *The Monstrous Races in Medieval Art and Thought*. Cambridge, MA: Harvard University Press, 1981.

Frye, Northrup. *Words with Power*. Markham, ON: Viking, 1990.

Fulk, R.D. *A History of Old English Meter*. Philadelphia: University of Pennsylvania Press, 1992.

Fulk, R.D. and Christopher M. Cain. *A History of Old English Literature*. Malden, MA: Blackwell, 2003.

Fyler, John M. *Language and the Declining World in Chaucer, Dante, and Jean de Meun*. Cambridge: Cambridge University Press, 2007.

Gameson, Richard, "Alfred the Great and the Destruction and Production of Christian Books." *Scriptorium* 49 (1995): 180–210.

Gardner, John. *The Construction of Christian Poetry in Old English*. Carbondale, IL: Southern Illinois University Press, 1974.

Garrison, Mary. "Alcuin of York." In *The Wiley-Blackwell Encyclopaedia of Anglo-Saxon England*. 2nd ed., edited by Michael Lapidge et al. Chichester: Wiley-Blackwell, 2014. 26–7.

Gatch, Milton McC. "The Office in Late Anglo-Saxon Monasticism." In *Learning and Literature in Anglo-Saxon England: Studies Presented to Peter Clemoes on the Occasion of his Sixty-Fifth Birthday*, edited by Michael Lapidge and Helmut Gneuss. Cambridge: Cambridge University Press, 1985. 341–62.

– "Noah's Raven in *Genesis A* and the Illustrated Old English Hexateuch." *Gesta* 14 (1975): 3–15.

Geary, Patrick J. *The Myth of Nations: The Medieval Origins of Europe*. Princeton: Princeton University Press, 2002.

– "Ethnic Identity as a Situational Construct in the Early Middle Ages." *Mitteilungen der anthropologischen Geselleschaft in Wein* 113 (1983): 15–23.

Gero, Stephen. "The Legend of the Fourth Son of Noah." *Harvard Theological Review* 73 (1980): 321–30.

Gesenius, Wilhelm. *Gesenius' Hebrew Grammar, as Edited and Enlarged by the Late E. Kautzsch*. 2nd English ed. Translated by A.E. Cowley. Oxford: Clarendon Press, 1910.

Getz, Robert. "The Old English Daniel, Line 499b." *Notes and Queries* 59.3 (2012): 305–6.

Gilbert, Gary. "The List of Nations in Acts 2: Roman Propaganda and the Lukan Response." *Journal of Biblical Literature* 121 (2002): 497–529.

Gittos, Helen. "The Audience for Old English Texts: Ælfric, Rhetoric and 'the Edification of the Simple.'" *ASE* 43 (2014): 231–66.

Glare, P.G.W. et al., eds. *Oxford Latin Dictionary*. 2nd ed. 2 vols. Oxford: Oxford University Press, 2012.

Gneuss, Helmut. *Ælfric of Eynsham: His Life, Times, and Writings*. Translated by Michael Lapidge. Old English Newsletter Subsida 34. Kalamazoo, MI: Medieval Institue Publications, 2009.

– "Anglo-Saxon Libraries from the Conversion to the Benedictine Reform." In *Books and Libraries in Early England*. Aldershot: Variorum, 1996. Ch. 2. 645–88.

– "King Alfred and the History of Anglo-Saxon Libraries." In *Books and Libraries in Early England*. Aldershot: Variorum, 1996. Ch. 3. 29–49.

– "Die Benediktinerregal in England und ihre altenglische Übersetzung." In *Language and History in Early England*. Aldershot: Variorum, 1996. Ch. 8. 263–84.

– "Latin Hymns in Medieval England: Future Research." In *Books and Libraries in Early England*. Aldershot: Variorum, 1996. Ch. 11. 407–24.

– *Hymnar und Hymnen in englischen Mittelalter*. Tübingen: Max Niermeyer, 1968.

Gneuss, Helmut, and Michael Lapidge. *Anglo-Saxon Manuscripts: A Bibliographical Handlist of Manuscripts and Manuscript Fragments Written or Owned in England up to 1100*. Toronto: University of Toronto Press, 2014.

Godden, Malcolm. "The Old English Orosius and its Sources." *Anglia* 129 (2011): 297–320.

– "Did King Alfred Write Anything?" *Medium Ævum* 76 (2007): 1–23.

– "The Relations of Wulfstan and Ælfric: A Reassessment." In *Wulfstan, Archbishop of York: The Proceedings of the Second Alcuin Conference*, edited by Matthew Townend. Turnhout: Brepols, 2004. 353–74.

– *Ælfric's Catholic Homilies: Introduction, Commentary and Glossary*. EETS s.s. 18. Oxford: Oxford University Press, 2000.

– "Apocalypse and Invasion in Late Anglo-Saxon England." In *From Anglo-Saxon to Early Middle English: Studies Presented to E.G. Stanley*, edited by Malcolm Godden, Douglas Gray and Terry Hoad. Oxford: Clarendon Press, 1994. 130–62.

Goetz, Hans-Erner. "*Gens*: Terminology and Perception of the 'Germanic' Peoples from Late Antiquity to the Early Middle Ages." In *The Construction of Communities in the Early Middle Ages: Texts, Resources and Artefacts*, edited by Richard Corradini, Max Diesenberger and Helmut Reimitz. Leiden: Brill, 2003. 39–63.

Goffart, Walter. "Bede's *uera lex historiae* Explained." *ASE* 34 (2005): 111–16.
– "The *Historia Ecclesiastica*: Bede's Agenda and Ours." *Haskins Society Journal* 2 (1990): 29–45.
– "Foreigners in the *Historiae* of Gregory of Tours." *Rome's Fall and After.* London: Hambledon Press, 1989. 275–91.
– "From *Historiae* to *Historia Francorum* and Back Again: Aspects of the Textual History of Gregory of Tours." *Rome's Fall and After.* London: Hambledon Press, 1989. 255–74.
– "The Supposedly 'Frankish' Table of Nations: An Edition and Study." *Rome's Fall and After.* London: Hambledon Press, 1989. 133–65.
– *The Narrators of Barbarian History (A.D. 550–800): Jordanes, Gregory of Tours, Bede, and Paul the Deacon.* Princeton, NJ: Princeton University Press, 1988; rpt. 2009.
Goldenberg, David M. *The Curse of Ham: Race and Slavery in Early Judaism, Christianity, and Islam.* Princeton: Princeton University Press, 2003.
– "Scythian-Barbarian: The Permutations of a Classical Topos in Jewish and Christian Texts of Late Antiquity." *Journal of Jewish Studies* 49 (1998): 87–102.
Gorman, Michael. "The Canon of Bede's Works and the World of Ps. Bede." *Revue Bénédictine* 11 (2001): 399–445.
Goukowsky, Paul. *Essai sur les origines du mythe d'Alexandre (336–270 av. J.-C.).* Vol. 1: *Les origines politique.* Nancy: Université de Nancy II, 1978.
Gransden, Antonia. "Traditionalism and Continuity during the Last Century of Anglo-Saxon Monasticism." *Journal of Ecclesiastical History* 40 (1989): 159–207.
Greenfield, Stanley B., and Daniel G. Calder. *A New Critical History of Old English Literature.* New York: New York University Press, 1986.
Gretsch, Mechthild. *Ælfric and the Cult of Saints in Late Anglo-Saxon England.* CSASE 34. Cambridge: Cambridge University Press, 2005.
– *The Intellectual Foundations of the English Benedictine Reform.* CSASE 25. Cambridge: Cambridge University Press, 1999.
– "Der liturgische Wortschatz in Æthelwold's Übersetzung der Benediktinerregal und sprachliche Normierung in spätaltenglischer Zeit." *Anglia* 111 (1993): 310–54.
– "The Benedictine Rule in Old English: A Document of Bishop Æthelwold's Reform Politics." In *Words, Texts and Manuscripts: Studies in Anglo-Saxon Culture Presented to Helmut Gneuss*, edited by Michael Korhammer. Cambridge: D.S. Brewer, 1992. 131–58.
– "Æthelwold's Translation of the *Regula Sancti Benedicti* and its Latin Exemplar." *ASE* 3 (1974): 125–51.
– *Die Regula Sancti Benedicti in England und ihre altenglische Übersetzung.* Munich: Wilhelm Fink, 1973.

Grinda, Klaus. "The Myth of Circe in King Alfred's *Boethius.*" Translated by Paul Battles. In *Old English Prose: Basic Readings*, edited by Paul E. Szarmach. New York: Garland Publishing, 2000. 237–65.

Grocock, Christopher, "Bede and the Golden Age of Latin Prose in Northumbria." In *Northumbria's Golden Age*, edited by Jane Hawkes and Susan Mills. Stroud: Sutton, 1999. 371–81.

Grosjean, Paul. "Confusa Caligo, Remarques sur les Hisperica Famina." *Celtica* 3 (1956): 35–85.

Hall, Alaric. "Interlinguistic Communication in Bede's *Historia Ecclesiastica Gentis Anglorum.*" In *Interfaces between Language and Culture in Medieval England: A Festschrift for Matti Kilpiö*, edited by Alaric Hall, Olga Timofeeva, Ágnes Kiricsi, and Bethany Fox. Leiden: Brill, 2010. 37–80.

Hall, J.R. "'The Old English Epic of Redemption': Twenty-Five-Year Retrospective." In *The Poems of MS Junius 11*, edited by R.M. Liuzza. New York: Routledge, 2002. 53–68.

– "The Old English Epic of Redemption: The Theological Unity of MS Junius 11." In *The Poems of MS Junius 11*, edited by R.M. Liuzza. New York: Routledge, 2002. 20–52.

– "On the Bibliographic Unity of Bodleian MS Junius 11." *American Notes and Queries* 24 (1986): 104–7.

Hall, Thomas N. "Biblical and Patristic Learning." In *A Companion to Anglo-Saxon Literature*, edited by Philip Pulsiano and Elaine Treharne. Oxford: Blackwell, 2011. 327–44.

Hanning, Robert W. *The Vision of History in Early Britain From Gildas to Geoffrey of Monmouth*. New York: Columbia University Press, 1966.

Harbus, Antonia. "Nebuchadnezzar's Dreams in the Old English *Daniel.*" In *The Poems of MS Junius 11*, edited by R.M. Liuzza. New York: Routledge, 2002. 261–86.

Harnack, Adolf. *The Expansion of Christianity in the First Three Centuries*. Vol. 1. Translated by James Moffatt. London: Williams & Norgate, 1904.

Harris, Stephen J. *Race and Ethnicity in Anglo-Saxon Literature*. New York: Routledge, 2003.

– "Bede and Gregory's Allusive Angles." *Criticism* 44 (2002): 271–89.

– "The Alfredian World History and Anglo-Saxon Identity." *JEGP* 100 (2001): 482–510.

Hartley, J.E. "North." In *The International Standard Bible Encyclopedia*, edited by Geoffrey W. Bromiley et al. Vol. 3: K–P. Grand Rapids, MI: William B. Eerdmans, 1986. 550–1.

Hartman, Megan E. "The Limits of Conservative Composition in Old English Poetry." In *The Dating of Beowulf: A Reassessment*, edited by Leornard Neidorf. Cambridge: D.S. Brewer, 2014. 79–96.

Hauser, Alan J., and Duane F. Watson. "Introduction and Overview." In *A History of Biblical Interpretation*. Vol. 1: *The Ancient Period*. Grand Rapids, MI: Eerdmans, 2004. 1–54.

Hay, Denys. *Europe: The Emergence of an Idea*. Rev. ed. Edinburgh: Edinburgh University Press, 1968.

Haynes, Stephen R. *Noah's Curse: The Biblical Justification of American Slavery*. Oxford: Oxford University Press, 2002.

Heuchan, Valerie. "All Things to All Men: Representations of the Apostle Paul in Anglo-Saxon Literature." PhD diss. University of Toronto, 2010.

Hieatt, Constance B. "Divisions: Theme and Structure in *Genesis A*." *Neuphilologische Mitteilungen* 81 (1980): 243–51.

Higham, N.J. and D.H. Hill, eds. *Edward the Elder, 899–924*. London: Routledge, 2001.

Hill, Joyce. "Ælfric: His Life and Work." In *A Companion to Ælfric*, edited by Hugh Magennis and Mary Swan. Leiden: Brill, 2009. 35–65.

– "Archbishop Wulfstan: Reformer?" In *Wulfstan, Archbishop of York: The Proceedings of the Second Alcuin Conference*, edited by Matthew Townend. Turnhout: Brepols, 2004. 309–24.

– "The Benedictine Reform and Beyond." In *A Companion to Anglo-Saxon Literature*, edited by Phillip Pulsiano and Elaine Treharne. Oxford: Blackwell, 2001. 151–69.

– *Bede and the Benedictine Reform*. Jarrow Lecture, 1998.

– "Monastic Reform and the Secular Church: Ælfric's Pastoral Letters in Context." In *England in the Eleventh Century: Proceedings of the 1990 Harlaxton Symposium*, edited by Carola Hicks. Stamford: Paul Watkins, 1992. 103–17.

Hill, Paul. *The Age of Athelstan: Britain's Forgotten History*. Stroud: Tempus, 2004.

Hill, Thomas D. "The Myth of the Ark-Born Son and the West-Saxon Royal Genealogical Tables." *Harvard Theological Review* 80 (1987): 379–83.

Hillier, Richard. *Arator on the Acts of the Apostles: A Baptismal Commentary*. Oxford: Clarendon Press, 1993.

Horowitz, Wayne. *Mesopotamian Cosmic Geography*. Winona Lake, IN: Eisenbrauns, 1998.

Houghton, John William. "(Re)Sounding Brass: Alcuin's New Castings in the Questions and Answers on Genesis." *Proceedings of the PMR Conference* 16–7 (1994): 149–61.

Howe, Nicholas. "From Bede's World to 'Bede's World.'" In *Writing the Map of Anglo-Saxon England: Essays in Cultural Geography*. New Haven, CT: Yale University Press, 2008. 125–48.

– "Rome as Capital of Anglo-Saxon England." *Writing the Map of Anglo-Saxon England: Essays in Cultural Geography*. New Haven, CT: Yale University Press, 2008. 101–24.

– "An Angle on this Earth: Sense of Place in Anglo-Saxon England." *Bulletin of the John Rylands University Library of Manchester* 82 (2000): 3–27.
– *Migration and Mythmaking in Anglo-Saxon England.* New Haven, CT: Yale University Press, 1989.
– "Aldhelm's Engimata and Isidorian Etymology." *ASE* 14 (1985): 37–59.
Howlett, D.R., R.E. Latham, et al., eds. *Dictionary of Medieval Latin from British Sources.* London: Oxford University Press, 1975–2013.
Hume, Kathryn. "The Concept of the Hall in Old English Poetry." *ASE* 3 (1974): 63–74.
Huppé, Bernard F. *Doctrine and Poetry: Augustine's Influence on Old English Poetry.* New York: State University of New York, 1959.
Hurt, James. *Ælfric.* New York: Twayne Publishers, 1972.
Innes, Matthew. "Teutons or Trojans? The Carolingians and the Germanic Past." In *The Uses of the Past in the Early Middle Ages*, edited by Yitzhak Hen and Matthew Innes. Cambridge: Cambridge University Press, 2000. 227–49.
Inowlocki, Sabrina. "Josephus' Rewriting of the Babel Narrative (Gen 11:1–9)." *Journal for the Study of Judaism* 37 (2006): 169–91.
Irvine, Susan. "Hanging by a Thread: Ælfric's Saints' Lives and the *Hengen.*" In *Hagiography in Anglo-Saxon England: Adopting and Adapting Saints' Lives into Old English Prose (c. 950–1150)*, edited by Loredana Lazzari, Patrizia Lendinara and Claudia Di Sciacca. Barcelona: Fédération Internationale des Instituts d'Études Médiévales, 2014. 67–94.
– "Wrestling with Hercules: King Alfred and the Classical Past." In *Court Culture in the Early Middle Ages: The Proceedings of the First Alcuin Conference*, edited by Catherine Cubitt. Turnhout: Brepols, 2003. 171–87.
– "Ulysses and Circe in King Alfred's *Boethius*: A Classical Myth Transformed." In *Studies in English Language and Literature: "Doubt Wisely" Papers in Honour of E.G. Stanley*, edited by M.J. Toswell and E.M. Tyler. London: Routledge, 1996. 387–401.
Isaac, Benjamin, Joseph Ziegler, and Miriam Eliav-Feldon. "Introduction." In *The Origins of Racism in the West*, edited by Miriam Eliav-Feldon, Benjamin Isaac and Joseph Ziegler. Cambridge: Cambridge University Press, 2009. 1–31.
Isaacs, Neil D. *Structural Principles in Old English Poetry.* Knoxville, TN: University of Tennessee Press, 1968.
Jeffrey, David Lyle. *A Dictionary of Biblical Tradition in English Literature.* Grand Rapids, MI: Eerdmans, 1992.
John, Eric. *Orbis Britanniae and Other Studies.* Leicester: Leicester University Press, 1966.
Johnson, Aaron P. *Ethnicity and Argument in Eusebius'* Praeparatio evangelica. Oxford: Oxford University Press, 2006.

Johnson, Lesley. "Imagining Communities: Medieval and Modern." In *Concepts of National Identity in the Middle Ages*, edited by Simon Forde, Lesley Johnson, and Alan V. Murray. Leeds: University of Leeds, 1995. 1–19.

Jones, Charles W. "Some Introductory Remarks on Bede's Commentary on Genesis." *Sacris Erudiri* 19 (1967–70): 115–98.

Jones, Christopher A. "Ælfric and the Limits of 'Benedictine Reform.'" In *A Companion to Ælfric*, edited by Hugh Magennis and Mary Swan. Leiden: Brill, 2009. 67–108.

– "Wulfstan's Liturgical Interests." In *Wulfstan, Archbishop of York: The Proceedings of the Second Alcuin Conference*, edited by Matthew Townend. Turnhout: Brepols, 2004. 325–52.

– "*Meatim Sed et Rustica*: Ælfric of Eynsham as a Medieval Latin Author." *Journal of Medieval Latin* 8 (1998): 1–57.

Jost, D.A. "Biblical Source of Old English Daniel 1–78." *English Language Notes* 15 (1978): 257–62.

Jost, Karl. *Wulfstanstudien*. Schweizer anglistische Arbeiten 23. Bern: Francke, 1950.

Jullien, Marie-Hélène and Françoise Perelman. *Clavis des auteurs Latins du moyen âge, territoire français, 735–987*. Vol. 2: *Alcuin*. Turnhout: Brepols, 1999.

Karkov, Catherine E. *The Ruler Portraits of Anglo-Saxon England*. Woodbridge: Boydell Press, 2004.

– *Text and Picture in Anglo-Saxon England: Narrative Strategies in the Junius 11 Manuscript*. CSASE 31. Cambridge: Cambridge University Press, 2001.

Keenan, Hugh T. "*The Ruin* as Babylon." *Tennessee Studies in Literature* 11 (1966): 109–17.

Ker, N.R. *Catalogue of Manuscripts containing Anglo-Saxon*. Oxford: Clarendon Press, 1957; rpt. 1990.

– "The Handwriting of Archbishop Wulfstan." In *Books, Collectors and Libraries: Studies in the Medieval Heritage*, edited by Andrew G. Watson. London: Hambledon Press, 1985. 9–27.

Kerlouegan, François. *Le De excidio Britanniae de Gildas: Les destinées de la culture latine dans l'ile de Bretagne au VIe siècle*. Paris: Publications de la Sorbonne, 1987.

Keynes, Simon. "An Abbot, an Archbishop, and the Viking Raids of 1006–7 and 1009–12." *ASE* 36 (2007): 151–220.

– "Between Bede and the *Chronicle*: London, BL, Cotton Vespasian B.vi, fols. 104–9." In *Latin Learning and English Lore: Studies in Anglo-Saxon Literature for Michael Lapidge*. 2 vols. edited by Katherine O'Brien O'Keeffe and Andy Orchard. Toronto: University of Toronto Press, 2005. Vol. 1. 47–67.

– "England, 900–1016." In *The New Cambridge Medieval History*, vol. 3: *c. 900–c.1024*, edited by Timothy Reuter. Cambridge: Cambridge University Press, 2000. 456–84.
– "King Athelstan's Books." In *Learning and Literature in Anglo-Saxon England: Studies Presented to Peter Clemoes on the Occasion of his Sixty-Fifth Birthday*, edited by Michael Lapidge and Helmut Gneuss. Cambridge: Cambridge University Press, 1985. 143–201.
Keynes, Simon, and Michael Lapidge. *Alfred the Great: Asser's* Life of Alfred *and Other Contemporary Sources*. London: Penguin, 1983; rpt 2004.
Khalaf, Omar. "A Study on the Translator's Omissions and Instances of Adaptation in the *Old English Orosius*: The Case of Alexander the Great." *Filologia Germanica* 5 (2013): 195–222.
Kintgen, Eugune R. "Echoic Repetition in Old English Poetry, especially *The Dream of the Rood*." *Neuphilologische Mitteilungen* 75 (1974): 202–23.
Kleist, Aaron. "An Annotated Bibliography of Ælfrician Studies: 1983–1996." In *Old English Prose: Basic Readings*, edited by Paul E. Szarmach. New York: Garland Publishing, 2000. 503–52.
Kornexl, Lucia. "The *Regularis Concordia* and its Old English Gloss." *ASE* 24 (1995): 95–130.
– *Die "Regularis concordia" und ihre altenglische Interlinearversion*. Munich: Fink, 1993.
Ladner, Gerhart B. "On Roman Attitudes towards Barbarians in Late Antiquity." *Viator* 7 (1976): 1–26.
Laistner, M.L.W. *Thought and Letters in Western Europe, A.D. 500 to 900*. Ithaca, NY: Cornell University Press, 1931.
– "Notes on Greek from the Lectures of a Ninth Century Monastery Teacher." *Bulletin of the John Rylands Library* 7 (1923): 421–56.
Lapidge, Michael. "The Career of Aldhelm." *ASE* 36 (2007): 15–69.
– "Versifying the Bible in the Middle Ages." In *The Text in the Community: Essays on Medieval Works, Manuscripts, Authors, and Readers*, edited by Jill Mann and Maura Nolan. Notre Dame, IN: University of Notre Dame Press, 2006. 11–40.
– *The Anglo-Saxon Library*. Oxford: Oxford University Press, 2006.
– *The Cult of Swithun*. Winchester Studies 4.ii: The Anglo-Saxon Minsters of Winchester. Oxford: Clarendon Press, 2003.
– "The Career of Archbishop Theodore." *Anglo-Latin Literature, 600–899*. London: Hambledon Press, 1996. 93–121.
– "The Study of Greek at the School of Canterbury." *Anglo-Latin Literature, 600–899*. London: Hambledon Press, 1996. 123–39.
– "The School of Theodore and Hadrian." *Anglo-Latin Literature, 600–899*. London: Hambledon Press, 1996. 141–68.

– "Theodore and Anglo-Latin Octosyllabic Verse." *Anglo-Latin Literature, 600–899*. London: Hambledon Press, 1996. 225–45.
– "Byrhtferth of Ramsey and the Early Sections of the *Historia Regum* attributed to Symeon of Durham." *Anglo-Latin Literature, 600–899*. London: Hambledon Press, 1996. 317–42.
– "Bede's Metrical *Vita S. Cuthberti*." *Anglo-Latin Literature, 600–899*. London: Hambledon Press, 1996. 339–55.
– "Latin Learning in Ninth-Century England." *Anglo-Latin Literature, 600–899*. London: Hambledon Press, 1996. 409–54.
– ed. *Archbishop Theodore: Commemorative Studies on his Life and Influence*. CSASE 11. Cambridge: Cambridge University Press, 1995.
– "Schools, Learning and Literature in Tenth-Century England." *Anglo-Latin Literature 900–1066*. London: Hambledon Press, 1993. 1–48.
– "Some Latin Poems as Evidence for the Reign of Athelstan." *Anglo-Latin Literature 900–1066*. London: Hambledon Press, 1993. 49–86.
– "Israel the Grammarian in Anglo-Saxon England." *Anglo-Latin Literature 900–1066*. London: Hambledon Press, 1993. 87–104.
– "The Hermeneutic Style in Tenth-Century Anglo-Latin Literature." *Anglo-Latin Literature 900–1066*. London: Hambledon Press, 1993. 105–49.
Lapidge, Michael et al., eds. *The Wiley-Blackwell Encyclopaedia of Anglo-Saxon England*. 2nd ed. Chichester: Wiley-Blackwell, 2014.
Law, Viven. *Wisdom, Authority and Grammar in the Seventh Century: Decoding Virgilius Maro Grammaticus*. Cambridge: Cambridge University Press, 1995.
Leclercq, Jean. *The Love of Learning and the Desire for God: A Study of Monastic Culture*. 3rd ed. Translated by Catharine Misrahi. New York: Fordham University Press, 1982.
Lee, Alvin A. *The Guest-Hall of Eden: Four Essays on the Design of Old English Poetry*. New Haven, CT: Yale University Press, 1972.
Lee, Anne Thompson. "*The Ruin*: Bath or Babylon?" *Neuphilologische Mitteilungen* 74 (1973): 443–55.
Lees, Clare A. *Tradition and Belief: Religious Writing in Late Anglo-Saxon England*. Minneapolis, MN: University of Minnesota Press, 1999.
– "The Dissemination of Alcuin's *De virtutibus et vitiis liber* in Old English: A Preliminary Study." *Leeds Studies in English* ns 16 (1985): 174–89.
Lendinara, Patrizia. "Forgetten Missionaries: St Augustine of Canterbury in Anglo-Saxon and Post-Conquest England." In *Hagiography in Anglo-Saxon England: Adopting and Adapting Saints' Lives into Old English Prose (c. 950–1150)*, edited by Loredana Lazzari, Patrizia Lendinara, and Claudia Di Sciacca. Barcelona: Fédération Internationale des Instituts d'Études Médiévales, 2014. 365–497.
Leneghan, Francis. "*Translatio Imperii*: The Old English *Orosius* and the Rise of Wessex." *Anglia* 133 (2015): 656–705.

Levison, Wilhelm. *England and the Continent in the Eighth Century*. Oxford: Clarendon Press, 1946.

Lewis, Charlton T. and Charles Short, eds. *A Latin Dictionary*. Oxford: Clarendon Press, 1879; rpt. 2002.

Lionarons, Joyce Tally. *The Homiletic Writings of Archbishop Wulfstan*. Woodbridge: D.S. Brewer, 2010.

Liuzza, R.M. "The Tower of Babel: *The Wanderer* and the Ruins of History." *Studies in the Literary Imagination* 36 (2003): 1–35.

Livesey, Steven J., and Richard H. Rouse. "Nimrod the Astronomer." *Traditio* 37 (1981): 203–66.

Lockett, Leslie. "An Integrated Re-examination of the Dating of Oxford, Bodleian Library, Junius 11." *ASE* 31 (2002): 141–73.

Loomis, Laura Hibbard. "The Holy Relics of Charlemagne and King Athelstan: The Lances of Longinus and St Mauricius." *Speculum* 25 (1950): 437–56.

Love, Rosalind. "The Library of the Venerable Bede." In *The Cambridge History of the Book in Britain*. Vol. 1: *c. 400–1100*, edited by Richard Gameson. Cambridge: Cambridge University Press, 2012. 606–32.

Lucas, Peter J. "On the Incomplete Ending of *Daniel* and the Addition of *Christ and Satan* to MS Junius 11." *Anglia* 97 (1979): 46–59.

Lynch, Kevin M. "The Venerable Bede's Knowledge of Greek." *Traditio* 39 (1983): 432–9.

Magennis, Hugh. "Ælfric Scholarship." In *A Companion to Ælfric*, edited by Hugh Magennis and Mary Swan. Leiden: Brill, 2009. 5–34.

– "Ælfric and Heroic Literature." In *The Power of Words: Anglo-Saxon Studies to Donald G. Scragg on His Seventieth Birthday*, edited by Jonathan Wilcox and Hugh Magennis. Morgantown, WV: West Virginia University Press, 2006. 31–60.

– *Images of Community in Old English Poetry*. CSASE 18. Cambridge: Cambridge University Press, 1996.

Major, Tristan. "The Number Seventy-Two: Biblical and Hellenistic Beginnings to the Early Middle Ages." *Sacris Erudiri* 52 (2013): 7–45.

– "Saturn's First Riddle in *Solomon and Saturn II*: An Orientalist Conflation." *Neophilologus* 96 (2012): 301–13.

– "Words, Wit, and Wordplay in the Latin Works of the Venerable Bede." *Journal of Medieval Latin* 22 (2012): 185–216.

– "Rebuilding the Tower of Babel: Ælfric and Bible Translation." *Florilegium* 23 (2006): 47–60.

Manitius, Max. *Geschichte der lateinischen Literatur des Mittelalters*. 3 vols. Munich: C.H. Beck, 1911–31.

Marsden, Richard. "Ælfric as Translator: The Old English Prose *Genesis*." *Anglia* 109 (1991): 319–58.

Martin, Lawrence T. "Bede as a Linguistic Scholar." *American Benedictine Review* 35 (1984): 204–17.
– "The Influence of Arator in Anglo-Saxon England." *Proceedings of the PMR Conference* 7 (1982): 75–81.
McBrine, Patrick. "The Journey Motif in the Poems of the Vercelli Book." In *New Readings in the Vercelli Book*, edited by Samantha Zacher and Andy Orchard. Toronto: University of Toronto Press, 2009. 289–317.
McCready, William D. "Bede and the Isidorian Legacy." *Mediaeval Studies* 57 (1995): 41–73.
– "Bede, Isidore, and the *Epistola Cuthberti*." *Traditio* 50 (1995): 75–94.
McDonald, Lee M., and James A. Sanders, eds. *The Canon Debate*. Peabody, MA: Hendrickson, 2002.
McNally, Robert E. "The 'Tres Linguae Sacrae' in Early Irish Bible Exegesis." *Theological Studies* 19 (1958): 395–403.
Meaney, Audrey L. "'And we forbeodað eornostlice ælcne hæðenscipe': Wulfstan and Late Anglo-Saxon and Norse 'Heathenism.'" In *Wulfstan, Archbishop of York: The Proceedings of the Second Alcuin Conference*, edited by Matthew Townend. Turnhout: Brepols, 2004. 461–500.
Mehan, Uppinder, and David Townsend. "'Nation' and the Gaze of the Other in Eight-Century Northumbria." *Comparative Literature* 53 (2001): 1–26.
Mellinkoff, Ruth. "Cain's Monstrous Progeny in *Beowulf*: Part II, Post-Diluvian Survival." *ASE* 9 (1980): 83–97.
– "Cain's Monstrous Progeny in *Beowulf*: Part I, Noachic Tradition." *ASE* 8 (1979): 143–62.
Menner, Robert J. "Nimrod and the Wolf in the Old English *Solomon and Saturn*." *JEGP* 37 (1938): 332–54.
Merrills, A.H. *History and Geography in Late Antiquity*. Cambridge: Cambridge University Press, 2005.
Metzger, Bruce M. *The Canon of the New Testament: Its Origin, Development, and Significance*. Oxford: Clarendon Press, 1987.
– "Ancient Astrological Geography and Acts 2:9–11." In *Apostolic History and the Gospel: Biblical and Historical Essays Presented to F.F. Bruce*, edited by W. Ward Gasque and Ralph P. Martin. Exeter: Paternoster Press, 1970. 123–33.
– "Seventy or Seventy-Two Disciples?" *Historical and Literary Studies: Pagan, Jewish, and Christian*. Grand Rapids, MI: Eerdmans, 1968. 67–76.
Meyvaert, Paul. "Le libellus responsionum à Augustin de Cantorbéry: une oeuvre authentique de saint Grégoire le Grand." In *Grégoire le Grand*, edited by Jacques Fontaine et al. Paris: Éditions du Centre National de la Recherche Scientifique, 1986. 543–50.

– "Bede the Scholar." In *Famulus Christi: Essays in Commemoration of the Thirteenth Centenary of the Birth of the Venerable Bede*, edited by Gerald Bonner. London: SPCK, 1976. 40–69.
– "Bede's Text of the *Libellus Responsionum* of Gregory the Great to Augustine of Canterbury." In *England before the Conquest: Studies in Primary Sources Presented to Dorothy Whitelock*, edited by Peter Clemoes and Kathleen Hughes. Cambridge: Cambridge University Press, 1971. 15–33.
– "Diversity Within Unity: A Gregorian Theme." *The Heythrop Journal* 4 (1963): 141–62.
Michelet, Fabienne L. *Creation, Migration, and Conquest: Imaginary Geography and Sense of Space in Old English Literature*. Oxford: Oxford University Press, 2006.
Mikkeli, Heikki. *Europe as an Idea and an Identity*. Basingstoke: MacMillan Press, 1998.
Mohrmann, Christine. "The Ever-Recurring Problem of Language in the Church." *Études sur le latin des chrétiens*. Vol. 4. Rome: Storia e Letteratura, 1977. 143–59.
– "Linguistische Probleme bei den Kirchenvätern." *Études sur le latin des chrétiens*. Vol. 4. Rome: Storia e Letteratura, 1977. 175–92.
– "'Tertium genus' les relations judaïsme, antiquité, christianisme reflétées dans la langue des Chrétiens." *Études sur le latin des chrétiens*. Vol. 4. Rome: Storia e Letteratura, 1977. 195–210.
– "Linguistic Problems in the Early Christian Church." *Études sur le latin des chrétiens*. Vol. 3. Rome: Edizioni di Storia e Letteratura, 1965. 171–96.
Molyneaux, George. *The Formation of the English Kingdom in the Tenth Century*. Oxford: Oxford University Press, 2015.
Murdoch, Brian. *The Medieval Popular Bible: Expansions of Genesis in the Middle Ages*. Cambridge: D.S. Brewer, 2003.
Neidorf, Leonard. "Cain, Cam, Jutes, Giants, and the Textual Criticism of *Beowulf*." *Studies in Philology* 112 (2015): 599–632.
Neiman, David. "Ethiopia and Kush: Biblical and Ancient Greek Geography." *The Ancient World* 3 (1980): 34–42.
Nightingale, John. "Oswald, Fleury and Continental Reform." In *St Oswald of Worcester: Life and Influence*, edited by Nicholas Brooks and Catherine Cubitt. London: Leicester University Press, 1996. 23–45.
O'Brien, Bruce R. *Reversing Babel: Translation among the English during an Age of Conquests, c. 800 to c. 1200*. Newark, DE: University of Delaware Press, 2011.
O'Brien O'Keeffe, Katherine. "The Geographic List of *Solomon and Saturn II*." *ASE* 20 (1991): 123–41.

– "The Use of Bede's Writings on Genesis in Alcuin's *Interrogationes*." *Sacris Erudiri* 23 (1978): 463–83.
– "The Book of Genesis in Anglo-Saxon England." PhD diss. University of Pennsylvania, 1975.
O'Leary, Aideen M. "Apostolic *Passiones* in Early Anglo-Saxon England." In *Apocryphal Texts and Traditions in Anglo-Saxon England*, edited by Kathryn Powell and Donald Scragg. Cambridge: D.S. Brewer, 2003. 103–19.
O'Neill, Patrick P. "On the Date, Provenance and Relationship of the 'Solomon and Saturn' Dialogues." *ASE* 26 (1997): 139–68.
O'Reilly, Jennifer. "Islands and Idols at the Ends of the Earth: Exegesis and Conversion in Bede's *Historia ecclesiastica*." In *Bède le vénérable entre tradition et postérité / The Venerable Bede: Tradition and Posterity*, edited by Stéphane Lebecq, Michel Perrin, and Olivier Szerwiniack. Lille: Ceges—Université Charles-de-Gaulle—Lille 3, 2005. 119–45.
Okamura, Jonathan Y. "Situational Ethnicity." *Ethnic and Racial Studies* 4.4 (1981): 452–65.
Olsen, Karin. "'Him þæs grim lean becom': The Theme of Infertility in *Genesis A*." In *Verbal Encounters: Anglo-Saxon and Old Norse Studies for Roberta Frank*, edited by Antonina Harbus and Russell Poole. Toronto: University of Toronto Press, 2005. 127–43.
Orchard, Andy. "Wulfstan's Library." In *The Cambridge History of the Book in Britain*. Vol. 1: *c. 400–1100*, edited by Richard Gameson. Cambridge: Cambridge University Press, 2012. 694–700.
– "Intoxication, Fornication, and Multiplication: The Burgeoning Text of Genesis A." In *Text, Image, Interpretation: Studies in Anglo-Saxon Literature and its Insular Context in Honour of Éamonn Ó Carragáin*, edited by Alastair Minnis and Jane Roberts. Turnhout: Brepols, 2007. 333–54.
– "Re-editing Wulfstan: Where's the Point?" In *Wulfstan, Archbishop of York: The Proceedings of the Second Alcuin Conference*, edited by Matthew Townend. Turnhout: Brepols, 2004. 63–91.
– *A Critical Companion to Beowulf*. Cambridge: D.S. Brewer, 2003; rpt. 2004.
– "Latin and the Vernacular Languages: The Creation of a Bilingual Textual Culture." In *After Rome*, edited by Thomas Charles-Edwards. Oxford: Oxford University Press, 2003. 191–219.
– "On Editing Wulfstan." In *Early Medieval Texts and Interpretations: Studies Presented to Donald G. Scragg*, edited by Elaine Treharne and Susan Rosser. Tempe, AZ: Arizona Center for Medieval and Renaissance Studies, 2003. 311–40.
– *Pride and Prodigies: Studies in the Monsters of the* Beowulf-*Manuscript*. Toronto: University of Toronto Press, 2003.

– "Conspicuous Heroism: Abraham, Prudentius, and the Old English Verse *Genesis*." In *The Poems of MS Junius 11*, edited by R.M. Liuzza. New York: Routledge, 2002. 119–36.
– "Old Sources, New Resources: Finding the Right Formula for Boniface." *ASE* 30 (2001): 15–38.
– "Wulfstan, the Homilist." In *The Wiley-Blackwell Encyclopaedia of Anglo-Saxon England*, 2nd ed., edited by Michael Lapidge et al. Chichester: Wiley-Blackwell, 2014. 514–15.
– *Dictionary of Norse Myth and Legend*. London: Cassell, 1997.
– *The Poetic Art of Aldhelm*. CSASE 8. Cambridge: Cambridge University Press, 1994.
– "Crying Wolf: Oral Style and the *Sermones Lupi*." *ASE* 21 (1992): 239–64.
Oswald, Dana M. *Monsters, Gender and Sexuality in Medieval English Literature*. Woodbridge: D.S. Brewer, 2010.
Otten, Kurt. *König Alfreds Boethius*. Tübingen: Niemeyer, 1964.
Overing, Gillian R. "Nebuchadenzzar's Conversion in the Old English *Daniel*: A Psychological Portrait." *Papers on Language and Literature* 20 (1984): 3–14.
Pons-Sanz, Sara M. *Norse-Derived Vocabulary in Late Old English Texts: Wulfstan's Works, a Case Study*. Odense: University Press of Southern Denmark, 2007.
Porteous, Norman W. *Daniel*. Old Testament Library. Philadelphia: Westminster Press, 1965.
Portnoy, Phyllis. "*Daniel* and the Dew-Laden Wind: Sources and Structures." In *Old English Literature and the Old Testament*, edited by Michael Fox and Manish Sharma. Toronto: University of Toronto Press, 2012. 195–226.
– *The Remnant: Essays on a Theme in Old English Verse*. London: Runetree Press, 2005.
– "Biblical Remnants in Hebrew, Greek, Latin, and Old English." In *Daimonopylai: Essays in Classics and the Classical Tradition Presented to Edmund G. Berry*, edited by Rory B. Egan and Mark Joyal. Winnipeg: University of Manitoba Centre for Hellenic Civilization, 2004. 319–40.
– "'Remnant' and 'Ritual': The Place of *Daniel* and *Christ and Satan* in the Junius Epic." *English Studies* 75 (1994): 408–21.
Powell, Kathryn. "Orientalist Fantasy in the Poetic Dialogues of *Solomon and Saturn*." *ASE* 34 (2005): 117–43.
– "The Anglo-Saxon Imaginary of the East: A Psychoanalytic Exploration of the Image of the East in Old English Literature." PhD diss. University of Notre Dame, 2001.
Pratt, David. "The Voice of the King in 'King Edgar's Establishment of Monasteries.'" *ASE* 41 (2012): 145–204.

– *The Political Thought of King Alfred the Great*. Cambridge: Cambridge University Press, 2007.

Radner, Hugo. "The Christian Mystery of Sun and Moon." In *Greek Myths and Christian Mystery*. Translated by Brian Battershaw. London: Burns and Oates, 1963. 89–176.

Ramsay, Nigel, Margaret Sparks, and Tim Tatton-Brown, eds. *St Dunstan: His Life, Times and Cult*. Woodbridge: Boydell Press, 1992.

Raw, Barbara C. "The Construction of Oxford, Bodleian Library, Junius 11." *ASE* 13 (1984): 187–207.

– *The Art and Background of Old English Poetry*. New York: St Martin's Press, 1978.

– "The Probable Derivation of Most of the Illustrations in Junius 11 from an Illustrated Old Saxon *Genesis*." *ASE* 5 (1976): 133–48.

Regan, Catharine A. "Evangelicalism as the Informing Principle of Cynewulf's 'Elene.'" *Traditio* 29 (1973): 27–52.

Reinsma, Luke M. *Ælfric: An Annotated Bibliography*. New York: Garland Publishing, 1987.

Remley, Paul G. "Aldhelm as Old English Poet: *Exodus*, Asser, and the *Dicta Ælfredi*." In *Latin Learning and English Lore: Studies in Anglo-Saxon Literature for Michael Lapidge*. 2 vols, edited by Katherine O'Brien O'Keeffe and Andy Orchard. Toronto: University of Toronto Press, 2005. Vol. 1. 90–108.

– *Old English Biblical Verse: Studies in* Genesis, Exodus *and* Daniel. CSASE 16. Cambridge: Cambridge University Press, 1996.

– "The Latin Textual Basis of *Genesis A*." *ASE* 17 (1988): 163–89.

Resnick, Irven M. "'Lingua Dei, lingua hominis': Sacred Language and Medieval Texts." *Viator* 21 (1990): 51–74.

Reynolds, Susan. *Kingdoms and Communities in Western Europe 900–1300*. 2nd ed. Oxford: Clarendon Press, 1997.

– "Medieval *Origines Gentium* and the Community of the Realm." *History* 68 (1983): 475–390.

Robinson, Fred C. "The Significance of Names in Old English Literature." *Anglia* 86 (1968): 14–58.

Robinson, J. Armitage. *The Times of Saint Dunstan*. Oxford: Clarendon Press, 1923.

Rollason, David. *Saints and Relics in Anglo-Saxon England*. Oxford: Basil Blackwell, 1989.

Romaine, Suzanne. *Language in Society: An Introduction to Linguistics*. 2nd ed. Oxford: Oxford University Press, 2000.

Romm, James. "Continents, Climates, and Cultures: Greek Theories of Global Structure." In *Geography and Ethnography: Perceptions of the World in*

Pre-Modern Societies, edited by Kurt A. Raaflaub and Richard J.A. Talbert. Chichester: Wiley-Blackwell, 2010. 215–35.

– *The Edges of the Earth in Ancient Thought: Geography, Exploration, and Fiction*. Princeton: Princeton University Press, 1992.

Ross, Allen P. "The Table of Nations in Genesis 10—Its Content." *Bibliotheca Sacra* 138 (1981): 22–34.

Rudolf, Winfried. "Style and Composition of Napier XVIII – A Matter of Person or a Matter of Purpose?" In *Authors, Heroes, and Lovers: Essays on Medieval English Literature and Language*, edited by Thomas Honegger. Bern: Peter Lang, 2001. 107–49.

Rumble, Alexander R. "Edward the Elder and the Churches of Winchester and Wessex." In *Edward the Elder, 899–924*, edited by N.J. Higham and D.H. Hill. London: Routledge, 2001. 230–47.

Sauer, Hans. "Die 72 Völker und Sprachen der Welt: Ein mittelalterlicher Topos in der englischen Literatur." *Anglia* 101 (1983): 29–48.

Sawyer, P.H. *Anglo-Saxon Charters: An Annotated List and Bibliography*. London: Offices of the Royal Historical Society, 1968.

Schaar, Claes. *Critical Studies in the Cynewulf Group*. Lund: C.W.K. Gleerup, 1949.

Scheil, Andrew P. *Babylon under Western Eyes: A Study of Allusion and Myth*. Toronto: Toronto University Press, 2016.

– *The Footsteps of Israel: Understanding Jews in Anglo-Saxon England*. Ann Arbor, MI: University of Michigan Press, 2004.

– "Babylon and Anglo-Saxon England." *Studies in the Literary Imagination* 36 (2003): 37–58.

Schepss, G. "Zu König Alfreds *Boethius*." *Archiv für das Studium der neueren Sprachen und Literaturen* 94 (1895): 149–60.

Schmidt, F. "Jewish Representations of the Inhabited Earth During the Hellenistic and Roman Periods." In *Greece and Rome in Eretz Israel*, edited by A. Kasher, U. Rappaport, and G. Fuks. Jerusalem: Yad Itzhak Ben-Zvi and the Israel Exploration Society, 1990.

Schwind, Johannes. *Arator-Studien*. Hypomnemata 94. Göttingen: Vandenhoeck & Ruprecht, 1990.

Scott, James M. *Geography in Early Judaism and Christianity: The Book of Jubilees*. Cambridge: Cambridge University Press, 2002.

– *Paul and the Nations: The Old Testament and Jewish Background of Paul's Mission to the Nations with Special Reference to the Destination of Galatians*. Tübingen: Mohr-Siebeck, 1995.

Scully, Diarmuid. "Bede, Orosius and Gildas on the Early History of Britain." *Bède le vénérable entre tradition et postérité / The Venerable Bede: Tradition and Posterity*, edited by Stéphane Lebecq, Michel Perrin and Olivier Szerwiniack. Lille: Ceges—Université Charles-de-Gaulle—Lille 3, 2005. 31–42.

Sharma, Manish. "Nebuchadnezzar and the Defiance of Measure in the Old English *Daniel*." *English Studies* 86 (2005): 103–26.

Shanzer, Danuta. "Bede's Style: A Neglected Historiographical Model for the Style of the Historia Ecclesiastica?" In *Sources of Wisdom: Old English and Early Medieval Latin Studies in Honour of Thomas D. Hill*, edited by Charles D. Wright, Frederick M. Biggs, and Thomas N. Hall. Toronto: University of Toronto Press, 2007. 329–52.

Sharpe, Richard. "The Varieties of Bede's Prose." In *Aspects of the Language of Latin Prose*, edited by Tobias Reinhardt, Michael Lapidge and J.N. Adams. Proceedings of the British Academy 129. Oxford: Oxford University Press, 2005. 339–55.

Sherman, Phillip Michael. *Babel's Tower Translated: Genesis 11 and Ancient Jewish Interpretation*. Leiden: Brill, 2013.

Shippey, T.A. *Old English Verse*. London: Hutchinson University Library, 1972.

Smith, Anthony D. "The Politics of Culture: Ethnicity and Nationalism." In *Companion Encyclopedia of Anthropology*, edited by Tim Ingold. London: Routledge, 1994. 706–33.

– *The Ethnic Origins of Nations*. New York: Basil Blackwell, 1986.

Smith, Jeremy. "Alfred and Ælfric: Wisdom and Poetry in Anglo-Saxon Education." *Revista canaria de estudios ingleses* 16 (1988): 9–20.

Snowden, Frank M., Jr. *Blacks in Antiquity: Ethiopians in the Greco-Roman Experience*. Cambridge, MS: Belknap Press of Harvard University Press, 1970.

Solo, Harry Jay. "The Twice-Told Tale: A Reconsideration of the Syntax and Style of the Old English *Daniel*." *Papers on Language and Literature* 9 (1973): 347–64.

Souter, Alexander, ed. *A Glossary of Later Latin to 600 A.D.* Oxford: Clarendon, 1949; rpt. 1964.

Speyer, Wolfgang. "Gigant." In *Reallexikon für Antike und Christentum*. Vol. 10, edited by Theodor Klauser. Stuttgart: Hiersemann, 1978. 1247–76.

Stanton, Robert. "Linguistic Fragmentation and Redemption before King Alfred." *Yearbook of English Studies* 36 (2006): 12–26.

– *The Culture of Translation in Anglo-Saxon England*. Cambridge: D.S. Brewer, 2002.

Stanley, E.G. "Hæthenra Hyht in Beowulf." In *Studies in Old English Literature in Honor of Arthur G. Brodeur*, edited by Stanley B. Greenfield. Eugene, OR: University of Oregon Books, 1963. 136–51.

Steen, Janie. *Verse and Virtuosity: The Adaptation of Latin Rhetoric in Old English Poetry*. Toronto: University of Toronto Press, 2008.

Steinova, Evina. "Munich, Bayerische Staatsbibliothek, Clm 6298: A New Witness of the Biblical Comentaries from the Canterbury School." *ASE* 43 (2014): 45–55.

Stévanovitch, Colette. "Envelope Patterns in *Genesis A* and *B*." *Neophilologus* 80 (1996): 465–78.

Stevenson, Jane Barbara. "Theodore and the *Laterculus Malalianus*." In *Archbishop Theodore: Commemorative Studies on his Life and Influence*, edited by Michael Lapidge. CSASE 11. Cambridge: Cambridge University Press, 1995. 204–21.

Stodnick, Jacqueline A. "The Interests of Compounding: *Angelcynn* to *Engla land* in the *Anglo-Saxon Chronicle*." In *The Power of Words: Anglo-Saxon Studies to Donald G. Scragg on his Seventieth Birthday*, edited by Jonathan Wilcox and Hugh Magennis. Morgantown, WV: West Virginia University Press, 2006. 337–67.

Sutcliffe, E.F. "The Venerable Bede's Knowledge of Hebrew." *Biblica* 16 (1935): 300–6.

Swanton, Michael. *English Poetry Before Chaucer*. 2nd ed. Exeter: Exeter University Press, 2002.

Symons, Thomas. "*Regularis Concordia*: History and Deviation." In *Tenth-Century Studies: Essays in Commemoration of the Millennium of the Council of Winchester and* Regularis Concordia, edited by David Parsons. London: Phillimore, 1975. 37–59 and 214–17.

– "Sources of the *Regularis Concordia*." *Downside Review* 59 (1941): 14–36, 143–70 and 264–89.

Szurszewski, Diane Elizabeth. "Ælfric's De falsiis diis: A Source-Analogue Study with Editions and Translations." PhD diss. University of North Carolina Chapel Hill, 1997.

Thiel, Matthias. *Grundlagen und Gestalt der Hebräischkenntnisse des frühen Mittelalters*. Biblioteca degli Studi Medievali 4. Spoleto: Centro Italiano di Studi sull'Alto Medioevo, 1973.

Thümmel, Hans Georg. "Poseidonios und die Geschichte." *Klio* 66 (1984): 558–61.

Treschow, Michael. "The Prologue to Alfred's Law Code: Instruction in the Spirit of Mercy." *Florilegium* 13 (1994): 79–110.

Treschow, Michael, et al. "King Alfred's Scholarly Writings and the Authorship of the First Fifty Prose Psalms." *The Heroic Age* 12 (2009).

Tugene, Georges. *L'idée de nation chez Bède le Vénérable*. Collection des Études Augustiniennes – Série Moyen Âge et Temps Modernes 37. Paris: Institut d'Études Augustiniennes, 2001.

Tunberg, Jennifer Morrish, "Scribes, Scribal Habits, Abbreviations, and Word-Separation." In *The Copenhagen Wulfstan Collection: Copenhagen, Kongelige*

Bibliotek Gl.Kgl.Sam. 1595, edited by J.E. Cross and Jennifer Morrish Tunberg. EEMF 25. Copenhagen: Rosenkilde, 1993. 31–49.
– "Dated and Datable Manuscripts copied in England during the Ninth Century: A Preliminary List," *Mediaeval Studies* 50 (1988): 512–38.
– "King Alfred's Letter as a Source on Learning in England." In *Studies in Earlier Old English Prose*, edited by Paul E. Szarmach. Albany, NY: State University of New York Press, 1986. 87–110.
Turner, Denis. "Allegory in Christian Late Antiquity." In *The Cambridge Companion to Allegory*, edited by Rita Copeland and Peter T. Struck. Cambridge: Cambridge University Press, 2010. 71–82.
Twomey, Michael W. "Pseudo-Methodius Revelations." In *Sources of Anglo-Saxon Literary Culture: The Apocrypha*, edited by Frederick M. Biggs. Instrumenta Anglistica Mediaevalia 1. Kalamazoo, MI: Medieval Institute Publications, 2007. 19.
– "The *Revelationes* of Pseudo-Methodius and Scriptural Study at Salisbury in the Eleventh Century." In *Source of Wisdom: Old English and Early Medieval Latin Studies in Honour of Thomas D. Hill*, edited by Charles D. Wright, Frederick M. Biggs, and Thomas N. Hall. Toronto: University of Toronto Press, 2007. 370–86.
Tyler, Elizabeth M. "Trojans in Anglo-Saxon England: Precedent without Descent." *Review of English Studies* 64 (2013): 1–20.
Ure, James M. "The *Benedictine Office* and the Metrical Paraphrase of the Lord's Prayer in MS. C.C.C.C. 201." *The Review of English Studies* 4 (1953): 354–6.
VanderKam, James C. "Putting Them in their Place: Geography as an Evaluative Tool." In *From Revelation to Canon: Studies in the Hebrew Bible and Second Temple Literature*. Leiden: Brill, 2002. 476–99.
Van der Toorn, K., and P.W. van der Horst. "Nimrod before and after the Bible." *Harvard Theological Review* 83 (1990): 1–29.
Van Oort, Johannes. *Jerusalem and Babylon: A Study into Augustine's* City of God *and the Sources of his Doctrine of the Two Cities*. Supplements to Vigiliae Christianae 14. Leiden: Brill, 1991.
Vawter, Bruce. *On Genesis: A New Reading*. Garden City, NY: Doubleday & Co., 1977.
Verheyden, Joseph. "How Many Were Sent According to Lk 10,1?" In *Luke and his Readers: Festschrift A. Denaux*, edited by R. Bieringer, G. Van Belle and J. Verheyden. Leuven: Leuven University Press, 2005. 193–238.
Walbank, F.W. *A Historical Companion on Polybius*. Vol. 3. Oxford: Clarendon Press, 1979.
Walbers, Birte. "Number and Measurement in Anglo-Saxon Christian Culture: Editions and Studies of Numerical Notes in Eight Anglo-Saxon Manuscripts, c. 800–c. 1150." PhD diss, University of York, 2012.

Wallace-Hadrill, D.S. *Eusebius of Caesarea*. London: Mowbray, 1960.

Wallach, Luitpold. *Alcuin and Charlemagne: Studies in Carolingian History and Literature*. Ithaca, NY: Cornell University Press, 1959; rpt. 1968.

Weelendorf, Jonas. "The Interplay of Pagan and Christian Traditions in Icelandic Settlement Myths." *JEGP* 109 (2010): 1–21.

Wellhausen, Julius. *Die Composition des Hexateuchs und der historischen Bücher des alten Testaments*. 4th ed. Berlin: de Gruyter & Co., 1963.

Wenham, Gordon J. *Genesis 1–15*. Word Biblical Commentary 1. Nashville, TN: Thomas Nelson, 1987.

Westrem, Scott D. "Against Gog and Magog." In *Text and Territory: Geographical Imagination in the European Middle Ages*, edited by Sylvia Tomasch and Sealy Gilles. Philadelphia, PA: University of Pennsylvania Press, 1998. 54–75.

Wetherbee, Winthrop. "Some Implications of Bede's Latin Style." In *Bede and Anglo-Saxon England: Papers in Honour of the 1300th Anniversary of the Birth of Bede, Given at Cornell University in 1973 and 1974*, edited by Robert T. Farrell. Oxford: British Archaeological Reports, 1978. 23–31.

Whitbread, L. "The Old English Poems of the *Benedictine Office* and Some Related Questions." *Anglia* 80 (1962): 37–49.

Whitelock, Dorothy. "The Authorship of the Account of King Edgar's Establishment of the Monasteries." *History, Law and Literature in 10th–11th Century England*. London: Variorum, 1981. Ch. 7. 125–36.

– "The Prose of Alfred's Reign." In *Continuations and Beginnings: Studies in Old English Literature*, edited by Eric Gerald Stanley. London: Nelson, 1966. 67–103.

– *After Bede*. Jarrow Lecture, 1960.

Whitford, David M. *The Curse of Ham in the Early Modern Era: The Bible and the Justifications for Slavery*. Farnham: Ashgate, 2009.

Wieland, Gernot Rudolf. "Bilingual Education in Anglo-Saxon England: Alfred to Æthelweard." In *Mehrsprachigkeit im Mittelalter: Kulturelle, literarische, sprachliche und didaktische Konstellationen in europäischer Perspektive*, edited by Michael Baldzuhn and Christine Putzo. Berlin: de Gruyter, 2011. 35–57.

– "A New Look at the Poem 'Archalis clamare triumuir.'" In *Insignis Sophiae Arcator: Essays in Honour of Michael W. Herren on his 65th Birthday*, edited by Gernot R. Wieland, Carin Ruff and Ross G. Arthur. Turnhout: Brepols, 2006. 178–92.

– *The Latin Glosses on Arator and Prudentius in Cambridge University Library MS GG.5.35*. Toronto: PIMS, 1983.

Wilcox, Jonathan. "A Reluctant Translator in Late Anglo-Saxon England: Ælfric and Maccabees." *Proceedings of the Medieval Association of the Midwest* 2 (1994 for 1993): 1–18.

Williams, David. *Deformed Discourse: The Function of the Monster in Mediaeval Thought and Literature*. Exeter: University of Exeter Press, 1996.

Willmes, Ansgar. "Bedas Bibelauslegung." *Archiv für Kulturgeschichte* 44 (1962): 281–314.

Wilson, G.H. "South." In *The International Standard Bible Encyclopedia*, edited by Geoffrey W. Bromiley et al. Vol. 4: Q–Z. Grand Rapids, MI: William B. Eerdmans, 1988. 590.

Wilson, Michael J. "The Rhetoric of *Genesis A*." PhD diss. Kent State University, 2002.

Winterbottom, Michael. Review of Jane Stevenson, *The "Laterculus Malalianus" and the School of Archbishop Theodore*. *Notes and Queries* 43 (1996): 457–9.

– "Aldhelm's Prose Style and its Origins." *ASE* 6 (1977): 39–76.

Wolfram, Herwig. "*Origo et religio*: Ethnic Traditions and Literature in Early Medieval Texts." *From Roman Provinces to Medieval Kingdoms: Rewriting Histories*, edited by Thomas F.X. Noble. London: Routledge, 2006. 70–90.

– *The Roman Empire and Its Germanic Peoples*. Translated by Thomas Dunlap. Berkley, CA: University of California Press, 1997.

Wood, Ian. "Defining the Franks: Frankish Origins in Early Medieval Historiography." In *Concepts of National Identity in the Middle Ages*, edited by Simon Forde, Lesley Johnson, and Alan V. Murray. Leeds: Leeds Studies in English, 1995. 46–57.

Wood, Michael. "A Carolingian Scholar in the Court of King Æthelstan." In *England and the Continent in the Tenth Century: Studies in Honour of Wilhelm Levison (1876–1947)*, edited by David Rollason, Conrad Leyser and Hannah Williams. Turnhout: Brepols, 2010. 135–62.

– "'Stand Firm Against the Monsters': Kingship and Learning in the Empire of King Æthelstan." In *Lay Intellectuals in the Carolingian World*, edited by Janet L. Nelson and Patrick Wormald. Cambridge: Cambridge University Press, 2007. 192–217.

– "The Making of King Aethelstan's Empire: An English Charlemagne?" In *Ideal and Reality in Frankish and Anglo-Saxon Society: Studies Presented to J.M. Wallace-Hadrill*, edited by Patrick Wormald with Donald Bullough and Roger Collins. Oxford: Basil Blackwell, 1983. 250–72.

Woodward, David. "Medieval *Mappaemundi*." In *The History of Cartography*. Vol. 1: *Cartography in Prehistoric, Ancient, and Medieval Europe and the Mediterranean*, edited by J.B. Harley and David Woodward. Chicago: University of Chicago Press, 1987. 286–370.

– "Reality, Symbolism, Time, and Space in Medieval World Maps." *Annals of the Association of American Geographers* 75 (1985): 510–21.

Wormald, Patrick. "Æthelwold and his Continental Counterparts: Contact, Comparison, Contrast." In *The Times of Bede: Studies in Early English*

Christian Society and its Historian, edited by Stephen Baxter. Oxford: Blackwell, 2006. 169–206.

– "Bede, the *Bretwaldas* and the Origins of the *gens Anglorum*." In *The Times of Bede: Studies in Early English Christian Society and its Historian*, edited by Stephen Baxter. Oxford: Blackwell, 2006. 106–34.

– "Wulfstan (d. 1023)." In *Oxford Dictionary of National Biography*. Online ed., edited by Lawrence Goldman. Oxford: Oxford University Press, 2004.

– "Archbishop Wulfstan and the Holiness of Society." In *Legal Culture in the Early Medieval West: Law as Text, Image and Experience*. London: Hambledon Press, 1999. 225–51.

– *The Making of English Law: King Alfred to the Twelfth Century*. Vol. I: *Legislation and its Limits*. Oxford: Blackwell, 1999.

Wrenn, C.L. *A Study of Old English Literature*. London: George C. Harrap & Co., 1967.

Wright, Charles D. "*Genesis A* ad litteram." In *Old English Literature and the Old Testament*, edited by Michael Fox and Manish Sharma. Toronto: University of Toronto Press, 2012. 121–71.

– "Blood of Abel and the Branches of Sin: *Genesis A*, *Maxims I* and Aldhelm's *Carmen de uirginitate*." *ASE* 25 (1996): 7–19.

– "Hiberno-Latin and Irish-Influenced Biblical Commentaries, Florilegia, and Homily Collections." In *Sources of Anglo-Saxon Literary Culture: A Trial Version*, edited by Frederick M. Biggs, Thomas D. Hill, and Paul E. Szarmach. MRTS 74. Binghamton, NY: Center for Medieval and Early Renaissance Studies, State University of New York at Binghamton, 1990. 87–123.

– "'Insulae Gentium': Biblical Influence on Old English Poetic Vocabulary." In *Magister Regis: Studies in Honor of Robert Earl Kaske*, edited by Arthur Groos. New York: Fordham University Press, 1986. 9–21.

Yorke, Barbara, ed. *Bishop Æthelwold: His Career and Influence*. Woodbridge: Boydell Press, 1988; rpt, 1997.

Young, Jean I. "Two Notes on the *Later Genesis*." In *The Anglo-Saxons: Studies in Some Aspects of their History and Culture presented to Bruce Dickins*, edited by Peter Clemoes. London: Bowes & Bowes, 1959. 204–11.

Zientara, Benedykt. "Populus – Gens – Natio. Einige Probleme aus dem Bereich der ethnischen Terminologie des frühen Mittelalters." In *Nationalismus in vorindustrieller Zeit*, edited by Otto Dann. Munich: R. Oldenbourg, 1986. 11–20.

Index

Toronto Anglo-Saxon Series

1 *Preaching the Converted: The Style and Rhetoric of the Vercelli Book Homilies*, Samantha Zacher
2 *Say What I Am Called: The Old English Riddles of the Exeter Book and the Anglo-Latin Riddle Tradition*, Dieter Bitterli
3 *The Aesthetics of Nostalgia: Historical Representation in Anglo-Saxon Verse*, Renée Trilling
4 *New Readings in the Vercelli Book*, edited by Samantha Zacher and Andy Orchard
5 *Authors, Audiences, and Old English Verse*, Thomas A. Bredehoft
6 *On Aesthetics in* Beowulf *and Other Old English Poems*, edited by John M. Hill
7 *Old English Metre: An Introduction*, Jun Terasawa
8 *Anglo-Saxon Psychologies in the Vernacular and Latin Traditions*, Leslie Lockett
9 *The Body Legal in Barbarian Law*, Lisi Oliver
10 *Old English Literature and the Old Testament*, edited by Michael Fox and Manish Sharma
11 *Stealing Obedience: Narratives of Agency and Identity in Later Anglo-Saxon England*, Katherine O'Brien O'Keeffe
12 *Traditional Subjectivities: The Old English Poetics of Mentality*, Britt Mize
13 *Land and Book: Literature and Land Tenure in Anglo-Saxon England*, Scott T. Smith
14 *Writing Women Saints in Anglo-Saxon England*, edited by Paul E. Szarmach
15 *Anglo-Saxon Manuscripts: A Bibliographical Handlist of Manuscripts and Manuscript Fragments Written or Owned in England up to 1100*, Helmut Gneuss and Michael Lapidge
16 *The King's Body: Burial and Succession in Anglo-Saxon England*, Nicole Marafioti

17 *From Lawmen to Plowmen: Anglo-Saxon Legal Tradition and the School of Langland*, Stephen Yeager
18 *The Politics of Language: Byrhtferth, Ælfric, and the Multilingual Identity of the Benedictine Reform*, Rebecca Stephenson
19 *Weaving Words and Binding Bodies: The Poetics of Human Experience in Old English Literature*, Megan Cavell
20 *Joinings: Compound Words in Old English Literature*, Jonathan Davis-Secord
21 *Imagining the Jew in Anglo-Saxon Literature and Culture*, edited by Samantha Zacher
22 *Latinity and Identity in Anglo-Saxon Literature*, edited by Rebecca Stephenson and Emily Thornbury
23 *Inhabited Spaces: Anglo-Saxon Constructions of Place*, Nicole Guenther Discenza
24 *England in Europe: English Royal Women and Literary Patronage, c.1000–c.1150*, Elizabeth M. Tyler
25 *Undoing Babel: The Tower of Babel in Anglo-Saxon Literature*, Tristan Major

www.ingramcontent.com/pod-product-compliance
Lightning Source LLC
LaVergne TN
LVHW090152080826
844660LV00013B/777/J

* 9 7 8 1 4 8 7 5 0 0 5 4 2 *